...NEEDED IN EVERY HOME

EQUIVALENT MEASURES

Speck	Less than ⅛ teasp.
⅓ of ¼ teasp.	Pinch*
⅓ of ½ teasp.	Pinch*
½ of ¼ teasp.	⅛ teasp.
3 teasp.	1 tablesp.
⅓ of 1 tablesp. . . .	1 teasp.
⅓ of 2 tablesp. . . .	2 teasp.
⅓ of 5 tablesp. . . .	1 tablesp. + 2 teasp.
⅓ of 7 tablesp. . . .	2 tablesp. + 1 teasp.
½ of 1 tablesp. . . .	1½ teasp.
½ of 3 tablesp. . . .	1 tablesp. + 1½ teasp.
½ of 5 tablesp. . . .	2 tablesp. + 1½ teasp.
½ of 7 tablesp. . . .	3 tablesp. + 1½ teasp.
2 tablesp.	⅛ cup
4 tablesp.	¼ cup
5 tablesp + 1 teasp. . . .	⅓ cup
8 tablesp.	½ cup
10 tablesp. + 2 teasp. . .	⅔ cup
12 tablesp.	¾ cup
16 tablesp.	1 cup
⅓ of ¼ cup	1 tablesp. + 1 teasp.
⅓ of ⅓ cup	1 tablesp. + 2⅓ teasp.
⅓ of ½ cup	2 tablesp. + 2 teasp.
⅓ of ⅔ cup	3 tablesp. + 1⅔ teasp.
⅓ of ¾ cup	¼ cup
½ of ¼ cup	2 tablesp.
½ of ⅓ cup	2 tablesp. + 2 teasp.
½ of ½ cup	¼ cup
½ of ⅔ cup	⅓ cup
½ of ¾ cup	6 tablesp.
2 cups	1 pt.
2 pt.	1 qt.
1 qt.	4 cups

A pinch is as much as can be taken between tip of finger and thumb.

Dry Measure

2 pints = 1 quart
8 quarts = 1 peck
4 pecks = 1 bushel

Liquid Measure

16 fluid ounces or 4 gills = 1 pint
32 fluid ounces or 2 pints = 1 quart
4 quarts = 1 gallon (U.S.)
31½ gallons = 1 barrel
63 gallons = 1 hogshead

Area

144 square inches = 1 square foot
9 square feet = 1 square yard
160 square rods or 10 square chains = 1 acre
640 acres = 1 square mile
A square 208.71 ft. on each side = 1 acre or
    43,560 sq. ft.

WEDDING ANNIVERSARIES

1st—paper, plastics
2nd—cotton
3rd—leather or any leather-like article
4th—linen, silk, rayon or nylon or other
    synthetic silk
5th—wood
6th—iron
7th—wool, copper, or brass
8th—bronze or electrical appliances
9th—pottery or china
10th—tin or aluminum
11th—steel
12th—silk, nylon, linen
13th—lace
14th—ivory or agate
15th—crystal or glass
20th—china
25th—silver
30th—pearls
35th—coral or jade
40th—rubies or garnets
45th—sapphires or tourmalines
50th—gold
55th—emeralds or turquoise
60th—diamonds or gold
75th—diamonds or gold

BIRTHSTONES AND FLOWERS OF THE MONTHS

	Birthstone	Flower
January	garnet	carnation or snowdrop
February	amethyst	violet or primrose
March	bloodstone or aquamarine	jonquil or daffodil
April	diamond	sweet pea or daisy
May	emerald	lily of the valley or hawthorn
June	pearl, moonstone or alexandrite	rose or honey-suckle
July	ruby	larkspur or water lily
August	sardonyx or peridot	poppy or gladiolus
September	sapphire	aster or morning glory
October	opal or tourma-line	calendula or cosmos
November	topaz	chrysanthemum
December	turquoise or zircon	narcissus or holly

GOOD
HOUSEKEEPING'S
GUIDE FOR
YOUNG
HOMEMAKERS

AN UP-TO-THE-MINUTE
HANDBOOK
OF SUCCESSFUL
HOME MANAGEMENT

•

Edited by
William Laas
with the Editors of
GOOD HOUSEKEEPING

Harper & Row, Publishers

GOOD HOUSEKEEPING'S GUIDE FOR YOUNG HOMEMAKERS

 New York, Evanston, and London

CONTENTS
by Categories

Articles contained in the *Guide* are listed here and grouped for convenience in general areas of interest. Each main article will be found *in alphabetical place* in the book. For information on appliances, for example, see *Appliance Trouble Shooting* under "A," *Dishwashers* under "D," etc. For information on items within main articles, refer to the *Index* for the page number.

EDITOR'S FOREWORD

Homemaker—no other word in the language so precisely suggests what a young married woman is expected to *do*.

When a wife not gainfully employed is asked her occupation, she answers, "Homemaker" or "Housewife"—but not just "Wife," and never "Unemployed." Running a successful home today is a full-time occupation, and a proud one. The truth is that modern homemaking demands more skills and higher levels of competence than many a salaried trade. Not long ago the Chase Manhattan Bank of New York estimated the worth of a housewife's work in equivalent wages at $8,285.68 a year, or $159.34 per 99-hour week. The bank listed a dozen different jobs, such as nursemaid, 44.5 hours @ $1.25—cook, 13.1 hours @ $2.50. Food buyer, seamstress, dietitian, housekeeper, laundress, practical nurse, handyman, gardener, chauffeur—even this list falls short of the actuality.

In modern America, a high standard of living and a bewildering wealth of consumer goods have relegated traditional "woman's work" to the elementary class. Cooking and sewing are just the beginning of desirable know-how. Today's young woman has to be a sort of engineer and manager as well. She copes with a host of intricate appliances that replace the household servants of the past. She shops in a lush supermarket forest of new materials, new foods, new processes, and magical chemicals. She has to know a bit about money: charge accounts, installment buying, taxes, insurance. She has to understand automobiles, home safety, the decorative arts, private schooling, telephone rates, beauty and fashion, diet and health—to name just a few of her multitude of necessary interests. Even the wife of many years' experience may feel a sense of bafflement at how much there is to know.

GOOD HOUSEKEEPING'S GUIDE FOR YOUNG HOMEMAKERS is designed to help fill this vital need for authentic up-to-date information. It is for the modern housewife who is constantly looking for the easy—or better—way to beat the system, save work, save headaches, save money, and keep her husband happy. Not a cookbook, not even a household hint book in the familiar sense, this Guide answers precisely those questions most likely to lead to a call for help. And it makes the answers easy to find by arranging the basic subject matter in alphabetical order throughout the book.

The unexcelled editorial resources of *Good Housekeeping*, including its famous Institute for the investigation and confirmation of advertised claims, have been combed for basic information. In cookery, for example, this Guide offers no specific recipes, but it does tell how to make a recipe work. It offers sound *basic* advice on the buying, storage, and preparation of food, as authoritative as it is often novel.

That popular department of *Good Housekeeping*, "The Better Way" has provided the last word on such diverse but relevant subjects as money and credit; how to choose a piece of furniture; how to recognize the value of a house (and proceed to buy or sell it); new ideas in every field from antiques through emergency childbirth to zippers.

All this is arranged in an A-B-C format which we believe makes this an indispensable handbook for daily use. Everyone from time to time needs to "look it up," and this book provides the quickest possible source of answers whether you're pondering a purchase or faced with emergency first aid. Also, it provides good reading. Any bride imbued with real curiosity will, upon opening to almost any item, find enough fascinating information to keep her engrossed by the hour.

WILLIAM LAAS
May 1966

IT'S EASY TO USE
THIS BOOK

A unique feature of this *Guide* is an arrangement of material that combines the quick-reference, A-B-C order of a dictionary with the handiness of finding related information in one place.

The book contains approximately 175 articles or entries that appear in alphabetical order (e.g., Antiques, Appliance Trouble Shooting, Bank Accounts, etc.). Often, you can quickly locate the subject of your interest simply by looking it up as in a dictionary. Numerous cross-references appear throughout the text. If you don't find what you need in this way, look for it in the Index. The Index lists thousands of items that appear as subsections or brief treatments within a more comprehensive article.

For example, "apples" are not separately listed, but it would probably occur to you to look for them under *Fruit*. If you look up apples in the Index, you will be referred to *Fruits* and to related entries, *Fruit Dictionary* and *Fresh Fruits and Vegetables*. These give information not only about apples, but about other fruits you might want to consider at the same time. They also broaden your general knowledge of the buying, storage, etc., of apples and other fresh produce.

In the Contents by Categories, all articles contained in the book are listed in functional groups. This is helpful when you want basic information about a subject. If about to move into a new home, you might consult the contents under such categories as FURNISHINGS and APPLIANCES; then turn to each article of interest in its alphabetical place.

In some cases individual items appear in alphabetical order within one article. You will find "ink" so listed under *Stain Removal*. This enables you to find a particular stain quickly among the more than fifty included, along with basic guidance on stain removal.

Illustrations frequently are presented in functional groupings. "Chippendale," for instance, is shown under *Chairs*, *Tables*, etc. This enables you to compare Chippendale with other types and styles of furniture at the same time as you look it up.

Note: For aids in an emergency, turn first to Contents by Categories, under EMERGENCIES.

GOOD HOUSEKEEPING'S GUIDE FOR YOUNG HOMEMAKERS

ANTIQUES | See also AUCTIONS; FURNISHING A HOME; FURNITURE BUYING GUIDE

How old is an antique? Anything over 100 years old? Anything made by handcraftsmen before the age of mass production? Anything that is old?

Actually, there is no single, precise answer. The kind of item under consideration is vitally important in determining whether it is to be classified as an antique. For example, furniture that is 150 years old usually is considered antique. Chinese porcelain, though, which is 300 years old might be considered to be relatively "new" by the knowledgeable collector. According to some experts, many so-called "antique shops" are simply stores that deal in "old" objects.

The year 1830 is used as the dividing line by the United States Customs Service in exempting from duty imported articles made before that time. However, carpets and rugs must have been made before 1700 and musical instruments before 1801 to qualify for the customs exemption. The 1830 date was adopted when customs regulations were revised in 1930. It was apparently selected because it was felt that the age of mass production, replacing individual handwork, began at that time.

It requires considerable knowledge to identify antiques. If you want an expert opinion on some item, you can get it—for a fee—from qualified appraisers or, in a few places, free from museums.

APPLIANCE TROUBLE SHOOTING | See also ELECTRIC APPLIANCES

Peter Sellers, the British comedian, has made a career of doing film battle with inanimate objects that refuse to work. The modern housewife with a dozen appliances under her daily management may sometimes wonder if that's really so funny. Yet in an amazing number of cases, balkiness in a device of any kind is not the fault of the device but of failure to use it properly. (Mr. Sellers doesn't *have* to bump into those hat racks!)

Every year, a truly staggering sum is spent in this country for first aid to misunderstood or mistreated appliances. Manufacturers have surveys to prove that users' ignorance is to blame for *one-third to one-half* of all service calls—which they politely list under "consumer education" or "instruction needed" visits. Obviously, if you know what's most likely to go wrong and what preventive steps can help avoid mishaps, you'll save yourself grief and expense.

Here are a few of the simpler problems women complain about, followed by trouble-shooting measures. Have you ever wondered:

Why the refrigerator or freezer door is suddenly hard to open? The last time you closed it, you probably slammed it just hard enough to create a partial vacuum.

Why a sewing machine jams or tangles on the first few stitches? This happens when you don't start properly. Begin sewing with the needle at its highest point, and hold the thread ends to the back for the first stitch or two. Don't push or pull the fabric.

Why a vacuum cleaner won't pick up dirt? The brush is worn, or packed with dirt and threads or, more likely, the cleaner is just too full of dirt. The efficiency of any vacuum cleaner drops way down when the bag is more than half full.

Why the toaster sometimes just won't toast? If you have a good toaster, this happens because of low voltage. Within your house or in your area, there just isn't enough power, especially during peak use, as at breakfast time. Turn off some lights or other appliances and it may work.

How to cut out unnecessary repair bills? First, of course, never buy from a dealer who cannot direct you to an authorized parts and service agency. Buy only when you have assurance that good service will be available when you need it; and see to it that expert installation gets you off to a good start.

Never call before you check the instruction book. After you've read it (and some of them are mighty heavy going) keep it handy—always. Along with the facts you must know to get the most from your machine, there's a list of points to check before you call for help. The melting freezer that's simply unplugged; the oven that won't turn on because the clock was flipped from "manual" to "automatic" in cleaning—these things can happen.

Don't fight an appliance. It doesn't pay. People have been known to kick, shake, punch, and carve up appliances—with provocation, perhaps. But the records show that some homes call for more than average service attention, and rough handling is suspected. Appliances are not particularly delicate, but they do contain parts that work better and longer with reasonably respectful care. It is worthwhile to be especially gentle when you are removing, cleaning and replacing parts, turning dials and switches, opening and closing doors and lids.

AUTOMATIC WASHERS

Check the instruction book for recommended water temperature and the type and amount of detergent. Often, hotter water and more detergent are the cure for gray washes. Take time to go through pockets and trouser cuffs for foreign objects. A penny in the washer pump or a pebble scraping the tub can mean an expensive repair.

Control knobs and buttons: Be sure you turn them the right way. The replacement of timing mechanisms is an all-too-frequent—and expensive—repair. Reminder: control knobs should not be used by children as playthings.

Installation: See that the washer is connected to a separate electric circuit—grounded for safety's sake—and leveled to prevent harmful vibration. Hot and cold water valves should be within easy reach. The drain hose must allow water to flow freely, and be securely attached to a sink or other drain in order to prevent flooding.

DISHWASHERS

Poor cleaning: The water may not be hot enough. Or the water pressure may be too low. An ample supply of hot water between 150 and 160 degrees under a pressure flow of 15 to 20 pounds per square inch is needed for best results. If pressure is insufficient, call the water company.

If the dishes in one section don't come out as clean as they should, be sure the water flow isn't blocked by large platters, etc. Improper loading can also cause filming and spotting.

Use only the recommended detergents. If hard water is a problem, experiment with several detergents, in varying amounts, to determine which is best suited to your water condition.

Silver and aluminum may be spotted and discolored if undissolved detergent is accidentally sprinkled on them. Do place the detergent on the floor of the dishwasher or in the specified detergent cup, so the water will dissolve it completely before it reaches silverware.

DRYERS

With the instruction book's help, learn the best way of setting your timer to avoid overdrying, shrinkage, and wrinkling. If you get poor results on automatic damp or dry shut-offs, a service call may be needed to adjust the thermostat—but first be sure you're drying the kind of load recommended, and have made the proper settings.

There isn't too much that can go wrong with a dryer, but do take care to *clean the lint trap regularly,* and other parts as the book recommends. If the dryer begins to show signs of poor performance (abnormal temperature, odd noises, etc.) have it checked right away.

RANGES

Before you decide the oven or top-stove thermostats of a new range need adjusting, make sure you're using pans that are in good condition. Dark, warped, or worn-thin pans can affect cooking results to a surprising degree. On the range-top, flat-bottom pans should be used. In the oven, bright, satin-finish baking pans give better browning than dark, discolored pans.

(If cakes are unevenly baked, check the range to see whether it needs leveling.) When using foil sheets to catch drips in the oven, be sure they're not so large as to restrict heat flow. The same goes for oversize cookie sheets.

All manufacturers report the automatic oven-clock switch as a prime cause of unnecessary calls. If your oven refuses to heat, check this switch first—it's usually labeled Automatic–Manual—and be sure it's turned on.

Burners and elements are removable, in many ranges, to make cleaning easier, but often service calls are made merely to connect a burner or plug in a removable electric element. So be sure to replace, gently but firmly, all parts removed for cleaning.

While most finishes are durable, avoid using abrasives or allowing spills from acid foods to dry on any range surface.

Excessive heat may be a matter of poor insulation; if it is, we're afraid you'll just have to bear with it. But the cause might be improperly adjusted controls, which a serviceman can remedy.

Remember that modern ranges don't need to be preheated for a half hour before baking, or electric top-stove units turned on minutes ahead of actual cooking. Most of the newer ovens preheat in ten minutes for baking; you can skip the preheating entirely for roasting meats.

REFRIGERATORS, FREEZERS

Here are points to check if the inside seems warm or the ice is melting. First, is the control set on "cold"? Now make sure the wall plug is fully pushed into the socket and that the fuse (or circuit breaker) hasn't blown. If everything's in order and the machine still isn't functioning, call for service.

Too much frost: Often a summer complaint, merely means that the weather is extra humid. If you haven't an automatic defroster, you must do the job yourself, weekly, depending on the climate (less often in winter). **Never use sharp tools.** You may puncture the cooling refrigerant tubes. This is an expensive repair.

Noises and smells: Manufacturers have reported service calls to clean refrigerators, clean out melted frost drains, level noisy units, even to remove toys from behind or under the refrigerator. You can save money by tracking down the source of trouble yourself.

Cleaning: Two words of caution here. Acids from spilled food may cause damage, so wipe up spills immediately. Avoid abrasive cleaners, especially on the ice trays; these are specially coated so they won't stick.

AUCTIONS | See also ANTIQUES; FURNISHING
A HOME; FURNITURE BUYING GUIDE

Auction galleries and country barns annually draw many thousands of people for a combination of bargain-hunting and entertainment. The odds are heavily against buying a rare piece of furniture or a painting of an old master at a low price. These pointers, however, may aid your search for bargains.

Inspect before you bid. Reputable auctioneers offer the public a chance to inspect sale items several days or hours before the auction. Avoid those who don't allow this privilege. Keep in mind that everything at an auction may not be from a single estate. The auction notice carries the name of the consignor of the bulk of the items, but the small print may read "and others" or "et al." meaning that the auctioneer has added other items— often those he has not been able to sell before.

Set a limit on your top price. Remember that delivery and repair costs are extra, also taxes. Set a value on the item, based on your previous examination of similar merchandise in retail stores. Some galleries also give the appraisal price, but this is only an aid in setting value. If you are apt to be carried away during the bidding, leave a bid with the auctioneer and stay home. If no bid at the sale tops yours, you get what you want at a price one step above the final bid made—even if it is lower than the bid you left.

Buy out of season. For instance, consider buying wrought-iron furniture or garden equipment when there is snow on the ground; or fireplace equipment during a heat wave.

In the summer, while others flock to the more informal country auctions, you may find few bidders at city auctions—good places to find bargains in large pieces of furniture, such as grand pianos or Gothic dining room tables which are difficult to fit into city apartments.

Know the terms of the sale. Printed in the catalogue or announced at the auction, these specify the amount of deposit required in order to bid, how much must be paid at the time a bid is accepted, settlement of disputes between bidders, time allowed for removal, etc.

Don't bid on impulse. Be sure you need the item and can use it. When inspecting, measure the piece, note colors, patterns and textures to determine that it fits into your home. You can question the auctioneer at any time. You may ask him whether the sale item is perfect, to repeat a description, to designate whether the sale is by individual pieces or as a lot, to call off his last bid, or to verify that it is your bid he has just acknowledged.

Sit where you can spot the antique dealers. A dealer's interest in an item is generally a good indication of its value. Dealers realize this and try to disguise their bidding. They usually sit up front, stand in the rear, or lounge near the platform. Some experts say that high-priced pieces that interest a dealer are potentially the best bargains.

BANK ACCOUNTS | See also CREDIT AND DEBT

The services of a bank have become virtually an essential of modern household management. Certainly, the easiest and safest way to pay bills is to write a check. Most salaries today are paid by check, which means you must have some place to cash it. Many wage-earners pay sizable fees for check cashing which a bank would do free if they had an account. Know something about banks, how they work, and how best to use them.

A **regular checking account** requires a minimum balance. You deposit $100, $300, $500, or $1,000, as required by the bank, and agree to maintain the account at least at that level. Each check you write is an order to the bank to pay some of your money as and to whom you direct. Thus, you can send payment through the mails without risk of loss. The returned check, endorsed on the back by its recipient, is the equivalent of a written receipt. It provides a record you can keep as proof of payment or for tax purposes, and the bank's monthly statement of your deposits and checks is helpful in budget planning.

Since the bank earns money on your deposits, sometimes this is enough to cover the cost of the service. If not, a small service charge (sc) appears on the monthly statement, varying according to the activity of the account. The bank makes no charge for cashing checks, handling savings bond purchases, and other convenient services. A relationship with a commercial bank is also helpful when you need to borrow money or transact other financial business.

In **special checking accounts** no minimum balance is required beyond sufficient funds to cover any checks you issue. The bank charges a fixed fee (usually 10 cents per check), but will cash other checks for you at no charge, up to the amount in the account.

A **savings account** is a time deposit that pays you a stated rate of interest. No checks may be issued against it; money may be withdrawn only by presenting the passbook. Mutual savings banks, chartered in only eighteen (mostly northeastern) states, specialize in this form of banking and do their best to make small depositors comfortable. On request, the bank will give you its own check (called a cashier's or bank check) instead of a cash withdrawal. Some provide bill paying and other services as complete as many families need. The compound interest you receive on a savings account can add up to a sizable bonus each year.

A **savings and loan association** (or "building and loan") is not a bank; when you open an account you buy a share in the association and receive dividends on its earnings. The rate of return is equal to or higher than interest paid by a bank. As a practical matter, savings and loan accounts may be used for cashing checks, etc., much like any savings account. Technically, a savings bank or savings and loan may demand thirty days' notice or more for withdrawals—but this is rarely applied.

In choosing a safe place to deposit your money, look for insignia identifying the institution as a member of the Federal Deposit Insurance Corporation in the case of banks, or of the Federal Savings and Loan Insurance Corporation in the case of savings and loan. These government-backed agencies insure your account up to $10,000 in case of bank failure. No insured depositor has ever lost money; others unfortunately have.

OTHER WAYS TO PAY BILLS

If you have no bank account, most banks will sell you a cashier's check or bank money order at the teller's window for the cash and a small fee. A postal money order is the same thing issued by a United States post office, generally at somewhat higher fees.

A *traveler's check* is for carrying on your person as "non-stealable money." Upon purchasing the check you sign it for identification; upon cashing it you sign it again. Therefore, it will usually be accepted by strangers, because without your second signature it is valueless if stolen or lost. The cost is 75 cents to $1 for $100.

FACTS TO KNOW ABOUT CHECKS

Once you sign a check, it becomes an order to pay which is almost as good as money. Therefore, never write a check to "Cash"—which means anyone can cash it—unless you are at the teller's window or in a store where you are about to receive the money or equivalent value. For the same reason, never endorse a check made out to you (or countersign a traveler's check) until you are sure of value received. Your endorsing signature legally testifies that you *have* received value. If sending an endorsed check through the mail, write "Pay to (recipient's name)" above your endorsing signature so that only he can cash it.

A check takes twenty-four to forty-eight hours or longer to "clear"—that is, to come back from its recipient through his bank to your bank, which thereupon charges it against your account. During this interim you can stop payment—that is, order your bank not to honor the check—but you should have a good reason. Banks become very unhappy if the privilege is abused.

They get downright unpleasant if checks are deliberately written against nonexistent funds. Overdrawing an account, issuing "rubber" checks that "bounce," is considered a dishonest practice.

On request, your bank will *certify* your check, which means the bank sets aside the money to cover it and guarantees payment. A certified check will be accepted as cash in legal transactions, buying a car, etc., which require transfer of a substantial amount of money between strangers.

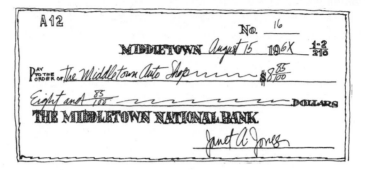

How to write a check that cannot be raised: Once you make out a check, there's no way to *guarantee* that the amount won't be altered. But there *are* some ways to reduce the risk. The American Bankers Association suggests that you:

1. Leave no space between the dollar sign and the first figure of the number, or between the last figure of the number and the following fraction (showing the amount in cents).

2. Begin writing out the amount as close to the left side of the check as possible. (If there's any discrepancy between the written amount and the amount in numbers, the spelled-out section is usually considered correct.)

3. Leave no space between the spelled-out amount and the following fraction, or insert the word "and."

4. Fill in remaining space with a wavy line.

Bank tellers watch for such telltale signs of a check's having been raised as erasures, squeezed-in numbers, and differences in handwriting.

Safe deposit boxes are rented in bank vaults for storage of your valuable papers, such as stock or bond certificates, wills, birth and marriage records, deeds on property; or for jewelry, rare coins, etc., and cash. Only you have the key to the box, and it may not be opened by anyone at any time without your authority, except by order of a court of law. It offers protection against possibly disastrous loss by fire or burglary if the valuables were kept at home.

Banking by mail has become big business. An estimated 40 per cent of all savings and loan business is transacted by mail, and this method represents the fifth in importance in basic banking services.

The advantages are obvious. Customers do not have to make special trips to the bank; they do not have to stand in line; and they can do this kind of banking twenty-four hours a day. Savings institutions often pay the postage (both ways) to encourage using the corner mailbox as a teller's window. They say mail loan payments and deposits can be handled in a more orderly fashion.

There are a few precautions to observe. The American Bankers Association recommends:

1. Never send currency or coins unless necessary, and then use registered mail. If necessary, tape coins so they do not slide around in the envelope.

2. Endorse checks "for deposit only" or to your bank.

3. Keep a record of checks sent for deposit. (Although it happens only rarely, checks can be lost in the mails or even destroyed in transportation accidents.) Unless mail is registered, the post office is not liable for financial losses. If a mail deposit is lost, have the maker of the check immediately stop payment, and request that he issue another.

Many banks furnish special forms for deposits, withdrawals, and loan payments. In the case of a deposit, however, banks will accept written and signed instructions on any notepaper.

Making your money work: Since a checking account pays no interest, or virtually none, good money managers open a second, interest-bearing account for savings. Both accounts may be in one commercial bank, but generally a mutual savings bank or savings and loan association pays more interest. If, hopefully, your checking account builds up beyond the balance needed to pay bills, you should immediately transfer the excess to savings. (Merely write a check and deposit it in your savings account.)

Time any withdrawals to catch the end of an interest period, which may be the last day of every month, or of every three months, or of every six months. This way your money will grow steadily at compound interest while it "rests." Have the accrued interest entered in your savings passbook at least once a year.

Recent consumer surveys show that many families use a savings account as a revolving fund for major purchases. If they intend to buy a car, refrigerator, fur coat, etc., they first accumulate the price of it in savings. By paying cash, the buyer avoids the finance charges that come with installment buying. Not all is a clear saving, however, since the bank interest is sacrificed.

To illustrate in round figures: A man might finance a $3,000 car loan for three years at $98 a month. His payments include a $540 finance charge. If he pays cash instead, he saves the $540. But he loses about $360 in compound interest (at 4 per cent for three years) had he left the $3,000 in the bank. His net saving becomes $180.

The revolving fund saver, though, immediately begins to rebuild his account by depositing the $98 a month he would have paid as installments on the car. In effect, he pays the $540 finance charge back to himself instead of to a lender. In three years, with accumulating interest, he winds up with about $3,750, plus the car.

Alternatively, in many cases, he may leave his savings intact to draw interest while borrowing the same amount from the bank as a passbook loan. He repays the bank in monthly installments at a net charge much less than the normal cost of consumer financing.

A **Christmas Club** (trade name of a corporation that sells the plan to banks) is for less systematic savers than the foregoing. It sets a fifty-week schedule of regular deposits in any amount from 50 cents to $20, usually ending in November. Little or no interest may be paid, and a penalty may be charged for withdrawing the money ahead of time. Nevertheless, millions of people, including children, find they need this psychological incentive to put aside some savings each week. They use club accounts not only for Christmas money, but for a vacation, taxes, investment, and other purposes.

BARGAIN SALES | See also AUCTIONS

January is a bargain hunter's dream month. In many parts of the country, department stores have white sales (sheets, pillowcases, and so on), fur sales, and general storewide clearance sales during January. Not all department stores have the same sales at the same time, but tradition, usually based on practical business considerations, has set aside some months as appropriate for placing certain merchandise on the bargain list.

It is not always possible to tell by reading an advertisement whether a sale or special offer really does represent a saving over the regular price of the merchandise. Various groups, including Better Business Bureaus, retail associations, and the Federal Trade Commission, work to prevent misleading price advertising—so-called "sales" which, in effect, do not really provide bargains. To detect whether the sale is a worthwhile one is a matter of knowing the store and its reputation, the merchandise lines that it carries, and of having the time to shop carefully.

According to the National Retail Merchants Association, many department stores schedule regular sales in these months:

January. White sales, fur sales, storewide clearance sales.
February. Washington's Birthday specials, furniture sales.
March. Housewares sales.
May. White sales.
July. Post-July Fourth clearance of summer merchandise, furniture sales.
August. Furniture sales continue, fur sales, white sales.
October. Columbus Day specials. Anniversary or other storewide sales.
November. Pre-Christmas value promotions.

If you need something which you know is on sale, and the value appears to be good, do not waste any time getting to the store. Sale merchandise is frequently on a first-come, first-serve basis.

BAROMETERS | See WEATHER

BEDDING | See also BEDS

All furnishing purchases are important, but the buying of bedding is uniquely so. A good mattress and bedsprings, smooth sheets, plump pillows, and warm coverings are the foundation of the restful sleep everyone needs to maintain good health.

MATTRESSES

The best mattress for you is one that satisfies your ideas of comfort. Some people prefer a firm or "hard" mattress—one that is fairly unyielding. Others like a "soft" or a "medium" mattress. Don't hesitate to make a "rest test" in the store; it's expected. Stretch right out and stay there until you get the feel of the mattress.

Federal law requires that labels list the materials used. Buy a mattress made by a reputable manufacturer and sold by a reliable dealer. Don't expect to get a $79.50 mattress for $39.50. There are no such bargains.

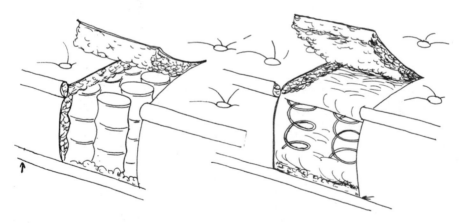

In most cases it's best to buy a new box spring with a new mattress; they are designed to work together. A mattress may not give proper support if used with an old or unsuitable spring. Some foam mattresses, only 4 inches thick, must be used with an extra-high box spring to reach normal bed height. The firmness rating (medium, firm, extra firm) also applies to both. A soft box spring, as sometimes found in a low-priced bedding set, may actually detract from the support capability of a firm mattress.

Innerspring mattresses are constructed in two major ways—the open-coil or Bonnell type, and the pocketed coil or Marshall type. The largest percentage of mattresses on the market is of the open-coil type. Coil counts range from 220 to 1,000 (for a full-sized mattress); the complexity of the method of joining the coils is often proportionate to the cost and quality. In general, a comfortable sleeping surface is one which "gives" to conform to the curves and contours of the body, yet provides positive, firm, over-all support. The coils should be strengthened to prevent edge sag.

In **open-coil** construction, coil units are made of high-carbon wire. The heavier the gauge, the firmer the mattress. Standard mattresses (full size) usually have 220 or more coils. A mattress with 300 or more coils may prove noticeably better over a period of time. Coil count may go as high as 1,000; but unless a mattress has been well assembled and insulated, it may not be as good as one with fewer coils but better construction. If coils crowd and touch each other, the result will be a noisy mattress.

In **pocketed coil** construction, each spring is sewed into its own pocket of muslin. Strips of these pocketed springs are wound back and forth to make up the unit. Full-size Marshall units usually contain about 800 coils. Each spring should work independently with little effect on adjacent ones, so allowance is made for body contours, and over-all support remains uniform.

The **padding** is usually all-cotton felt; sometimes a layer of curled hair or foam is added. Insulating material keeps the padding from working down into the coils and prevents "coil feel." This may be wire link or mesh, sisal pads, quilted cotton felt with a cloth backing, or multi-layer cellulose pad with a net backing.

Many of the lower priced mattresses are **machine-filled.** Components (springs, insulation, and padding) have been laid together and fed into a machine which inserts them into a pre-sewn bag, much as a sausage skin is stuffed. The open end is then sewed shut. The disadvantage is that not enough attention can be paid to adequate fastening of the components, and they may tend to shift during use.

Better mattresses have prebuilt borders, and for ease in handling and turning, have study, firmly attached handles.

Foam mattresses may be made of natural latex, foam rubber, or a plastic foam called polyurethane. Density or firmness can be controlled in the manufacturing process. Foam mattresses are ideal for allergy sufferers. They collect no dust, are moth, vermin, and mold-proof.

Urethane foam costs less than latex foam and does not have the same properties. Latex foam is molded to shape, whereas urethane foam is made in a large bulk from which slabs are cut to size.

Latex has excellent compression resistance, will keep its supporting power through years of service. Good quality urethane foam also will give you long-term resilience and firmness. However, it is much lighter in weight than latex; take care not to buy one that's too light. It may shift off the spring, and bed linens may not stay in place.

A bed board under a soft mattress will make it feel firmer, but you do not get the proper support provided by a good firm mattress, and you will not benefit from the box spring.

The **outer fabric** should be firmly woven and sturdy. High count 8-ounce ticking is best. Fabric below 5-ounce weight will not wear well. A woven pattern is more durable than printed material; printed ticking also tends to fade. Damask is sometimes used, but must be very heavy to be durable. Quilted covers and fancy ticking improve appearance but not performance.

Sizes: A mattress should be at least 6 inches longer than the sleeper, and wide enough not to be confining. When two people sleep on a standard double bed, each has only the width of a baby's crib (27 inches). Consider oversize bedding if you are 5 feet, 10 inches or taller. Standard sizes are 75 inches long by 54 inches wide for a full bed, 38 inches wide for a twin. The same widths are available in extra long (80-inch) mattresses. Queen size is 60 by 80 inches; king size is 72 to 78 inches wide, by 80 to 84 inches long.

Care. A good mattress is a long-term investment. Protect it with a washable pad. Occasionally vacuum lint and dust off the innerspring type with a hand vacuum cleaner, or the small nozzle attachment of your floor cleaner. Innerspring mattresses should be turned occasionally to distribute wear and to restore component materials to their original resilience. Alternate the turning—side-to-side one time, end-to-end the next. An occasional airing is beneficial, too, particularly in humid climates. Foam mattresses require no special care. They don't need turning or airing.

BED SPRINGS

When you lie on a mattress your weight will depress the springs below it several inches. Therefore, careful selection of a spring is important for comfort as well as long service.

A good box spring should start with a solid wood frame; each row of springs should be supported by a slat. Spring count can vary from fewer than 100 to as many as 1,000 (full-size bed). As in mattresses, construction methods vary widely from the coil-over-coil approach to complicated tying arrangements. Any box spring, regardless of its inner construction, should have a good layer of insulation, and generally a thin layer of padding covered by a durable dustproof ticking. You should not be able to feel the coils when you run your hand over the surface of a box spring. If the mattress was designed for a certain type of bed spring, then you should buy the set.

MATTRESS PADS

Mattress pads vary considerably in quality. Better ones will have close, neat stitching in a quilted pattern that keeps the filling from shifting. Edges should be tape bound and double stitched; the fabric should be Sanforized or preshrunk. The best filler is bleached cotton or a synthetic fiber such as polyester or nylon. Some pads are plastic-coated or -covered, so they can be sponged off between washings. There is also a combination pad and mattress cover which fits somewhat like a fitted sheet, and protects the sides and ends of the mattress as well as the top.

PILLOWS

Pillows are filled with one of the following:

Down. The more down in a pillow, the more expensive it is apt to be. Down comes from the undercoating of a duck or goose, is very soft and fluffy, and has no quill. Eiderdown is very expensive but the softest of the down fillings; goose down runs it a close and practical second. By blending feathers and down in varying proportions, degrees of firmness can be varied to suit every taste—the more feathers, the firmer the pillow. For example: 75 per cent goose down, 25 goose feathers produces a pillow which is satisfactorily soft, and the feathers have the desirable effect of keeping the down stirred up—discouraging its matting or packing.

Feathers. Even without down, goose feathers make a fine pillow. They may be white or gray; color makes no difference in the filling qualities. Duck feathers are smaller, make a heavier pillow, and are not as strong as goose feathers. Both are desirable fillings because they have a natural arch or curl that gives long-term resiliency.

Turkey and chicken feathers are straight and must be artificially curled for fluffiness. This results in a less durable pillow, since the feathers will mat down quickly when the curl comes out. "Crushed feathers" is a term sometimes used to describe this filling.

Batting. Pillows filled with batting made from polyester or acrylic fibers have some special advantages. They are non-allergenic, mothproof, odorless, and easy to wash. They have good resiliency and are lightweight. Filling should be in the form of a one-piece batting, not clumps or fibers. A one-piece batting is less apt to lump in use.

Foam pillows of natural latex or man-made polyurethane are very buoyant, non-allergenic, and unaffected by moths and mildew. One-piece forms are superior to shredded foam. Some latex foam pillows are made with one soft side, the other side harder.

A good pillow **covering** fabric is ticking or closely woven, 8-ounce twill. The seams of better pillows are welted for greater strength. If the covering is nylon or acetate, it should be a heavy, twill-type taffeta; lighter weights tend to fray and pull out at the seams.

HOW TO JUDGE A GOOD PILLOW

A good pillow will not be too heavy. Compare by weighing them on your hand. Heaviness is often a sign of poor quality filling.

It should be resilient. Check by putting your weight on two hands centered on the pillow. A good pillow will not stay dented, but come back to shape.

It should be buoyant, so that your head will not sink too far down when you sleep. Test by holding one end and shaking vigorously. The filling should not shift or settle at the other end.

Feel the pillow to be sure it isn't lumpy. Pound it; there should be no dust. Smell it; never buy one that has an odor.

Check the covering. It should be firmly woven so the filling can't leak out or dust filter in.

SHEETS AND PILLOW CASES

Percale sheets are woven of finer threads than muslin, and their texture, therefore, is softer. The use of combed yarns accounts for their smooth, silky feeling. Combing is a process that straightens the fibers and eliminates short fibers before the cotton is twisted into thread. The best wearing sheets, muslin or percale, are those with the highest thread count.

> MUSLIN: 112, lightweight, poor durability
> 128, medium weight, fair durability
> 140, heavy weight, excellent durability
> PERCALE: 180, lightweight, good durability
> 200 (and higher), lightweight, very fine
> and smooth, very good durability

Get the **right size.** Flat sheets may be purchased in lengths of 90, 99, and 108 inches for a regular 75-inch bed; 113 or 120 inches for extra long beds. Since flat sheets usually shrink about 6 per cent in length, the 108-inch-long sheet is the best choice for a standard 75-inch bed. After allowing for hems and shrinkage, there will still be 6 or 7 inches of tuck-in length at each end. In deciding on width, allow about 6 inches of tuck-under at each side of the mattress. Standard widths run 63 or 72 inches for single beds; 72 inches for a three-quarter or twin bed; 81 or 90 inches for a double bed. A 108-inch width is best for oversize beds.

Fitted sheets are made to fit oversize as well as standard size beds. You will find them labeled Full, Twin, King, Queen. Check corners of fitted sheets to make sure they are reinforced to prevent tearing. Many are made with elasticized corners which make them easier to put on and take off. Fitted sheets should be Sanforized or have some other shrink resistant finish so they will keep their fit after laundering.

The most frequently used **pillowcase** sizes are 42 by 36, 42 by 38½, and 45 by 38½ inches. To determine the right choice of case for your pillow, measure its width, double this measurement, add another 2 or 3 inches. For example, a pillow measuring 20 inches across needs a case marked 42 inches. A smaller case would make the pillow too compressed; a larger one, too untidy.

You'll find it convenient to have six sheets for each bed and three cases for each pillow. This will allow for a set in use, a set in the laundry, and a set in the closet.

BLANKETS

The warmth of a blanket does not depend so much on its weight as on its construction. A good blanket is made with a lofty nap or with a cellular weave (thermal type) that traps body heat and keeps out cold air. "Fiber woven" refers to blankets made by a quicker and more economical process than weaving.

All-wool blankets have excellent warmth-retaining qualities and their nap will stay resilient through years of use if the blankets are laundered properly. Special finishes have been developed for wool blankets to make them mothproof, machine-washable and dryable with minimal shrinkage.

Acrylic blankets such as Acrilan, Creslan, and Orlon retain warmth well and are lightweight. Because these fabrics resist shrinkage and distortion, they may be machine laundered and dryer dried. Acrylic fabrics are also not affected by moths or mildew, are nonallergenic. Blankets of acrylic tend to shed or pill more than wool. Fiber-Sealed Orlon and "Nap Guard" are two names to look for; blankets carrying these labels have been treated for retention of nap. Acrylic blankets are soft but not as springy as wool. Their plus values lie in ease of care and light weight combined with good warmth retention.

Rayon blankets and blends containing rayon are less expensive, but washing tends to disturb the nap causing them to shed or look shaggy. Rayon blend blankets bearing an Avisco Integrity Tag have been made with good quality rayon and will perform better than cheaper ones. Finishes such as "Nap Guard" are used also on rayon blankets to minimize shedding.

Cotton blankets are lightweight and soft with a slight nap. They're good blankets for summer when high warmth retention is not needed or desired. There is a thermal blanket made of cotton with a cellular weave, however, which retains warmth extremely well.

Electric blankets can be regulated to supply the exact degree of warmth you want. They weigh very little, and one cover is all you need. On the latest models, once a comfortable setting has been found, the thermostatic control needs no further adjustment, no matter how room temperature varies. Use of an electric blanket will add about fifty cents a month to your electric bill. Prices vary according to materials used and blanket size. Be sure an electric blanket you buy has a UL (Underwriters' Laboratories) seal, which assures you it is safe to use. A word of caution with electric blankets: *Do not use moth preventives or dry-clean.* Either one could damage the wiring.

Blanket size for twin bed is 65 by 90 inches; for double bed, 80 by 90.

The utility size, 72 by 90 inches, is a good choice since it can be used on either twin or double beds. King size blankets measure 90 by 108 inches.

BEDS | See also BEDDING

Comfort, convenience, and style are of prime importance when selecting a bed. Each of these 11 basic types of bed serves a specific purpose of style or convenience:

1. Canopy four-poster. The canopy frame is optional; without it the bed is called a *four-poster*. The delicate design, reflecting late Sheraton influence, dates back to the eighteenth century.

2. Brass bed. This late nineteenth century headboard consists of brass-plated tubing wrought in an ornate pattern. Contemporary adaptations are usually lower in height and somewhat less intricate in design.

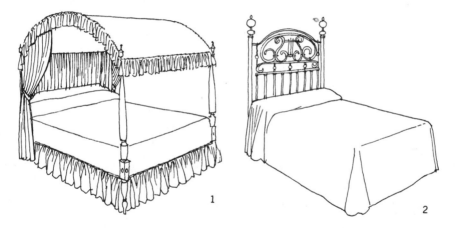

3. Daybeds are available in both traditional and modern styles, and are particularly appropriate for bed-sitting rooms or den-guest rooms. To dress the bed for day use, round bolsters are usually placed at each end.

4. **Wrought iron.** The headboard shown is a contemporary version of a late Victorian style. Victorians referred to metal work of this type as "iron lace" and used wrought-iron furniture indoors and out. Modern versions are often made of aluminum, as well as of iron.

5. **Twin swing bed.** Twin box springs and mattresses are mounted on metal frames attached to an oversize headboard to form an outsize double bed. Casters on the frames allow the units to swing apart for ease in making the beds.

6. **Recess wall bed.** When not in use, this space-saving bed can be folded upright into the wall. Bed frames are made in twin or full size, use standard mattresses, and will fit into a recess as shallow as 12 inches.

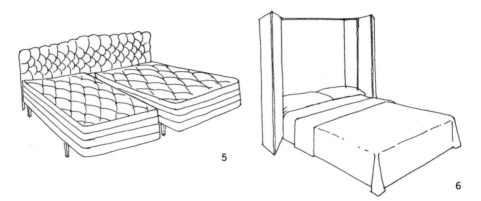

5

6

7. **Bunk beds** are particularly useful in children's rooms. They may be placed one above the other, as shown, or separated and used as twin beds. A ladder is provided to climb to the upper bunk.

8. **Roll-away cot.** This cot folds compactly to 16 inches thick and 45 inches high; casters on the base allow it to be rolled out of sight for storage.

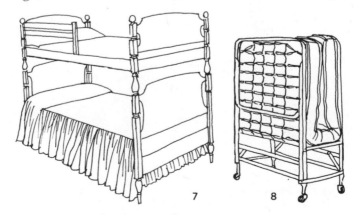

7   8

The bed opens to standard height and is supported by folding legs at each end. Bed frames are made in widths of 30, 36, 39, and 48 inches. Cots are extremely useful in small houses or apartments with limited space.

9. **Convertible sofa beds.** The no-guest-room problem is often solved by a sofa that converts into a bed for overnight guests. It is available in a wide variety of styles and fabric coverings.

10. **Trundle bed.** Sleeping space for two is provided by this modern version of the old trundle bed. During the day, one bed slides out of sight beneath the other; at night, the lower bed is pulled out and raised to the same height as its twin.

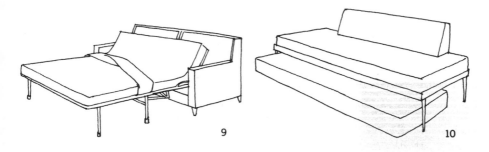

BIRDS FOR PETS |

How to tell singers from swingers. Because they are entertaining and usually easy to tame, songbirds or "talking" birds can make fine household pets if they are chosen carefully. Some have beautiful colors and exotic plumage; some are noted for their full-throated, lovely songs or talented mimicry of anything they hear.

A list of popular pet birds follows. Prices depend not only on the breed but on the particular bird's beauty and demonstrated talent. For example, a parakeet may cost anywhere from $3 to $15, and a myna bird from $22 up to several hundred dollars. Before buying, it is a good idea to shop more than one pet store.

Canaries are the most talented singers of all, but *only the males sing*. To be certain you have a singer, hear his song before you take him home. If you plan to purchase a pair of singing canaries, cage them separately. Two males in the same cage will not sing and will almost certainly fight.

Cockateels are parrot beauties in saffron-gray and white, with red and yellow touches. Comparatively quiet birds, cockateels can be taught to talk and perform tricks, but they are admired mainly for their exotic appearance.

Conures are miniature or dwarf parrots, about 6 inches high. Clowning, colorful birds with powerful beaks, they can be trained and taught to talk as well as some larger parrots.

Doves are gentle and retiring. They have a plump charm and like to sit in their cages and coo sweetly. They are usually sold in pairs, but single birds manage nicely. Their coloring and personality are subdued.

Finches are tiny, jewel-like, perky birds enjoyed primarily for their color. Their bouncy, cavorting movements are amusing to watch. Most are not good songbirds.

Java temple birds, are also called Java sparrows, ricebirds, or paddybirds. Slightly larger than a canary, this charcoal-grey and pink bird is handsome and entertaining. It has a soft, bell-like song and a "whistle" to which it jumps up and down. Easily finger tamed, it is a good choice for children.

Lovebirds, playful and pretty, live up to their name with cuddling and mutual chattering. They resemble parakeets in color and cleverness, but have short tails. They are larger with a chubby charm of their own. Buy only one lovebird if you want it to talk and do tricks.

Mynas, the best talkers of the bird world, will imitate anything from a siren or telephone ring to another bird or human voice. Though clever, they are not particularly pretty (black with a large yellow beak). Mynas are not seed-eaters and must be fed heartier fare, such as dog food, fruit, or specially packaged myna food. Cages require more frequent cleaning. Mynas already trained to talk are much more expensive.

Parakeets or budgerigars are small and colorful, ranging from albino-white and pastels to yellow-greens and the popular blues. Affectionate and highly intelligent birds, they can be taught to pull a wagon, walk a ladder, ring a bell, and do many other tricks. All parakeets can be taught to talk, but young birds (eight to ten weeks) are easiest to teach. Identify a parakeet of three months or younger by the lines or ridges across its forehead. These are absent on older birds.

Ravens are clever, amusing, crowlike birds. They can be hand-tamed with proper training. Versatile and loyal pets, they can be taught to talk in an almost human voice, but the vocabulary will probably be limited to about fifteen words. (Parakeets and mynas can learn many more words.) Like mynas, ravens need hearty food and require frequent cage cleaning.

Waxbills, members of the weaverbird family, come in many colors. The vivid-feathered Lady Gouldian is the most expensive.

Here are guidelines for buying:

Be certain you pick a healthy bird. Beware of a puffed-up bird that looks like a ball of feathers. Choose one that is in good feather, bright and chirpy, clear-eyed and active. It should sit up straight on its perch and have a good grip.

A cage should be large enough for the bird to stretch its wings, exercise and play freely. A metal cage is generally considered the most durable and easiest to care for. Most cages come equipped with perches, swings, food and water cups. You may want to include such inexpensive accessories as a treat cup, weekend food and drink cups, bird bath, cuttlebone, treat cake, millet spray, and perch cleaner.

Remember that all birds are highly susceptible to drafts, strong sunlight, and sudden temperature changes, although some can withstand variations in heat or cold. Keep the bird in a comfortable, temperature-controlled room—not the kitchen, where appliances, cupboards, and open windows are potential dangers.

BREAD |

Although it is rarely homemade today, bread is still very much the staff of life. When made from enriched or whole wheat flour, it can be an inexpensive source of a number of important nutrients. The Food and Drug Administration has established standards for five types of bread—white, enriched, milk, raisin, and whole wheat; these standards specify the bread's ingredients, moisture content, weight, and proper labeling. This directory may help you understand the differences in nutrition among breads.

White bread must contain flour, water (or other specified liquid), salt, and yeast. It may also have one or more of certain other ingredients (such as shortening, milk, eggs, sugar, etc.). When wheat is milled into white flour, four important nutrients—thiamine, riboflavin, niacin, and iron—are greatly reduced. White bread is considerably lower in these nutrients than whole wheat or enriched bread.

Enriched bread has the same essential and optional ingredients as plain white bread, plus specified amounts of iron and the three B vitamins—thiamine, riboflavin, and niacin—which are added to bring the nutritional level of enriched bread up to that of whole wheat bread. It may also have added Vitamin D and calcium. Most white bread available today is enriched.

Milk bread is plain white bread made with milk as the only liquid ingredient. It is higher in calcium but about the same as white bread in the other nutrients.

Raisin bread is also made from the same basic formula as white bread, but it must have 50 pounds of raisins for each 100 pounds of flour. If not enriched, it is on a nutritional level with plain white bread, although the raisins increase the iron content somewhat.

Whole wheat bread is made with whole wheat flour rather than white flour. Whole wheat flour retains its iron and B vitamins.

Cracked wheat bread is made of part cracked wheat flour and part white flour. The more cracked wheat flour the bread contains, the higher nutritional value it will have. As in wheat bread and American rye, the type of flour that predominates will be mentioned first in the list of ingredients on the label.

Wheat bread contains part whole wheat and part white flour. Its nutritional value depends on the amount of whole wheat flour used.

Pumpernickel, a compact dark bread, is made of dark rye flour and rye meal. Nutritionally, it approaches whole wheat bread.

American rye contains white and rye flours. Again, the nutritive value is determined by the proportion of the two flours used.

STORING BREAD AND ROLLS

Today you can buy an assortment of breads and rolls—packaged ready-to-eats, brown-and-serves, frozen, and refrigerated—at either your market or bakery. In storing these breads keep the following pointers in mind:

If they're **frozen** breads, rolls, or coffeecakes, store them in your freezer until time to heat and serve as label directs.

If they're **refrigerated** rolls or biscuits, in tubelike containers, all ready to bake, store them on one of the refrigerator shelves—not in the door. For best results use before the expiration date on the container.

If packaged **brown-and-serve** or **baked** loaf breads and rolls, store them, preferably in your freezer, where properly wrapped, they will retain moisture and flavor, remain free of mold, and keep their freshness for several weeks. As a second choice, store wrapped bread in a clean, dry, ventilated breadbox at room temperature, away from such heat-producing equipment as range, refrigerator, radiator, etc. Stored this way, these breads will stay acceptably fresh for several days, but are more subject to mold than bread stored in the refrigerator or freezer.

The least desirable place to store wrapped bread is in the food compartment of the refrigerator. Here it retains moisture and is less subject to mold, but it stales more readily than in the breadbox.

If you use packaged hot roll **mix,** complete with yeast, or packaged biscuit or muffin mix, follow the label directions for storing on the pantry shelf until used for rolls, tea rings, date twists, pizza, biscuits, muffins, etc.

If it is frozen bread **dough,** follow the label directions for storing and for making white, wheat, rye, raisin, and other bread loaves and rolls.

BRUSHES |

One cleaning aid that is often not used to best advantage is the brush. This familiar tool has received attention from designers in recent years, and today is more functional than ever. Pictured are some new brush styles and some old types in new materials.

1. The **outside window washing brush** has a long, telescoping handle that attaches to a hose. A container in the handle holds detergent. The amount of suds can be regulated with a dial switch. The brush spins from

BRUSHES

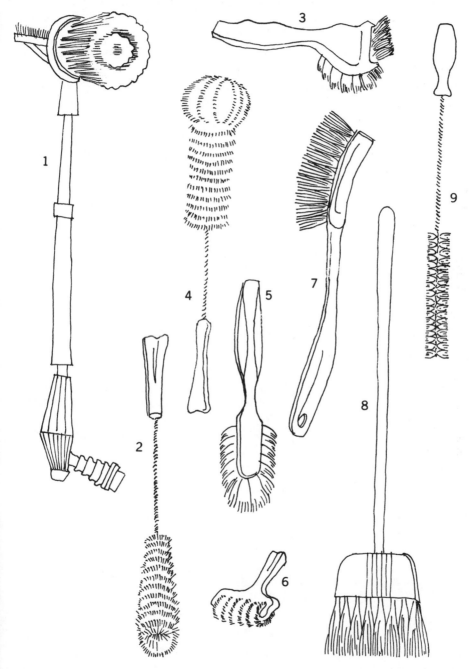

water pressure. Some models come with a squeegee on one side, extensions to reach high windows, and other features.

2. The **baby-bottle brush** has a flared tip and long handle to clean the bottle before sanitizing. It can be sterilized.

3. The **pot and pan brush** has two sides. One brush surface has natural fiber bristles to scrub, the other has brass wire bristles to scour.

4. The **tumbler brush** has a swirl of nylon tufts at the end, and a long handle to reach the bottom curves of vacuum bottles, kettles, fruit jars, and other deep narrow containers.

5. The **dishwasher brush** with its round head and springy bristles makes dishwashing easier.

6. The **comb-cleaning brush** bristles reach between the comb's teeth. It can be used wet or dry.

7. The **stove and appliance brush** has long, brass wire bristles to scrub out crevices, dents, and dimples of stove burners, waffle irons, and other metal surfaces.

8. The **plastic broom** has bristle tips that have been split. This enables it to gather the finest dust and dirt particles.

9. The **percolator brush** is long and thin, with stiff bristles to clean oils out of spouts and hollow stems of coffeepots and teapots.

Other useful brushes include:

The **Venetian blind duster,** which has three fingers of long bristles to dust two slats at a time. The brush head can be dusted clean or washed with soap and water.

The **barbecue grill cleaner** comes with a stiff wire brush on one side to scour and a metal scraper on the other side to clean flat surfaces. The scraper has notched corners to clean grill rods.

The **scrub brush** has a plastic block that is comfortable to hold and will not be damaged by water. Its bristles are crimped plastic that stays stiff.

The **duster brush** has the same type of split-tip plastic bristles as the broom mentioned above. It sweeps up tiny particles from window ledges, counters, etc.

The **radiator duster** is flat-sided with long, soft bristles. Its long handle reaches into radiator crevices.

The **outdoor broom washer** attaches to a hose. The operation is similar to the outside window washer. Its plastic bristles resist acids and solvents.

The **ceiling and wall duster brush** fits on any standard-threaded handle. Long, soft bristles reach around molding and cornice surfaces.

CANNED FISH |

Tuna, America's most popular canned sea food, is an excellent source of the same fine protein you find in meat, eggs, cheese, and poultry. Kinds include albacore, prized for its white meat; yellowfin, greatest in size and abundance; skipjack, the smallest, but second only to yellowfin in the canned pack; and bluefin, a favorite of sportsmen. Look also for the style of pack:

Solid pack, in which free flakes shall not exceed 18 per cent, is ideal for cold plates, etc. *Chunks* are pieces, not less than 50 per cent of which, by weight, are retained in a half-inch mesh screen. It is fine for salads and other dishes where small pieces are desirable. *Flakes* are pieces, more than 50 per cent of which will pass through a half-inch mesh screen. *Grated tuna* consists of particles, not a paste, which pass through a half-inch mesh screen. Excellent for sandwich fillings, canapés, etc. Cans are available in three sizes, 13 ounces and smaller.

Most domestic tuna is packed in such vegetable oils as corn, cottonseed, or soybean. Some also comes in vegetable broth. Dietetic tuna, with its low salt content, is packed in distilled water with no salt added.

Salmon, another pantry shelf favorite, comes in three can sizes, 1 pound and smaller. Always check the label for the variety best suited to your needs, using the guide below:

1. For salads, canapés, or open-face sandwiches in which a rich salmon color and large firm flakes are important, choose:

      Sockeye: red   Blueback: medium red   Coho: silver

2. For closed sandwiches or creamed salmon dishes choose Chinook or king salmon. Both of these range in color from deep salmon to light pink and are a good buy.

3. For delicate soups or bisques, pink salmon is especially suitable in both color and flake.

4. For croquettes, fish cakes, casseroles, and other dishes where color is not important, try chum or keta. They are light pink and have large, coarse flakes.

Sardines, those little fish of the sea which we enjoy as hors d'oeuvres and in sandwiches, come from Maine, where they are packed in vegetable oil, mustard sauce, or tomato sauce, in 3¾- or 4-ounce cans. Pacific sardines, which are larger than Maine sardines, are packed, for the most part, in tomato sauce in 1-pound cans. From Norway and Portugal come tiny sardines (brisling or sprat) neatly packed in oils (such as olive) for a special flavor.

Browse through your grocer's shelves, too, for canned tomato herring, gefilte fish balls or patties, halibut, oysters, saurel, smoked clams and oysters—the list is endless!

CANNED SOUPS |

Canned condensed soups have been a cook-saving staple on the pantry shelf for generations. Today, with the addition of frozen soups and an ever-increasing variety of styles, they provide fine eating at the turn of a can opener. They may be served singly or in combination, or "individualized" by the addition of a favorite herb, tasty leftovers, etc.

In addition, canned soups or broths may be used as the stock for creating interesting sauces and exotic dishes. A whole new school of cookery has grown up around the American housewife's ability to duplicate French or Chinese or New England masterpieces without the labor of locating and preparing the basic ingredients.

Milk soups (prepared with milk): Cheddar-cheese soup, cream-of-asparagus, cream-of-celery, cream-of-chicken, beef-noodle, mushroom, pea, and vegetable. In the *frozen group* are: clam chowder (New England style), cream-of-potato, cream-of-shrimp, and oyster stew.

Meat, sea food, and legume soups: Bean with bacon, beef, beef broth, black bean, chicken-vegetable, chili-beef, consommé, green pea, onion, pepper pot, Scotch broth, split pea with ham, vegetable-bean, vegetable-beef, turkey-vegetable, etc. In the *frozen group* are: cream-of-shrimp, green pea with ham, oyster stew, old fashioned vegetable with beef, etc.

Vegetable soups: Chicken-vegetable, clam chowder (Manhattan style), cream-of-asparagus, cream-of-vegetable, green pea, minestrone, onion, cream-of-potato, Scotch broth, tomato, tomato-rice, vegetable, vegetable-bean, vegetable-beef, vegetarian vegetable, *frozen* cream-of-potato, etc.

Cereal soups (containing macaroni, rice, barley): Alphabet, beef-noodle, chicken gumbo, chicken-noodle, chicken-rice, Scotch broth, tomato-rice, turkey-noodle, minestrone, noodles with ground beef, etc.

SOUP MIXES

Soup mixes got their start in this country with the successful dehydrating and packaging of a chicken-noodle variety traditional with European cooks. Today, mixes include beef and many vegetable combinations. Packaged dry soup mixes keep indefinitely and take up little space, which makes them a favorite with skiers, hikers, and campers. Just add hot water and that steaming bowl of soup is ready.

A newcomer to this family comes in special, hermetically sealed cans to protect the flavor—two cans to the carton of the same or different soups. Just as freezing permitted introduction of certain hard-to-preserve soup flavors, this method adds scope. The chicken-noodle mix, for example, contains diced chicken which has been freeze-dried for fuller flavor.

BOUILLON CUBES

Beef or chicken bouillon cubes are valuable both as stock in cookery and to make a bracing hot broth drink for a cold day. Note that in using either cubes or canned soup as a stock, you can give the result an individual touch by the judicious addition of herbs, spices, and seasonings. Some of the finest dishes of famous chefs are prepared in just this way.

CANS AND CAN SIZES |

Knowing these facts can help you to get the most out of canned food products.

You may safely keep unused canned food in the opened can if it is promptly refrigerated. The can and its contents are sterilized when processed. The can will be safer than the dish to which these portions would otherwise be transferred.

Dents and rust on a can do not mean that the contents are spoiled. Some grocers sell such cans at a lower price than usual. If the rust or dent has actually perforated the can, it must be discarded.

A can that has swelled should be discarded. This could indicate production of gases by bacteria left in the food by inadequate sterilization in processing.

The liquid in a can of vegetables is not worthless. Don't throw it out. It contains about one-fifth of the vegetables' vitamins and minerals.

Never heat an unopened can. Heat can build up pressure inside the can and may cause it to burst. For campfire cooking, always puncture the top of the can before heating.

The occasional darkening on the inside of a can is caused by the action of components of certain foods on the lining. It is not dangerous.

Canned foods last indefinitely—as long as there is no break in the can.

In this age of self-service food stores, women have become increasingly dependent on labels as a guide to buying. Well-known canners word the labels to give you a clear picture of what's inside the can. The can size; the variety, style, color, maturity, and amount of food in the can (ingredients are listed according to proportion—the most, first); the number of servings; kind of syrup; uses; etc., are noted. This helps you buy what you want and the amount you need.

Of course, you must judge flavor for yourself. If certain brands satisfy you, remember their names. Canned tuna, for example, comes in several styles.

CAN AND JAR SIZES

BUFFET	PICNIC	VACUUM	NO. 300	NO. 303
8 oz.	10½ oz.	12 oz.	14-16 oz.	16-17 oz.
1 cup	1¼ cups	1½ cups	1¾ cups	2 cups

NO. 2	NO. 2½	46-OUNCE	NO. 10
1 lb. 4 oz. or 1 pt. 2 fl. oz.	1 lb. 13 oz.	3 lbs. 3 oz. or 1 qt. 14 fl. oz.	6½ to 7¼ lbs.
2½ cups	3½ cups	5¾ cups	12 to 13 cups

CAR PROBLEMS | See also DRIVING TIPS; GASOLINE AND OIL

It has happened to many drivers, perhaps to you: your car's horn gets stuck, keeps blowing. What should you do? Or you are driving in a sudden rainstorm and must go through a flooded spot in water up to the hubcaps. According to the American Automobile Association, the Automotive Safety Foundation, and the National Safety Council, here are practical ways to handle some of the most common problems that call for trouble shooting on the road.

Stuck accelerator. If you take your foot off the gas but the car fails to slow down, the accelerator may be stuck. Immediately turn off the ignition or—preferable if your car has power steering or power brakes—shift into low so the motor will help slow the car. (Power-equipped cars remain easier to control when the engine is running.) Slow gradually and get off the road. Unless the sticking is easily explained—an object wedged against the pedal, or lack of lubrication—do not drive farther until the car has been checked by a mechanic.

If your car brakes fail. One of the most terrifying driving experiences is sudden brake failure. Safety experts and automobile manufacturers suggest you follow these steps to stop your car:

Take your foot off the accelerator. Then apply the parking brake. This is the most important thing to remember. Yet, in the tension of the moment, many people forget about the car's second brake system. It will slow you down and eventually stop you, if it is in good working order.

Shift to a lower gear. Shifting down should be progressive—that is, from third to second to first—if possible, to avoid damage to the transmission. With an automatic transmission, shift the selector lever into low.

Pump the brakes hard, even if the brake pedal has gone to the floor. Enough hydraulic brake fluid may be left to build up pressure to give you temporary braking action.

Look for a surface of sand, dirt, water, or any material which may help to reduce your speed. In the country, look for a side road or aim for a soft spot on the bank of a hill. In the city, you may be able to slow down by rubbing your tires against a curb.

To avoid brake failure, have your brakes checked and maintained regularly. Brake fluid level should be checked every 1,000 miles and the brakes should be checked for adjustment or possible relining every 5,000 miles. In addition, watch for these signs of possible trouble: swerving of the car when brakes are applied; soft, spongy brake action; noisiness, squealing, or scratchy metal sounds; and brake pedals that must be pushed close to the floorboards before they work.

Locked bumpers. This happens frequently in parking or unparking maneuvers. If your bumper becomes lightly locked with that of another car, rock the bottom car up and down by pressing both hands on a fender. Should this fail to disengage them, try lifting the top bumper with a jack. If neither works, call a serviceman. Be careful that your hands and body are not pinched between the cars.

Frozen door lock. Do not force the key; it may snap. Heat it over a match or cigarette lighter or by holding it in your hand for several seconds. Put the key in the lock and attempt to turn it gently. Repeat if necessary.

Flood. When you must drive through deep puddles of water, keep your left foot lightly on the brake as you proceed and depress it enough to stop or practically stop the car. This friction heat keeps the brake linings dry. If they do become wet, dry them by periodically applying the brakes. Drive slowly until they take hold again.

Stuck horn. Lift the hood and find the horn, usually in front of and to one side of the radiator. Hit it sharply several times. If it continues to sound, pull out one or both of the wires attached to the horn. Then have it promptly repaired.

Overheated radiator. Escaping steam, often on the under side of the radiator, is the most usual sign of overheating. Another is the temperature gauge on the instrument panel registering at its highest point. Stop as soon as possible. Running an overheated car any distance may severely damage the engine.

If you have water handy and want to check the level in the radiator, be very careful about removing the radiator cap. Hot water and steam may spurt out. With a cloth, slowly loosen the cap, standing at arm's length from it. Turn the cap slightly in a counterclockwise direction, step back and wait. After you hear the pressure release, turn the cap the rest of the way to remove it.

If the water level is low, let the engine cool for several minutes before you add water. Use hot water if available. Keep the engine idling as you pour. (Be certain that the car's transmission is in neutral and the hand brake engaged.) If you have no water, wait until the gauge indicates normal temperature before starting the engine again. Drive slowly until you reach a source of water, stopping again if necessary for another cool-off period. Should the car overheat with a full radiator, the cause could be any of several conditions requiring service attention.

Car does not start. Make sure, first, that you are not out of gas, that the ignition key is fully on, and that the transmission is in the proper gear for starting. If switching the ignition key does not turn the motor, the battery may be dead. Try the horn and lights. Their failure to work properly indicates a battery too weak for starting.

When the motor turns but does not catch, and you smell gas, the carburetor may be flooded. Press the accelerator to the floor, hold it there without pumping, and turn on the ignition. If the car does not start in ten or fifteen seconds, switch off the ignition, take your foot off the accelerator, wait a few minutes, and repeat.

CARPETS | See RUGS AND CARPETS

CARVING GUIDE | See also HOLIDAY DINNER

How to carve a turkey. It *can* be done neatly and with a minimum of struggle. We suggest showing your husband these suggestions before you set the holiday bird before him—or even the chicken for a family meal.

1. Place roast fowl before carver, with legs to right. Starting at side facing him, he cuts leg from body, bending it back with left hand.

2. Next he lifts leg to side plate nearby. While holding leg with left hand, he severs thighbone from drumstick, just over round bone, as shown.

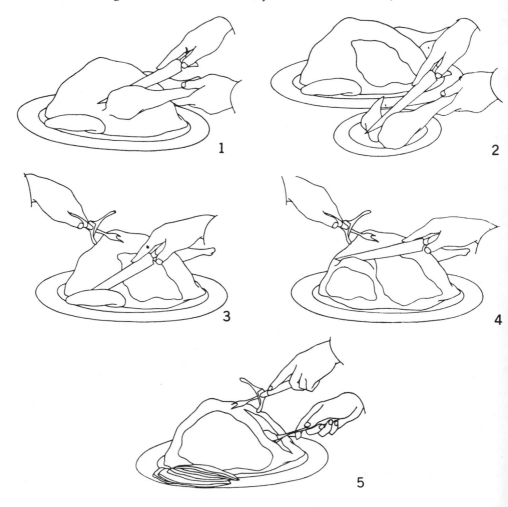

1

2

3

4

5

3. He slices all meat from drumstick and thigh. Then, with fork astride breastbone, he cuts down sharply where wing joins body, severing wing completely.

4. Now, starting just above joint from which wing was removed, he cuts thin slices of white meat, working upward, always cutting parallel to breastbone.

5. After breast has been sliced, it's easy to reach stuffing. For second servings, carver turns platter and carves other side of bird.

With an electric slicing knife, the procedure is the same except that at the start, place the bird on a cutting board.

How to carve roast beef. A standing rib roast will be easier to carve if the butcher has cut the backbone from the ribs—and if your knife is razor sharp!

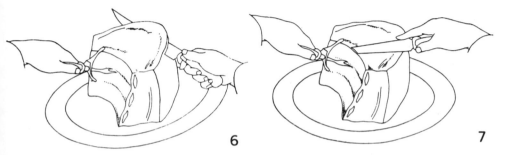

6   7

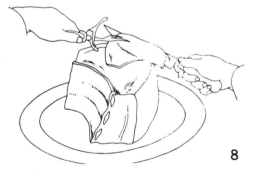

8

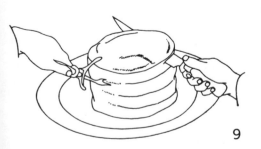

9   10

6. Place the roast (wide end down) before the carver with the rib side to his left. He inserts the fork between the two top ribs.

7. Start cutting quarter-inch-thick slices from the right outside edge toward the rib side. When the blade touches the rib, use the tip of the knife to cut along the length of the bone to loosen the meat slice.

8. Slide the knife under the slice, and steadying it with the fork, lift it to the side of the platter. Continue until there are slices for everyone. Reinsert the fork lower in the meat as necessary.

With *rolled rib roast,* proceed as follows:

9. Do not remove the cords from the roast before carving. Insert the fork into the left side about one or two inches below the top. Start slicing across the meat grain, from the right side toward the fork.

10. Make the first slice fairly thick to get a level surface. Use the knife and fork to lift each slice to the side of the platter. Move the fork lower in the meat for each slice, and sever the cords one at a time as they are reached.

Leg of lamb. Note that one side of the leg bone is thicker, meatier than the other. Place before carver with thin section facing him and shank (protruding bone) to right.

11. Insert fork in large end of leg and cut a few lengthwise slices from thin side. Now turn the leg so it rests firmly on this cut surface.

12. This puts thick meaty section upright, with shank pointing up. With fork in large end of roast, start slicing from right end, close to shank. Slice straight down to leg bone. Cut as many parallel slices as needed.

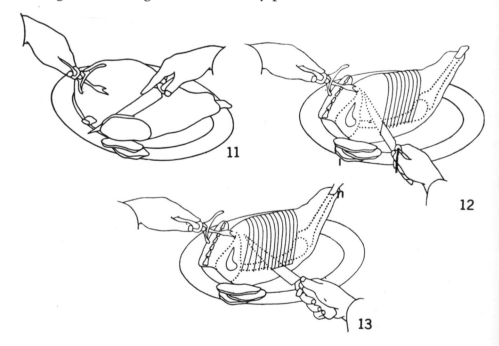

13. With fork still in place, run carving knife along leg bone under the slices. This releases all slices at one time, ready for serving.

Whole ham. Place before host with scored side up and shank end to right. Thinner section will be toward him if the ham is a left leg, will face away from him if a right leg. Proceed as with leg of lamb, first cutting two or three slices from thin side to serve as a base for turning ham upright (Ill. 14). For additional servings, turn ham back to original position (scored side up) and carve at right angles to bone (Ill. 15).

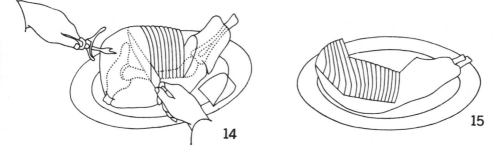

14   15

Loin of pork. For easier carving, butcher should saw across the base of the ribs to loosen backbone.

16. As soon as loin is roasted, in the kitchen, place on cutting board with rib side up. Holding it with fork, remove backbone by running knife along it, close and parallel.

17. Place roast on platter with ribs facing carver, resting on surface just cut. He holds it with fork at top and makes vertical slices beginning at right end. For first slice, keep blade close to left side of first rib. Next slice will be boneless; others will alternate, some boneless, some containing a rib.

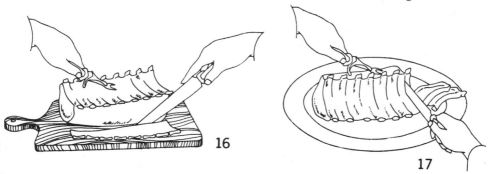

16   17

Steak (T-bone, porterhouse, etc.): Set before carver with tapered end at left.

18. Cut around bone closely with point of knife; remove bone to side of platter.

19. With knife at right angles to platter, cut across full width of steak to make 1-inch slices, until entire steak including tapered end is sliced. (*Note:* Although they look alike, the center slices are apt to be best and may be served to an honored guest.)

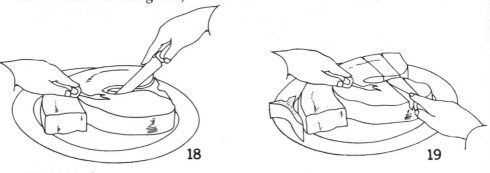

18   19

CHAIRS |

Each of the chair styles shown represents a basic traditional design. All are available either in the basic form or in an adaptation or modification of the original. Most are made in both armchair and side-chair forms.

1. **Boston rocker.** Benjamin Franklin is credited with inventing the rocking chair. All-wooden type may be painted and decorated.

2. **Victorian.** Exposed wooden frames, sometimes elaborately carved; upholstery may be velvet, needlepoint, or other formal fabric.

3. **Hepplewhite.** Shield-back side chair, tapered legs, upholstered seat. Many variations are made.

4. **Queen Anne.** Cabriole legs and vase-form of splat back are characteristic. Seats are sometimes of woven rush, more often upholstered.

5. **Duncan Phyfe.** Lyre back is favorite form; removable slip seat may be upholstered in striped satin, other fabric, or leather.

6. **Louis XVI.** Wooden frames, usually carved in classical motifs, sometimes painted and/or gilded. Upholstery is usually of tapestry, brocade, satin, damask, or other formal fabric.

7. **Ladder-back.** At least four slats, arranged ladder fashion, form the back. Usually it has rush seat.

8. **American Empire**. Has upholstered slip seat. Graceful wooden frame may be solid or veneer.

9. **Sheraton.** Wooden frame, upholstered seat, a classically designed back. In this example, upholsterer's nails form pattern on seat edge.

10. **Chippendale.** Elaborately carved wooden frame is typical; legs may be straight; seat upholstered in leather or fabric. Many variations.

11. **Windsor.** Chair shown is called "bow back." Captain's chair was developed from the design, minus bow over back. Many variations.

12. **Hitchcock.** "Fancy" chairs named for the famous maker. Painted wooden frames may be decorated. Seats often made of rush.

CHAIRS

1   2   3   4

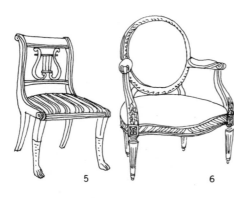

5   6   7   8

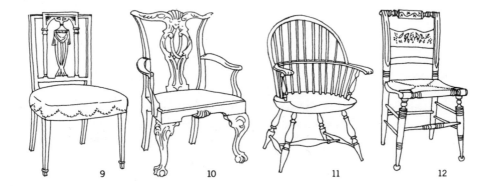

9   10   11   12

13. **Louis XV.** Exposed wooden frame carved in graceful curves. Upholstered back, sides, seat, and armrests make it quite comfortable.

14. **Wing.** Style introduced during early part of eighteenth century. High back and sides offered protection against ever-present drafts.

15. **Directoire.** Developed after French Revolution, emphasizes classic simplicity of ancient Greek and Roman lines.

HOW TO BUY A CHAIR THAT REALLY FITS

You won't find one chair that is equally comfortable for every person who sits in it. But for the perfect lounging chair for yourself, experts advise that you follow these rules:

1. Start with seat height and depth, the most critical dimensions. Your feet should reach the floor while your back easily touches the chair back. Be sure there is no pressure under your thighs close to the knees; this can hinder circulation.

2. The seat should slant somewhat from the front to the back and be flat or slightly curved from the sides. It should meet the back at an angle greater than 90 degrees.

3. About six or seven inches above the seat, the back should curve in to meet and support the curve of your spine.

4. The back should be high enough to support your shoulder blades, but not so high that it pushes the neck forward. And it should be flat or slightly raised in the center so that shoulders are not pushed forward.

5. Armrests should support elbows and lower arms. If rests are too high, they'll push shoulders up and forward. If too low, they'll be useless.

6. The seat should be wide enough to permit movement, but not so wide that you must stretch for the armrests.

7. The center of the seat should not be too soft or the front edge too hard. A firm, resilient material is the best cushioning.

Most adults will be comfortable in chairs that conform to the general rules above and have these dimensions: seat—15 to 16 inches high (when the cushion is compressed), 18 to 19 inches deep, 20 to 22 inches wide; back— at least 18 inches high; armrests—about 14 inches long, 7 to 9 inches above the seat.

CHARGE ACCOUNTS | See also CREDIT AND DEBT

Millions of Americans say "charge it" when shopping. When used wisely, a charge account can be a great convenience. You do not have to carry large sums of money; you can often order by telephone or by mail; you don't have to wait for change; and the monthly bill is a permanent record of your purchases.

Not all charge accounts are the same. The knowledgeable shopper weighs the cost of the various types to determine which to use—and how frequently. Too, she makes certain in advance how much she can safely afford to spend. These are the main types of charge accounts:

Regular. This is the oldest type. Generally, the customer is billed at the end of the month or on a certain day of each month following her purchase. Payment is due ten to thirty days later. There are no service charges. The store considers the cost of extending credit in setting prices for its merchandise.

Option. This is a variation of the regular account with a time limit. If the customer pays the full amount by an agreed date, there is no service charge. Or she may elect to pay in six to ten monthly installments plus a service charge of 1½ per cent per month on the unpaid balance.

Revolving. Technically, this is a form of installment credit rather than a true charge account. The customer agrees to a maximum amount she may charge, generally from $100 to $500, or more by special arrangement. A time limit is set on repayment, usually from six to twelve months. Each month the customer pays a certain percentage of what she owes. If she buys more merchandise, the monthly payments become larger. For example, on a ten-month plan a customer may charge $200 in purchases and pay $20 a month. If she charges an additional $100, the monthly payments increase to $30. A service charge of 1½ per cent a month on the unpaid balance is added to the bill.

Coupon or scrip. In decreasing use today, this plan also limits the customer to a maximum amount. She receives a book of coupons or scrip, which she uses as cash in buying merchandise. She agrees to pay for the book within a fixed period. When scrip is issued, a service charge of up to 10 per cent is made.

Lay-away. This is really a savings plan. The store retains the merchandise until you pay for it in installments or in a lump sum. For instance, a fur coat bought on a lay-away at an August sale would be held until November.

The customer would have these three months to pay for it, at no service charge.

With regular and option accounts, there is usually a limit to how much the customer may charge—although the store may set this limit without telling you. The idea is to keep a family from overextending its credit (which see). In applying for the account, a customer usually must give details of income, employment, bank references, and other charge accounts. The store checks the applicant's payment record with the local credit bureau. (Does she pay her bills promptly and in full?) Through the Associated Credit Bureaus of America, a person new in a community is checked by contacting the credit bureau where she lived previously.

In many cities, customers receive a charge plate or card. Sometimes it is usable for identification in several stores. If it's lost, the customer should notify the store *immediately*. Generally, the customer is not responsible for charges made against the lost card after such notice.

Growing use of charge accounts is being made by teenagers. The minimum age is usually fourteen or fifteen, with maximum credit limited to $25 or $30 or sometimes $50. To respect the obvious ethics in the situation (and because by most state laws teenagers are minors), the store either requires a parent's permission or notifies the parents that an account has been opened.

CHEESE DICTIONARY |

* Varieties so marked are made in the United States and are normally available.

NATURAL CHEESES

KIND, ORIGIN, SHAPE	DESCRIPTION	USES
*Bel Paese Circular cake	Surface: slate gray Interior: light yellow. Soft to solid consistency Flavor: mild	Dessert—with fruit or crackers
*Blue Wheels Portions	Danish blue cheese, imported from Denmark, is creamy white with blue-green veins, made from cows' milk. Blue cheese is also made in U.S.A.	Dessert—with crackers or fruit Salads—popular in tossed ones Salad dressings Appetizers—as a spread
*Brick Rectangular Slices Sticks	Surface: yellowish brown Interior: white to light cream. Pliable body and somewhat open texture Flavor: mild to pronounced	Sandwiches—especially for lunch or lunch box With cold cuts—used sliced, to round out meat platters

*Caciocavallo (originally from Italy) Made in a number of unusual shapes, often in pairs	Surface: light brown and par-affined Interior: rather hard, dry. Very solid. body and texture Flavor: somewhat salty, smoky	As table cheese when fresh For grating and cooking when fully cured
*Camembert (originally from France) Portion servings	Surface: thin, whitish crust Interior: soft, creamy, yellow-ish. Before serving, soften at room temperature until almost fluid. Eat crust Flavor: luscious flavor all its own	Dessert or salad—the univer-sal favorite with crackers or such fruits as pears, ap-ples, etc.
*Chantelle (trade-mark name) Wheel shape	Surface: red-coated Interior: cream to light orange. Semihard. Rather open texture Flavor: mild to pronounced, depending on age	With cold meats As dessert or party refresh-ment—with crackers or fruits, etc.
*Cheddar Circular cake or cylin-drical Rectangular blocks or bars Sticks, wedges, slices, shredded	Surface: waxed yellow-brown or unwaxed Interior: light cream to orange. Close texture. Few, if any, irregular small openings Flavor: mild when fresh; sharp and pleasing when cured or aged	Sandwiches—a favorite filling With pies and cobblers Salads—adds heartiness to tossed salads In salad dressings In dishes such as soufflés, cas-seroles, etc.
*Cottage Bulk or packages	Made from skim milk, coagu-lated by pure lactic-acid bacteria culture. Some have cream added. White Flavor: pleasing, slightly acid. Other flavors: chive, pine-apple, fruit salad, vegetable salad	Salads—adds heartiness to fruit and vegetable ones. Season with chives, pickle relish, diced tomatoes, etc. Sandwiches
*Cream Packages, loaf, bars, glasses, plastic dishes, etc.	Made from a mixture of cream and milk with minimum fat content of 33 per cent. Comes with chives, relish, pimento, dates, bacon, pine-apple, etc., added. Flavor: delicate, slightly acid	Breakfast spread Sandwiches Salads—adds heartiness to fruit and vegetable ones Salad dressings Dessert—with crackers and jelly
*Edam (originally from Holland) Round ball	Surface: red-coated Interior: body and texture usually somewhat grainy Flavor: mild. Slightly salty when fresh, pronounced when cured	Dessert—popular in wedges, with fruit or salad Appetizer or nibbler. To serve, cut off top; hollow out cen-ter; dice; refill

NATURAL CHEESES

Kind, Origin, Shape	Description	Uses
*Gorgonzola Cylindrical	Blue-mold cheese made from cows' milk Surface: clay color Interior: blue streaks produced by mold spores Flavor: rich, piquant, when fully cured	Salads and salad dressings—add cheese, crumbled Dessert—with fruit, salad, or crackers
*Gouda (originally from Holland) Ellipsoid	Made from partly skimmed milk Surface: usually red Interior: if imported, solid; often contains small round holes. If domestic (baby Gouda), softer, closer body Flavor: often slightly acid	Same as Edam
*Liederkranz (trade-mark name) Rectangular packages	Surface: russet Interior: creamy yellow, soft Flavor and odor: robust	Appetizer—on crackers, toast, etc. With salad, crackers Dessert—with crackers, fruit
*Limburger (originally from Belgium) Cubical; rectangular In jars	Surface: grayish brown Interior and flavor: when fresh, is white, odorless, and tasteless. As curing progresses, odor, flavor, and color develop strongly	Sandwiches—especially good with rye, pumpernickel, or other dark breads; or on crackers Nice appetizer
*Mozzarella (originally from Italy) Irregularly spherical	Made from cows' milk. Semi-soft. Light cream colored Flavor: mild	Especially enjoyed in main dishes such as eggplant or veal parmigiana, pizza, etc., because of elastic quality of melted cheese
*Muenster (originally from Germany) Cylindrical Slices Sticks	Surface: yellowish tan Interior: white when fresh. Turns light cream when fully cured Flavor: mild to pronounced	Sandwiches—good with rye or pumpernickel bread Appetizers or nibblers—nice with scallions, carrot or cucumber sticks, radishes
*Mysost (Gjetost or primost) Cubical; rectangular	Made from whey. White to brown Flavor and odor: sweet flavor, distinct odor	Serve thin slices on bread or crackers, at lunch, supper, etc.
*Neufchatel (originally from France) 2- or 3-lb. loaves	Resembles cream cheese with lower fat content—20 per cent minimum. White. Soft Flavor: mild	Sandwiches or salads Nibblers or light refreshments—good on crackers

Oka (Port du Salut) (made in Canada) Circular cakes, 1 and 5 lbs.	Made from cows' milk Surface: russet Interior: creamy yellow. Semi-soft Flavor: robust	Dessert—especially good with port wine
*Parmesan (Reggiano) Cylindrical Grated; shredded	Surface: black or very dark green Interior: light yellow, with green tinge. Very hard Flavor: mild, unless cheese is old	Grated—serve with Italian spaghetti; on soups such as onion and minestrone; in all kinds of cookery
*Provolone (originally from Italy) Pear, ball, or sausage shape, tied with rope Slices	Includes such as Provolette, Provoloni, Salami, etc. Flavor: sharp	Dessert or nibbler—with crackers
*Ricotta (originally from Italy)	Made from whey, with whole or skim milk added. Soft texture Flavor: mild	Popularly used in ravioli, la-sagna, etc.
Roquefort (made in France) Cylinders, 4½ to 6 lb. Portions	Made from sheep's milk Surface: yellowish-brown rind Interior: white, with blue-green mold. Semisoft Flavor: spicy	Dessert—superb with pears or other fruit, crackers, nuts, etc. Salad dressings—crumble into French dressing; or blend with mayonnaise Appetizers, nibblers—blend with cream or cream cheese to make spread, filling for stuffed celery, etc.
*Swiss—domestic (originally from Switzerland) Wheels or blocks Slices Portions	Surface: grayish brown Interior: white or slightly glossy cream color. Round, shiny holes throughout Flavor: mild, nut-sweet to ro-bust. Also with sapsago, caraway	Sandwiches Sliced—with cold meats Salads—adds heartiness to fruit or vegetable ones In dishes such as Swiss-cheese pies, fondue

NOTE: Natural cheeses such as Cheddar, Swiss, brick, etc., may now be purchased in factory-wrapped packages in a variety of sizes—also conveniently sliced. The flavor of all natural cheeses, except cream and cottage cheeses, is enhanced if the cheese stands at room temperature a while before serving. (Cut into servings if needed.)

PROCESS CHEESES

Kind, Origin, Shape	Description	Uses
*Packaged Process Cheese ¼- to 5-lb packages	Made by mixing 2 or more "wheels" of same variety of cheese, or 2 or more varieties (except cream or Neufchatel cheese), into a homogeneous mass, with aid of heat and with (or without) water, salt, harmless coloring, and emulsifying agent. Must be heated to pasteurizing temperature during manufacturing, and labeled "process cheese." Flavors: Cheddar, white Cheddar, pimento, Swiss, brick, Limburger, sharp, caraway, Gruyère, etc.	Cookery—because it melts easily Sandwiches—process cheeses slice well
*Packaged Process Cheese Slices 6 oz. and 12 oz. packages	The same cheese as packaged process cheese, but sold in sliced form. Packaged for easy separation Flavors: Cheddar (mild and sharp), Swiss, Gruyère, caraway, pimento, etc.	Sandwiches Any dish calling for process cheese
*Gruyère Portion servings Slices in 6 oz. packages	This light-yellow process cheese is solid and has no holes. Its flavor is similar to, but slightly sharper than, Swiss cheese	Portions: for dessert or as nibblers—with crackers or fruit Slices: for sandwiches, rabbits, cheeseburgers, and to top casseroles
*Process-Cheese Spreads Jars and packages, or loaf, as dips, etc.	These flavored process-cheese spreads and blends have a soft spreading consistency Flavors: pineapple, pimento, blue, relish, olive-pimento, Swiss, Cheddar, sharp, Limburger, smoked, bacon, clam, onion, dill pickle, etc.	Sandwiches Salads Nibblers Sauces, etc.
*Process-Cheese Foods (or cheese-food compounds) Packages Loaf, slices, links, etc.	Flavor: deliciously mild to sharp. Process cheese foods are made of Cheddar cheese with milk solids added. Pimento, bacon, smoke, garlic may be added to links	Sauces Sandwich spreads—they melt smoothly and evenly To slice as nibblers
*Process Grated Cheese In canisters or glass jars	Two types: Cheddar; also Italian, in Parmesan and Parmesan Romano	Cheddar—for au gratin dishes, soups, etc. Italian—for sprinkling on salads, etc.

*Process Smoked Cheese	A process-cheese food that is hickory-smoked or has smoke-flavored solids added	Appetizer or nibbler—delicious served thinly sliced or cubed Also nice on soups, casseroles, veal dishes, etc.
*Triple-use Cheese Spread or Sauce In jars or glasses	A pasteurized process-cheese spread. Can be spread, spooned, or heated	Sauce—delicious on vegetables, meats, etc. Spread—tasty on bread, crackers, etc.

CHESTS |

The chest, originally devised strictly as a means of storing possessions, has now, with various changes and embellishments, become ornamental as well as useful. Here are ten basic styles, each with its own marks of identification in design, finish, and ornament.

1. **French Provincial,** usually seen in fruit wood or light finishes. Elaborate hardware, curved feet and top, plus scroll carving, are identifying marks.

2. **Captain's** chest, originally used in military campaigns. Usually done in mahogany or teak. Brass hardware and corners are characteristic.

1

2

3. **French Empire,** generally seen in fruit wood, occasionally with lacquer panels or trim. Classic motifs are nearly always used.

4. **Hepplewhite,** one of the greats of the eighteenth century. Bow front, circular brass pulls, and beveled trim distinguish this style.

3

4

5. **Chippendale,** has serpentine front. Chinese influences in legs and fret-work carving. Nearly always in mahogany, with simple pulls, graduated drawers.

6. **Early American** chest of simple lines. Usually made of pine, frequently painted. Four-panel front, straight legs, and low height are characteristic of this style.

5

6

7. **Victorian,** usually done in dark woods, such as mahogany or walnut. Wooden pulls, ornate carving, and a marble top are typical.

7

8

8. **Louis XV** chest, or commode, represents peak of French elegance. Often painted and trimmed with bronze; sometimes seen in fruit woods.

9. **Sheraton,** another outstanding eighteenth century design. Usually done in fruit wood or mahogany, with fluted columns, vase legs, and bowed front.

10. **Contemporary** chest frequently combines drawer and cabinet space. Often of teak, the finish is usually hand rubbed. Danish design is illustrated.

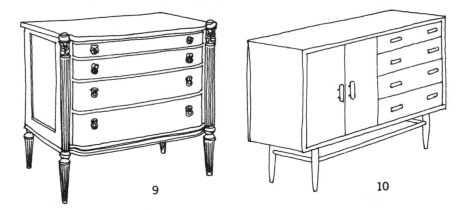

9   10

CHILDBIRTH, EMERGENCY |

Most babies are born in hospitals. Some are born under medical care at home. But a few do arrive under emergency conditions without medical assistance. In these cases, it is important that the mother and the person called upon to help with the delivery know what should be done.

A birth is a natural process. An inexperienced person's role is to let nature take its course while trying to reassure the mother, to maintain sanitary conditions, and to see that the baby is handled carefully.

The birth of a baby involves three stages. In emergency situations, certain measures should be taken at each stage. A person called upon to assist should first determine the stage of labor and then act accordingly. Do not panic, and of course, get medical help as soon as possible.

BEGINNING OF LABOR

The first sign is the start of labor pains. This stage may last for as long as eighteen hours for a mother having her first child. It may last only two or three hours, or even less for those who have had children. There is time to prepare a clean surface for the mother to lie on, and a bed for the baby.

First pains are usually felt in the lower back, and later felt as contractions in the lower abdomen. At first, the contractions are mild and irregular. These contractions of the womb (uterus) are nature's way of pushing open the mouth of the womb (cervix) so that the baby can come down the birth canal. Early labor pains may be brief and from ten to twenty minutes apart, or they may even stop temporarily.

The mother should rest between contractions. Water or nourishing liquids can be given, but solid foods should not be given. To prepare for the birth and because a slight, watery, bloodstained discharge normally accompanies labor pains, cleanse the mother's skin on the inner thighs, rectal area, and around—but not in—the vagina with soapy water. She also should be encouraged to urinate frequently and have a bowel movement if possible.

THE BIRTH

As the baby moves down the birth canal, labor contractions increase until they come at two to three-minute intervals. Frequently, the bag of water which surrounds the baby in the womb breaks at this stage. However, this may occur earlier. Normally, about a pint of water may gush out.

The mother should lie down and prepare for birth. Those assisting should scrub their hands with soap and water, if possible. The mother and those helping should keep their hands away from the birth canal opening.

As the baby begins to appear, the person helping should support the baby with his hands and arms to keep the infant above the fluid or waste material on the bed. No attempt should be made to pull out the baby in any way. As the head and neck appear, two conditions may occur which must be corrected:

If a membrane from the water sac is over the baby's head or face, it should be taken between the fingers and torn so that the water will run out and the baby can breathe.

If the umbilical cord (running from the baby's navel to the placenta, a membrane structure in the womb) is around the baby's neck, try to slip it gently over his head or down over his body to prevent strangulation. Do not pull on the cord.

When the baby's body is free from the mother, it still is attached by the umbilical cord. The cord does not have to be cut immediately. The first thing to do at this point is to make sure that the baby starts to breathe. Babies are born with fluid in their noses and throats which must be drained. Hold the baby gently but firmly by the ankles (a towel or cloth wrapped around the ankles will help prevent your grip from slipping) and raise the lower part of his body higher than the head. Leave the cord slack and do not pull on it.

Most babies begin to cry and breathe when the fluid is drained, but it may be necessary to stroke his throat toward the mouth with your free hand to clear the fluid. If the baby does not begin to cry or breathe, mouth-to-mouth respiration should be begun immediately. Breathe very gently into the baby's mouth in a short puff every five seconds. Stop as soon as breathing begins.

Then wrap the baby in a towel, blanket, or other soft cloth—the cleanest you can find. Place him on his right side across the mother's abdomen, with his head lowered and facing away from the mother's face. The third stage of labor now follows.

AFTER THE BIRTH

The placenta (afterbirth) is a round, flat structure about six to eight inches in diameter. This breaks free from the womb and must be expelled along the same channel through which the birth occurred. The mother undergoes slight contractions while the placenta is expelled. This usually takes twenty to thirty minutes. During this time, do not pull on the cord.

When the placenta is expelled, it still is attached by the cord to the baby. Wrap the afterbirth separately, allowing the cord to hang loosely from the baby. Place the wrapped placenta beside the baby and wrap them together securely in a blanket so the placenta will not drop and pull on the cord.

Some bleeding occurs during childbirth and when the placenta is expelled. Place a sanitary pad or clean cloth between the mother's legs and have her keep her legs together to exert pressure. If bleeding increases, gently massage her abdomen. Stop when the womb feels firm.

Keep the baby warm but don't overdo it. Use covered hot water bottles if necessary and available. Do not worry about feeding or bathing the baby. Newborn infants do not require food for the first eight to twelve hours.

In emergency births, medical assistance should be sought as soon as possible. In almost all cases, this will be available before it is necessary to cut the umbilical cord, which should be done only under sanitary conditions. (If it should be necessary to cut the cord after the placenta is expelled, firmly tie a cord or clean cloth strip about four inches from the baby's navel and cut on the placental side with a knife or scissors sterilized by boiling or in a flame.)

In some situations, sterile receiving blankets and sanitary pads are not available. Articles of the mother's clothing or the cleanest pieces of cloth available can be used to wrap the baby. A clean handkerchief or any paper tissues can be used instead of a sanitary pad.

CHILDREN'S PARTIES |

Giving a party for preschool children requires tailoring activities to the particular age group. What pleased a two-year-old will not be good for the three-, four-, or five-year-olds. More important than any rules in helping children to have a good time is a real love and understanding of their ways. Careful planning is necessary to reduce confusion and disappointment, rather than leaving it up to chance that everything will come off well.

The **three-year-old's** notion of a party is vague and undemanding. He is, at his best, a friendly, agreeable, sociable little creature who likes to play beside (but not necessarily with) his contemporaries. Though less grabby than he was six months earlier, he is still not beyond the age of fighting over possessions. Group activity is likely to be marked by sudden squalls and squabbles, so that adult supervision is necessary.

The opportunity to play at someone else's house, plenty of toys, some simple refreshments, and a gift or favor for himself will satisfy this age better than any attempt to make him take part in games. He loves surprises, so long as they are not too complex. Some children of this age cannot hold up socially as well or as long as others. An especially shy or difficult child may arrive late or leave early to avoid undue strain.

Five or six children, both boys and girls, are a sufficient number, and one hour and a half sufficient time (say from 11:30 to 1:00 o'clock). Mothers of shy or boisterous children may need to stay for the party; but other children will often behave better without their mothers.

The party begins with opening and playing with the presents and the host's toys. Children this age sometimes play together, but there will be much solitary play. Then refreshments are served on a coffee table with the children seated on small chairs. Each receives a small favor just before going to the table, and is served very small sandwiches and milk. The cake is shown, the candles blown out, and each child given a small piece with ice cream. Then they return to the playroom for informal play, and again are given a small party gift.

Each phase of the party (play, refreshment, play) takes about half an hour. Balloons used for decoration are handed to each child as he leaves with his mother, a final present that helps get him out the door happily. Many children will be overstimulated, so this is an important touch.

It is most important not to try to make this party too formal. Have the mothers solve any problems which arise by separating the children; this is no time for discipline or teaching good manners or exacting justice. The host has a right to act like a child, too (not like a host). Relaxed good humor will bridge most little crises.

A **four-year-old** tends to be a creature of boundless energy, enthusiasm, and appetite for the new and different and exciting. He loves an occasion, and a party is just the kind of occasion he loves best. Though he may be hard to control when things are going badly, he can be cooperative if things are going his way.

It is easy to entertain a four-year-old. He is appreciative of adult attention; he tends to accept quite uncritically the games you suggest, the food you serve, the favors and surprises you provide. The keys to success are speed, simplicity, and novelty. Speed because the children react quickly and fatigue rapidly; simplicity because they are not mature enough to understand complex games; novelty because they now have a notion of what a party is, and expect something more than just to go and play. The surprise should be something simple, such as a distribution of favors.

Six to eight guests make a good number and an hour and a half is a good length for this party (ideally, from 3:30 to 5:00 P.M., after the nap and not too close to dinnertime). An adult helper for the mother should be available, possibly one of the guest's mothers who feels she should stay with her child. The party starts in an atmosphere resembling a nursery school playroom, with a good assortment of large toys which may be borrowed for the occasion. The host opens presents as they are given to him. After ten or fifteen minutes, each child is given a favor, such as a fireman's hat, as he goes into another room for refreshments.

Small sandwiches are served, so that children may eat several (better than half-eating one big one). Or just ice cream, cake, and milk, and simple favors such as a toy frying pan filled with candy. Blown-up balloons clustered on the wall are handed to the children as they finish eating. They return to the playroom to play with the balloons and other toys, and again are given special surprise favors. These are wrapped separately and presented in a big cloth bag that the children reach into, taking turns. They are still too young even for the simplest formal games.

Leave taking should be planned carefully, because by the end of a party most four-year-olds are tired and excitable and may go to pieces if they have to wait to be called for. Be especially careful that the party does not last too long. Expect guest children to blow out the candles before the host does, or to want to take their "gifts" back home with them, to spill things, etc. Avoid confusion by giving out the favors and surprises at different times, rather than all at the table.

The **five-year-old** seems very self-contained and capable, but this is deceptive. When faced with something new or difficult, he may need a surprising amount of assistance. Adult help should be immediately available to show him how to take part in games and carry out directions. The five-year-old is not especially sociable; he may keep to himself in a strange situation, or rely a good deal on a best friend. Thus, it will usually work out best to provide initial activity which is more or less solitary, and even after this warming-up period, not to expect too much group cooperation.

It is wise to provide some games which involve considerable charging about the house by the guests. Getting rid of excess energy is a problem even at this age, as it will be later. Some key theme, such as a Valentine, Halloween, or Indian motif helps make the party exciting. Six is a good number of guests, because at this age children find it hard to wait for turns or attention. And preferably have all boys or all girls, though a co-ed group will still work out all right. At least two adults should be in charge, and the party may last for two hours (perhaps 4:00 to 6:00 P.M.).

A PARTY SCHEDULE

Have all materials and props ready, and activities planned for every minute. Here is a suggested schedule for a party of five-year-old girls:

4:00–4:15.   Guests assemble for relatively quiet, solitary activity, such as making things with pipe cleaners or clay.

4:15–4:30.   Game of Spider allows children to get adjusted to one another without much mingling. Strings are wound around the house, in and out of furniture. Each child follows her own string, winding it onto a spool as she climbs over and under the furniture, which she must not move. Finally she finds a present at the end of her string.

4:30–5:10.   Game of Clues. Mother reads aloud the clues, which might be "under something yellow in the living room," "under something green in the bedroom," etc. The whole group looks for them; the last clue leads to a treasure for each person. This can be materials for making something, such as a Valentine hat. All this charging around has tired the children, so now they are content to sit quietly making whatever their treasure suggests.

5:10–5:15.   Marching to music. Five-year-olds love a birthday march around the party area, to the music of a record, a piano, or the singing of a rousing song. Simple rhythm instruments for each child add to the fun. This is an activity both boys and girls like, and gives them a further opportunity to work off steam.

5:15–5:45.   Refreshments at the regular dining table, with tablecloth and napkins, but paper plates. A good menu includes small sandwiches, milk, and some crunchy food, such as carrot sticks or celery; then cake and ice cream. Don't try anything fancy and don't give a choice of foods.

5:45–6:00.   Some planned, sedentary activity such as coloring books until all parents arrive.

It is very important to avoid long waits between activities; five-year-olds are not good at improvising. At the beginning of the party especially, keep them occupied without making much demand on them for sociability. Be sure to provide each guest with a sturdy bag for his presents and favors; at this age children become very upset if they think their things are lost. A party is very important to them; the host may become overexcited just in anticipation; and you may have to overlook some less-than-ideal behavior.

If the party is for boys, games should be greatly simplified. Boys need a chance to be physically active and boisterous, but find it hard to follow a complicated Spider or make complicated things. They need to move from one activity to another more rapidly than girls do.

CHRISTMAS TREES |

How to buy: To suit your needs—whether you live in a small apartment or in a large house—a tree should be the right size, have good color, and stay fresh. Douglas fir and Scotch pine are most popular because they have good needle retention. Spruce, which sheds its needles after a few days indoors, makes a better outdoor tree. These check points can help you to select a tree:

Bounce the butt on the ground. If the needles fall, the tree is dry.

Pull some needles at the end of a branch to check whether they have good resistance to being plucked. Also make sure the needles are pliable and the color of the foliage meets with your approval.

Rub your fingers across the stump. If the stump is sticky with resin, the tree has been kept fresh.

Check the shape and whether the branches are broken.

Larger trees are more expensive. A day or two before Christmas, prices usually drop sharply if sellers still have a plentiful supply. At this time, though, the best-shaped trees may have been sold. If you buy early to get the freshest and most shapely tree, it should be stored properly.

How to store: Cut one inch off the butt and place the tree in a pail of water.

Stand it outdoors away from sunlight and wind, or in an unheated garage or basement.

If the tree is leaning against a wall, turn it daily to avoid bending the branches unevenly on one side.

To set up: When you set up the tree, cut another inch or two off the butt. Use a standard that will not tip and has a water well. The trunk base should be submerged and the container kept filled. Before decorating, support sagging branches with wire attached to the trunk. Additional branches can be wired into any bare spot by securing them to the trunk and to the branches just above and below.

Hazard: Fire is the main danger posed by both artificial plastic and natural Christmas trees. A tree should not be placed near a fireplace, heater, or so that it blocks a door or stairway. The National Fire Protection Association also suggests:

1. Decorations should be noncombustible, like glass and metal. Combustible materials—paper, cotton, etc.—should be "flameproofed."

2. Electrical toys which spark or those that use flammable fuels should not be used near the tree.

3. Never place lighted candles on a tree. Check lighting sets for frayed wiring and broken sockets. Use sets which have the Underwriters' Laboratories (UL) seal.

4. On metal trees, use flood—not string—lights to avoid shocks.

5. Turn tree lights off when no one will be home or when you go to bed.

6. Artificial snow or other materials should be flame-resistant.

A tree should be discarded outdoors the day after New Year's, or earlier if the tree becomes dry and the needles turn brown and fall.

CLOTHES STORAGE |

A leading architect once commented that *no* house ever has enough closet space; the question is whether your storage problem is worse than usual, or merely tolerable. There are many ways, though, of organizing closets and their contents to take full advantage of the space available.

In recent years, manufacturers have developed a number of storage aids which make closet arrangements much simpler and which permit closets to absorb extra clothing with no apparent loss in efficiency. Many of these devices make it possible to hang such things as hats, handbags, and shoes. Others can restore order to the jumble that often comes from stacking things on shelves.

Belts can be hooked—twenty at a time—on a revolving belt rack which hangs from a closet rod.

Handbags are suspended from a rack with ten hooks (which also holds belts). A garment bag with five shelves can also be used to store handbags. A third type of handbag holder has four pouches, one below the other.

Hats can be hung in a round garment bag with shelf space for four hats.

Linens also hang in garment bags that have five shelves. These could, of course, be used to hold anything that can be put on a shelf.

Shoes may be stored in several ways. There are garment-type bags with shelf space for ten or twenty pairs. Another type that has pockets lining the inside of the bag rather than the shelves, holds twenty pairs. A smaller enclosed shoebag is round. In its center is a revolving unit with pockets for ten pairs of shoes. Shoes can also be hung on revolving trees with pockets which are not enclosed. A fifth type of shoe bag has pouches attached to either side of a central stem.

Shoes in open hangers should be placed in the closet so they do not soil clothes. Stackable boxes, available in clear or decorated plastic, come in two styles. One has pull-out drawers, the other style has a lid.

Lingerie. Similar, larger boxes are available for storing lingerie, sweaters, blouses, scarves, etc.

Skirts, blouses, and suits double up on hangers that attach one below the other. An improvement over former skirt trees, these hangers can be detached individually to remove a single garment. At the same time, as many as six blouses or skirts or three suits can hang in little more space than one garment would take.

Sweater and skirt combination garment bags have shelves at the top for sweaters and a rod at the bottom to hold skirts.

Umbrellas may be kept in a revolving unit with four pockets suspended from a single hook.

If you find your closets filled with clothing you use infrequently or seasonally, you might have use for a garment rack in an attic or storeroom.

These range in size from three to five feet long and cost anywhere from five to twenty dollars. Several models have hat and shoe racks. One of the longer ones has four shelves for flat storage. Most can be taken apart easily and folded into a box when not in use.

Another solution to the same problem (other than the well-known under-bed storage boxes) is a unit with nine cardboard bins which rest on a three-shelf metal frame.

CLOTHING SIZES |

Ready-to-wear clothing should be selected to fit without alteration if possible. Certain alterations are easily made—such as sleeve length or looseness at the waist—but extensive alterations are always risky as well as expensive. Never buy a dress or other garment if the shoulder line must be altered; if shoulders are too narrow and armholes too tight; or if the waistline comes at the wrong place for your figure.

Following are basic ready-to-wear sizes for women's clothes, and for men's and children's clothing that women often buy.

WOMEN'S SIZES

Junior sizes 3, 5, 7, 9, 11, 13 (and less commonly, 15) are for the young figure with small or medium frame, small and short waist, high bust, round hips, and slight shoulders, height 5'4" to 5'6".

Junior petites (also 3 to 15) fit the 5' to 5'4" woman with very small frame and the same proportions as juniors.

Misses sizes 6, 8, 10, 12, 14, 16, 18 (and less commonly, 20) are for the woman of average or slightly above average height (5'5" to 5'8"), fairly even proportions, with small to medium frame and waist at the middle of the torso.

Petite sizes 8 to 20 are for women shorter than 5'5" in the same proportions as misses.

Tall sizes 8 to 20 are another variation of misses sizes for women 5'7" or taller, with longer waist and skirt lengths.

Half sizes 10½, 12½, 14½, 16½, 18½, 20½, 22½, 24½ (and less commonly, 26½) are for women under 5'5", fully proportioned, with short waist, full bust, and narrow shoulders. They are available in both youthful and mature styles.

Women's regular sizes 38, 40, 42, 44, 46, 48, 50, 52 are for medium to tall women (5'5" to 5'9") with mature figure, longer waisted and fuller through the bust, waist, and hips than half sizes.

Note that dress sizes are an approximation. Two garments of the same size, but made by different manufacturers, may be quite different when measured in inches. Sizes at the extremes of each range, such as junior 15, misses 20, etc., are manufactured in smaller quantity than the more typical sizes and may be relatively hard to find. Today, for example, former women's sizes 34 and 36 are generally labeled as misses sizes 14 and 16.

Shoe sizes consist of a number designating length and a letter designating width in proportion to length. Size 7B, for example, is approximately the same *width* as 6½C, a shorter shoe, or 7½A, a longer one.

If a shoe fits correctly, you should have enough room at the tip to wiggle your big toe while standing. But the instep should be sufficiently snug so as not to bulge under your ankle while walking; neither should the shoe slip off your heel. Note that your foot can increase a full size between morning and night, because of the weight you put on it during an active day. Use shoe sizes as a general guide only; obviously one should never buy a shoe unless it's a comfortable fit.

Hosiery sizes correspond approximately to shoe size as follows:

Shoes	Below 4½B	4½B to 5½AA	5½A to 6D	6E to 7C	7D to 8B	Above 8B
Hosiery	8½	9	9½	10	10½	11

Denier refers to fineness of yarn—the lower the denier number, the thinner the yarn. Fifteen denier is half as thick as 30 denier, and thus not as strong. *Needle count* and *gauge* refer to fineness of fabric—the higher the number, the closer (and stronger) the knit fabric. A 474 needle count is stronger than 400.

Glove sizes measure the length of your hand in inches (6, 6½, 7, etc.). Leather gloves come in quarter-sizes, fabric gloves in half-sizes only. The right hand is usually one-quarter size larger than the left, or vice versa in a left-handed person. Use the longer hand for fitting, first turning any ring settings toward the palm. The terms "one-button," "two-button," etc., refer to the length in inches of the arm part of the glove, beginning at the base of the thumb. A 2-button glove is wrist length; 10-button is elbow length; 20-button is shoulder length.

MEN'S SIZES

Outer clothing for men—suits, coats, jackets, hats, etc.—rarely can be bought without a personal fitting. But here are sizes of some men's items that are often purchased for them in absentia:

Dress-shirt size is designated by collar and sleeve length in inches. A 16-33 shirt has a 16-inch collar and 33-inch sleeve; a 16-32 has the same collar but a 32-inch sleeve. Other dimensions are in proportion. In selecting a shirt, lean slightly to the generous side in collar size; a too-tight shirt is both uncomfortable and ugly. Sleeve length is measured from base of neck at top center back, not from armhole.

The term "custom," properly used, means a shirt made to order from a hand-fitted individual pattern, a luxury item highly prized by men who can afford it. An approximation of the custom shirt, much less expensive, is made in some specialty shops by assembling collar, sleeves, yoke, etc., of standard pattern but in the individual's sizes. These appeal to men whose dimensions vary markedly from the average, causing them difficulty in finding a good ready-to-wear fit.

Sport shirts are labeled small, medium, large, and extra-large by neck size: S (14-14½); M (15-15½); L (16-16½); XL (17-17½).

Underwear sizes. Boxer shorts are based on the waistband in inches (28, 30, 32, 34, etc.). Undershirts go by chest sizes: small (34-36), medium (38-40), large (42-44), X-large (46). The undershirt should be long enough to fall 8 inches or more below the waist. Knit briefs are sized by waist measurement as follows: small (30-32), medium (34-36), large (38-40), X-large (42-44).

Pajamas usually are designated A, B, C, or D as to chest size: A (34-36"), B (38-40"), C (42-44"), D (46-48"). Pajamas well fitted at the shoulders but otherwise on the loose side make for comfortable sleep.

Socks correspond to men's shoe sizes as follows:

Shoes	5 to 5½	6 to 7	7½ to 8	8½ to 9	9½ to 10	10½ to 11½	12 to 13	Above 13
Hosiery	9	10	10½	11	11½	12	13	Outsize

"A" and "B" widths can wear a half-size smaller; "E" and "EE" widths can wear two half-sizes larger. Stretchable socks sized small, medium, and large will span two or three of the above sizes and fit neatly when put on.

CHILDREN'S SIZES

The correct way to fit a child with clothing is to measure his height and weight. Size designations roughly parallel a child's age, in months for infants and in years for older children; but it is not at all uncommon for a child to be either smaller or larger than average for his age.

Buy infants' clothes a size or two larger than necessary, with the exception of waterproof pants, which must fit closely. As a child grows, always favor slightly larger sizes—not only for economy, but because tight-fitting garments may interfere with a child's normal activity or even, as in the case of the feet, cause actual injury.

Following are the height-weight measurements for five size classifications included in the Commercial Standards recognized by the garment industry:

INFANTS

Height (in.)	24	26½	29	31½	34	36½
Weight (lbs.)	13	18	22	26	29	32
Size		3	6	12	18	24	36

TODDLERS

Height (in.)	31	34	37	40
Weight (lbs.)	25	29	34	38
Size	1	2	3	4

CHILDREN

Height (in.)	34	37	40	43	46	48
Weight (lbs.)	29	34	38	44	49	54
Size	2	3 or 3L	4	5	6	6X

GIRLS

Height (in.)	50	52	54	56	58½	61
Weight (lbs.)	60	67	75	83	95	107
Size	7	8	9	10	12	14

BOYS

Height (in.)	48	50	52	54	56	58	59½	61	62½	64	65	66	67	68
Weight (lbs.)	54	59	65	73	80	87	93	100	107	115	121	126	132	138
Size		7	8	9	10	11	12	13	14	15	16	17	18	19	20

The right size for a child is judged by fit and comfort. A garment bearing the indicated size may not always fit, either because of variation in measurement by the manufacturer or because the child's body proportions are nonstandard. Also, many children wear one size in some styles and a different size in other styles. If possible, take the child to the store to try on garments; otherwise it is best to select only those that can be taken out on approval.

CHILDREN'S SHOES AND SOCKS

Foot length (in.)	3½	4	4½	5	5½	6	6½	7
Shoe size	1	1½-2½	3-4	4½-5½	6-7	7½-8½	9-10	10½-11½
Sock size	4	4½	5	5½	6	6½	7	7½

Foot length (in.)	7½	8
Shoe size	12-13	13½-1½
Sock size	8	8½

Note: For shoe widths E or wider, buy a half-size larger socks than above.

When buying shoes for a child, always have both feet measured. One foot usually is slightly larger than the other, and the larger foot determines the size. Encourage your child to sit, stand, and walk in the shoes before making your selection. A foot expands in both length and width when weight is put on it. A properly fitted shoe will be comfortable as soon as the child tries it on.

Look for adequate space beyond the big toe and enough width and height to allow all five toes to lie normally. Also check for generous height and width across the widest part of the shoe, where the foot flexes. If the shoe does not correspond to the foot shape, the fit is wrong. The counter and back should be slightly bulbous to avoid heel irritation. If any area feels tight, cuts, or rubs, don't buy the shoes—keep looking.

Since a child's foot grows rapidly, allow enough room in new shoes for maximum growth. Then check regularly to make sure both shoes and socks are large enough. Ill-fitting shoes lose their shape, but a far more important consideration is the permanent injury they can do to a child's foot. The following chart shows the *average* frequency of size change in growing children; however, a particular youngster's feet may change as many as three sizes during any one period. Immediately discard shoes that are too small; they have been outgrown even if not actually worn out.

Age (yrs.)	2 to 6	6 to 10	10 to 12	12 to 15	15 to 20
Size change every	1-2 mos.	2-3 mos.	3-4 mos.	4-5 mos.	6 mos.

CLOTHING, WHAT TO WEAR | See also CLOTHING SIZES; COTTONS; FIGURE CARE; WOOL

The secret of being well dressed is not simply a matter of being able to afford an expensive wardrobe. Even if you have a limited budget, it is possible to be well dressed for almost every occasion. This can be accomplished by following certain fundamental rules in planning your wardrobe and in selecting clothes.

You probably observe many of these rules without thinking about them. The first requirement, though, can be the hardest for some women; take a long, objective look at yourself. Note your good and bad features. Each woman is different in size, proportion, and personality. A style that is right for one woman may be entirely wrong for another. But clothes can be used to balance and cover figure faults.

A **slim** woman can wear bulky, full fabrics, and styles with round, curving lines.

A **heavy** woman should wear smooth—but not clingy—fabrics, dark colors, conservative prints, and vertical stripes.

A **tall,** slim woman should avoid vertical lines. She can wear big accessories and bright colors or a contrasting top and bottom.

A **short** woman can gain an effect of height with straight skirts, short jackets, and one-color outfits.

Hip-length separates or waistless dresses are best for **short-waisted** women. Those with **narrow shoulders** can use shoulder padding and fuller sleeves. Women with **short necks** need wide or deep necklines, collars that stand away from the throat, and collarless coats.

Regardless of your size and shape, an indispensable guide to being well dressed is simplicity. Uncomplicated clothes, practical colors, a limited amount of jewelry, and unpretentious accessories are suitable for almost any occasion. In your own wardrobe it is probably simple and casual clothes that have been most comfortable and flattering.

Start by making an inventory of your clothes. Try on every garment and eliminate those which are outdated, ill-fitting, or just don't suit you. Keep in mind the places you go and the things you do most often. Then plan how to fill in the gaps in your wardrobe. Study women's magazines, newspapers, and store selections for fashion trends. Look for long-lasting styles and lines suited to your figure. Plan to spend the most money on clothes you will wear most often. It is usually better to buy one good dress than two inexpensive ones.

When you shop, wear the shoes and undergarments that you would wear with the dress you expect to buy. Look for the finishing touches that mean quality. These include well-made buttonholes and belt, seams at least one-half inch wide, and an adequate, even hem. If you are trying to match or co-ordinate colors and textures with a dress you already have, snip off a small piece of material from a seam and take it along.

Proper fit is essential to being well dressed. Be sure to look in the correct size range. When you find comfortable clothes you like, look for the same label in future shopping. The manufacturer's styles may change, but the basic measurements will usually be the same.

Test the fit by walking and sitting in the garment. The lines should be smooth, but not tight. There should be no hard or sharp wrinkles and the garment should not bind or pinch anywhere. The collar should set properly at the neck. You should be able to move your arms freely without tension across the shoulders and armholes. The sleeves must hang straight from the shoulders. If the dress has a normal waistline, it should never feel high or low. The skirt should fit smoothly without spanning or sagging. The right skirt length, though dictated by fashion, may vary an inch or two, depending on the shape of your legs, fullness of the skirt, and proportion of the dress.

BASIC WARDROBE FOR TRAVEL

Selecting a vacation wardrobe can pose problems for the inexperienced traveler. Careful planning is important, especially if your budget and luggage weight are limited. The climate and location of your vacation area as well as the nature of your trip and planned activities should be considered. For an average two-to-four-week vacation trip, this is a basic list:

1 topcoat
1 simple suit
2 daytime dresses
1 after-five dress
1 skirt or dress for evening wear
1 dress-up and 2 simple tops
1 cardigan sweater
2 changes of sleepwear
1 robe and folding slippers
3 pairs of nylon stockings

3-4 pairs of shoes, including 1 dress
  and 1 walking
2 handbags: 1 large travel and 1 small
  dressy
2 sets of lingerie
3 pairs of gloves
2-3 chiffon or silk scarves
1 packable hat or veil
Your favorite jewelry
Rainwear

A practical travel wardrobe is color-coordinated and versatile. Plan it around a basic color scheme so that a few garments can be mixed to form several outfits. Simple, comfortable clothes in neutral or dark colors are good for traveling because they don't show soil readily. They are easily brightened or dressed up with scarves and jewelry. (It is a good idea to have bright color accents in your accessories rather than in the clothes themselves.)

Jersey knits and other knitted garments are excellent for travel because they are wrinkle resistant. Wash-and-wear fabrics minimize care problems. Many synthetics and synthetic blends wash easily and require little or no ironing.

Variations of the basic wardrobe may be made to suit different types of vacations. For instance, fashions in larger cities are often sophisticated but quite simple and uncluttered. Casual, informal styles are more common in smaller towns and in the country. At a resort, emphasis is on beachwear and play clothes during the day but softer, more feminine clothes for the evening. For trips to the mountains, national parks, or camps, you will want clothes suitable for hiking, riding, or other outdoor sports as well as casual dresses.

CLUB MEETINGS | See also FOOD PLANNING IN QUANTITY

If you're planning a meeting for your club, here are pointers to help make it run smoothly—a meeting too good to miss.

The larger the audience, the happier the speaker—and the happier the meeting. Be sure to notify members of the day, hour, and place—but not too far in advance. Brief the speaker well ahead on the probable size and interests of the audience, desired length of the speech, and the time it will begin. Let her know if there's to be a question-and-answer period afterward.

Ask if her program requires any advance setup. And tell her what's being arranged to take care of her when she arrives. (It's best to send a club member to meet her.)

Get there early in the day, if possible, to set the lights and test the microphone. If a projector is to be used, have the person operating it sit nearby. Assign someone to take care of the lights and/or windows—all unobtrusively, of course.

In introducing the speaker, be brief but enthusiastic. Be sure you know how to pronounce her name correctly, the work she's doing, the organization she represents, and her title. Give her due credit but no flowery flattery. Let the speaker be the one to discuss the main topic.

Well served refreshments increase attendance and generally make people feel closer. Keep the work down to a minimum, perhaps by using paper cups and dishes in gay colors that suggest the program's theme.

SUGGESTED FOODS TO SERVE

With coffee: pecan tartlets—warm coffeecake with assorted fresh finger fruits—assorted cheeses and crisp crackers—apple turnovers with lemon sauce—jelly roll à la mode—vanilla ice cream topped with hot mincemeat—individual caramel custards—snack tray of figs, dates, nuts, and cheese chunks.

With tea: fresh fruit cup with cinnamon toast triangles—hot gingerbread—cream cheese and kumquats—tiny wedges of pumpkin and mince pie—melba toast with guava jam and cream cheese.

With other beverages: *lemonade,* homemade ice cream sandwiches; *cold cider,* hot gingerbread—raisins with salted peanuts; *French chocolate,* coconut macaroons; *eggnog,* pound cake and salted almonds.

Without beverage: hot onion soup with cheese toast—*pots de crème* in demitasse cups with crisp cookies—wine jelly with butter cookies or vanilla ice cream balls in a bowl with assorted toppings (wedges of lemon or lime; shaker of nutmeg; instant coffee; shaved unsweetened chocolate; flaked coconut).

With a foreign flavor: *Italian,* bisque tortoni and coffee with twist of lemon peel; *Mexican,* pralines with coffee or chocolate—tiny bunches of grapes; *Chinese,* fortune cookies—pineapple on picks dipped in coconut—salted almonds, and tea; *French,* crêpes suzette—frozen crêpes in sauce, and coffee.

COFFEE |

A good cup of coffee is an essential part of the day for millions of people. Here are basic facts on how coffee is made to get it the way you like it:

Blends. Most commercial coffee is made of numerous varieties of coffee beans. Usually, blends contain a large proportion of Brazilian beans, with some from other parts of Latin America and small amounts from Africa. Colombian, Jamaican, or other varieties may be featured in a particular blend.

Roasting. Green coffee beans are heated at very high temperatures until they are various shades of brown. The darker the roast, the more burnt the flavor and the more bitter the taste. The combination of the blend and roasting produces the distinctive aroma and flavor of coffee. Coffee sold in the East and South is generally darker than that sold in the Midwest and West.

Grinds. Roasted coffee beans are ground into particles of prescribed sizes which determine the amount of time it takes water to go through them. Regular is the coarsest grind and is used in percolator coffee makers. Agitated water mixes with coffee for six to eight minutes. Drip or all-purpose is a medium grind for drip coffee makers, but usable in other types. Water takes about four to six minutes to pass through the coffee. Fine is a very fine grind for vacuum coffee makers. Water and coffee mix for from one to three minutes.

Instant coffee is a dry, soluble extract, obtained by removing the water from a strong coffee brew. Practically all widely distributed brands today consist of just the dehydrated brew, with no added ingredients. Make it as the label directs. When only one or two cups are needed, it is convenient to make the coffee right in the cup. However, when several cups are to be served, make it all at once in a pot, then let the brew stand over very low heat for four or five minutes.

Decaffeinated coffee. Green coffee beans are softened with steam and then soaked in a solvent which removes 97 per cent of the caffeine. The beans are drained, steamed again to remove traces of the solvent, and dried. The beans are then roasted and ground in the same manner as other coffee, or extracted as an instant coffee.

Coffee and chicory. A blend popular in the South and among some Europeans, in which the chicory enhances the coffee flavor.

Cereal beverages. For those who do not drink coffee, there are hot-drink products made from roasted cereals. They come in two forms: one you prepare as you would regular coffee, the other as you would an instant type.

The Coffee Brewing Center, a research organization sponsored by coffee growers, suggests this formula for making regular coffee: per serving, two level measuring tablespoons or one standard measure of coffee to three-fourths of a measuring cup of water—six ounces. Stronger coffees are served in small cups and in many homes after dinner. They include:

Demitasse. This can be made with American coffees in any coffee maker. One-half cup of water is used for every two level measuring tablespoons of coffee.

Italian coffee. Beans are roasted longer, which brings oil to the surface and makes them dark. The beans are finely ground for *macchinettas* (drip pots). The grind may be even finer for espresso makers in which steam is forced through the coffee.

French café filtre can be made with Italian-roast coffee in a drip-type coffee maker.

These additions give variety to after-dinner coffees:

One inch of vanilla bean (vanilla extract won't do) or two crushed cardamon seeds can be added to ground coffee before brewing (for four to six cups).

Cinnamon sticks, cloves, or all-spice berries can be steeped in coffee after it has been made.

Ginger, nutmeg, red sugar, cinnamon, grated orange peel, or shaved bitter chocolate can be used as a garnish on whipped cream or milk coffee topping. A twist of lemon can be served with black coffee. Some people like to blend American roast with the darker, richer Italian or Spanish roast.

GOOD COFFEE TIPS

Use only fresh coffee. Oxygen in the air destroys coffee flavor, and produces staleness. To be sure ground coffee is fresh:

Buy it in a vacuum-sealed can.

Or, if it's not vacuum-packed, be sure it was roasted and ground within the last day.

Don't stock coffee unless it's in a vacuum-sealed can, unopened.

After opening a can or bag of coffee, use it up within a week if possible.

If a little coffee is left over at the end of the week, don't mix it with a fresh supply.

Store coffee in the refrigerator, in a tightly lidded can or a glass jar with screw-on top.

COOKED MEATS | See MEAT

COTTONS |

Do you know how cotton fabrics differ, or what descriptive terms such as Sanforized and vat-dyed really mean? This glossary can help you in your cotton shopping:

Combed cotton is made of long, fine yarns which are "combed" to remove impurities and short lengths of fiber. The fabric is smooth and very fine when made of quality fibers such as Sea Island, Egyptian, and Pima.

Mercerized cotton is yarn or fabric which has a special finish to make it lustrous and strong.

Sanforized cotton is a trademark indicating the fabric has a special finish to make it shrink-resistant—shrinkage not to exceed 1 per cent.

Wash-and-wear cotton garments can be worn, washed, and worn again with little or no ironing throughout their wearable life.

Vat-dyed cottons are solid-colored or printed fabrics that will not bleed and are highly resistant to fading in washing.

LIGHTWEIGHT COTTONS

Batiste is soft, sheer fabric made of mercerized yarns. It is used for lingerie and infants' wear.

Dotted swiss is sheer and crisp with small dots woven in at intervals. It is used for dresses and curtains.

Gingham usually has a woven check or plaid pattern. Tissue gingham is very lightweight and sheer. It is used for dresses, play clothes, and blouses.

Muslin ranges from sheer fabric to heavier sheeting. Muslin sheets have 120 or 140 threads per inch and are durable, but not as fine and smooth as percale sheets.

Plissé has a puckered or blistered effect applied by a special process that stays in if not ironed out. It usually comes in stripes or designs, and is used for sleepwear and underwear.

Seersucker, usually striped, has a permanent woven-in pucker. It is used for men's and women's suits and sportswear.

MEDIUM-WEIGHT COTTONS

Broadcloth is tightly woven with a fine crosswise rib. Shirts, blouses, and dresses are made from it.

Chambray is woven with colored lengthwise yarns and white crosswise yarns and has a mottled-color effect. It is used for workshirts, and in lighter weights for dresses and sportswear.

Indian madras usually has a hand-woven plaid pattern of muted tones. Bleeding madras gives a different effect after each washing. Some madras, however, is colorfast. Madras is used for sportswear and men's shirts.

Percale has a smooth finish and is used for dresses, sports shirts, and sleepwear. Percale sheeting must have at least 180 threads per inch; the higher this count, the smoother and "silkier" the sheet.

Piqué has raised cords or welts running crosswise. Birdseye piqué has a pronounced raised diamond effect on the surface. Waffle piqué has a raised honeycomb effect. It is used for blouses and dresses.

Poplin is similar to broadcloth, but has a heavier crosswise rib. It is used for jackets, slacks, and sportswear.

HEAVYWEIGHT COTTONS

Denim usually has a blue thread running lengthwise and a white thread running crosswise. It is used for work clothes, and in lighter weights for sportswear.

Duck, also called canvas, is very durable and tightly woven. It is used for uniforms, sportswear, lawn furniture, and awnings.

Hopsacking is a rough-surface fabric made with a loose basket weave. It is used for sportswear and dresses.

Ticking usually is woven with alternating colored and white stripes. It is used for mattress covering, sportswear, and pillow covering.

CREAM | See MILK AND CREAM

CREDIT AND DEBT | See also CHARGE ACCOUNTS;
HOME REMODELING LOANS; MORTGAGES

How much credit can you afford? Can you buy a new car on time payments? Should you borrow to finance a vacation trip?

The matter of money—making it, borrowing it, spending it—is so subject to variables that there is no single rule of thumb to cover all cases.

A middle-aged man and wife with a paid-up house and no dependents conceivably could safely borrow—on a two-year loan—up to 25 or 30 per cent of the man's annual income of $7,500. On the other hand, a young married couple with two incomes exceeding $7,500 probably should not borrow more than 10 to 15 per cent. Why? The wife may have a baby, cutting the family income sharply at the same time that expenses rise.

A key factor in family credit is *discretionary income*. This is the money you have left each month after paying fixed expenses, such as rent (or mortgage payments), food, clothing, utilities, fuel, taxes, insurance, transportation, etc. Subtract that total from your husband's take-home pay. Then keep in mind that, if possible, regular savings should go into a fund for unpredictable emergencies. What is left is your discretionary income.

The next step is to look at yourself as a bank would if you went to it for a loan. Lenders weigh several factors in deciding whether a borrower will repay a loan without difficulty. Among them are:

Debts. How much money is owed already—on installment purchases; other bank, insurance, or finance-company loans; unpaid charge accounts, etc. (Mortgage payments usually are not viewed as debts, but as rent.) For example, Mr. Johnson already has obligations of $500 a year. The bank estimates that he can spend $1,000, or 15 per cent, of his income on credit. So he probably could not get a one-year loan for more than $500.

Income. In general, and there *are* exceptions, people earning $5,000 or more a year are considered better risks than those earning less. The lower the income, the more (in terms of percentage) which must be spent on basic necessities, and the less money available for credit repayment.

Assets. Is there money to repay the loan if the borrower loses his job?

To determine this, lenders require a borrower to list money in bank accounts, and to detail other assets such as cars, stocks, bonds, unmortgaged home—even though no collateral may be required for the loan itself.

Credit record. How have previous debts been repaid? Promptly? Or is there a pattern of slowness or possibly default on some payments? In examining your own family record on this score, be honest with yourself. You may find you have a tendency to overestimate your ability to repay.

Job. The best risks are considered to be people in executive or supervisory positions or in skilled work. Also considered is the stability of the particular industry. Is it subject to seasonal slumps? Is it a dying industry with future firings likely? Lenders also tend to be apprehensive about anyone who switches frequently from job to job, staying on each for a short time.

Age. In general, lenders view people who are thirty-five to fifty-five years old as the most desirable credit risks. At this age, people tend to be settled in their habits, have seniority in jobs, possibly own their homes, and have had experience in judging how far to extend credit without getting into trouble.

Family status. If you are happily married, the lender (or you) need not fear the financial upset a divorce or separation would bring. Children are also important. The more children, the heavier your regular expenses—and the greater the possibility of unexpected bills. The increase in expenses as children grow older has to be taken into account. If you are a working wife, you may think your earnings will help to repay credit. Lenders, though, generally do not put too much emphasis on such income if a woman is still in her childbearing years.

Where you live. The longer (preferably four years or more) that you have lived at the same address, and in the same area, the better the risk from a lender's viewpoint. To him this indicates stability and probably a circle of friends and neighbors who might be able to help you to cope with emergencies.

Reason for borrowing. If it is for what appears to be a constructive purpose, most lenders feel the borrower will be conscientious in repaying.

COSTS OF BORROWING

Buying on credit has become part of our national way of life. Few young homemakers realize, however, just what interest and charges they pay when they buy on time, use some types of charge accounts, or take out a small loan.

Determining the exact cost of credit in terms of *true* interest (simple annual interest), or even in dollars and cents, can be difficult. Several rather complicated mathematical formulas may be used. Some simple principles that help to lower these costs are:

Make the down payment as large as possible.

Shorten the repayment period as much as possible.

Make payments on schedule. Avoid penalty charges and possible repossession of merchandise.

The simplest type of loan—and usually the lowest in cost—is a **term note.** You borrow a set amount of money for a specific period and pay a set rate of interest. If you borrow $100 from a bank at 6 per cent for a year, you would repay $106—in a lump sum—at the end of the year.

Most small personal loans are not term notes but **installment notes.** An installment loan is usually discounted—that is, the interest charges are deducted from the amount borrowed at the time the loan is made. If you borrowed $100 on a 6 per cent discount loan for one year, the bank would keep $6 and give you $94. You would repay the loan at $8.33 monthly. The true annual interest on this loan is about 12 per cent. Why? You pay the borrowing charge in full for a year. But as you repay the loan monthly, you really do not have use of the full $100 for a year. Consequently, the interest *rate* increases as less is owed on the debt, becomes almost double the announced rate.

In **time buying** you are usually quoted a monthly interest rate. The annual interest rate is at least twelve times that amount.

Annual interest on installment-buying plans and revolving charge accounts can involve rates which are higher than you think they are. (Charges may also include bookkeeping fees.) If a $100 radio is bought on time, you might pay $10 down and have 12 monthly payments of $9. The total cost of the radio would be $118. The true annual interest rate is 33 per cent. On charge accounts, where the interest is levied on the unpaid balance, the rate varies. If there is a 1 per cent monthly charge, the true annual interest is 12 per cent.

THE MANY WAYS TO BORROW MONEY

Commercial bank. Loans by commercial banks are known by many names, including *personal, home improvement,* and *automobile.* You may be able to borrow as much as $5,000 for as long as 36 months on just your signature if your credit rating is good and your income large enough. (Loans for special purposes, such as a major home improvement, can bring larger amounts for up to 60 months.) Interest rates on these loans are usually stated in discount terms, frequently 4½ to 6 per cent. This is about 8 to 12 per cent true interest. For home improvement, a loan insured by the Federal Housing Administration may be available at a lower rate.

Collateral. If you provide collateral, such as stocks, bonds, or the cash value of a life insurance policy, you can obtain a lower rate of interest or get a bank loan you might not have been able to get otherwise. Interest rates are on either a simple or discount basis. In either case, true interest would usually be about 5 to 8 per cent.

Savings account. The institution in which your money is deposited usually will lend up to 85 or 90 per cent of the amount saved. The borrower surrenders his passbook until the loan is repaid, but he continues to receive interest for the *total* deposited sum. Rates are lower because the lender assumes no risk. Bank charges vary widely from 5 to 8 per cent simple interest, but in dollars may work out to less than they pay *you*. A savings and loan association usually charges from ½ to 1 per cent above the current dividend it is paying.

Borrowing from **small loan** companies is more costly than from a bank. This is because finance companies charge higher basic interest (they are not as selective in loan risks as banks), which is calculated *monthly* on the unpaid balance of a loan. For example, if $100 were borrowed at 3 per cent a month on the unpaid balance, you might arrange to repay it at $10 a month, plus interest. Hence the first payment would be $13, the second $12.70, the third $12.40, and so on. At the end of 10 months, the $100 would have been returned and $16.60 paid in interest. The true *annual* interest rate would be 36 per cent.

Education. The majority of banks offer special loans for education purposes. Rates are about 6 to 12 per cent simple interest. If the loan is made directly to a student, interest charges and repayment usually do not begin until after his graduation.

Revolving credit. Some banks will open a standing loan to a borrower's credit up to a possible $5,000, issue blank checks, and charge interest *only* when checks are written. The charge is about 1 per cent monthly or 12 per cent true interest annually.

Life insurance. Insurance companies allow loans up to nearly the full amount of a policy's *cash value* (a smaller amount than *face value*). Rates range from 5 to 6 per cent simple interest. The borrower repays as he wants although interest must be paid annually. Should he die before the loan is repaid, the insurance company deducts the loan and any outstanding interest from the face amount of the policy due to the beneficiary.

Credit unions. More than fourteen million persons belong to credit unions. Membership is limited to those having a common association, generally employment. Credit unions sell shares to members and use some of the money to make loans to them at favorable rates.

CURTAINS | See also INTERIOR DECORATORS; WINDOWS; WINDOW TREATMENTS

Selecting sash curtains means deciding among fabrics, each of which has desirable properties but none of which has them all. For example, cotton curtains may be permitted to hang for months without washing, since it is easy to restore their whiteness and crispness with bleach and starch. Nylon curtains, on the other hand, may lose their prettiness with such rigorous laundering, therefore must be taken down more often than cotton for gentle washing. Here are features to consider:

Cotton curtains in organdy, lace, or net wear well and are easily revived, but must be starched and ironed after each washing. Lace or net curtains must be put on stretchers to restore their shape, which is not an easy job.

Nylon curtains are now made of yarns that stay crisp longer than formerly, even after repeated washings. They should be made of bright (not semidull) yarn to resist the weakening and damaging effects of sunlight. They need little or no ironing.

Fiberglas curtains are not affected by sunlight, mildew, or insects, need no drying or ironing, but in sooty city locations they may become grey and grimy. Soaking in hot, sudsy water and chlorine bleach helps whiten them.

Dacron and **Orlon fibers** make sheer and beautiful curtains, but can be difficult to whiten if they hang too long. Hot water or long soaking makes them lose their crispness, as it does nylon. Don't permit any more soiling than can be removed by a quick plunge into suds or washer. A steam iron restores crispness.

CAFÉ CURTAINS

Café curtains extending only to the sill are popular, inexpensive, and can be used charmingly without shades or blinds. They work well with infor-

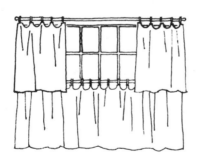

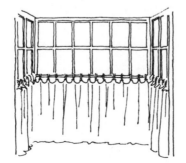

mal, contemporary interiors, in plain or printed fabrics, lined or unlined. Two tiers of different colors, may be teamed on the same window. Hang them by rings on poles of brass or other ornamental metal, making sure they are easy to pull from side to side. Flexibility in affording control of light and air, and in being easy to hang or take down, are their chief virtues.

TIPS ON CURTAINS

Choose preshrunk materials for curtains, and measure the length after putting up curtain rods. Allow an extra inch for heading above the rod. Measure from top of rod to the sill; or to the lower edge of the trim below the sill; or to the floor; any of these lengths is proper. Each panel of curtains, whether straight hanging or tied back, should be the width of the rod. Crisscross curtain panels should be twice the width of the rod for proper fullness. Plain or sheer curtains need more fullness than patterned ones.

In buying ready-made curtains, look for straight hems, full ruffles, square corners, and good construction. Be sure that rods and fixtures are smooth and free from rust. Protect the fabric from the heat of radiators by a suitable radiator cover. If curtains are made to hang at either end, turn them after each laundering; otherwise the bottoms will wear out first. Tie back curtains in children's rooms so they will not be pulled out of shape, and pin back or remove any curtain whenever windows are washed.

DENTISTRY |

A child's first visit to a dentist may establish his attitude toward dental care for the rest of his life. Consequently, parents should carefully prepare a child for that first dental checkup. Barring injuries to the mouth or problems such as gum infections, a child should have his first dental examination as soon as he has all his first teeth. This is generally between the ages of two and three.

The appointment, if possible, should be early in the day or after a nap, when the child is not tired and is less likely to be upset by the new experience. Pedodontists, dentists who specialize in treating children, suggest that a few days before the appointment parents should tell the child about it, calmly and casually. The explanation should be frank and simple: he is going to see the dentist, the man who helps keep teeth clean and healthy.

Parents often defeat their own purpose by making such statements as "Don't worry, the dentist won't hurt you." The child may connect the word "hurt" with the dentist and may become frightened. Do not try to reassure the child by saying, "All he will do today is look." If it is necessary to do more, the child's confidence in the dentist or in the parent may be damaged.

It is also unwise to mislead a child by making him think it is going to be a great treat. A ride in a chair that goes up and down like an elevator is fun, but that is not why the child is seeing the dentist.

Many dentists prefer to have mothers remain out of the treatment room. However, if the dentist feels a mother will be reassuring to a badly frightened child, he may invite her in. If so, she should remain quiet. To do his job, a dentist must be able to form a calm and confident relationship with the child. An overanxious mother, continually interrupting to rephrase the dentist's instructions, will only make the child more nervous and difficult to examine and treat.

DENTAL SPECIALTIES

Like medical doctors who concentrate in one area of work, some dentists specialize in particular problems. General practitioners (or family dentists) often consult with specialists or refer patients to them directly. In all, eight fields of specialization in dentistry are officially recognized by the American Dental Association:

Orthodontics includes the largest group of dental specialists. The orthodontist diagnoses and treats irregularities in tooth position and jaw relationship, primarily malocclusion—abnormal tooth arrangement or faulty bite. The orthodontist is often thought of as the specialist in "braces," which dentists prefer to call orthodontic appliances.

These appliances are made of metal or plastic and help to straighten teeth by applying mechanical force against them, gradually changing their position. Appliances may be removable or cemented in place. When the teeth are straightened, the orthodontist may apply a retainer to hold them in their new positions while new bone forms around the teeth.

Since irregular or protruding teeth may be unattractive, a person with malocclusion is often affected psychologically as well as physically. According to the American Dental Association, several surveys have shown that about half the children in any given age group need some form of orthodontic treatment.

Oral surgery deals with any surgery of the oral cavity and the surrounding structures. A major activity of the oral surgeon is exodontia, or extraction of teeth. He may also be involved in treating fractures of the facial bones, especially the upper and lower jaws, and diagnosis and removal of tumors and cysts. A family dentist usually performs routine extractions. An oral surgeon may be needed to perform more difficult or complicated ones, or larger scale extractions in which several teeth are removed. He also performs operations to improve the shape of the ridges of the jaw to receive artificial dentures.

Periodontics is the treatment of diseases of the gums and other tissues which support the teeth. Periodontal disease is the greatest single cause of loss of teeth after age 35. It develops slowly in two stages. The early stage, gingivitis, is characterized by tender, inflamed, or bleeding gums. In the later stage, periodontitis (sometimes called pyorrhea), the inflammation spreads along the roots and the gums may separate from the teeth. The bone structure supporting the teeth is destroyed if the disease is not treated, and teeth are eventually lost.

In the early stage, treatment of periodontal disease involves removal of calculus deposits, or tartar, from around the teeth. In more advanced stages, various medical and surgical techniques are used. In some cases, splints and other appliances are used to reduce the movement of loose teeth or to lessen the effects of harmful mouth habits, such as clenching or grinding the teeth during the day or during sleep.

Pedodontics is dentistry for children. Pedodontists use various techniques to eliminate—if present—a child's fear of dentistry and to teach the importance of dental care and prevention of tooth decay. They may use charts and models to explain just what they will do and how it will be done. They may try to eliminate such habits as thumb sucking and lip biting, which eventually may cause dental disorder. Children who are physically or mentally handicapped frequently pose special problems in dental care and often are treated by a pedodontist.

Prosthodontics deals with artificial replacement of missing teeth. A prosthodontist designs and constructs full and partial dentures, bridges (to replace one or more missing teeth), and other artificial devices. Routine prosthodontic work is usually performed by the family dentist.

Oral pathology is the study of abnormal changes or diseases of oral tissue. The oral pathologist is a diagnostician who makes microscopic studies of tissue and performs other tests (for example, blood tests). He frequently examines patients himself. Further treatment usually depends on his findings.

Endodontics is concerned with the treatment of the dental pulp or tooth nerve.

Public health dentistry is concerned with controlling oral disease in mass populations by applying preventive techniques, such as fluoridation of water supplies and by establishing treatment programs and clinics.

Dental authorities emphasize that it is not wise to attempt to choose a dental specialist by yourself. Your family dentist, says the American Dental Association, is best qualified to determine whether you need a specialist for a particular dental problem.

WISDOM TEETH

Dentists call these third molars, but because they usually begin to appear during the late teens—when a person presumably is becoming wiser—they have become popularly known as wisdom teeth. Here is why they cause trouble:

Unlike other teeth, a wisdom tooth is in a position where it cannot be reached easily. Hence, it is difficult, if not impossible in some instances, to fill; and it may have to be removed if it becomes decayed. If a wisdom tooth is painful, it is frequently because of decay and not usually, as many people believe, because the tooth is impacted.

An impacted tooth is one that is prevented from completely breaking through the surface of the gum because it is blocked by bone, fibrous tissue, or another tooth. It is not necessarily painful or troublesome, and occasionally corrects itself. However, pain can be caused by the pressure of the impacted tooth on the roots of nearby teeth or tissue.

When a wisdom tooth is partly erupted or near the surface and there is an opening into the space around it, food particles carrying infection frequently get into the opening. These particles are difficult to remove and are likely to cause decay and infection of surrounding tissue. Because of this, if the third molar is impacted, its chances of decaying are increased considerably. A dentist foreseeing trouble in later life may recommend removal of wisdom teeth in adolescence.

DESKS |

The desk form originated when a writing box was placed on a frame. The basic styles are made with various styling details, in a variety of woods and finishes.

1. **Tambour** is named for sliding top, consisting of strips of wood on a flexible backing. Upper section is removable; handles on sides are for carrying lower section. Example shown is late Sheraton.

2. **Block-front** style originated in eighteenth century in Rhode Island, is named for block-form carving of front. Shell carving on slant-top lid and intricate interior carving are typical.

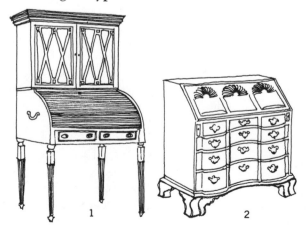

3. **Pedestal desk,** with work surface supported by two columns of drawers, has ornamental brass pulls, tooled-leather top. Modern flat-topped desks are inspired by this Chippendale style.

4. **Schoolmaster's** desk of pine with butterfly hinges, turned legs, H-form stretchers. Slant top has book-rest, lifts to allow access to storage space. Style shown is primitive American, dates from about 1715.

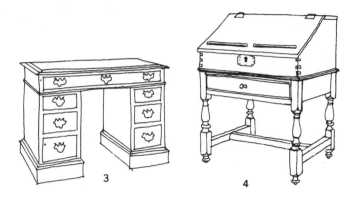

5. **Queen Anne desk-on-frame** really consists of two separate pieces—a removable "writing box" on a lowboy frame. Example shown is early eighteenth century, with shell-carved cabriole legs.

6. **George Washington desk,** generously proportioned, dates from about 1790. Letter file at each side of top. False drawers at ends look like real drawers in front.

7. **Secretary** with removable glass-paned bookcase above, storage drawers below a slant-top drop-leaf writing compartment. Style shown is Chippendale with bracket feet, broken-pediment top.

8. **French-Provincial escritoire** of fruitwood with wood-paneled bookcase above a graceful slant-top writing desk. This form is derived from Louis XV.

7   8

9. **Contemporary kneehole desk** with simple tapered legs, flush drawers, molding gallery around three sides of top.

10. **Writing table,** often called lady's desk, is small and delicate in scale. Usually has compartmented filing area above writing surface, one big drawer below. Example is Hepplewhite.

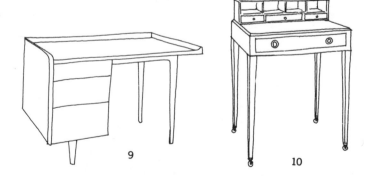

9   10

DIET FOR YOUNG CHILDREN | See also MENU PLANNING; VITAMINS AND MINERALS

Three meals a day, 7 days a week, 365 days in a year make a total of 1,095 meals to be prepared. No wonder the average mother runs out of ideas for feeding her children! A child develops slowly, his capacity for food changes, he can have a wider variety as he grows older; but the basic food requirements must be met each day.

See the section on planning menus for a discussion of nutrients in a properly balanced diet. When you market for the family, the same foods may be used for the children with careful planning. Many fortunately are available in small cans or jars specifically processed as "baby food." Your doctor will advise you if a special problem, such as an allergy, makes variations necessary. The following guidelines will help you to handle many common child-feeding problems.

Milk is particularly important. Besides calcium, which is needed for strong bones and teeth, it supplies high-quality protein and important B vitamins. Whole or skim, evaporated, or whole or nonfat dry milk may be used. Raw milk must be pasteurized for drinking, to avoid needless risk of infection. Pasteurization does *not* materially affect the nutrients in milk. (When raw milk is specified for medical reasons, it is available as "certified" milk drawn from rigidly inspected herds.)

Water should be given to children as a habit when they wake up in the morning. If the child tends to be constipated, he may also have prune or another fruit juice before breakfast.

The quantity of food given should be regulated by the child's appetite. When he is not hungry, he should not be forced to eat, or even cajoled. Let him wait for the next meal. But if he still seems hungry at the end of a meal, offer second helpings of vegetable, fruit, or milk.

While eating, a child should sit comfortably either at a low table with his feet on the floor, or in a high-chair. Silverware should be small enough for him to handle, yet enough like the adult type so that later he can make the adjustment easily. Meals should be served attractively, and good table manners should be encouraged. A child will eat better when he enjoys the occasion.

MENUS AT VARIOUS AGES

12 to 14 months:

BREAKFAST

4 to 5 tbsp. whole-grain or enriched cereal, with milk
Whole-grain or enriched bread, buttered
1 cup milk
Fruit: mashed banana, applesauce, puréed prunes, or stewed pears;
    or any commercial "baby food" or junior fruits

MIDMORNING

⅓ to ½ cup orange juice or ¾ cup tomato juice

NOON

2 to 3 tbsp. baked potato
3 to 5 tbsp. chopped or puréed vegetable (except corn)

Finely chopped, strained, or mashed meat, chicken, or fish; *or* 1 soft-cooked or mashed hard-cooked egg; *or* cottage cheese. (Start with a very small quantity; if the child accepts the food with no adverse symptoms, increase the quantity slightly each time.) Commercial baby or junior meats may be used.

1 cup milk

½ to 1 slice whole-grain or enriched bread, buttered

3 to 5 tbsp. custard pudding; *or* gelatin dessert; *or* stewed fruits; *or* commercial baby or junior fruits

MIDAFTERNOON (after nap)

Fruit juice or raw apple slices, with zwieback or whole-grain cracker

SUPPER

3 to 5 tbsp. cooked cereal with milk; *or* creamed vegetable; *or* 1 egg if not eaten at noon; *or* rice, macaroni, spaghetti

½ to 1 slice toast, dried bread, or zwieback, buttered

1 cup milk

2 to 3 tbsp. stewed fruit or mashed banana; or commercial or junior fruits

(*Note:* Also use 1 cup milk throughout day in cooking foods.)

14 months to 2½ years:

BREAKFAST

Whole-grain or enriched cereal, with milk, and sugar or other sweetening; *or* 1 egg, soft- or hard-cooked, poached, or scrambled

(*Note:* Include at least 5 eggs a week at breakfast or supper.)

1 slice crisp, drained bacon

Fruit juices or cooked fruit

½ to 1 slice whole-grain or enriched bread, buttered

1 cup milk (also use 1 cup milk during day in cooking)

MIDMORNING

½ cup orange juice or up to 1 cup tomato juice

NOON

1 baked potato with butter or margarine

1 chopped or mashed cooked vegetable

1 raw vegetable for chewing

2 to 3 tbsp. chopped or ground cooked meat, chicken, liver, or fish

½ to 1 slice bread, buttered

1 cup milk (either as drink or used in preparing food)

Dessert of raw fruit, seeded and skinned; *or* a custard, gelatin, *or* pudding

MIDAFTERNOON (after nap)

1 glass of milk, with fruit *or* zwieback if hungry (permits reducing amount of fluid intake at supper)

SUPPER

1 egg (if cereal served for breakfast)

1 cup milk (if not served after nap)

Sandwiches: cream cheese and jelly, grated vegetable, peanut butter
Dessert choice as for noon meal
(*Note:* Also use 1 cup milk throughout day in cooking foods.)

2½ to 4 years:

The regimen is less strict now as to menus; if your child prefers beef stew for breakfast, let him have it. Note that the daily one-quart ration of milk need not be taken as a beverage. It is just as effective in soups, puddings, etc.; eaten as cheese; or as nonfat dry milk added to cereals and other foods. A child may drink his milk before, after, or with the main course as he likes best. But he should be taught to drink it slowly, when his mouth is empty, and not use it to gulp down a mouthful of food. Menus may be devised from the following list:

Any kind of meat, fish, or poultry in any form from chopped to a chop, including some liver, kidneys, sweetbreads, or brains.

Any whole-grain or enriched bread, adding variety with corn or raisin breads; serve with butter or margarine.

Any whole-grain or enriched cereals, including the macaroni family.

Cheese: Any kind of mild flavor.

Eggs: At least five per week, any style. Most children like "coddled" eggs: brought to a boil, then removed from heat and allowed to stand in hot water two to five minutes.

Any vegetables except coarse, fibrous ones such as tough root vegetables, whole kernels of corn, raw cucumber, radishes. Garnish with sprigs of parsley, which the child should learn to eat. No need to chop vegetables after 3½ years.

Any fruit, raw or cooked, including dried fruits if well cooked. Fruit juice at least once daily, fresh, frozen, or canned.

Sandwich combinations such as cream cheese with honey or jelly; lettuce and tomato; grated carrot and raisins; peanut butter and jelly; hard-cooked egg; any of these with added chopped parsley.

Salad dressing including mayonnaise, lemon juice and oil, or sweetened lemon juice.

Desserts as in earlier years, plus ice cream occasionally, always followed with something crisp to chew on, such as zwieback, carrot strips, celery, apple, etc.

Water. All the child wants, but preferably *between* meals and *before* 4 P.M., so that the child may find it easier to remain dry through the night.

DINNERWARE | See also GLASSWARE; WINES AND LIQUORS

In setting the contemporary table, a complete set of dishes all of one pattern is no longer considered essential. For informal dining, the modern hostess may change the dinnerware with each course. China may be mingled with silver hollow ware (vegetable dishes, gravy boat, etc.), or with dessert and salad plates of glass. Many discriminating hostesses exercise imagination to create interesting combinations of harmonizing or contrasting color and pattern. For formal dining, however, a basic service for twelve might include the following:

12 service plates (11-12 in.)	12 coupe soup plates (8-9 in.)
12 dinner plates (10-11 in.)	12 rim soup plates (8-9 in.)
12 luncheon plates (9-10 in.)	12 cups and saucers
12 salad plates (8-9 in.)	1 round vegetable dish
12 pie plates (7-8 in.)	1 oval platter (10-11 in.)
12 bread and butter plates (5-6 in.)	1 chop platter (12-15 in.)
12 fruit dishes (5-6 in.)	1 oval platter (14-17 in.)

China, also called porcelain, is nonporous and resistant to chipping or cracking. Typical restaurant dishes are *vitrified china,* rather thick and opaque. Fine china is made of finer clays fired at high temperature, translucent and delicate in appearance. *Bone china* gets its name from the addition of bone ash to give it whiteness.

Earthenware, made of coarser clays, is porous in texture and less chip-resistant than china. It becomes *pottery* when thick or heavy and decorated in bold designs.

Melamine dinnerware is made of the smooth, hard material also seen on kitchen counter tops. Light in weight and extremely resistant to breakage, it is often used outdoors but should not be confused with *picnicware,* made of a styrene plastic that cracks more easily than melamine. Decorations are an intrinsic part of the material and will not wear off in dishwashing, but scouring with harsh abrasives and scoring with sharp knives should be avoided. Some melamine is susceptible to tea and coffee stains if allowed to stand too long before rinsing, and must be kept away from direct heat of the oven or range.

Glazing, a glasslike coating, importantly affects china quality. If the decorations are applied before glazing ("underglaze"), they will last as long as the dishes. If applied on top of the glazing ("overglaze"), they are more vulnerable and on low-priced dishes may soon wear off. Even on high-quality overglaze ware, the patterns may not withstand the forceful action and hot water of an automatic dishwasher. Gold decorations always are overglaze, and should be washed carefully by hand.

Open stock refers to patterns which the store can supply in individual units; it does not mean that the pattern will be available indefinitely. You may wish to add additional pieces to your set from time to time, or to replace breakage. Some patterns of famous potteries have been current for generations. This is an important point to check when buying dinnerware.

DISHWASHERS | See also APPLIANCE TROUBLE SHOOTING

All dishwashers need very hot water (150° to 160° F.) and special low-sudsing detergents. (These aren't just desirable—both are essential for good results and sanitation.) Somewhere inside each machine (bottom, top, sides, or middle) are one or more motor- or water-driven devices designed to dash the water at the dishes with enough force to "scrub" them clean. In the 40 minutes or so the machine operates, it fills, sprays and drains several times and then dries.

All dishwashers have racks with a maze of padded "fingers" sticking up to prop dishes and glassware in the right positions for washing. Besides these, there are open areas for inverted cups, deep bowls, pans, etc., and a basket for silverware and tools. (You'll find pictures in the instruction books that show you how to load the different items.) There's usually plenty of leeway in loading, the only sin being to nest or pile items so the water can't get to them. It's something like loading a sinkside dish drainer, but on a grander scale.

When you're shopping, shoo the salesman away long enough to practice with the racks a little. Be easy and natural about your loading. Try positioning imaginary plates, cups, glasses, platter, bowls, saucepan, serving pieces in any order that suits you. You'll notice that you load some models from the top into a tub. In others, the rack or racks roll out and you can load from all sides except the back. In either case, you should have easy access to every part of the dishwasher.

Some dishwashers hold more than others. It goes without saying that a machine rated at fifteen place settings will hold far more than one rated at eight. But don't let the difference of a place setting or two influence you too much. More important than its precise rating is the machine's general roominess and flexibility. Small families note: unless you're short on dishes, you'll probably wash only once a day, so scale the size you buy to a three-meal load.

All dishwashers today can be loaded without meticulous rinsing. It's enough just to scrape or shake foods off, under the cold-water tap if that's easier. If you don't plan to wash for hours, there is a precautionary prewash or prerinse on most machines.

Some dishwashers have booster heaters. This means that in addition to the heat going on during drying, it boosts the wash and/or rinse water temperature if it needs it. The heat, incidentally, may come from a gas or electric unit inside the machine. This is an excellent feature for any home with a somewhat unreliable water-heating system. Or for homes with small children, where keeping the tap water hot enough for the dishwasher might constitute a hazard. However, improving your hot-water-heating system may be less expensive in the long run, since these "booster" dishwashers usually cost more to buy and operate than conventional models.

All dishwashers will wash pots, pans, and cooking utensils provided there is no burned-on or baked-on soil. If this surprises or disappoints you, look at it this way. Some pans, after a meal, are merely smeary or greasy. These can go into the machine any time there's room. Or you can scour off crusty soil and then leave final cleanup and drying to the machine. Dishwashers with pot-and-pan cycles encourage you to put all pans in the machine. Then, at the end of the cycle (which does not include drying), finish off by hand any pans that are not clean, the soil presumably having been softened up by the dishwasher.

Almost any kind of cooking and serving ware you wash in the sink can be put in the dishwasher with no ill effects, *except*: woodenware or colored aluminum, unless the manufacturer explicitly advises machine washing; heat-sensitive plastics (but melamine dinnerware can be machine washed); flatware with cemented handles. Fading of china patterns and metallic trim on both china and glassware may be of concern unless patterns are applied under the glaze. To find out for sure how your china will fare, check with the manufacturer or a detergent maker.

All dishwashers have a single or double cup into which you put one or two tablespoonfuls of automatic-dishwasher detergent. The models with two detergent cups will give the dishes a double wash if you want it. Most machines come with one or more sample packages of detergent tucked inside. You may have to experiment with a few brands to find the ones most compatible with your water supply. Some models additionally offer hidden tanks that hold about a month's supply of a rinse additive, extra assurance of good results in problem-water areas. One machine has storage for both detergent and rinse aid, and injects both automatically.

Dishwashers pretty much keep themselves clean. You may have to rinse a strainer screen in the bottom if large food particles have accumulated. Spills on the rubber or vinyl gasket around the door or lid may have to be sponged off, since this strip isn't exposed to the washing. Service shouldn't pose much of a problem either, once the machine is properly installed. But it's well to find out where you can get service when you need it.

FIVE DISHWASHER STYLES

Undercounter, the true built-in that slides in under the kitchen counter, usually next to the sink. One built-in can be installed on a low-base cabinet which brings the machine above counter height, a more comfortable loading level for tall families.

Freestanding comes complete with cabinet and top, but is otherwise the same as the undercounter model.

Dishwasher-sink includes an undercounter machine, under-sink cabinet and 48-inch sink top. A new version of this is a dishwasher with a sink directly on top of it, and all in a mere 24 inches.

Portable, the popular wheel-around model with hoses that snap on and off the sink faucet for use. It parks anywhere in the kitchen the rest of the time. Most are low enough to roll under a 36-inch-high counter or table. They are available with a variety of tops, even maple for cutting-board convenience.

Convertible, a portable that can be plumbed and wired in permanently when you remodel or move. It is larger than most portables, actually free-standing, but on wheels and with hoses.

Finishes and colors can now be found, or ordered, to match almost any kitchen scheme.

HOW TO GET THE MOST OUT OF A DISHWASHER

In addition to easing a woman's work load, automatic dishwashers have definite health benefits. The use of water that is much too hot for hand washing, vigorous washing action, and special detergents combine to reduce bacteria. If you have a dishwasher, here are suggestions to help you get the most value from it:

Scrape large food particles from dishes before putting them in the dishwasher. If the waste screen needs frequent cleaning, too much food is being left on dishes.

The hot water heater should be set to give water of 140 to 150 degrees in the dishwasher. Normally, a setting of 150 to 160 degrees will achieve this.

The heater should be big enough to supply adequate hot water. Most dealers or plumbers will advise you on the proper size for your needs.

If installing a heater, keep the distance between heater and dishwasher as short as possible. The prewash cycle clears the pipes of cold water. Let the water run from the faucet until it is hot before starting the dishwasher.

Rack your dishes as the manufacturer suggests. Water and detergents should reach them on every surface. Try not to handle the eating surfaces of dishes and silverware when removing them from the dishwasher.

Use detergents recommended by the manufacturer. These are low sudsing and too strong for hand washing, but have the best sanitary effect in an automatic dishwasher.

Hard water may leave a film on the inside of the dishwasher and spots on glasses and dishes. Try increasing the amount of detergent up to two tablespoonfuls, or adding a rinse aid. In extreme cases you may need a mechanical water-softening system.

Do not skip the drying cycle to towel-dry dishes. If you are in a hurry, wait five to ten minutes after the wash-and-rinse cycles. Heat in the washer will evaporate most of the water from the dishes.

Watch for indications that the dishwasher is not working properly. Unused or caked detergent left in the dispenser, and bits of soil and a filmy appearance on the dishes after washing are signs of trouble.

Dishes heavily filmed or spotted? This may be caused by too much detergent, water not hot enough, or the dishwasher improperly loaded. Remove heavy film and spots this way:

Wash dishes and glasses as usual, but don't let them dry. Remove all metal articles—silver, pans, cutlery, etc.—because the next step would corrode them. Set ¾ cup of liquid chlorine bleach on the lower rack. Run the dishwasher through the wash-and-rinse cycles, but don't let the dishes dry. Next, place 2 cups of vinegar in a bowl on the lower rack, and run the machine through a full cycle. *Note:* Bleach used too often can injure china and dishwasher parts. Do not use more than once a month.

Black spots on silver are often caused by sprinkling detergent directly on it. Avoid this. Use silver polish to remove spots.

To remove coffee or tea stains from china cups, wash by hand, using ½ cup of chlorine bleach in 3 cups of warm water. For plastic cups, use a special stain remover. Follow the package directions.

If detergent doesn't dissolve, be sure to rack dishes so that the water force can hit the detergent cup. Add the detergent to the dry cup just before starting the dishwasher; if it stands too long in the cup, it may not dissolve well.

DISHWASHING | See also DISHWASHERS

The invention of detergents has taken most of the scrubbing out of dishwashing. They penetrate grease, lift off food particles, clean well in hard water and soft, and make most towel drying unnecessary. Here are some tips on bringing sparkle to your dishes with minimum effort:

Make light suds by being economical with the detergent; mountains of suds simply waste your time in rinsing off dishes and sink. To keep suds level down, add detergent after the dishpan is filled.

Just *before* serving dinner, empty your broiler, roasting pan, and other cooking utensils of grease and put them to *soak* in hot water with a few drops of detergent. This lightens the cleanup job later.

Use water as *hot* as your hands can stand (hotter if you wear gloves). Wash glasses and silverware first, then cups and saucers, then plates, with cooking utensils last.

Rinse in very hot water, too, and place on a rack to drain dry. Silverware and some glasses may need drying with a lintless towel to avoid streaks and spots. Also, silverware and kitchen knives should not be soaked in water more than a few minutes.

Own a variety of dishwashing tools besides a sponge and/or dishcloth, including:

> Pot scrubber of wire brush or plastic bristle, with handle.
> Rubber plate scraper.
> Copper or plastic ball to remove sticky foods.
> Silverware caddie (hooks onto drain rack).
> Special cleaners for copper, silver, rust, and coffee stains.
> Steel-wool soap pads.
> Cellulose dish mop (with long handle for deep things).

Cleaning crystal hollowware. The term "hollowware" refers to decanters, vases, fancy bottles, etc., of patterned or cut glass which may develop a milky, cloudy base, or trap dirt in their crevices. The haze usually comes from lime deposits in the water. Place some uncooked rice in the container, add several tablespoons of vinegar; shake well; then empty. If it is still milky, refill with a warm detergent solution, add more vinegar, and let it soak overnight. Rinse and repeat if necessary.

If the bottle has contained vinegar or wine, use a solution of several tablespoonfuls of ammonia to a quart of water; let it stand for an hour or so to remove the film. Vases that have contained flowers may be deodorized with a little chlorine bleach in the wash water.

BURNED UTENSILS

To remove burnt-on food from a cooking utensil of aluminum, stainless steel, porcelainized cast iron, ceramic, or heatproof glass, partly fill with water and a little detergent, and simmer on the range for ten minutes. As it simmers (boiling will raise too much foam), scrape and loosen the burnt particles with a wooden spoon. Then empty the utensil and remove any remaining crust with a steel-wool soap pad.

Burned enamel pans, however, should be cleaned with household cleanser and a sponge.

A rainbow-like discoloration of stainless steel utensils is a heat tint, caused by overheating when empty of food or water. It won't come off, but you can remove the brownish film that often accompanies the tint. Soak a dishcloth with full-strength ammonia (try not to breathe it in), and cover the film with the cloth for 15 to 30 minutes. Then wash the utensil in the regular way.

Stainless utensils may be discolored or even pitted by prolonged contact with mustard, mayonnaise, vinegar, or pickling brine. Scrub with household cleanser; any remaining slight discoloration usually fades in time.

Darkened aluminum may be lightened by boiling 2 teaspoons cream of tartar to 1 quart water in the pan for 10 minutes. Then use steel-wool pad.

Stains in Teflon may be lightened by boiling 2 tablespoons of baking soda, ½ cup of liquid household bleach, and 1 cup of water in the pan. Then wash in warm suds. Don't let the solution contact any surface other than Teflon. Remember to rub it with 1 teaspoon of salad oil before using again.

WOODEN BOWLS

Your cherished wooden salad bowls and other woodenware should *never* be soaked in water or washed in the dishwasher. Wash quickly by hand in warm, not hot, slightly sudsy water and dry immediately with a towel. (One exception is a specially finished ware of solid elm. If you are unsure, don't experiment.) When a bowl becomes crazed, chipped, or cracked it is not only unsightly but unsanitary and must be discarded. A worn (but not cracked) inner finish may be restored as follows:

First remove all the old finish with sandpaper. Then mix one tablespoon of mineral oil with half a tablespoon of powdered pumice stone. Rub this into the inside of the bowl with cheesecloth until the wood feels dry and smooth (about half an hour). Let it dry for twenty-four hours, remove the dust, and repeat the process. You may have to repeat ten or a dozen times. When satisfied, wash the bowl in the normal way. Do not wax, polish, or shellac it.

DRAPERIES AND DECORATIVE FABRICS | See also CURTAINS; WINDOWS

Select drapery to suit the type of window. There are two accepted lengths: to the sill or to the floor. Have plenty of fullness; skimpy draperies are rarely pleasing. Never split 50-inch material; use one 36-inch width or more for each panel, even if you must buy a cheaper fabric.

Lining improves the appearance of most draperies, and protects the material from sunlight and fading. Modern fade-resistant "miracle" fibers, however, will wear very well unlined.

Good solid-color fabrics for drapery might include heavy faille, satin or sateen, velvet or velveteen, rough-textured and diagonally woven fabrics, plain or textured corduroy, self-patterned damask in silk, cotton, or a synthetic material. Good figured fabrics include the florals (chintz, etc.), striped (satin to bedticking), and geometric patterns (on linen, etc.), either modern or traditional.

Sash curtains are not strictly necessary with Venetian or bamboo blinds, but make most rooms look more intimate. Draperies may be omitted by using full, crisp, ruffled, tied-back organdy or tailored sheer curtains on the windows, or sheeting for a more informal effect. A popular contemporary treatment uses one fabric of casement-type cloth, pleated and unlined.

An effective way to give a room a warm, peaceful setting is to use fabrics similar to drapery or upholstery for other purposes. A number of unusual—and inexpensive—approaches are possible, following these general rules:

Use only one pattern—particularly if it is a large design—in a room.

For accent, use bright colors in small amounts.

A tightly woven fabric wears better for upholstery than a loose weave, even if the material is heavy.

A lightweight or loosely woven fabric will drape better than a tightly woven, heavy fabric.

When buying fabric, check colorfastness, cleaning instructions, and shrinkage.

Take samples of fabric home to try in a room in both daylight and artificial light.

Know how much you need and exactly what you want before ordering. Get an extra yard if there is a large pattern.

In decorating, be sure patterns repeat evenly, or, if there is a large motif, that it is centered on the upholstery.

Consider using synthetic leathers and hide furs, stretch fabrics and other manmade fibers instead of conventional upholstery coverings. Keep in mind unexpected—but effective—materials such as burlap, denim, duck, terry cloth, felt, corduroy, mattress ticking, or sailcloth for home use. Many of these come in a range of colors and very wide widths, and are inexpensive.

In many cases, fabric-dyeing processes have been improved to make colors sun- and colorfast. There also are fabric lines in which prints, stripes, and solid colors are coordinated to match. Many materials are coated, or can be treated for a small expense, to be water, oil, and stain resistant.

Use a vivid color or rich-looking material to cover a wastebasket, pillow, lampshade, desk set, picture mat, or books and portfolios. Doors, cabinets, or panels of a screen room-divider can be decorative features when covered with a pattern which is used elsewhere in a room.

Almost all materials, including the newer paper-backed types, can be pasted, tacked, or stapled on a wall. You can create a dado on the lower part of a wall with fabric, covering the tacking with wood molding, braid, or guimpe trim. Hang drapery from the ceiling on traverse rods or café rods to separate a dining area or a guest sleeping space.

Mill-end shops (located in or near most large cities) often have good buys in odd-size remnants. Sailcloth and heavy duck may be less expensive when bought from a commercial awning shop or a tentmaker. Dress goods, such as cotton, silk, velvet, or woolen coating, may be bought on sale and used successfully in decorating. But bear in mind that dress-goods widths are different from drapery or upholstery material widths.

SLIPCOVERS

A washable slipcover on a sofa or chair has a prominent place in decorating a room, as well as many practical advantages. Used on new furniture, it protects the permanent upholstery and permits changing your color scheme at will at modest cost. It can modernize or freshen the appearance of old furniture.

Whether you make the slipcovers yourself or have them custom made, choose a good grade of fabric. Don't economize on material which may stretch out of shape or shrink after washing or cleaning. Buy a preshrunk fabric or have the shrinking done before making the slipcover, to insure a good fit.

Avoid a clash of patterns, especially with a patterned rug or wallpaper in the same room. It's better to use one slipcover fabric throughout than a "set" of two or three flower patterns that are not different enough to complement each other. A combination of one flowered pattern with, for example, stripes or a plain texture would be more effective. Select easily washable or cleanable materials, avoiding wool (which attracts moths) and high-pile fabrics (which attract dust).

Place figures symmetrically on the backs and seats. The skirt of the slipcover should reach to or just clear the floor. Use matching cords on all seams; or on a plain material, use heavier cords, welts, or fringe in a contrasting color.

DRIVING TIPS | See also CAR PROBLEMS; DRIVING WITH CHILDREN

Most automobile accidents are caused, at least in part, by improper driving. Safety experts, including those of the National Safety Council and the Division of Accident Prevention of the Public Health Service, say possibly the worst driving sins contributing to accidents are:

Speed not suitable for conditions. This major cause of fatal accidents includes driving too fast for prevailing road and weather conditions; and driving too slow to conform to traffic flow.

Following the car ahead too closely. Experts urge a minimum distance between cars of one car length for every ten miles per hour of speed.

Failure to yield right of way. The right of way is a permissive system for orderly procedure in traffic, never an absolute right to go first. Generally, the car to your right at an intersection proceeds before you do. The safe driver, however, always *yields* the right of way to a car already in the intersection, or closer to it; to pedestrians; and in any case of question or possible hazard. Emergency vehicles have the right of way regardless of location.

Improper passing. Serious accidents are caused by switching lanes without signaling and without regard for other cars; by passing on the right; by passing on or too near a curve or the crest of a hill; or by driving on the wrong side of the road.

Car neglect. Even a careful driver is a menace to himself and others if any operating part of a car is defective. Have your brakes, steering, etc., checked periodically and at any sign of mechanical trouble.

Inattention. Driving is a full-time job. Stay alert with your eyes on the road at all times and keep both hands on the wheel. Don't drive when fatigued.

Driving under the influence of liquor or drugs. Even a small amount of liquor can diminish driving ability. Labels on many drugs warn not to drive after taking them. They include antihistamines, tranquilizers, and amphetamines (such as benzedrine); and practically any drug sold only on prescription.

Improper turns and signals. Turns must be made from specified lanes and at safe speeds. Be sure to signal correctly and not too early or too late.

NIGHT DRIVING TIPS

The rate of fatal automobile accidents is almost three times higher between dusk and dawn than it is during daylight. Safety experts say, though, that many of these fatalities can be averted if certain basic precautions are observed. They include:

Visibility. Keep the windshield, back window, headlights and taillights clean to maintain good visibility for yourself and drivers of other cars. Clean windows also help to reduce eyestrain and fatigue. Reflective tape or paint on the bumper or trunk of a car and reflective license plates (used by some states) make cars more visible at night. Turn your headlights on at dusk, and use the parking lights only for parking purposes. Dim your lights when approaching or following another car. Too, use directional signals well in advance of any turn. Keep the headlights on (dimmed) in inclement weather.

Never wear tinted glasses to reduce headlight glare. To prevent temporary glare blindness from the bright lights of an oncoming car, look to the right shoulder of the road and slow down. Confusing glare in the car can be reduced if you keep your instrument-panel lights dim and don't use the dome light or other light sources when moving. Have your headlight alignment checked regularly.

Speed. The greater your speed, the farther ahead you must see—possibly beyond your vision range at night—and the longer it takes to stop. So, drive at least 10 miles an hour slower at night than you normally do during the day under similar road conditions. Reduce speed additionally during bad weather. Know the approximate length of your headlight beam, and control your speed so you can stop safely within its visibility range. (You need about 188 feet to stop at 50 mph; 272 feet at 60 mph under favorable conditions.)

On a clear, straight road, a driver can see ahead about 250 to 275 feet. However, the headlights of an approaching car gradually reduce this visual distance to about 90 feet when it passes by. Don't try to pass a car in fog. Use extra caution and reduce speeds sharply on poor, curved, or unfamiliar roads.

Stops. If at all possible, never stop on a traveled roadway at night. In emergencies, pull off the road as far as possible. Alert approaching traffic by placing lights or flares behind you. (Flags or reflectors may also be used.) Turn on parking lights, the left-turn blinker, and the inside dome light. New cars have an emergency flasher, which blinks both turning signals. Don't walk on the road. Have equipment on hand for night emergencies. These items should include a flashlight with spare bulbs and batteries, any type of safety markers (flares, flags, etc.), and extra fuses and bulbs for the car's lighting system.

Physical condition. Drive at night only if you feel well and rested. Physical or mental fatigue, eyestrain, emotional upsets, and liquor add greatly to the usual difficulties of night driving. If you feel drowsy, have someone take over the wheel. If another driver is not available, stop as soon as possible to get fresh air and to rest or nap. Always keep a window partly open. On long drives, avoid overeating and make frequent rest stops. Be sure your eyes are checked regularly.

WINTER DRIVING TIPS

Road conditions change in severe winter weather, and so should your driving techniques. Observe these rules to have better control of your car on ice or snow.

Starting. Spinning wheels on ice or snow polishes the surface and reduces traction. So, start slowly, applying gentle pressure on the gas pedal. With a manual gear shift, start in second or even in high. Try to keep the front wheels straight. If this is not possible, rotate the steering wheel back and forth to open a path for the front tires. If the back wheels are blocked by deep snow, try rocking by alternately shifting from forward to reverse gear but with a light touch on the accelerator so the wheels will not spin and dig into the snow.

Under way. Keep speed reduced until you can feel the conditions of the road. If your car skids when you stop, or slides sideways on turns, use extreme caution. Some of the most slippery driving conditions occur just at freezing temperature (32° F.) when new ice may be forming on wet roads or old ice or snow is melting on the surface. Keep more than the usual distance between you and the car ahead. Slow in advance of a curve without braking, if possible. Do not turn the wheel sharply. If the rear wheels start to skid sideways, steer in the direction of the skid, *not away from it.* Turn the steering wheel slowly on a slow skid; fast on a fast skid. Do not overcorrect, and beware of the counterskid.

Plan ahead to maintain as even a speed as possible to avoid loss of traction. If you see a red traffic signal up ahead, try to approach it just as it is about to turn green so you will not have to come to a full stop. If you are approaching a hill, remember that if you stop on it or slow down too much, you may not be able to proceed. If the wheels of your car should spin, your only recourse is to back down or turn around—a ticklish operation. Instead, maneuver for road room from a distance. If there is another car ahead of you, let it get well ahead. Then work up sufficient momentum when you reach the hill to get you over the crest. *Go slow but keep going is the winter driver's formula.*

Stopping. To slow or stop, lightly pump the brake pedal—that is, push down several times in rapid succession. This allows you to maintain steering ability and keeps the wheels from locking, which occurs if brakes are applied suddenly. Remember, on ice or snow, three to twelve times the usual stopping distance is needed.

Winter car care. Both rear and front windows should be clear of ice and snow for visibility. Keep your lights clean, and drive so you can stop within their range. Lights should be on low beam in snow to reduce glare. If you are stuck in a snowbank, turn off the motor because exhaust fumes may become trapped under the car and drift into the automobile.

SUMMER DRIVING TIPS

On vacations, drivers often travel on unfamiliar roads and under conditions they do not normally face during the rest of the year. If your family is planning a motor trip, these driving tips may be helpful:

Mountains and hills. When going downhill, never disengage the clutch or put the car out of gear and coast. Instead, shift to a lower gear, or to "low" with automatic transmission. On long upgrades, watch the water temperature gauge for overheating. If the radiator overheats, turn off to the side of the pavement and wait for it to cool. Moderate speeds lessen the chance of overheating.

Condition of car. Have your car checked thoroughly before leaving home. Be alert for symptoms of trouble. Constant driving at high speeds can increase tire pressure to the blowout point. Be sure tires are in good condition and are checked frequently for correct air pressure.

Expressways. Special rules and precautions must be observed on expressways. For example, high speeds are maintained and you must adjust yours to the pace set by traffic in your lane.

Schedule. Start early in the day to avoid some of the traffic and heat. Plan frequent stops, at least every two or three hours, to break the monotony. Safety experts recommend that you limit driving time to a maximum of six to eight hours a day.

Comfort. Proper posture and seat adjustment and a back pillow or an air-cooled cushion can add driving comfort. Occasional applications of an astringent to wrists, palms, forehead, and neck give some relief from heat discomfort. Seat belts, also, in addition to their safety value, lessen fatigue.

DRIVING WITH CHILDREN | See also DRIVING TIPS; LEARNING TO DRIVE

On a family automobile trip, children pose special car-safety problems that require careful attention from parents. In the same sense that you teach children to eat and play properly, you must teach them proper behavior in a car. You also should use available safety devices. Authorities stress that some form of restraining device—bassinet, harness, or seat belt—is probably the single most effective safety device for children in cars.

Infants. Until a child is able to sit up, he should ride in a bassinet placed in the rear seat, running from front to back of the car. (No child should ride while sitting on an adult's lap.) One end of the bassinet is secured by bails or hooks over the back of the front seat and the other rests on the rear seat. The baby should be held in the bassinet by either a nylon net covering attached to the top of the bassinet, or a harness.

Eight months to six years. Harnesses can be used from the time children sit up until they weigh fifty pounds. Harnesses come in a variety of styles and most permit the child to sit, stand, and lie down. The harness holds the child at the shoulder and chest areas and around the pelvis—never around the waist or abdomen alone. It attaches to another strap which is bolted to the car and prevents the seat from falling forward and crushing the child.

The harness should fit snugly and be adjustable to allow for growth. The child should not be able to turn around in the harness, nor should he be able to open it.

It is a good idea when buying seat belts or harnesses to insist on certification that they meet minimum Society of Automotive Engineers (SAE) standards. Such certification may appear as the identifying seal of either Underwriters' Laboratories (UL) or the American Seat Belt Council.

These specifications rule out the use of front seats secured by hooks or bails over the back of the seat. The Institute of Transportation and Traffic Engineering (ITTE) at the University of California concluded: "During a collision their design provides what amounts to a built-in injury-producing structure."

The rear seat is the safest place for the child to ride and the best place to install harnesses. A harness and adult belt can be installed in the same seat to allow for a change of passengers. Harnesses cost about as much as seat belts—from nine to twelve dollars or more, plus installation.

A harness should be used every time a child rides in the car. Check the fit at each wearing and keep slack at a minimum.

Four years and older. Although most four- to six-year-olds wear a harness, some children prefer seat belts. A four-year-old should be able to use an adult seat belt. The belt must fit snugly over the pelvic area and not around the waist. Seating the youngster on a cushion often helps to achieve a good fit by taking up some of the belt length, and at the same time, it enables the child to see out the window.

Other precautions. All sharp, loose objects should be removed from the car. The back-window shelf of many cars contains things which can cause serious head injury if hurled through the air, as they would be in an accident or sudden stop. Remove any unnecessary hard or sharp objects from the dashboard or other parts of the car. A padded dashboard is a good safety measure, now standard on new U.S. cars. Packages and groceries should be placed in the trunk or on the floor where they cannot be thrown against the child.

Special locks to prevent children from opening car doors are available. One type has a switch operated from the driver's seat which locks and unlocks all doors. Another lock cannot be opened by the inside handle. Station wagons can be equipped with a rear-window screen to help prevent a child from falling out, and to keep him from reaching and releasing the tail-gate handle.

A child must learn that a car is not a playground. He should be taught to keep his hands off the dashboard, handles, locks, steering wheel, and driver. Arms, head, and toys must be kept inside the car. Although children may want toys and food, especially on long trips, don't give them food on a stick, and toys should be small and soft.

Teach children to enter and leave the car from the curb side. Check that all fingers are inside before shutting and locking doors. When stopping to pick up or drop off passengers, put the car in neutral or "park," and use the emergency brake. Before leaving the car, always turn off the ignition, remove the keys, and use the emergency brake. Never leave a child alone in a car.

DRY CLEANING | See also STAIN REMOVAL

Called "dry" because it does not use water, dry cleaning is a method of washing and rinsing garments in a fluid that dissolves or loosens general soil and some stains. The cleaning fluid evaporates quickly from the fabric, and unlike water, does not remove creases or pleats. Dry cleaning is specified for materials that would fade, shrink, or stretch out of shape in water, or that would be difficult to iron. Stains not removed by the fluid bath are removed by "spotting"—a special technique involving expert knowledge of fabrics, dyes, finishes, and the chemistry of stains.

Dry cleaning generally is a job for the professional. As a practical matter, dry cleaning at home should be limited to a safe cleaning fluid, to simple items such as blouses, sweaters, gloves, etc., to the removal of fresh stains, or to pretreating spots on a fabric before laundering.

Clothes badly soiled by perspiration or food stains require gentle hand laundering before being dry cleaned, which the professional calls "wet cleaning." He measures the garment first, then restores it to the original dimensions with special pressing equipment. He also removes plastic buttons, belts held together by adhesives, or other items that cleaning fluids would dissolve.

Send clothes to the cleaner before they become badly soiled, and as soon as possible after being stained. (Old stains are often impossible to remove.) Pin a note to the garment identifying the stain if you can. Don't press stained garments between dry cleanings, and remember to remove every-thing from the pockets. If you notice yellowing at the neckband, call it to the cleaner's attention for special work by the "spotter." A cleaner can't restore faded colors or prevent the fume fading that gives acetate clothing an off-color cast.

Have clothing cleaned before storing. It removes stains that would set with age, and food stains that attract moths, silver fish, or other destructive insects.

When selecting a dry cleaner, don't be taken in by fancifully described processes and cut-rate prices. A dry cleaner is best judged by the quality of his work. Inspect your newly clean clothes. If you are dealing with a good dry cleaner, clothes should have no cleaning solvent odor, no fabric shine, and no dulling of color, or "graying down" if the garment is white. In addition, slacks and trousers should be neatly creased, and pleated skirts should hang straight, with no crooked or uneven pleating. Double creases can be avoided when the right equipment and trained pressers are employed.

A good cleaning job can also be determined by the absence of impression marks at seams, pockets, and buttons. In really careful dry cleaning, buttons are removed and resewn instead of pressing them into the fabric, leaving ugly marks and possibly damaging the buttons.

Bagginess, often noticeable at the knees of trousers, can be taken out by a special finishing. A good cleaner will do this and also brush out dirt particles and lint that have collected in cuffs. He'll repair small rips and tears as well.

Remember, though, that shrinkage isn't always his fault. Some things will shrink no matter how carefully they're treated, especially if they're so soiled that the cleaner has to use soap and water to remove some of the soil. And in the case of spot removal, there are stains and certain kinds of materials that simply won't respond. Cleaners who display an up-to-date plaque stating membership in a dry-cleaning association—for example, the National Institute of Dry Cleaning—have access to the latest techniques for cleaning all kinds of materials.

A final reminder: remember that a dry cleaner is not responsible for the loss of articles left in pockets.

Self-service dry cleaners provide coin-operated machines that work much like washing machines. Cost savings are considerable: from $1.50 to $2.00 per 8-pound load, for which commercial cleaners charge $6.00 to $8.00. One load consists of 8 to 10 dresses, sweaters, etc., or 3 to 4 suits.

Garments and colors can be mixed, with certain precautions against linting. Turn soft, dark items inside out and place them in a mesh bag. Also pretest extra-bright colors or ask the shop attendant for advice on color-fastness.

The solvent used—perchlorethylene—is nonflammable. Toxic fumes are kept away from customers by venting; also, the machines cannot be opened while in operation. The clothes are lightly sprayed with water mist, especially on spots or soiled areas, before you put them in the machine. About 90 per cent of stains will come out, but not mildew, scorch, lipstick, ink, or stains which have been set. These take spotting by an expert.

Even fancy things such as beaded blouses, chiffon, tulle, and cashmere sweaters are acceptable in the machines, as are blankets and slipcovers; but not leather, fur, rubber, angora, pillows, or some plastic buttons. Creases, pleats, and ruffles stay sharp, but dry cleaning does not remove deep-set wrinkles. Touch these up with a steam iron. Also minimize wrinkling by carrying clothes home on hangers.

DURABLE PRESS GARMENTS | See WASH AND WEAR

EGGS |

Eggs, the American breakfast mainstay, are equally suitable for luncheon, supper, and snacks. A "friendly" food, they go with everything and combine tastefully with other foods. The sensitive egg responds to care and gentle, respectful handling. Too often it is the victim of thoughtless cruelty in cooking. "Do right by the egg, and it does more than right by you."

Be a choosy buyer. If possible, buy from a dealer who keeps eggs in refrigerated display cases. Heat lowers egg quality rapidly. For example, eggs left 4 days in a warm store (70° to 80° F.) lose as much freshness as those kept several weeks in a refrigerator. In higher midsummer temperatures, such losses occur even more rapidly.

The carton should carry a label with a trusted brand name or trademark, or the letters "U.S." Such eggs have been graded for quality and size. *If they have been properly stored,* their label is a reliable buying guide. Egg grades are established by the United States Department of Agriculture. (Check with your county or state agriculture department to see if your state has its own grading program.)

By all means, take advantage of locally produced eggs. But be sure the "egg man" handles them properly and guarantees their quality. With eggs, "fresh" implies high quality rather than time laid. In some states the term "fresh" may legally identify Grade AA and Grade A eggs, but may not signify B and C grade eggs. Grade A eggs are most commonly available. Age alone does not determine the quality or "freshness." Equally important are the conditions of storage. Eggs should be kept covered and cold. The grade also is determined in part by Madame Hen.

QUALITY AND FOOD VALUE

Grade AA or Grade A eggs are top quality, with a large amount of firm white, and a well-rounded, high-standing yolk. While good for all uses, their high quality and freshness are most appreciated for poaching, frying, or boiling in the shell.

Grade B and Grade C eggs have thinner whites, and the yolks tend to flatten out. Many families find it pays to buy these lower grade, lower priced eggs for making omelets and salad dressings, scrambling, thickening sauces, baking, and combining with such other foods as tomatoes, cheese, onions, etc. They offer the same food value as top-grade eggs.

Shell color does not indicate food value or quality of contents, yet it influences egg prices in some localities. There is absolutely no reason for paying a higher price for a particular shell color. Often you can save money by buying brown eggs where white ones are in greater demand, and vice versa. Differences in flavor are negligible.

While shell color is determined chiefly by the breed of hen, yolk color is influenced by the feed. Modern management and scientific feeds have pretty much standardized yolk color—to a middle-of-the-road yellow.

Egg size and quality are not related. And don't let your eye deceive you. A round-shaped egg, though appearing smaller, may actually weigh more than a larger appearing, long, oval egg. "Large" eggs (two ounces each, or 24 ounces to the dozen) make up the bulk of the market supply. The established legal weight classes are indicated in the table below:

Egg Size	Minimum Net Weight Per Dozen
Jumbo	1 lb. 14 oz.
Extra large	1 lb. 11 oz.
Large	1 lb. 8 oz.
Medium	1 lb. 5 oz.
Small	1 lb. 2 oz.
Pullet	15 oz.

Since eggs do not roll off nature's production line in absolute uniformity, slight tolerances are permitted within the dozen.

Seasons and prices: Prices have steadied and seasonal market supplies of eggs have leveled off as modern poultry management has modified seasonal fluctuations in egg production. When different-size eggs of like quality are offered at retail counters, consumers often find a price advantage in selecting the size most plentiful at the time.

Large eggs are preferred for use at breakfast and for main dishes at luncheon and dinner. Medium and small eggs are excellent for out-of-hand eating (such as hard-cooked eggs for lunch boxes, picnics, and deviled eggs). Most standard recipes are based on the use of large and medium eggs.

For babies: Strained egg yolks have now joined the huge family of canned foods for babies.

To keep eggs: Since eggs lose quality rapidly in a warm kitchen, get them into your refrigerator quickly. Make sure each rests with broad end up. Don't keep them long—use them. Remove from refrigeration only as many eggs as you are going to use at one time.

ELECTRIC APPLIANCES | See also APPLIANCE TROUBLE SHOOTING

Although the modern housewife needs no engineering degree to operate her array of household appliances, it does help to know at least this much about electricity: Appliances that heat electrically use vastly more current than light bulbs, radio and TV, or electric motors. Your breakfast toaster may use nearly ten times as much current while it's on than the most powerful vacuum cleaners, while your electric iron requires more watts than a dozen light bulbs plus the radio. Air conditioners ("heat pumps") are also heavy users of current. Here is a table of approximate wattages:

Electric roaster	1,650	Portable heater	1,000
Electric ironer	1,650	Television	300
Air conditioner	850 to 1,400 and up	Refrigerator	150
Automatic toaster	1,200	Vacuum cleaner	125
Waffle iron	1,200	Radio	100
Electric skillet	1,200	Mixer or blender	100
Coffee maker	1,000	Electric fan	100
Automatic hand iron	1,000	Light bulb	25 to 150

These wattages also measure the cost of operating the various appliances. You buy electricity by the kilowatt-hour, which means the use of 1,000 watts (a kilowatt) for 1 hour (or 500 watts for 2 hours; 100 watts for 10 hours, etc.). Your electric bill may indicate the kw-h rate, or you can ask the power company business office. Often the rate decreases on a sliding scale; the more current you use, the less it costs per kilowatt-hour. In some places high-wattage appliances such as an electric range or water heater receive a "wholesale" rate that makes the cost of current comparable with other fuels.

Fuses and circuit breakers are safety devices to prevent fire by cutting off the current before the wires get hot. Never plug in a toaster, iron, or other heat appliance without disconnecting all other appliances from the same outlet or circuit. An overloaded circuit will blow a fuse or trip a circuit breaker—the commonest cause of unnecessary service calls.

Sometimes this happens because of momentary overloading. For example, at the instant a refrigerator turns itself on it takes an extra "surge" of current. If fuses blow repeatedly, your house may need rewiring. Never let anyone by-pass the fuses in your house or replace them with higher wattage fuses. Also, in buying an appliance, be sure it bears the safety seal of Underwriters' Laboratories.

SMALL APPLIANCES

Mixers. An electric mixer can be a third hand in your kitchen, but consider a permanent place for it since its usefulness will depend upon its being handy at all times. A portable hand mixer may be the solution.

On a stand mixer look for chrome plated beater blades and beater ejector; attachments: juicer, meat grinder, dough hook; variety of speeds.

On a portable hand mixer look for three speeds; variety of colors; beater ejector; wall mount for storage, or a stand and turntable; detachable cords; drink-mixer attachments; heel rest.

Blenders. No longer just a drink mixer, a blender will purée, chop, grate, crumb, shred, or combine a wide variety of foods, and has given rise to a whole new school of cookery. With its stainless steel blades whirling at speeds up to 18,000 revolutions per second, it reduces tedious jobs to seconds and makes possible gourmet dishes you otherwise might not attempt.

Look for speed control with from two to ten settings; container that holds more than one quart; optional half-pint jars for blending cheese spreads, baby foods, etc.; heat-resistant glass or rugged plastic containers, with opening from the bottom for removing thick mixtures; close-fitting cover (some are in two parts to permit adding ingredients during blending); handle, pouring spout, measuring cup with ounce markings on the container; high-powered motor, and sharp, stainless steel blades; rubber-tipped feet for stability; timer; and heating element.

Height and shape: One blender is only 10½ inches high, another has a wide bottom for greater capacity. (*Note:* A blender will shave cracked ice, but whole ice cubes may damage the blade.)

Can openers. Since the average family opens eight hundred cans a year, a device that quickly and cleanly cuts the top off a can of any size or shape (even sardine cans) is a convenience. Electric ones come in wall or table models. Look for a brand of a reputable manufacturer; ability to puncture the lid with little effort (a strong push may splatter contents); magnetic lid holder, swiveled to get a firm grip on any lid (won't work on aluminum cans); removable cutting wheel and lid holder for easy cleaning; smooth exterior and other well-made parts for better service; additional features such as built-in knife sharpener; cord holder. Some models are wholly automatic: you insert a lid, press a lever, and that's all.

Coffee makers. These are usually of the percolator type, though one makes coffee by the vacuum principle. It may be stainless steel, chrome, aluminum, glass, glass ceramic, or plastic.

Look for sizes ranging from five to one hundred cups; most popular is ten cup; simple design or immersibility for easy cleaning; brew selector for mild to strong coffee, and light to indicate when coffee is ready; glass tube that shows amount of coffee in the pot.

Note: Because flavor is so important in coffee, daily washing of the coffee maker with clean, hot suds is necessary. Simple rinsing will not remove clinging coffee oils which eventually darken the pot, and become rancid and bitter. Use a small percolator brush to clean the stem and spout. Wipe dry and keep unassembled between uses, with cover removed and inner parts exposed to air. When stains accumulate, use a special coffee-stain remover according to the manufacturer's directions.

Toasters vary widely in quality, so brand reputation rather than price is a key factor in selection.

Look for automatic pop-up feature; control of toasting from light to dark (some four-slice models are paired, making two slices light, two slices dark); easily cleaned crumb tray; automatic toast-lowering device; wide slots to hold English muffins or home-sliced bread; reheat setting with which to warm toast.

Electric skillets or frying pans are fairly deep, usually square (but round models are available), and have a cover.

Look for automatic temperature controls; cooking guide of suggested temperatures; immersibility in water; vented cover; high-domed cover for extra capacity when needed; stay-cool handles; nonstick surfaces on some models; broiling unit in cover; deep-fat frying basket.

Griddles are larger and shallower than skillets and usually have a provision for drainage of fat. Their size ranges up to 200 square inches of cooking area. Other qualities are similar to skillets.

Portable ovens vary in size from a small table baker that will do a few rolls or a frozen pie to a large roaster, which serves as a second oven for a large party or may be hooked up outdoors.

Portable broilers serve a similar purpose in augmenting the range broiler, or substituting for it to broil just a chop or two. Look for selection of heats, rack positions, timer, and easy-to-clean surfaces and parts. A *rotisserie* feature sometimes comes in combination with these.

Automatic waffle bakers are greatly improved with new, nonstick finish on the grids, and choice of heats for light or dark waffles. Look for a light which indicates when the waffle is done; and for removable grids for easy cleaning. Some have reversible grids which may be used as a griddle.

Electric slicing knives. Reasons for the popularity of the electric slicing knife include these:

You can carve meat and even slices of roast meat and fowl.

It's a dream come true, too, for cutting angel food cake, fresh bread, or stacks of sandwiches. It'll glide right through with no effort.

It's also just the thing for slicing thin or thick slices of fruits, vegetables, cheese, or cold cuts.

To use an electric knife, you merely guide it through the food. Fingertip control will set the twin blades in motion reciprocating up to 2,400 times a minute. Using a sawing motion or excessive pressure is actually a hindrance. Let the knife do the work.

To protect your china or counter tops, a wooden cutting board is a must with these knives. Cutting frozen food should not be attempted because the ice crystals or the package may damage the blades. And the knife itself is not practical for slicing very small items (such as radishes) or for paring fruits and vegetables. Moreover, the knife will cut meats to the bone but not through it.

The blades, which have hardened stainless steel serrated edges (and, by the way, should not be sharpened) are removable for easy cleaning. The nonimmersible handle which houses the motor can be wiped off easily with a damp cloth. Greaseguards on the blades prevent food from entering the motor. Some of the latest models are cordless.

ESTATE PLANNING | See also LIFE INSURANCE

Many people think of estate planning as something useful only for established wealthy families. In practice, though, estate planning can be valuable to nearly every family—even young couples who are just starting to acquire property.

Have you and your husband recently estimated how much your net assets are worth? If not, you may be surprised. A family which owns a home, car, and life-insurance policies probably has assets of at least $10,000. More than 60 per cent of American families are in this group. Many are worth considerably more.

But have you ever considered what would happen to those assets if your husband should die? Have arrangements been made for their transfer to his heirs in an orderly way best calculated to serve your family needs at a minimum of expense?

In addition to a will, estate planning involves consideration of such matters as life insurance, taxes, and how bank accounts and property are held by a husband and wife. Consequently, planning requires professional help. It may require the teamwork of an attorney, banker, accountant, and insurance agent. Why this is so can be demonstrated by the following variety of ways possible for property to be passed on to heirs:

By will, in which heirs, executors, and disposition of property are designated.

By joint ownership of property which passes to the survivor automatically.

By contract, such as life-insurance policies, annuities, trusts, or pension plans. In these cases, beneficiaries usually are named in the contract.

By state law (in the absence of a will) which specifies how an estate is divided among heirs according to the relationship to the deceased.

MAJOR CONSIDERATIONS IN ESTATE PLANNING

A will. Even though property is held jointly or a beneficiary is named in a contract, authorities recommend that *both* husband and wife make a will. If you and your husband die at the same time in an accident, the fact that you each left a will insures the disposition of your property according to your legal stipulations.

Although state laws differ, in some states a husband is considered to be the last to die in a common accident. Accordingly, a house owned jointly would be inherited by his relatives if there were no will. If a will does not name guardians for minor children and their property, a court appoints the guardians. The American Bar Association says that terms of a will should be stated clearly and should be prepared by an attorney.

Ready cash. Enough money should be immediately available in an estate to cover doctors' bills, funeral costs, administration expenses, and taxes. If such money is not available, it is possible that some property assets—perhaps a house—will have to be sold. The Institute of Life Insurance reports a study of 2,700 estates in the $10,000 class showed the average immediate cash need was $2,380. However, an average of only $1,110 was available to meet estate expenses. These immediate cash needs can be supplied by life insurance or by liquid assets such as a separate bank account in the survivor's name.

Taxes. The effect of taxes in possibly reducing an estate must be considered. Although federal taxes are not levied on an estate less than $60,000, some states impose inheritance taxes on lesser amounts. It is not unusual for an estate to exceed $60,000. In these cases, federal taxes may be eliminated or reduced by taking advantage of legal exemptions. Arrangements can be made to give money to heirs before death either under a gift-tax exemption or by paying a gift tax which is less than the estate tax. Trust funds may be established. These arrangements—because of taxes and legal considerations—should be made with professional help.

Estate affairs must be kept up to date. Wills should be revised to cover any new or changed family situations. Insurance policies should be changed if a beneficiary dies or if a different method of payment is advisable. Thought also should be given to naming an executor and/or a trustee. The trust departments of banks will act in these capacities. Your local bank trust officer can tell you the services available and the cost involved. There are minimum charges which may make these services uneconomic for small estates. In such cases, a trust officer can suggest an alternative procedure.

WHAT YOU SHOULD KNOW ABOUT WILLS

The subject of wills is one most people find difficult, or are reluctant, to discuss. In many families, neither the husband nor the wife has a will.

Young people, particularly, tend to ignore its importance. Wives may feel they haven't enough property of their own to worry about. This assumption is not correct. Unless you're perfectly content to have your property distributed according to the laws of your state—and you might be surprised to know what that can mean—you need a will.

You probably have more assets than you think. Some things, such as a house or a bank account which you own jointly with your husband, may not necessarily have rights of survivorship. This means that if you died, your husband would not automatically receive title to your half of the house or your part of the account. Instead, these things become part of your estate. Some states provide that when a wife dies intestate—that is, without a will—her husband receives only one-third of her property. The balance is divided among her children. If there are no children, the husband might get half the estate, the rest being shared by the wife's relatives. It's entirely possible that relatives you barely know might share in your estate if no will were left.

On a more personal level, there might be possessions you want specific persons to have. Perhaps there are family heirlooms which you desire your eldest child to inherit. If no will is made, there is no legal assurance that he'll get them. The possibility exists that, should a dispute arise concerning such personal effects, they might have to be sold at public auction in order to divide an estate.

In a will, you can name an executor (or executrix, if it's a woman) to be in charge of carrying out your wishes. If there's no will, a court appoints an administrator who handles that job. He does so according to state law and court instructions, which, though legal, often are not what you intended. Additional expenses also may be involved when an administrator is appointed. These costs come out of the estate.

Guardianship of minor children can be established, subject to court approval, by a will. For instance, you and your husband might intend that your sister be named guardian if you both died. Without wills to guide a court, it might name a different guardian.

Take into consideration the possibility that you and your husband might die together (for example, in an automobile or plane crash) or within a short time of each other. Such happenings are tragic enough, without additional complications and heartaches. A properly drawn will usually contains instructions on guardianship of children and property distribution in the specific instance of a double death.

Although trusts may be set up separately, many people include them in wills. Parents usually want to make sure that money and property left for children will be handled prudently and under mature supervision. Also, trusts often are used to reduce the tax liabilities of an estate.

Preparing a will is something that should be done by a lawyer. Although you can draw up your own will, there is better than a fifty-fifty chance that it will not be a legal document. Such handwritten wills (called holographic ones) are not legal in more than half the states; even where they are used, many are declared invalid in court for various reasons.

FIGURE CARE | See also MENU PLANNING

Personal grooming for health as well as good looks concerns the modern housewife as a practical matter. She must budget her time for it, shop wisely for cosmetics and beauty aids, and learn to use them for best results. She may find herself in the role of counselor to a growing daughter. Above all, a sensible regard for her everyday appearance contributes to a happy home. A lovely wife pleases husband and children, favorably impresses guests, and faces the outside world with confidence.

There are beauty experts who can literally make you over, but the first step is to realize that *you* are the best person to assign to the job. No matter how many experts you consult, you still have to brush your hair, cream your skin, coddle your hands. You have to exercise and diet, stand and move like a beauty. No one else can do these things for you. In daily housekeeping, care of the figure is perhaps the beautifying measure most often overlooked.

Silhouette. The first thing anyone notices about you is your over-all outline, a general sizing up of height, weight, proportions, posture. Find out how you compare to the ideal silhouette.

How tall are you? Have someone measure you accurately in your stocking feet. How much do you weigh? If possible, get on the scales, nude, before breakfast. How much should you weigh to look your prettiest?

HEIGHT	DESIRABLE WEIGHT		
	Small	Medium	Large
4'11"	94–101	98–110	106–122
5'	96–104	101–113	109–125
5'1"	99–107	104–116	112–128
5'2"	102–110	107–119	115–131
5'3"	105–113	110–122	118–134
5'4"	108–116	113–126	121–138
5'5"	111–119	116–130	125–142
5'6"	114–123	120–135	129–146
5'7"	118–127	124–139	133–150
5'8"	122–131	128–143	137–154
5'9"	126–135	132–147	141–158
5'10"	130–140	136–151	145–163
5'11"	134–144	140–155	149–168

(*Note:* This table assumes height with 2-inch heels and weight with 4 pounds of clothing. If measuring in the nude, deduct accordingly.)

Consider the size of your bones; a woman with a small frame should weigh less than one with a large frame. Look for your height on the preceding table (supplied by Metropolitan Life Insurance Company), and there's your weight for health and beauty.

DIET

Normal meals give women 1,600 to 2,200 calories a day. A reducing diet gives from 1,200 to 1,400; a gaining diet, from 2,600 to 2,800. Don't expect to lose or gain large amounts of weight in a hurry—slowly (1½ to 2 lbs. per week) does it. Always consult your doctor before embarking on a gaining or losing program.

To lose weight:

Cut down but don't omit breads, cereals, fats, and sugar. Use enriched or whole-grain bread, cereals, flour.

Eat *fruit* fresh and without sugar.

Eat plenty of *salad,* but go easy on dressing, or use a special low-calorie dressing.

Drink *skim milk* (liquified nonfat dry milk, or regular), or buttermilk instead of whole milk.

Don't skip meals, but eat less at mealtime, nothing between meals.

To gain weight:

Stimulate your appetite by fresh air and exercise. Or add dried brewer's yeast to cereals, hamburgers, etc. (its vitamin B_1 content peps up the desire for food).

Indulge yourself happily in favorite high calorie dishes, though with due regard for maintaining a balanced diet.

Between-meal snacks are fine—midmorning, midafternoon, and before bed.

Allow time for a hearty *breakfast.* (Yes, you can—it just takes planning.)

Try to *increase* the size of portions of all dishes.

Plenty of *sleep* is a must.

EXERCISE AND FIGURE

Exercise is important. Although it's almost impossible to exercise enough to take off extra pounds without watching the calories too, don't disregard the importance of regular, moderate exercise. It keeps your muscles in trim, encourages the proper posture, and stimulates circulation—all of which adds much to your looks.

The exercise habit is surprisingly easy and painless to establish. Parking your car a few blocks away from your destination, walking to the bus or subway stop beyond the nearest one, running up and down the stairs a few extra times a day—these simple readjustments can make a real difference.

A good figure. If you are overweight, you undoubtedly are also out of shape. If decidedly underweight, you probably have no figure to speak of. But even if your weight is ideal, you may bulge or flatten in the wrong places. Here is how to check your figure with a tape measure:

First, measure your wrist and jot this down. Now, your chest, above the bosom, should be 5½ times the wrist; an unbelted waist should be 4½ times the wrist. Hips, at their broadest point, should be 6 times the wrist. Your thigh at its fullest contour should be 3½ times your wrist. The knee above the bone should be 2½ times the wrist; the calf at its plumpest point, 2¼ times; and the ankle, 1¼ times your basic wrist measurement.

In comparing your figure to this guide rule, a difference of an inch or less may be ignored. You may have an unusually large hip bone or a small frame at the upper back which will give you a small chest dimension. But if you're over an inch out of shape in certain spots, exercise is the answer.

Although diet perfects your weight, exercise perfects your proportions. It tightens muscles, firms flesh, helps flabbiness, improves a bad shape, preserves a good shape. Consult books, pamphlets, or instructors on spot reducing, or try isometric exercises (below) to correct your problem spots.

Posture. Perhaps you never thought of it, but the way you sit, stand, and move is exercise. The way you brush your teeth, open the oven door, make a bed—that's exercise, too. If you do it incorrectly, it's bad exercise that makes a bad shape. If you do it correctly, it's good exercise that makes a pretty figure.

Stand sidewise in front of a long mirror (illustrations 1 and 2). Don't try to look your best; just take your natural pose. Now check what you see:

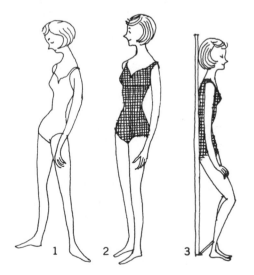

QUICK CHECK FOR FIGURE POINTS

Bad	Good
Head forward, neck curved	Neck straight from hairline to shoulders
Protruding shoulder blades	Shoulder blades flat
Chest caved in	Bosom high
Deep curve in lower back at waistline	Shallow curve in back at waistline
Abdomen bulging	Abdomen flat, buttocks normal
Feet turning out	Feet straight ahead

Before you can correct a slouchy, strained, or awkward carriage, you must learn the feeling of good body balance.

Back up against a wall with your heels three inches away, knees bent (illustration 3). Now straighten your knees, and tighten the thigh and pelvic muscles. This forces your waist to the wall, and flattens your back. Now pull your shoulder blades down (not back) one inch; lift and expand your lower ribs.

Do it twenty times a day, and each time walk away from the wall with head up, chest high, back curve flattened out, buttocks tucked under, and feet pointed ahead. See how your waistline and abdomen shrink when you make your natural muscle corset work.

Try this mirror game for a good carriage, the quickest way to a better figure (illustration 4):

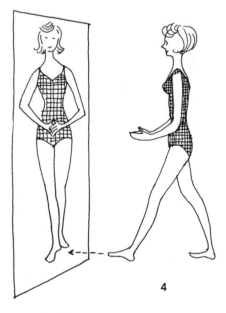

4

(1) Stand about twenty feet from a large or full-length mirror. (2) Bend your arms to touch the top of your hips, and press your palms together.

(3) Walk slowly toward the mirror, keeping your eyes only on the hands reflected in it. The object is to keep your hands moving steadily and directly forward. When they do, your posture will be good; you can't do it unless your body is upright and every part of your torso and legs moving correctly. Practice this every day, to teach your body the feeling of good posture.

Isometric exercises. Although exercise is important to good health, many people find calisthenics monotonous, or say they cannot find time in busy schedules. To meet the requirements of such people, a method called isometric exercising has become increasingly popular.

Isometric exercises require literally no movement of muscles. Instead, muscles are tensed against immovable objects. Physiologists have found that if a muscle is tensed to its maximum or near-maximum contraction for a short time (six to eight seconds) each day, its strength can be increased considerably.

Isometric exercises are of limited value. They are not meant to improve endurance or to benefit the circulatory or respiratory systems. The value of walking, swimming, and other activities should not be overlooked. Finally, persons with heart disease or other medical problems should seek a physician's advice before engaging in *any* stressful activity.

A distinct advantage of this exercise technique is that it can be performed almost anywhere, at any time, without special apparatus. For example, office workers can perform an isometric exercise while sitting at a desk, by pushing down against the desktop with both hands for about eight seconds. A woman can do this at home by pressing down on a tabletop.

While there are many kinds of isometric exercises, the ones below are well suited to promote gains in firmness and strength where these are needed by most women. Maintain tension for no more than eight seconds. Breathe deeply between exercises; do little breathing during a contraction. In the first few weeks, do not apply maximum effort. Use about one-half what you think is your full strength. Gradually increase effort until, after about six weeks, you are using maximum force for these exercises:

Clasp hands close to chest, palms together and elbows out to the side. Press hands together and hold for eight seconds. Using the same arm position, hook fingers close to chest. Pull hard and hold. These exercises benefit arms and chest.

Sit in a chair with your feet resting on the floor, legs bent at a 90-degree angle, left ankle crossed over right. Forcibly try to straighten your right leg while resisting with the left. Repeat with opposite leg (cross right ankle over left). These are good for upper-leg muscles.

Sit in a chair with another chair facing you. Extend your legs to full length with each ankle pressed against the outside of the legs of the chair opposite. Keeping your legs straight, push inward with your ankles against the chair legs. This is good for inner-thigh muscles. To benefit outer thigh muscles, place your ankles against inside of the chairlegs, and exert pressure outward.

Sit on the floor, knees bent, anchoring your feet by hooking them under a couch or sofa. Gradually lean back to approximately a 45-degree angle. Tighten your abdominal muscles while holding this position for eight counts.

TAKING THE STRAIN OUT OF HOUSEWORK

As you may have discovered, some household duties can be as strenuous as chopping wood. Here is a list showing how many calories you work off in normal activities:

1 to 2 calories per minute resting in bed, sitting, eating, talking on the telephone, hand sewing, knitting, typing, coffee klatching.

2 to 3 calories per minute dressing, washing hands, peeling potatoes, polishing furniture, playing the piano, strolling, driving a car.

3 to 5 calories per minute making beds, ironing, washing windows, wet mopping, hanging clothes, scrubbing floor on hands and knees, moderate walking.

Over 5 calories per minute carrying heavy loads up stairs, gardening, mowing with hand mower, rapid walking, playing tennis, chopping wood.

THE RIGHT WAY TO LIFT, PUSH, REACH, AND CARRY

Carrying luggage. Leaning to either side when carrying luggage is ungraceful and leads to early fatigue. Instead, walk erect, elbows slightly bent. Occasionally shift the luggage from hand to hand to avoid unnecessary strain. Instead of buying a big piece of luggage, get two smaller ones for easier balance. (Illustration 5).

5   6

Lifting from the floor. Do not bend from the waist to lift an object from the floor. This puts all the strain on the lower back muscles. Instead, bend the knees and squat down, keeping the back straight. If necessary, spread the knees or lower one knee to get closer to the object. Then use the leg muscles—the strongest in the body—to push up, holding the object close as you rise. (Illustration 6).

Lifting from table level. Instead of bending over the table, pull the object close to the body before attempting to lift. Keep the back erect. Maintain good balance by keeping the feet about twelve inches apart, with one foot half a pace forward. To move a typewriter, approach and lift it from the rear, thus keeping the heaviest part next to the body. Avoid sudden or unusual twisting when carrying a heavy object. (Illustration 7).

7

Pushing and pulling. Keep the back straight and let the legs do the work. Push at about the middle of an object, rather than near the top or bottom. Exert a smooth, steady force; avoid jerky or sudden motions. When moving upholstered chairs or similar furniture, slide them instead of attempting to lift or carry them. Whenever possible, use a small wagon, dolly, or even a lawn mower to transport heavy sacks and crates. (Illustration 8).

8

Reaching. Stretching is good exercise by itself, but it can be dangerous when you add extra weight by picking up something. The farther you reach, the greater the possibility of strain. Don't take chances by trying to reach a heavy object on a high shelf. Use a sturdy footstool. Stand close enough to the object to maintain your balance. Take boxes down one at a time unless they are empty or very light. When reaching high for a small object, use one hand for support. (Illustration 9.)

9

On stairs. Never carry a large object so that it blocks your vision when going up or down stairs. One hand should always be free to grasp a railing or provide balance and support. If the package cannot be carried on the side with one hand, either get help or try moving it down one step at a time. Also, don't try to consolidate the load to save steps. Instead, if possible, divide the load into smaller packages and make two or three trips. To avoid tottering backward, lean forward slightly when going upstairs. (Illustration 10.)

10

FIRST AID | See also CHILDBIRTH, EMERGENCY; POISONING;
STORMS AND DISASTERS

Your husband is badly cut by a power tool at home . . . a neighbor is accidentally overcome by carbon-monoxide fumes in her garage . . . your young daughter swallows a poisonous garden chemical that "looked like candy". . . .

These three emergency situations—heavy bleeding, breath stoppage, and oral poisoning—may be fast killers. There may be no time to fumble for a phone number, search for a neighbor, or wait for a doctor. There must be immediate action. But what action? The American Red Cross, in supplying this information, strongly recommends that everyone know and practice these basic steps. They can not only save lives, but the time saved in giving proper first-aid treatment can lessen body stress and promote quicker recoveries.

HEAVY BLEEDING

1. In arterial bleeding, death can occur in a minute or less. To stop heavy bleeding, place a thick, preferably sterile gauze, pad directly over the wound.

2. Hold or bandage this pad snugly in place. In an extreme emergency, a piece of clothing or even the bare hand pressed on the wound can stem bleeding.

3. After heavy bleeding has stopped, keep the victim quiet. The wounded limb should be elevated.

4. If professional aid is delayed for some time, have the victim slowly sip a solution of a level teaspoonful of salt and one-half teaspoonful of baking soda dissolved in a quart of water. This mixture or plain water counteracts both dehydration (loss of water) from excessive bleeding and the shock reaction which may follow the hemorrhage.

IF BREATHING HAS STOPPED

1. This may occur in cases of drowning, asphyxiation, suffocation, and other accidents. First, make sure the breathing passage is open. Remove visible foreign matter. Place the victim on his back, tilting his head back so that the chin is pointed upward, and then pull or push the jaw into a jutting-out position.

2. If breathing does not resume immediately, begin artificial respiration. The mouth-to-mouth method is the most effective one for the lone rescuer. Start with the head and jaw position described above. Then, open your mouth and place it tightly over the victim's mouth. At the same time, pinch his nostrils shut or make sure the nostrils are covered by your cheek.

3. For an adult, blow vigorously about twelve breaths per minute. (Air

may be blown through the victim's teeth even if they are clenched.) For an infant or small child, blow shallow breaths appropriate to the child's size, probably about twenty breaths per minute. If you fail to get air exchange, check the head and jaw position again. If you still fail to get air exchange, quickly turn the victim on his side and administer several sharp blows between the shoulder blades. This may dislodge any foreign matter that might be caught in the throat.

In cases of electric shock, drug poisoning, or carbon-monoxide poisoning, artificial respiration must often be carried on for long periods. It should be continued until the victim begins to breathe for himself or until a physician pronounces the victim dead.

ORAL POISONING

First-aid care varies with the type of substance involved. The majority of accidental poisonings can be cared for in the following manner:

1. Dilute the poison to minimize its effects. Milk or ordinary tap water is usually available and either or both should be given—four glasses or more for adults, and less to children. Milk protects the digestive tract lining somewhat and may slow the absorption of poison.

2. Induce vomiting by having victim drink a half glass of water that contains several teaspoons of milk of magnesia or baking soda. You can usually also cause vomiting by tickling the back of the victim's throat with your finger or with the blunt edge of a large spoon.

3. Give an antidote. The labels on containers of many poisonous substances show the recommended antidote. Such an antidote should be administered quickly—as directed. This can be given with the diluting fluid or after vomiting has occurred. Call your physician or Poison Control Center *as soon as possible* for specific instructions. Someone can do this while you give first aid. Consult phone book for Poison Control Center number.

Exceptions to the above procedures are poisoning cases of strong acids and alkalis, petroleum products (including kerosene), and when the person is in a coma or having convulsions. See POISONING article in this book.

FIRST-AID KIT

The Red Cross advises that you keep a freshly stocked one readily available. The so-called unit type, with dressings individually wrapped, prevents contamination and eliminates waste. These kits come in various sizes and can be found in most drugstores. In addition, the Red Cross urges that at least one person in every household take a Red Cross first-aid course to increase confidence and ability in an emergency situation. The Red Cross first-aid textbook, available for seventy-five cents from your local Red Cross chapter, is a good book to keep handy at all times.

MINOR INJURIES

Many minor injuries can be treated at home (or on a trip) to prevent complications. However, there is a point beyond which home treatment should not go. Cuts or blisters which become red or sore may be infected and should be treated by a physician. Sprains should be X-rayed to be sure the bone is not fractured, cracked, or chipped. When there is any question of major injury, temporary care (first aid) should be given until a physician sees the patient. For home treatment of minor ailments and injuries, the medical authorities suggest the following:

Cuts and scratches. Wash hands before treating minor wounds. Then cleanse the scratch, cut, or abrasion with soap and clean water. Use a sterile gauze pad for scrubbing dirt from a cut or scratch. After washing, hold a sterile pad over the wound until bleeding stops. Then bandage. Replace bandage as necessary to keep the wound clean and dry. Do not use an antiseptic on the wound, and never allow mouth contact. If the person hurt is not immunized against tetanus, consult a physician.

BITES AND STINGS

For bites of flies, gnats, mosquitoes, and most spiders, a paste made of baking soda (sodium bicarbonate) and cold cream helps relieve pain. Calamine lotion can be used to reduce itching. For *bee and wasp* stings, remove any stinger in the wound and apply ice or ice water for immediate relief. Then treat as above. If the person is allergic to bee or wasp venom, use a constricting band on an arm or leg above the sting, apply ice, and seek immediate medical treatment.

For chiggers, scrub affected area with a brush and soapy water. Bathe bites with a baking-soda solution or alcohol. Pick off *ticks* with tweezers if they are not embedded. If a tick has fastened itself to the skin, cover with a heavy oil (mineral, salad, or machine), wait until the tick disengages itself, then pick it off with tweezers. Gently scrub the area with soap and water.

Poisonous bites by snakes, scorpions, black-widow spiders, or tarantulas require medical attention. First aid for *snake bite*:

Have the victim remain quiet. Tie a constricting band above the bite, if it is on an arm or leg. The band should be tight enough only to stop the return flow of blood in surface vessels and not to shut off deeper circulation. To tell whether the band is properly adjusted, insert your finger under it; some oozing from the wound should continue.

Sterilize a knife or razor blade in a flame and carefully make a cut one-fourth to one-half inch long and one fourth of an inch deep through each fang wound, cutting longitudinally—up and down an arm or leg. A shallower crosscut then can be made through each wound. Be careful not to sever a tendon or muscle.

Apply suction for about an hour by mouth or with a suction cup. Venom is not a stomach poison, but it is advisable to spit or rinse fluid from your mouth.

Keep the injured part lower than the rest of the body. Apply ice or cold water compresses after stopping suction. Keep the constricting band on until medical help is available. Loosen the band for 1 minute every 15 minutes.

For poisonous spider or scorpion bites, use a constricting band on an arm or leg, and ice or cold compresses on the bite until medical help is available.

Bites of warm-blooded animals (cats, dogs, and wild pets that children adopt) can be dangerous because of the possibility of rabies. Wash the wound thoroughly, scrubbing with a sterile piece of gauze and soap and water. Then rinse and bandage. Consult a doctor on whether anti-rabies treatments should be started. The animal should be captured and isolated. Rabies treatments are extremely painful, not undertaken lightly.

OTHER ACCIDENTS

Bumps and bruises. Most bruises can be treated initially with a cold compress to reduce pain and swelling. After a bruise becomes discolored, as with a black eye, warm compresses help to dispel the discoloration. With a nosebleed, a person should remain quiet with his head back if sitting, or with head and shoulders raised if lying. Try to stop bleeding by lightly pinching the nostrils together or applying a cold, wet towel to the face.

All head bumps are serious. Keep the person lying down and quiet. If there is headache, dizziness, or loss of consciousness, call a doctor. Loosen constrictive clothing. Give no stimulants. Be sure air passages are not blocked.

Burns and blisters. For mild cases of sunburn where the skin is only reddened, cold cream or oils will ease pain. Wash your hands before applying it. A dry, covering dressing should be used if blisters appear. Extensive and severe cases should be treated by a doctor.

Thermal burns from a flame or hot stove can be treated at home if they are small and the skin is only reddened (first-degree burn). If the skin is not broken, immerse in clean, cold water or apply ice to relieve pain. Then place a sterile gauze pad soaked in a solution of baking soda and water (two tablespoons to a quart) over the burn and bandage loosely. If blisters form (second-degree burn), do not disturb or open the blisters. Cover the burn with the cleanest dry cloth available, to exclude air. Second-degree burns and those where the skin is burned deeply (third-degree burn) should be treated by a physician.

Severe burns are usually accompanied by shock. If a burn victim is pale, has irregular or shallow breathing, or nausea, first call a physician. Then have the patient lie down. If he is conscious and can swallow, give him plenty of nonalcoholic liquid (water, tea, or coffee) but do not force him to drink.

Rashes and itches. After contact with *poison ivy, oak,* or *sumac,* wash the exposed area thoroughly with soap and water. Repeat lathering and rinsing several times. Then sponge with rubbing alcohol. Do not scratch or rub affected area. Calamine lotion can help relieve itching.

Heat rash or prickly heat—small, raised red spots usually on the neck, shoulders, or chest—can be eased by powdering with talcum or cornstarch. Sponge-bathe lightly between powderings.

If a skin rash is accompanied by running nose, red eyes, and other symptoms usually associated with a cold, it may be a childhood communicable disease. Call a doctor.

Eye specks; splinters. Do not rub an eye in which a speck or foreign particle has lodged. Examine only after you have washed your hands. To extract, pull the lower lid down and if the particle is on the inside surface of the lid, gently lift it off with the corner of a clean handkerchief. If you do not find the particle on the lower lid, grasp the upper lashes gently, pull the upper lid forward and then down over the lower lid. This may sweep away the particle or flush it out with tears.

If the object in the eye is a splinter, piece of glass, or even a piece of straw that has penetrated and stuck in the eyeball, do not remove. Apply a sterile gauze pad or clean cloth lightly over the eye, and seek medical help.

To remove a *splinter* or sliver in the skin, first wash the skin and then pick the splinter out with tweezers, a needle, or a knife point which has been sterilized in a flame. Treat the wound as you would a cut or scratch.

Sprains. These should be X-rayed to make sure they are not fractures. For first aid, elevate the joint on a pillow. Cold, wet applications or an ice bag during the first half hour of injury may retard the swelling. Do not move the joint. If travel is necessary, use a splint or supportive bandage.

FISH BUYING GUIDE | See also SHELLFISH

Fish dinners once were the specialty of America's seacoasts and shores. Today there are such delicious quick-frozen fish, as well as canned fish to augment the supply of fresh fish, that families everywhere can enjoy this superb food. Modern marketing methods have eliminated the disagreeable cleaning chore and usually the pesky bones. Include fish regularly in your weekly menus for good nutrition.

FROZEN FISH

Frozen fish comes in three principal forms in most markets.

Fillets and steaks. Boned halibut, flounder, ocean perch, pike, cod, sole, whiting, catfish, etc., are so quickly frozen that their fresh flavor and fine food value are retained. All you do is thaw the package in the refrigerator for an hour or two, or just until the fish can be separated. Then broil, fry, or bake it until it is easily flaked with a fork, *but still moist*, as the label directs.

Breaded fish portions (also called fillets, cutlets, steaks, burgers, etc.) are equal-size portions of uncooked fish which have been dipped in batter, then breaded before quick-freezing. Fry, broil, or bake them as the package directs, while still frozen.

Heat-and-eat fish sticks. The cleaned fish is cut into sticks, breaded, fried until crisp and brown, or left uncooked, then quick-frozen. All you do is follow the instructions on the package before serving.

FRESH FISH

You're blessed if you have a good source at hand. Try fresh fish in these forms:

Steaks are cut crosswise from such fish as halibut, swordfish, salmon, and cod, and are about ¾" to 1" thick.

Fillets are sides or parts of fish, cut lengthwise and boned, with all or most of the skin removed.

Dressed whole. Look for fish with red gills; scales that adhere closely to the body, bright, bulging eyes; firm flesh; and fresh, sweet odor.

To store fresh fish, wrap it in wax paper, plastic, or foil, and refrigerate in the coldest section. Plan to use it the same day if possible.

AMOUNT OF FROZEN OR FRESH FISH TO BUY

For 2 servings	Cut of fish	For 4 servings
About ¾ lb.	fillets	about 1½ lbs.
About 1 lb.	steaks	about 2 lbs.
About 1½ lbs.	whole	about 3 lbs.

FISH TO BAKE

FILLETS

cod	ocean perch
flounder	sole
haddock	whiting

STEAKS

cod	pollock
haddock	salmon
halibut	swordfish

DRESSED WHOLE

bluefish	lake trout	shad
catfish	mackerel	Spanish mackerel
cod	mullet	whitefish
haddock	red snapper	yellow pike
hake	sea trout	

FISH TO BROIL

Order frozen or fresh fish fillets (¼″ to 1″ thick), or steaks (½″ to 1½″ thick), or whole fresh fish, with the lists below as guides. If frozen, thaw if and as the label directs.

FILLETS

bass	haddock	pollock
bluefish	hake	red snapper
carp	ling cod	sole
catfish	mackerel	Spanish mackerel
cod	ocean perch	whiting
flounder	pike	

STEAKS

bass	haddock	red snapper
cod	halibut	salmon
fresh tuna	muskellunge	swordfish

DRESSED WHOLE

bass	mullet	smelts
bluefish	pike	Spanish mackerel
butterfish	porgy	trout
carp	red snapper	whitefish
catfish	sea trout	whiting
flounder	shad	yellow pike
mackerel		

FISH TO FRY

Order frozen or fresh fish fillets or steaks, or dressed small whole fish from the list below. Thaw if and as the label directs.

FILLETS OR STEAKS

cod	ocean perch	shad (and/or shad roe)
flounder	pickerel	sole
haddock	pollock	swordfish
halibut	red snapper	tuna

DRESSED SMALL FISH

bass	pike	sunfish
butterfish	pompano	trout
lake herring	porgy	whitefish
mackerel	sand dab	whiting
perch	smelts	

FISH TO POACH

Choose a soft fish like flounder, Boston sole, ocean perch, haddock, or cod, if you can poach and serve in the same skillet. Halibut, bass, English sole, and pompano are firm enough to poach in a skillet and then transfer to a platter, if you prefer.

FLOOR CARE | See also FLOORING; STAIN REMOVAL

Most materials used on floors today may be kept spick and span with only occasional washings and waxings. Problems encountered, except with very old floors which should be refinished or replaced, often are the result of *too much* scrubbing and waxing, if not of neglect. New appliances and self-polishing waxes make the job easier; however, there is no magic finish for a floor that will give it a permanently bright look without regular maintenance. Here are suggested methods of floor care:

ALL FLOORS

Once or twice a week at least, vacuum, dry-mop, or sweep the floor to keep dirt from grinding in (a lightweight electric vacuum cleaner does this well). Wipe up fresh spills immediately to prevent tacking and stains. Dried-on spots or heel marks may be gently buffed with a moist steel-wool soap pad and polished with a paper towel or wiped up with a special floor-mark remover and buffer. Before a kitchen floor becomes badly soiled, damp-mop regularly with *cool* water. This won't disturb the wax, and will prolong the time between scrubbings. Repair worn wax patches, following the label directions.

Washing (except wood floors) may be done with an easy-wringing mop and hot, sudsy water. Caution: don't flood the floor, since water may loosen the adhesive that holds the floor-covering material in place. Consider an electric floor polisher-scrubber, which does this job with much less effort than getting down on your hands and knees. To clean with machines (with a dispenser), dispense enough detergent for an area about four feet square, then run over it with the whirling brushes as easily as with a vacuum cleaner. Then sponge-mop the suds up and repeat for another area.

Waxing (except wood floors) is best done today with self-polishing waxes which dry to a clear, colorless shine, and don't turn yellow. Experiment with various brands; they differ in shine, color, water and scuff resistance (see recommendations below for specific floorings). When light-colored floors turn yellow, the cause usually is a build-up of old wax that has become mixed with soil. With periodical use of the electric polisher-scrubber, wax build-up should present no problem. (If you do not own one, they may be rented for a dollar or two a day.)

Eventually it may be necessary to remove the old wax film and ground-in dirt. Wash the floor with a solution of one-half cup of detergent and one-half cup of ammonia to one gallon of hot water. Or use a special wax remover according to manufacturer's directions. Rinse well, let it dry thoroughly, then rewax the floor.

To wax a nonwood floor, first clean and dry it thoroughly. Apply self-polishing wax by "painting" it on with a slightly dampened, long-handled applicator. Pour a small pool on the floor and spread it with long, even strokes in a thin coat; never scrub or rub it in. When the first coat is dry (30 to 45 minutes), apply a second thin coat. Stay off the floor at least 50 minutes (or overnight, if possible), until it's completely dry (nonsticky). Although this type of wax will dry bright by itself, buffing with the electric polisher will improve some brands. If you can wait several hours before applying the second coat, so much the better.

Liquid and paste polishing wax requires buffing to shine. Pour a small pool of liquid wax on the floor and work it into a clean, dry cloth, such as a piece cut from a worn-out sheet. Then with the long-handled applicator (or tie it to the head of a mop), rub the cloth back and forth over the floor. If you use the electric polisher, pour pools of wax the size of a half-dollar, about a foot apart over a six-foot-square area at a time. Slowly draw the polisher through the wax to spread it evenly. Let dry half an hour before buffing.

To apply a paste polishing wax, spread it thinly on the waxing brushes with a butter knife, and apply to floor. Spread thinly and evenly; two thin coats are better than one heavy one. Let dry half an hour, or until no longer tacky, before buffing.

There are new products which wash and wax a nonwood floor in one operation.

WOOD FLOORS

Never wash a wood floor with water, even over a small area, since it may warp or crack the wood or raise the grain. For the same reason, do not use regular self-polishing waxes (which contain a high percentage of water). To clean the floor, use a polishing wax, either liquid or paste, or a self-polishing wax designed specifically for wood floors, containing a solvent that removes dirt as it waxes. Apply polishing wax as described above, or self-polishing wax according to the manufacturer's recommendations, following the grain of the wood.

Waxing is essential three or four times a year. Without it, the original wood finish of varnish, shellac, lacquer, or penetrating sealer will scratch and wear, and dirt will become embedded. Between waxings, wipe up tracked-in dirt or spills with a damp cloth, and rub difficult spots with a little wax. Dark spots on wood should come off, if still fresh, by careful

FLOOR COVERINGS

Type of Flooring	Characteristics	Care*	Approximate Cost per Sq. Ft. Installed
VINYL (tile or sheet)	Tough, nonporous, resistant to stains, wear. Comes in clear colors, special effects—including translucent three-dimensional.	When soiled (as with all floors listed) first vacuum clean, then damp-mop. Protect with self-polishing or liquid polishing wax in thin coat. So-called floor finishes, removable like wax, can also be used.	Tile: 85¢ to $1.15 Sheet: 55¢ to $1.10
VINYL ASBESTOS	Excellent all-around low-cost floor. Comes in attractive colors and designs; resists stains and wears well.	Use self-polishing or polishing wax to protect and make cleaning easier.	30¢ to 65¢
LINOLEUM (tile or sheet)	Inlaid linoleum is durable, long wearing, easy to clean. Embossed linoleum has texture interest, often resembles masonry.	Use liquid polishing wax or self-polishing wax to protect surface and provide gloss. Old linoleum may need two thin coats of wax to shine.	35¢ to 80¢
CORK TILE	Cork provides maximum quiet and cushiony comfort under foot. Cork with vinyl or urethane surface is highly resistant to wear, stains, washing; but natural cork is not suited for the abuse of kitchen traffic, water damage, etc.	Use liquid polishing wax for natural cork (it removes soil without water); and any type of wax for cork with vinyl or urethane finish.	Natural: 65¢ to $1.00 Vinyl-surfaced: $1.60 Urethane: $1.00 to $1.25

Type	Description	Care	Cost
ASPHALT TILE	Lowest in cost of the tile group. More susceptible, however, to dents and stains. Some types are grease resistant. Polymer-resin asphalt is grease resistant, longer wearing.	Use only self-polishing wax or water-based polishing wax. Avoid the use of solvents. Wipe up stains on regular asphalt speedily.	15¢ to 65¢
RUBBER TILE	Cushiony, comfortable flooring. Exceptionally quiet. Comes in clear colors. Requires consistent wax care to maintain appearance.	Use only self-polishing or water-based polishing wax unless the manufacturer suggests a polishing wax.	65¢ to 70¢
PRINTED FLOOR COVERINGS	Inexpensive. Need no installation; they unroll like a rug. Many styles. Vinyl-surfaced types wear longer.	Require little or no waxing, but to keep shiny, use self-polishing wax.	8¢ to 10¢
TERRAZZO, FLAGSTONE, MARBLE, CERAMIC	These handsome masonry materials make hard, durable floors. Terrazzo and flagstone are easier to clean when "sealed." New marble and ceramic tile need no special protection.	Special "sealer" sold by janitor-supply houses helps protect terrazzo, flagstone, and old marble. New marble and ceramic require only washing, occasional scrubbing.	Terrazzo: 50¢ to $1.75 Flagstone: 60¢ to $1.60 Marble: $4.00 to $12.00 Ceramic: $1.35 to $1.90

* For more information on washing and waxing, see FLOOR CARE; HOUSECLEANING.

treatment with vinegar. Let it stand three or four minutes; wipe dry; and repeat if necessary. Light (not deep) scratches often can be blended in with paste or liquid polishing wax, buffed well.

LINOLEUM AND VINYL FLOORS

Linoleum. Either self-polishing or polishing wax can be used. The first is preferable on kitchen floors, since it can be renewed by buffing between waxings, and removed easily by "suds-scrubbing" with the electric polisher.

Vinyl is exceptionally resistant to stains and wear, but waxing (either type) lessens scratches, and makes floors easier to clean.

Vinyl asbestos may be treated the same as vinyl.

TILE FLOORS

Asphalt tile. Use a self-polishing wax only. The solvents in most polishing waxes soften the tile; if you prefer such a wax, be sure it's recommended for asphalt tile on the label.

Rubber tile is not, in most cases, harmed by a polishing wax; but unless the manufacturer directs its use, apply self-polishing wax.

Cork tile is best protected by liquid polishing wax—liquid rather than paste because it's effective in removing soil and in depositing wax on the cork texture. But treat *vinyl-cork-tile* floors the same as vinyl.

Ceramic tile rarely warrants waxing of any kind. But old discolored tiles look cleaner after they're power scrubbed by machine.

OTHER FLOORS

Sealed-concrete floors, often colored or painted for interiors, may be waxed with either type of wax, for easier upkeep.

Terrazzo and **marble** floors, even if well sealed, are subject to staining unless protected with wax (either type). There is also a special sealer-type product of polishing waxes and resins for a slip-retardant finish. The same applies to *slate, brick,* or *flagstone* that has been sealed or glazed for indoor use; waxing enhances its color and protects it against wear.

FLOORING |

The surface of a floor—its pattern, color, and texture—is basic in the decorative scheme of a room. A wide choice of materials today makes it possible to combine beauty with practical factors of use, wear, and maintenance. Pick a flooring first for its adaptability to the hard or light use it will receive, and for ease in maintaining its good looks. Then consider these general guidelines:

In a small house or apartment, one floor material used throughout connected living areas will make rooms seem larger and keep the cost down. In a large open plan, breaks in floor pattern can be used to separate a dining area visually or to create a conversation corner. An extreme contrast in texture and color is effective when there is reason for it: for example, color insets can direct traffic, or a strip of clay tile under a window can logically set off house plants. Choice of flooring may modify the size or shape of a room, may be bold or neutral in color and pattern, may determine the mood and style of furnishings and fabrics.

Wooden strip flooring goes with any decoration, while block or parquet adds an interesting effect. Random plank has a colonial or rustic mood, while plywood flooring is economical if covered with carpeting.

Many troweled materials formerly confined to outdoor areas or to public and commercial buildings have entered the home with slab construction. These include concrete, terrazzo, and other compounds poured into place, which often need only sealing. The same is true of brick and natural stone, providing a wide range of effects.

New, man-made floor coverings, many in the do-it-yourself category, are particularly useful where basic house construction provides only a subfloor. The floor-coverings chart lists the various types and their characteristics, and approximate costs. (Page 118f.)

FLOUR |

The following descriptions will guide you in buying the right flour for your recipes. Don't buy more than you can use up in a reasonable length of time.

All-purpose flour (sometimes referred to as general-purpose, or family flour) comes in bags and gives good results in most types of home baking. It may be a blend of hard wheats, soft wheats, or both. It is usually enriched, as indicated on the label. Enriched flour contains thiamine, niacin, riboflavin, and iron in addition to energy-yielding carbohydrates and supplementary protein.

Today, all-purpose flour is being promoted in two ways: *unsifted,* for use in recipes that have been perfected for unsifted flour; *sifted,* for other recipes. The difference is important in measurement: 1 cup of unsifted flour may equal up to 1¼ cups of the same flour after sifting. To assure good results, use only recipes from a reliable source and follow to the letter, using sifted or unsifted flour as specified. Don't experiment!

Instant-type flours are the same high quality, nutritionally wholesome, all-purpose flours we've used for years, but in a convenient new form. They pour freely and evenly, dispense instantly in cold liquids, cannot be sifted (the flour slips right through the sifter), and mix instantly. In using them, carefully follow recipes that call for instant-type, instantized, or instant-blending flour.

Bread flour, which also comes in bags, is excellent for yeast breads, but is not as satisfactory for general use. It is made from hard wheats and has a higher gluten content than all-purpose flour. It is not as generally available as all-purpose and cake flours.

Cake flour comes in packages and makes especially delicate cakes. It is made from selected soft wheats and is especially milled to give a very fine flour.

Self-rising flour is an all-purpose or cake flour to which leavening and salt have been added in proper amounts for most home baking except yeast breads. When using, follow the recipes which appear on the label.

Whole wheat, entire wheat, and graham flours are synonymous terms. Such flours contain, in natural proportions, all the constituents of the entire cleaned wheat grain. Do not sift these flours before measuring.

FOOD PLANNING IN QUANTITY | See also CLUB MEETINGS

Community and social activities, church suppers, and many other events are built around the serving of food to a large number of people. The problem then arises of how much food to buy. Home experience does not provide a reliable guide, especially when it comes to items used only sparingly at home, such as cream or catsup. Also, four normal servings at home multiplied by ten may not necessarily equal forty servings for a crowd. The following guide to food purchasing in quantities for twenty-five, fifty, or a hundred persons will be helpful in planning social affairs for your group:

QUANTITIES TO SERVE 50 PERSONS

(*Note:* For 25 persons, divide amount indicated by 2. For 100 persons, multiply by 2.)

Food as Purchased	Approximate Amount for 50 Servings	Size of Each Serving
BEVERAGES AND DRINKS		
Coffee, instant	1½ small jars	¾ cup
Coffee, regular	1¼ lbs.	¾ cup
Cream for coffee	1 qt. and ½ pt.	1½ tbs.
Fruit-juice concentrates, frozen	9 6-oz. or 5 12-oz. cans	½ cup
Fruit or tomato juice, canned	4 46-oz. cans	½ cup
Half-and-half cream	1 qt. and 1 pt.	2 tbs.
Lemon for tea	5 large	1 thin slice
Lemonade concentrate, frozen	13 6-oz. cans	8 oz.
Punch	2 gals.	⅔ cup
Sugar, lump	1⅛ lbs.	2 lumps
Tea	¼ lb.	¾ cup

MEAT, POULTRY, FISH

Bacon	6 lbs.	2 slices
Beef, rolled rib roast	25 lbs. before boning	3 oz. cooked
Beef, standing rib roast	35 lbs.	4 oz. cooked
Chicken, to roast	35 to 40 lbs.	¾ lb.
Chicken, stewing, for dishes using cut-up, cooked chicken	20 to 25 lbs.	
Frankfurters	100	2
Fish fillets, frozen	13 1-lb. pkgs.	¼ lb.
Ham, canned, boned	1 14-lb. can	¼ lb.
Ham, bone in, to bake	22 to 25 lbs.	3 oz. cooked
Hamburgers	12½ to 15 lbs.	2½ to 3½ oz. cooked
Lamb, leg to roast	25 lbs.	3 to 4 oz. cooked
Meat, chopped, for meat loaf	12 lbs.	2 to 3 oz. cooked
Oysters, for scalloped oysters	6 qts.	½ cup cooked
Oysters, for stew	6 qts.	2 cups
Pork, chops (3 to 1 lb.)	17 lbs.	1 chop, ¾" thick
Pork, loin to roast	25 lbs.	4 to 5 oz. cooked
Sausage, bulk or links	12½ lbs.	2 to 3 oz. cooked
Turkey, for dishes using cut-up, cooked turkey	16 lbs.	
Turkey, to roast, to slice	35 to 40 lbs.	½ to ⅔ lb.
°Precooked boneless turkey roll	6½ lbs. solid pack for cold slices	2 oz.
	9-lb. roll in broth for hot dishes	2 oz.
Uncooked boneless turkey roll	2 4½- to 5-lb. rolls	2 oz.

° Order in advance from meatman or from local hotel and restaurant supplier.

VEGETABLES

Any canned vegetable	14 1-lb. cans *or* 11 1-lb.-4 oz. cans *or* 2 6½- to 7-lb.-5 oz. cans	½ cup
Asparagus spears, canned (medium-sized)	11 1-lb.-4 oz. cans	4 to 6 spears
Asparagus, market fresh	20 lbs.	4 to 5 stalks
Cabbage (in eighths)	15 lbs.	1 eighth
Carrots	16 lbs. (tops off)	⅓ lb.
Cauliflower	15 lbs. (flowerets only)	¼ lb.
Corn on the cob	50 ears	1 ear
Frozen vegetables	13 to 17 pkgs. (10 to 12 oz. each) *or* 7 to 8 16- to 24-oz. size	About ½ cup
Green beans (or wax), market fresh	12½ lbs.	¼ lb.
Onions, for creaming	15 lbs.	½ cup (3 or 4)
Potatoes, for creaming	12½ to 15 lbs.	½ cup
Potatoes, frozen French fries	16 9-oz. pkgs. *or* 8 16-oz. size	5 or 6 fries
Potatoes, mashed	25 lbs. *or* 2 family-size and 1 regular pkg. instant mashed potatoes	½ cup

Food as Purchased	Approximate Amount for 50 Servings	Size of Each Serving
Potatoes, to scallop	12½ lbs. *or* 10 pkgs. scalloped-potato mix	½ cup
Potatoes, sweet, glazed	25 lbs.	1 potato
RELISHES AND SALADS		
Cabbage, for slaw	12 to 15 lbs.	⅓ cup
Catsup	3 14-oz. *or* 2 20-oz. bottles	1 tbs.
Chicken salad	6¼ qts.	½ cup
Chili sauce	4 to 5 12-oz. bottles	1 tbs.
Cranberry sauce, jellied	6 1-lb. cans	½" slice
French dressing	1 to 1½ qt.	1½ to 2 tbs.
Fruit salad	9 qts.	¾ cup
Lettuce, for lettuce hearts	12 medium heads	⅕ head
Lettuce, leaf, for salad	6 heads	2 or 3 leaves
Mayonnaise or salad dressing	1 qt.	1 tbs.
Olives	2 qts.	2 olives
Pears, for salad	7 1-lb.-13 oz. cans	1 pear half
Pickles	2 qts.	2 small pickles
Potato salad	6¼ qts.	½ cup
Salmon, for salad	8 1-lb. cans	⅓ cup salad
Tuna, for salad	16 6½- or 7-oz. cans	⅓ cup salad
Tomatoes, for salad	30 medium	3 slices
SANDWICHES		
Beef, roast, sliced	4 lbs. 12 oz.	1 slice
Bread, sandwich	2 3-lb. loaves	2 slices
Ham, baked, sliced	4 lbs. 12 oz.	1 slice
Swiss cheese, sliced	3 lbs. 2 oz.	1 slice
MISCELLANEOUS		
Apples, cooking, for sauce	25 lbs.	½ cup
Applesauce, canned	14 1-lb.-4-oz. cans	½ cup
Brown bread, canned	8 11-oz. cans	1 slice, ½" thick
Bread (about 1-lb. loaf)	5 loaves	1½ slices
Butter or margarine	1 to 1¼ lbs.	1 pat, ½" thick
Cling-peach halves, canned	7 1-lb.-13 oz. cans	1 peach half
Crackers	1 lb.	2 crackers
Cream, heavy, to top desserts	1 qt.	1 rounded tbs., whipped
Fruits, frozen, to top ice cream	13 to 17 pkgs. (10- to 12-oz.)	¼ to ⅓ cup
Ice cream, brick or bulk	2 to 2½ gals.	about ⅙ qt.
Jelly	8 8-oz. glasses	about 1 tbs.
Noodles	8 6-oz. pkgs.	½ cup, cooked
Pies	9 pies	⅙ pie
Rice, packaged precooked	6 15-oz. pkgs.	¾ cup, cooked
Rice, regular uncooked white	3 qts. 1 cup	¾ cup, cooked
Rolls or biscuits	6½ doz.	1½
Soup, canned, condensed	20 10½-oz. cans	1 cup
Soup, mix	10 env.	about ¾ cup

FOOD STORAGE |

Good habits of food storage contribute to family well-being in two ways: money and health. Since the cost of food takes a large slice of every family budget, food saved is money saved; while wasted food is money thrown away in dribs and drabs. Yet obviously food should not be saved to the point where it spoils. These tips will help make your refrigerator and/or freezer more efficient in their food-preservation job.

PROTECT COOKED FOOD

Food that is cooked for later use, such as soups, custards, meat, meat stews, unstuffed poultry, etc., should be cooled quickly, kept covered while cooling, and refrigerated promptly. There are always large numbers of spoilage organisms—bacteria, yeast, and molds—in the air. If food is uncovered while cooling, the organisms will drop on the surface and by the time the food is cool enough to go into the refrigerator, spoilage may be started. Refrigeration will slow down, but not entirely stop the growth of these organisms. Cooling can be hastened by placing the covered container in cold water or directly in the refrigerator. Any dishes containing fish, milk, eggs, etc., should not be stored too long (more than forty-eight hours) even in the refrigerator.

Be sure to keep leftovers in clean, identifiable wrappings or containers. Many an aluminum "ball" has gone unnoticed in the back of the refrigerator until it was too late. Glass or plastic dishes, and wide-mouthed glass jars with tight lids are neat and handy.

It's quite safe to keep food in opened cans in the refrigerator. However, very acid foods such as tomatoes or grapefruit juice are best transferred to a nonmetallic container. They tend to pick up a taste from the can, which is undesirable though harmless.

PROTECT FRESH FOODS

Wash fruits and vegetables well, discarding the spoiled or bruised parts *before* refrigerating. Shake the excess water from salad greens; the few drops remaining will be just right for maintaining the desired humidity in the crisper.

Fresh meats should be wiped off with a damp paper towel (or a cloth) and stored in the meat drawer, or loosely wrapped in wax paper and stored in the coldest part of the refrigerator.

Fresh fish should be wrapped in aluminum foil or plastic film, or placed in a covered dish, to prevent transfer of odors. Don't keep fresh fish more than twenty-four hours. Cooked fish may be kept covered or wrapped for two days. (See chart, next page.)

FOOD STORAGE CHART

Type of Food	In Refrigerator 34°F. to 38°F.	In Freezer 0°	Special Handling
BUTTER, margarine	1 to 2 weeks	3 months	Tightly covered or wrapped.
CHEESE Cottage cheese, ricotta	3 to 5 days	2 to 3 months	Tightly wrapped or in closed containers. Frozen cheeses are likely to become crumbly. Do not freeze cream cheese or creamed cottage cheese.
Other soft cheeses	1 to 2 weeks	2 to 3 months	
Hard cheeses	3 to 6 months	6 months	
EGGS Whole, raw	1 week	6 to 8 months	In refrigerator, keep egg whites in covered container; egg yolks covered with water. Freeze whole eggs, yolks, or whites in covered containers. DO NOT FREEZE EGGS IN SHELLS.
Egg whites and egg yolks, raw	1 to 2 days	6 to 8 months	
Hard-cooked (in shells)	8 to 10 days	Do not freeze	
FISH Cod, flounder, haddock, halibut, pollock, shrimp	24 hours	4 months	Wrap fish ready for freezing in moisture- and vapor-resistant freezer wrap. Put two layers of wax paper between individual servings if wrapped together. Tape securely.
Mullet, ocean perch, sea trout, striped bass, shucked clams		3 months	
Salmon steaks, Pacific Ocean perch, crab meat		2 months	
Most cooked fish and cooked shellfish	1 to 2 days	3 months	
FRUITS Whole citrus fruits, apples	7 days	Do not freeze	Many fruits should be packed in sugar or syrup and ascorbic acid (vitamin C) before freezing. In refrigerator, keep fruits in crisper or store uncovered, according to type.
Most other fruits	3 to 5 days	10 to 12 months	
Fruit-juice concentrates	6 days	12 months	

	Refrigerator	Freezer	
MEATS			In refrigerator, keep meats loosely covered or wrapped. To freeze, wrap meat tightly in moisture- and vapor-resistant freezer wrap. Put two layers of wax paper between individual servings if wrapped together. Tape securely.
Beef, roasts, steaks	3 to 5 days	12 months	
Cooked meats	1 to 2 days	3 months	
Ground meat		1 to 3 months	
Variety meats (liver, kidney, heart, tongue)		1 to 3 months	See also storage guide under MEAT.
Pork, cured			
sliced ham	3 to 5 days	1 to 2 months	
whole ham	1 week	1 to 2 months	
bacon	1 week	2 to 3 weeks	
frankfurters	1 week	1 month	
Fresh pork (chops, roasts), and veal roasts	3 to 5 days	8 months	
Veal cutlets, chops	3 to 5 days	6 months	
POULTRY			For freezing, store liquid or semi-liquid cooked poultry dishes in tightly closed rigid containers. Keep other poultry dishes in moisture- and vapor-resistant freezer wrap.
Chicken			
whole		12 months	
cut up	1 to 2 days	6 months	
livers		3 months	
Turkey, duck, goose (whole); chicken and turkey, cooked (sliced meat and gravy)		6 months	
MILK, CREAM	3 days	Do not freeze	Keep in covered containers.
Ice Cream	2 days	1 month	
SOUPS, STEWS, CASSEROLES, BAKED GOODS	1 to 2 days	2 months	
VEGETABLES, SALAD GREENS	3 to 5 days	8 to 10 months (for many vegetables—not all)	Boil or blanch vegetables before freezing. Do not freeze crisp vegetables, radishes, or fresh whole tomatoes.
Canned (open) or leftover vegetables	1 to 3 days		
Root vegetables	1 to 2 weeks		

PLAN USE OF SPACE

Get into the habit of storing foods in approximately the same spots in the refrigerator—this is a time-saver because you won't have to search for standard items, and you won't overlook things until they have been kept too long for use. Also, don't take up valuable space with foods that don't need refrigeration. Catsup, peanut butter, jellies, hydrogenated shortenings, and many other foods will keep well at room temperature for a long time. When a refrigerator gets overcrowded, it will need defrosting often and will not do as efficient a cooling job.

No one can say exactly how long foods can be refrigerated without spoiling—too many variables are involved. The chart gives a general guide to the keeping limits of particular foods—how long they will retain the look, taste, and nourishment they had when they were bought. To make sure they work for you, take these precautions: *shop* in a store that refrigerates its perishables; *don't overload* refrigerator shelves; *defrost regularly* (unless the refrigerator is self-defrosting) when frost becomes ½ inch thick; *handle* and wrap or cover foods properly before refrigeration; and *promptly* refrigerate both fresh and leftover food.

SAVE TIME WITH YOUR FREEZER

When preparing soups, stews and casseroles, buy enough ingredients to make double the amount you'll eat right away, and freeze half. Here are some points to remember:

Cook the portion you plan to freeze until it's just tender. It will get the additional cooking it needs when it's reheated for serving. Be especially careful with rice, noodles, spaghetti, and the like.

You may freeze cooked meat which has already been frozen raw. The refreezing of such meat after thorough cooking is virtually a first-freezing for the cooked food. It will not cause spoilage or quality changes. (As a general rule, though, thawed frozen foods should not be refrozen.)

Season foods that are to be frozen more lightly than usual. You can add more seasoning at serving time.

Crisp toppings such as bread crumbs, potato chips, and grated cheese will be better if added when reheating for serving. Cooked white potatoes do not freeze well, so put them in later.

Cooked foods are at their best if eaten within a month or so of freezing.

If you have room in your freezer, use casserole dishes that can withstand sudden extreme changes in temperature (glass ovenware and glass ceramic, for instance). They let you do the whole cook-freeze-reheat process conveniently in the same dish.

Sandwiches and cookies freeze very well. Make extras, enclose them in freezer wrap, and freeze. Put them, still frozen, in a lunch box in the morning. They'll be thawed, and perfectly fresh and moist, by noon. If you butter both slices of bread from edge to edge, you'll find that moist fillings won't soak into the bread. Jelly, meat, cheese, and meat or sea-food salad (if not too moist) are good fillings for freezing.

Foods to avoid because they don't freeze well: tomatoes, hard-cooked eggs, lettuce, celery and other crisp vegetables, or salad greens; also mayonnaise and similar salad dressings.

FOOT CARE |

From 50 to 80 per cent of school-age children have foot problems. Usually the result of poor care or bad shoes, many of these problems become painful deformities by the time the children reach the age of twenty.

Weak feet, flat feet, ingrown toenails, athlete's foot, bunions, corns, calluses, warts, and leg cramps are common conditions requiring the care of a physician or podiatrist. Most damage is caused by the time children are six. Constant pressure in a wrong area is a major cause of foot problems. For example, an infant compelled to sleep continually in the same position may suffer damaging pressures on his feet. He should be turned over from time to time until he is able to turn himself.

Problems can also result from pajamas with tight feet, shoes and socks that are too tight, a blanket that is always tucked in snugly, or forcing a child to stand or walk too soon. Socks, after laundering, should be at least one-half inch longer than feet. Stretch socks and leotards may be too constricting if not fitted properly. Until children begin to stand, knit booties provide warmth when necessary and also permit the toes freedom to exercise.

A child seldom complains of painful feet, so it is up to parents to spot trouble. Check regularly for cracks between the toes, excessive perspiration or odor, blisters, warts, sores, ingrown toenails, and red, rough, or hard spots. Observe how he walks—trouble signs are: toeing in or out, bowed or knock-knees, poor posture, a lack of spring in his step, frequent and unnecessary falls, an unwillingness to take part in active games, and excessive eagerness to remove his shoes. By age five, a child should walk with toes pointing nearly straight ahead.

A physician should look carefully at feet during checkups. He can also check new shoes for proper fit and recommend exercises. Good foot care calls for daily scrubbing and thorough drying—especially between toes. Nails are cut straight across and no shorter than the end of the toe. Most gym shoes or sneakers do not offer enough protection to be worn all day, every day. Your physician or podiatrist may prescribe orthopedic shoes to correct a foot problem. However, it is not advisable to buy such shoes unless they have been prescribed.

PODIATRISTS (CHIROPODISTS)

At one time or another, more than seven out of ten people suffer from foot trouble. To treat it, a family physician may refer you to a podiatrist, or foot specialist. Modern podiatry (care of the feet)—far removed from the practice of nineteenth century itinerant corn cutters—is accepted today as an important branch of health care. Several states now require school children to have an annual foot examination. (The older name for a foot specialist, chiropodist, is now seldom seen.)

The podiatrist is not a medical doctor. He is, though, a practitioner trained in all phases of the care of the feet. Rigid laws control both his licensing and practice. His degree—either Doctor of Podiatry (Pod.D.) or Doctor of Surgical Chiropody (D.S.C.)—is earned after a course of study that includes two years of premedical undergraduate schooling and four years of professional training at one of the nation's five accredited schools of podiatry-chiropody. Some states also require a year's internship.

State laws vary, but in general, the nation's 8,100 podiatrists are licensed to perform various types of surgery on the foot (except amputations), as well as to treat some 75 foot ailments by means of casts, whirlpool and paraffin baths, and electric currents. They may use such testing tools as X rays, blood tests, and urinalysis. Some states prohibit the podiatrist's use of antibiotics, general anesthesia, and drugs containing narcotics. In any case, treatment of the foot cannot be separated from the care of the rest of the body. Hence, most physicians prefer that their patients keep them informed of any foot problem that may have to be treated by a podiatrist.

Such diseases as diabetes, hardening of the arteries, heart disease, anemia, gout, and kidney ailments may first show up in the feet and legs. Podiatrists cannot, of course, treat any general disease, but they are trained to refer patients to physicians when something other than a foot problem is indicated.

The earlier a foot ailment is detected, the easier it is to correct, and at less expense to the patient. Podiatrists point out that ill-fitting shoes, particularly among women, are a major contributing cause of foot trouble.

FRANKFURTERS | See also MEAT

Today the once lowly hot dog is one of America's finest meats. It's a combination of beef, pork, veal, and aromatic spices and seasonings, which are encased, then smoked over hickory or other hardwood. The casings may be natural or "skinless." If simply served, these sausages are as good for children as for grownups. They supply the same high-quality protein and meat values as roasts, chops, and steaks, and make a very thrifty buy.

You can't tell a good hot dog just by looking at it. A well-known brand name is your best buy. Some are all-beef, some kosher style. They have no waste. They are fully cooked, ready to eat, or to heat and eat. Some are sold by the link or portion of a pound. If they've been government inspected, several franks out of each five-pound carton carry a little band giving the packer's name and exact ingredients. Ask to see this label. There are also franks containing wheat or soy flour; the label usually declares such additions.

Regular-size franks average 9 to 10 per pound; dinner franks (larger), 5 per pound; cocktail franks (smaller), 26 to 28 per pound. Allow 1 or 2 regular-size franks per serving for lunch; 2 or 3 for dinner. To store, keep in original cellophane package in coldest part of regrigerator. Wrap bulk franks loosely in wax paper. Use within three or four days. You may freeze very fresh franks in their original package and keep them a week or so in the home freezer. If you plan to keep them a month, wrap in freezer-wrapping material.

FREEZERS | See also APPLIANCE TROUBLE SHOOTING;
FOOD STORAGE; REFRIGERATORS

Frozen foods are preserved by *quick*-freezing. This is done at a very low temperature, and the food must be kept at zero (F.) or below to retain its texture and flavor. Therefore, although foods will freeze at temperatures as high as 32° F., the freezing process is slow and may actually ruin the texture and flavor of the food. In a standard refrigerator, the freezer section is mainly useful for storing commercial frozen food packages unthawed. Check whether a freezer compartment goes to 0° F., as it must if you freeze home-prepared foods.

In a true home freezer, you can keep foods fresh and flavorful for months. You have a choice among three styles: **upright,** with shelves like a refrigerator; **chest** or horizontal type, opening from the top and containing baskets or dividers; and **combination** refrigerator-freezer, with 2 to 16 cubic feet of freezer space maintained at 0° F. The choice of type and size depends on floor space and on how you intend to use the freezer.

If you grow your own fruits and vegetables; if you want to avoid frequent market trips and buy in quantity; if you plan to cook and freeze whole meals . . . such projects will require plenty of freezer space. The chest type is lowest in cost per cubic foot; but if you look upon your freezer as an extra pantry, the upright type is convenient to use, or the combination type may have sufficient space.

In most homes, convenience rather than economy justifies a freezer (owners say they eat better when the foods they like are always at hand). But a freezer may also cut food costs if systematically managed. You can time your food buying when prices are lowest, whether for a bag of peaches or a side of beef. Some grocers, butchers, freezer-locker plants, and farmers offer discounts on quantity purchases. You need never waste any food, and you can cook inexpensive but time-consuming dishes ahead of time in sufficient quantity to freeze for half a dozen future meals.

TIPS ON HOME FREEZING

Freeze only good quality food, preferably at the height of the season. Poor quality food is not worth the trouble or the cost of electric current, and will not be improved by freezing. Freeze promptly and in small amounts, since overloading your freezer may result in slow freezing (follow directions in the instruction book). Put food awaiting freezing in the refrigerator; do not let it stand at room temperature.

Wrap food *only* in the moisture-proof, vapor-proof packaging materials and containers made especially for low temperatures. Seal sheet wrappings with freezer tape; improperly wrapped foods will shrink, lose moisture, flavor, and texture. Label and date each package. This is very important because later they may be impossible to identify, and you'll need the date to follow a first-in, first-out program in consuming the food.

Do not refreeze food that has been completely thawed, because it might have begun to spoil; it will certainly lose in flavor and quality. However, you can *cook* thawed food which has been frozen raw, such as a frozen turkey, and then safely refreeze the leftovers. Also, if a power failure should disconnect the freezer you can salvage partially thawed food as long as it still contains ice crystals (but immediately discard partly thawed fish or sea food). Discard anything that has the slightest "off" odor.

How long to keep food frozen depends on the quality and kind, the temperature, and the care taken in packaging. If you use the freezer every day, consuming the oldest foods first, you should have no problem. See the tables under FOOD STORAGE.

Consult cookbooks for special techniques of preparing food for freezing. Also write to the U.S. Department of Agriculture or your state extension service for bulletins on the best varieties of fruit and vegetables to grow in the garden. The size of your freezer determines how much you can freeze at one time—usually 4 to 6 pounds per cubic foot. Be sure to place each package in direct contact with a freezing surface until frozen.

FACTS ON FREEZER CARE

Defrosting is easier if you do not let the frost exceed half an inch or so and become icy. Remove the food from one wall or shelf, and place a folded newspaper at the bottom to catch the frost. With a plastic scraper (your gasoline station has them for windshields), scrape the frost from this section, then proceed to the next.

If the frost is thick and icy, remove all food packages and wrap them in newspapers and blankets to keep them frozen. Disconnect the freezer. Direct a fan into it to hasten melting, or use an electric defroster especially made for this purpose. Mop up the water with old towels, then wipe out the interior with clear warm water. Wipe dry before turning on the freezer.

Defrosting generally is necessary once or twice a year, depending on the humidity. You can reduce humidity by chilling cooked foods in cold water or in the refrigerator before freezing; and by planning your trips to the freezer to avoid opening the door or lid any more often than necessary.

If the power fails, keep the freezer tightly closed. In a fully loaded freezer all foods except ice cream will stay frozen for about two days; in a partially filled freezer, for about one day. Over a longer period, use dry ice or transfer the food to a locker plant. (See cautions above against refreezing thawed food.) In some localities you may want to buy food insurance against this calamity.

Spills inside a freezer must be left until defrosting time, since a wiping cloth will stick to the icy surface. But in a frostless freezer, rub the spill with a hot, damp dishcloth. It will stick at first, but keep rubbing and redampen as necessary—the warm cloth will stick less and less.

FRESH FRUITS AND VEGETABLES | See also FRUIT; FRUIT DICTIONARY; VEGETABLE BUYING GUIDE; VEGETABLE DICTIONARY

Selecting fresh fruits and vegetables for quality, nutritional value, and economy requires knowledge and care. Based on recommendations by the U.S. Department of Agriculture and the Defense Supply Agency of the Department of Defense, here is a shopping guide for fresh produce.

The best food buys are those in season. When fresh fruits and vegetables are plentiful, prices are usually lower for top quality. The women's pages of newspapers and market reports on radio or television regularly report which fruits and vegetables are at their peak in your area.

Inferior quality produce sold at reduced prices may involve excessive waste and prove less economical than higher priced foods in good condition. Quality sometimes can be judged by weight, as with citrus fruits. In these cases, the heavier the item for its size, the better the buy.

The fresher the produce, the higher the nutritional value. Perishable foods gradually lose nutrients and good flavor as they age, especially if they are not kept in a cool place. Shop at a market where there is a quick turnover to be better assured of freshness. Do not stock large quantities of highly perishable foods. Fresh fruits and vegetables should be firm and crisp.

Fresh fruits and vegetables are at their peak in texture, flavor, and food value when harvested at the proper stage of maturity (development) or ripeness. However, many fruits, including bananas, pears, peaches, plums, and avocados are picked in a mature-hard state and sometimes sold before they are fully ripened. If kept at room temperature, these fruits ripen to full flavor in a few days.

APPEARANCE

Most fruits yield slightly to moderate pressure when ready to eat. Unless fruits will be used immediately, do not buy them in a very ripe stage. Once started, deterioration progresses rapidly. Lack of full characteristic color may be a sign of immaturity or overmaturity. An overgrown appearance usually indicates overmaturity.

Some seed vegetables, such as peas and lima beans, should be well developed but not bulging or dry looking. Snap beans are best when seeds are immature. Medium-size, slender cucumbers are usually best; large, plump ones may be overmature. Oversize root vegetables may have a woody or tough texture. Soft or burst heads of cabbage are undesirable. Bud clusters on broccoli should be compact and show no signs of yellow flowering. Some vegetables, such as lettuce, onions, and celery, develop seed stems when overmature.

Mature fruits and berries appear plump and juicy. Fully ripe melons of most types usually have a distinct characteristic aroma and a yellowing rind.

Produce may be sold at lower prices if it is superficially defective or imperfect, although quality is unaffected. Learn to recognize the difference between good quality foods with surface defects and lower priced foods of inferior quality. Avoid produce with bruises or signs of decay and insect damage.

Examples of superficial defects which do not affect quality are brown, irregular marks (called scab) on avocados; scarring and discoloration on grapefruit and orange skins; slight discoloration or defects on outer leaves of some leafy vegetables; brown flecks on ripe bananas. An irregular shape does not affect food value or edible quality if the food item is otherwise in good condition.

A deep or rich color generally indicates highest food value and flavor. For example, the dark green outer leaves of leafy vegetables have more nutrients than the lighter colored inner ones. Also, bright orange carrots may provide more vitamin A than paler ones. Fruits and vegetables should be appropriately colored for their types.

CHOOSING FOR USE

Sometimes one variety of a fruit or vegetable is preferred over another for a specific use. For example, tart apples are best for cooking, and mild or sweet types are best for eating raw. Decide how you intend to use a certain food and then select the recommended variety.

Prewrapped and prepackaged fresh fruits and vegetables offer several advantages. Transparent film bags or overwrapped cartons keep root vegetables, greens, and other produce fresh longer because they reduce moisture loss and spoilage. The produce is protected from excessive handling by shoppers.

Cartons of small fruits or vegetables sometimes have a layer of good quality specimens on top which conceals produce of lesser quality. Watch out for stained, wet, or leaky cartons that indicate overripe or decaying contents.

FRUIT |

With more and more people becoming waistline conscious, and with better nutrition a national goal, the popularity of fruit has zoomed. Check your calorie charts to see what bargains fruits are!

Markets now display fresh fruit from all growing areas in this country and from many parts of the world, thanks to modern methods of packing fruit in protective boxes and hydro-cooling, right at the farm; then sending it to market under refrigeration.

Don't buy more fruit than you need for a few days. Be sure to ripen fruit to your liking before storing it in the refrigerator. The height of the local growing season is the best time to tuck some of your favorite fruits in the freezer, to can them, or to put them up as jams or jellies.

Frozen fruits. Hurry them home and into your freezer. (Take along an insulated bag when you shop.) They add delightful variety to your menus.

blueberries	raspberries
grapefruit sections	rhubarb
melon balls	sliced peaches
mixed fruit	strawberries, sliced or halved
pineapple chunks	whole strawberries with syrup

Most frozen fruits come sweetened and ready to eat or cook as is, or thawed. Check the label for sweetening and thawing directions. Usually it's best to thaw them almost, but not completely; a few ice crystals should remain for these fruits to be at their best for the table.

Canned or jar fruits. Explore your grocer's shelves. Many real time-savers are waiting for you—for example:

apples, sliced, baked, cinnamon rings, or applesauce	cling-peach halves or slices
apricots	pears
cherries, sweet or sour	pineapple—chunks, slices, tidbits, and crushed
grapefruit sections	purple plums
mandarin orange sections	fruit cocktail
fruits for salad	

Some fruits come sweetened and thickened, ready to use as ice cream toppings or pie fillings. If you're counting calories, many canned fruits come artificially sweetened, or canned only in fruit juice and/or water.

Dried fruits. Today's packaged dried prunes, apricots, peaches, pears, apples, etc. are so tender they can be eaten directly from the package. (They are partially cooked and pasteurized.) They don't need sugar and their cooking time is cut down too (see label directions). Store in the refrigerator. To chop dried fruits, use kitchen scissors, just snipping the meat from around the pits, if any.

Dates are an excellent energy food containing small amounts of the B vitamins and iron. They are very low in sodium. Packaged dates come pitted and unpitted from the Middle East and California—some in plastic containers. Delicious eaten as they are, they are also fine for salads, on cereals, in breads and cakes, cookies, etc. Chopped dates are small pieces, rolled in powdered sugar, ready to use in favorite bakings.

Dried figs. All American dried figs are grown and packed in California. They are available in several varieties:

Black Mission (black) figs are equally delicious as a confection, for stewing, and for other dishes. Calimyrna (large, light brown) may be used like black figs, are especially favored for eating out of hand. Kadota (light brown) are usually sold canned or fresh.

Raisins come from the grapes of the San Joaquin Valley in central California. Some are sun dried, others are specially dried indoors. They are ready for eating straight from the package or to use as a recipe ingredient. The most popular consumer-size packages are the 15-ounce and 1½-ounce cartons.

Modern packaging methods offer sufficient protection for the normal use of raisins in the home. And since they are available the year round, one can buy as one needs them, keeping the package on the pantry shelf, away from direct heat.

FRUIT DICTIONARY | See also FRESH FRUITS AND VEGETABLES

Apples are on the market the year round (at their peak from October to March). Listed below are some of the commercial leaders. Always store apples in a cold, dry place. About 3 or 4 apples equal 1 pound. To prepare, wash and dry them. Then eat them out of hand; or pare, core, and slice; or core and use whole.

VARIETY	COLOR	SEASON
FOR COOKING		
Rhode Island Greening	Green-yellow	September to March
Rome Beauty (baking only)	Medium red	November to May

FOR EATING

Delicious	Light red and striped with darker red	October to May

FOR COOKING AND EATING

Baldwin	Red, mottled with bright red	November to May
Gravenstein	Mostly green with pale red stripes	July to September
Grimes Golden	Yellow	September to January
Jonathan	Deep red	October to February
McIntosh	Bright red	September to May
Northern Spy	Striped bright red over yellow	October to May
Winesap	Dark red	January to June
Yellow Newtown	Greenish yellow or yellow	January to June

Apricots (May through August, at peak in June and July). Look for orange-yellow, plump, juicy apricots. About 8 to 16, depending on their size, equal 1 pound. Keep them in the refrigerator. To prepare apricots, wash, peel like peaches, then halve and slice them, or eat out of hand.

Avocados (all year; peak season for California avocados is February through April; for Florida avocados, September through November). When ripe, the avocado flesh is soft and mellow and yields readily to gentle pressure from the palms of the hands. If firm, you can hasten the softening by keeping the avocado in a warm room; then refrigerate.

Just before serving, cut in half lengthwise. Then hold between palms of hands and turn halves in opposite directions; next insert a sharp paring knife into the pit, lift out and discard it. Tear the glove-like skin from the halves; then slice crosswise or lengthwise. Or halve the avocado crosswise, turn halves, and pit as above; peel; then slice into rings. Or serve the halves unpeeled. To prevent darkening, immediately dip avocado slices into lemon juice; wrap any leftover avocado in wax paper or foil, and refrigerate.

Bananas (year round). Buy them by the hand or cluster, at whatever stage of ripeness you find them in the store; they'll finish ripening at home. About 3 bananas equal 1 pound. For baking, broiling, or frying, use firm bananas that are all yellow or slightly green-tipped. For eating, salads, desserts, milk shakes; or as an ingredient in cakes, cookies and breads, use fully ripe bananas, flecked with brown, or all yellow bananas.

Keep bananas at comfortable room temperature until they reach the desired stage of ripeness, then they may be refrigerated and held for several days. To prevent darkening, dip banana slices into acid fruit juice, such as lemon or pineapple juice.

BERRIES

Fresh berry time begins in April. The order of appearance is as follows:

Strawberries: Peak season, April through July. Limited amounts are available all year now, including midwinter.

Gooseberries: June and July.

Raspberries: June, July, and August. Limited amounts are available in September, October, and November.

Blackberries: May through August; best in June, July, and August.

Blueberries: May to September; most plentiful in July.

Loganberries: April through September. Peak in June.

Choose berries that are ripe, well-colored, and free from off-color spots. Before storing, pick over, removing spoiled ones; spread them on a tray and refrigerate uncovered. Just before using, place in a colander or sieve; gently run water over them. Drain well; hull. One quart yields about three and a half cups.

Cherries (May through August). Red, white, and black sweet cherries should be firm, shiny, plump, of fully ripe color, and free of spots. To store them, wash, drain and dry; then refrigerate.

Cranberries (September through March, most plentiful from October through December). Choose berries that are firm, plump, fresh-appearing, and with a high luster. You can refrigerate them; or freezer wrap, then freeze them for weeks.

Currants (July). Make sure they are not so ripe they fall off stems. Refrigerate on shallow tray. Use white or red currants for eating, salads, fruit cups, or desserts. Use black currants for jelly or jam. If serving clusters, wash, dry, then serve with or without stems.

Fresh figs (June through November, most plentiful in August, September, and October). They should be soft. Kadota figs should be greenish-yellow; Black Mission, purplish. Buy them slightly underripe; refrigerate until fully ripe, then they're ready to eat.

Grapes (June to April). Choose firm, fresh-looking bunches, in which plump grapes cling to their stems when gently shaken. Refrigerate. Always wash and drain grapes before eating.

CITRUS FRUITS

Grapefruit. Fresh Florida grapefruit are especially delicious from October through June. California and Arizona ship them the year round. They should be firm, well-shaped, heavy with juice, and thin-skinned.

The color varies from pale yellow to reddish-brown. Rust spots and green tinges do not affect the inner quality. Very often small grapefruit are sweeter and juicier than the large sizes. Small grapefruit can be easily reamed for fresh juice too. Grapefruit meat is white or pink, with or without seeds.

Under U.S. Department of Agriculture rulings, any grapefruit containing fewer than seventeen seeds is considered seedless. Store grapefruit in a cool place, preferably in the refrigerator.

Kumquats (November through February). They are a small orange-like fruit, resembling pecans in shape. Choose firm fruit, heavy for its size. Keep refrigerated.

Lemons (all year, from California and Arizona). A few drops of juice squeezed from a plump lemon wedge brings out the flavor of almost any meat, fish, poultry, vegetable, or salad. And since lemon contains virtually no sodium, it makes a fine seasoning for low-sodium diets, as well as for low-calorie diets. Keep refrigerated.

Limes (Florida, between June and September; California, between October and December). Look for limes that are green, not yellowish, and heavy for their size. Persian limes are the size and shape of lemons. The small round variety are Key limes. Keep them all refrigerated. Use like lemons.

Oranges (all year). The two important varieties from California are Valencias (May to November) and navel oranges (November to May). Navel oranges are not only easy to peel, they are also easy to section and eat out of hand. Valencias are rich in juice.

Florida ships Hamlins and Parson Browns (pale, thin-skinned juice fruit), and navel oranges from October to January. Pineapple oranges (high in color with a smooth peel) appear from December through February and are known for their full-flavored juice. Then comes the Valencia season, from February through June.

Florida is growing increasing quantities of temple oranges, first cousins to tangerines; these peel easily and are available from December through February. Tangelos, a hybrid between tangerines and grapefruit, but similar in appearance and flavor to oranges, are available from November to March. The Murcott honey orange (high in color, with a rough peel) is available from February through June.

Toward the end of the orange season the skin near the stem takes on a greenish tinge. This is not a sign of underripeness but is a peculiarity of citrus fruits. All oranges must pass state maturity requirements before they can be shipped. To enhance the eye appeal of certain varieties, Florida oranges are sometimes colored; such fruit is stamped "Color added."

Look for oranges that are firm and heavy for their size. If there are several persons in the family, and if storage space is available, it is economical to buy oranges by the box or bag.

Keep oranges in a cool place, refrigerating those to be used the next day for juice or salad.

Mandarin oranges, flavorful, whole segments of a tiny species of orange, are sold canned rather than fresh, ready for use. The rind, membrane, and seeds are removed before the sections are vacuum-sealed in light syrup.

Tangerines (November through May, peak December and January). Their deep-orange skin is loose and puffy, and peels easily. Select firm, heavy fruit for fruit bowls and to eat out of hand. Use sections in salads, fruit cocktails, etc. Tangerine juice and grated rind may be substituted for orange juice and rind. Keep refrigerated.

MELONS

Melons must be fully ripe to enjoy their flavor at their peak. Most ripe melons yield to pressure at the blossom end, and have a typical fragrance and yellowish tinge. Before storing, place in a paper bag or wax paper and refrigerate. To serve, halve them, scrape out seeds, then cut in quarters or smaller. Here are some of the varieties:

Cantaloupes (May into October; imported ones may come in earlier) may be round, oval, or oblong, usually with over-all netted skins, and are light gray in color. When ripe, they have a yellow ground color, a smooth scar on the stem end, a distinct aroma, and the blossom end yields to pressure.

Casabas (July into December) are large, rough-skinned, roundish, sometimes considerably pointed and deeply ridged. When fully ripe, their rind is golden yellow; the white flesh is very juicy and sweet. This melon weighs 4 to 10 pounds.

Cranshaws (June to November) have a fairly smooth rind, mottled with gold and green. Their flesh is bright salmon color, thick, and juicy. Weighs 4 to 8 pounds.

Honeyballs (May through August) are like honeydews but are rounder and smaller, with a slightly netted skin.

Honeydews (January to November, the peak being July through September) are large, round or oval, averaging about 6 pounds. Their smooth hard skin is without netting. When vine-ripened, they are creamy or yellowish in color, show softening at the blossom end, have smooth, well-rounded ridges next to the stem, and are definitely fragrant. Their green flesh is exceptionally sweet.

Papayas (all year) are melon-like in superficial characteristics—thin, smooth skin, spherical to oblong shape, center cavity packed with seeds. They are ready to eat when the rind is yellow and the fruit feels soft. They taste and look (on the inside) like cantaloupe.

Persians (July into November) look like large cantaloupes; are round, but have flat ends. They have a green rind with heavy netting. When ripe, the rind has a yellowish cast; the flesh is pink, not as sweet as honeydew or honeyball but resembling cantaloupe in flavor. This melon may weigh as much as 10 pounds.

Santa Claus or Christmas melons (winter) look like small oblong watermelons. They have a hard, thick, slightly netted green rind. Their light-yellow-to-green flesh is sweet. Signs of ripeness are light yellowing of the rind, and softness at blossom end.

Watermelons (May through September). Weigh 20 to 40 pounds, vary from round to long cylindrical in shape, and are green to light green, sometimes with stripes. When ripe, the underside of the watermelon begins to turn yellow, not light green; the flesh is crisp, juicy, and red. Your best guide to ripeness is to buy watermelon in halves or quarters, since a great many markets now sell them by the pound.

The small refrigerator-size watermelon, sometimes called New Hampshire Midget, is available from April to September. It may weigh 3 to 5 pounds, and resembles a cantaloupe in size and shape. Its color may vary from light to very dark green, usually with stripes. It ripens close to the rind, has texture like that of a larger watermelon. Refrigerate until served.

OTHER FRUITS

Nectarines (June, July, and August) are a kind of peach with a smooth skin like a plum; the skin is greenish-white with a faint blush. Choose firm fruit, free from cuts and bruises. Keep them refrigerated.

Peaches (late May to mid-October, peak in July and August) are white- or yellow-fleshed, either clingstone or freestone. Cling peaches are used for canning; freestones are fine for all uses.

Ripe peaches should be firm, but yield to gentle pressure, and should be free from brown spots or other signs of decay. The flesh should be either yellow or white, not green. About 4 peaches will weigh 1 pound. Keep them refrigerated. If the freestone variety does not peel easily, let stand in boiling water to cover, one to two minutes; then plunge into cold water; peel; remove pits. Pare cling peaches.

Pears (all year, peak August through October). Varieties of pears include:

Bartlett (July through October), bell-shaped; soft yellow; sweet; juicy.

Bosc (September through February), a russet variety, with long tapering neck.

Comice (October through February), green skin. Famous for size, superb quality, and beauty.

Anjou (October through May). Green skin, fine grain, spicy.

Nelis (February through June). Russet, very sweet, luscious.

When buying pears to eat, check softness by pressing slightly near the stem end. If they are not quite soft, let them ripen at room temperature in a paper bag or fruit bowl. When ripe, store in refrigerator. Slightly underripe pears are best for cooking. Pears need no peeling; just wash. Or halve, core, and slice them. If sliced and held before serving, coat with lemon juice or French dressing to prevent darkening.

Pineapple (all year, peak from March through June). Quality fruit is heavy for its size and has no signs of decay or mold at bottom or around the eyes. When ripe, the fruit has a sweet fragrance and golden-yellow flesh; center leaves loosen easily when pulled. Keep wrapped, in refrigerator.

Plums and prunes (plums from June through October; prunes a month later). Choose those that are plump and yield slightly to pressure. Refrigerate. About 12 to 15 plums or fresh prunes equal 1 pound. Wash, eat them as is, or cook. Prunes look like dark-skinned plums.

Rhubarb (January through July, peak during May and June). Early rhubarb has light-pink stalks; later rhubarb stalks are dark reddish green. Buy fresh crisp stalks; store in cool, dry place. Don't peel rhubarb unless it is tough and stringy. Before cooking, trim ends; discard leaves (they are not edible); and wash the stalks well.

UNUSUAL FRUITS

Have you ever been tempted to try some different fruits for your family but hesitated because you were not sure how to serve them or what they tasted like? If so, here are facts about several which you may want to try.

Guava (autumn). The common guava is round or pear-shaped, about two inches in diameter with a thin green or yellow skin. It has a pulpy core with many hard seeds. Guavas are sweet and slightly acid. They are often used in salads and pies and also can be eaten like apples. To prepare: wash, peel, remove core, and press the pulp through a coarse sieve; slice the outer flesh, and serve topped with the strained pulp.

Mango (May through August). A large, usually oval fruit, the mango has a thick, smooth skin, ranging in color from green to yellow to red. When ripe it tastes somewhat like an apricot-pineapple combination—sweet with a slight acidity. It can be eaten whole or sliced. To prepare: wash, peel, and slice meat from the pit. Scrape the fibrous flesh from around the pit and purée it. Serve the sliced mango with a dash of lime juice. Do not serve with alcoholic drinks.

Persimmon (October through December). This smooth-skinned, bright-orange fruit is oval, with one pointed and one flat end. It is the size of a large apple. Persimmons are best eaten fully ripe—when the flesh has a soft, jelly-like consistency and a sweet, chocolate-apricot flavor. They are usually eaten raw, peeled and seeded, but can be cooked.

Pomegranate (September into December). Often used as a decoration, the pomegranate is about the size of an apple. Color ranges from pale yellow to purple but is usually red. The firm, white flesh inside is not eaten. This flesh contains pockets of bright-red seeds which have a refreshing, sweet-sour flavor. Eat the seeds, discarding the pits, or use as garnish for salads and desserts. The juice is used in fruit drinks and punches. To open a pomegranate, slice off the calyx or stem end, and following the partition walls, divide the rind into segments. These may then be forced open and the seeds removed; or you may cut a core at one end and squeeze out the juice.

FRUIT JUICES AND DRINKS |

Today's canned or frozen fruit juices, ades, and fruit-drink bases come in almost endless variety of flavors and blends of flavors. They provide the pickup that Americans associate with breakfast or the first course of other meals, or a vitamin-rich beverage at any time. Keep a supply of fruit juices on hand—a good health habit to encourage in thirsty children. Here are hints on using and keeping juices at their best.

Straight or blended juices contain the fresh-fruit product, as close to the natural state as the canning art can achieve. Usually they are unsweetened, although sometimes sugar or a preservative may be added (read the label). Serve straight, or diluted a bit if a blander taste is desired. With the naturally sweeter types, such as pineapple or prune, a dash of lemon juice adds a tang. All may be converted into refreshing ades by mixing with ice, water, or carbonated water and a little sugar (or none).

Nectars, such as apricot, peach, pear-pineapple, etc., are similar to juices but of a thicker consistency because of the nature of the fruit.

Juice drinks and punches are blends of the various fruit juices named on the label, sweetened and diluted, ready to serve as a soft drink.

Fruit-drink bases, whether powder or liquid, come in a variety of flavors to be mixed with water. Some contain less than 15 per cent natural fruit juices, others are entirely synthetic. Often labeled "breakfast" drinks, some are artificially sweetened and low in calories.

Frozen juices, with one exception, are concentrates which are reconstituted by adding water. Lemon juice, whether bottled, canned, or frozen, comes at natural strength, and may be used in cooking or in drinks like the fresh juice.

Get frozen fruit juices home and into your freezer or freezer section of combination refrigerator-freezer as quickly as possible; they'll keep many months at 0° F. If stored in the freezing compartment of a conventional refrigerator, they'll keep several weeks. Never let unopened cans of frozen juice stand at room temperature—they may burst.

To reconstitute frozen juices, remove top of can and follow label directions. To bring out a juice's full fresh bouquet, shake or stir briskly and thoroughly before pouring. For best flavor, use within twenty-four hours after reconstituting. If using unreconstituted juice as an ingredient in recipes, let it thaw until just soft enough to be stirred well; then measure required amount.

Handle unopened canned juices with care. The best storage place is the coolest, driest spot you have. There, canned juices will keep their fresh flavor and vitamin content for months. Never store them near a range, pipes, or radiator.

Before you open canned juices, shake the can well to mix the juice. Puncture the top with a regular puncture-type opener; make a second opening on other side; then the juice will pour easily. Stir in a pitcher to aerate.

You can keep opened cans of juice on hand in your refrigerator—it's perfectly safe. But the flavor will last longer if you transfer them to covered jars.

FURNISHING A HOME | See also FURNITURE BUYING GUIDE; INTERIOR DECORATORS; WINDOWS

Shopping for furniture and decorating a home are adventures most women enjoy. But because there is such a wealth of furnishing and fabric types, styles, qualities, and materials, some guidelines are needed to eliminate confusion and guesswork. You can furnish an attractive home on practically any budget if you plan carefully and spend wisely.

In this Guide, see the section on furniture buying for shopping suggestions, and names of individual items of furniture such as beds, chairs, etc., for guides to basic style and selection. Here are points to consider:

Buy good quality. Major pieces of furniture—sofas, upholstered chairs, dining tables, beds, etc.—are long-range investments. When you move, they move with you. If you must economize, choose inexpensive rugs, curtains, and draperies which are apt to be replaced because they may not fit the floors and windows of future homes.

Pick a basic style. Decide in advance what kind of home you want— modern or traditional, or contemporary, which is a combination of the other two. In your budgeting, don't omit accessories—lamps, art objects, mirrors, etc.—which are essential to making a room look like home, and must be selected to harmonize with its style.

Consider the way you live. If you do much entertaining, you'll need plenty of seating space, small tables, and dancing space. Book and record collecting call for shelves and cabinets. A hi-fi, piano, or television set requires proper placement in order to function properly without being obtrusive. You'll want rooms that are easy to clean and care for. Develop a clear picture before you shop.

Think of colors. Good use of color can make a room look larger or better proportioned, can lighten a dark room or make too bright a room cooler. It can make a ceiling seem higher or lower, direct the eye to a focal point, or away from a defect. Color also has important psychological values, making a room cheerful, formal, or whatever your taste may dictate. Good rule of thumb: use soft or clear shades in large areas, more intense colors only for accent.

Shop before buying. Do a good deal of looking and collect samples of carpeting, floor tiles, fabrics, paint colors, etc. Note down the name of a store where you saw a sofa or table you liked, with the size, price, and other details. Don't be stampeded (even by an impatient husband) into buying until your whole plan is complete from wall color to mantel clock. But do let him inspect such basic items as chairs, couches, etc., for style and comfort.

Measure rooms accurately. With a tape measure, get the dimensions of the room to be furnished, including door openings and other breaks in the wall space. On a large sheet of paper, draw the room on a scale of one inch to one foot: a 12-by-14-foot room becomes 12 inches by 14 inches. Cut out pieces of colored paper on the same scale to represent furniture: a 6-foot sofa becomes 6 inches. By placing its outline on the room drawing you can see *if* the sofa fits and *where.* Also measure each window (they might be of slightly different sizes) for curtains and draperies.

Allow time for deliveries. Except when you buy a floor sample (the actual piece on display at the store), or a standard, generally inexpensive item stocked in a warehouse, your furniture will be ordered specially from the factory. Cutting, assembling, and transporting it may take six to eight weeks.

Arrange furniture for convenience and beauty. Failure to consider both needs together is a very common mistake. Don't crowd any room, especially with large pieces that are difficult to move. In your plan create "conversation groups" of furniture so your guests can talk to one another naturally. Have a coffee table for your sofa and small tables near each chair for snacks, ash trays, etc. Arrange lamps for good lighting, avoiding both glare and dark, unlighted corners. Leave enough space for easy passage through doorways and from one side of the room to another.

Balance heavy pieces to please the eye. A large sofa on one wall, with nothing as big opposite, makes a room seem to tilt. But a smaller piece of a dark color may balance it visually, because dark colors look heavier. A large picture or hanging on the opposite wall also may give balance. Always place rugs or large furniture at right angles to the wall, not "catty corner." Use your room drawing and colored paper outlines for experiment, to avoid misjudgments and the back-breaking job of pushing heavy pieces around to fit.

FURNISHING A BACHELOR APARTMENT

The career girl—or a bachelor—who lives in a small apartment is often faced with making one room plus bath and Pullman kitchen serve as three: bedroom, sitting room, and dining room. The illusion of space can be created by careful shopping for furniture and by simple uncluttered decorating. Here are some ideas:

Buy a divan (*a* in plan) which slides part way under a fitted table top. Placed in a corner with a lamp on the table (*b*), the combination resembles a sofa with end table. At night the divan is pulled out for sleeping. A second divan can be added on the other wall (*c*) to create a conversation corner.

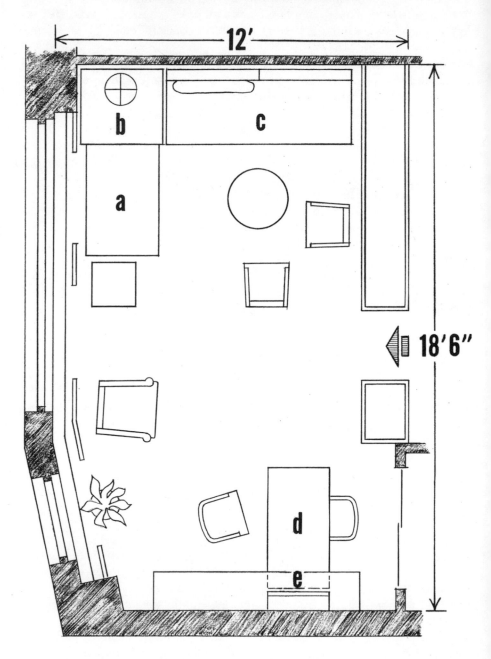

Cover the divans to match the walls, making them less conspicuous. But paint one wall a different color from the other three to add dimension to the room, and choose a contrasting color as floor covering.

At the opposite end of the room a portable table can be pulled out for meals or work (*d*). When not in use it can be stored part way under a laminated-plastic wall-hung shelf (*e*) which can also serve as a buffet.

Cove lighting behind a stained-glass panel can be used to give the illusion of daylight shimmering through.

Mirrors placed on opposite walls so that they reflect each other will add depth to your room.

A sofa and four chairs can be fitted into a room only 11 feet by 15½ feet without crowding if they are small in scale and simple in design. These qualities are essential in a room of this size, but they also make the pieces easily usable in a future, larger home. Here again your dual mirrors will help to create a seemingly endless vista.

A captain's chest can be fitted into a niche created by a built-in bookshelf, and it can be flanked by storage cupboard units.

FURNITURE BUYING GUIDE | See also FURNISHING A HOME

First make a list of furnishings room by room, the following being typical of the items usually needed:

LIVING ROOM

1 sofa or day bed	4 lamp tables (2 flanking sofa, 1 for each large chair)
2 large easy chairs	
2 light pull-up armchairs	1 large coffee or cocktail table
1 desk or writing table	1 magazine stand or nest of tables

DINING ROOM (if separate)

1 adjustable table seating 8	1 serving table, sideboard, console, or chest for service
8 chairs (including 2 armchairs)	

(*Note:* Cover armchairs to match living-room chairs; use as extras.)

HALL

1 console or chest with mirror above it	2 chairs or 1 bench

BEDROOM

1 double bed, or twin beds	2 night tables holding lamps
1 chest, or 1 double or triple chest	1 or 2 side chairs
1 dressing table with bench	1 large chair with ottoman to match

WOOD FURNITURE

A widespread misconception is that furniture made of solid pieces of wood is somehow better than veneered furniture, which is made of thinly sliced laminated woods. The veneer is the visible surface layer, made of choice wood with a decorative grain. Each has its advantages. Veneered wood has distinctive patterns, and modern adhesive techniques assure durability. Solid wood is heavier and lends itself to carved or shaped surfaces; also in better grades it can be refinished more satisfactorily.

A matched set of furniture for a flat price often seems attractive. But decorators point out that matching woods may become monotonous and seem unimaginative. Different styles and woods can often be mixed attractively, and you may want to collect one piece at a time.

The furniture style you choose depends on personal taste and preferences. Rely on your own judgment; furniture should reflect your personality, not that of friends or neighbors, or relatives. If you like casual living, you probably will be attracted to furniture with contemporary lines. If you are more conservative, you may want traditional styles. Features to check when you shop for furniture:

The wood should have an attractive, interesting grain. All visible surfaces should be smooth to the touch and free of scratches and dents. Veneered surfaces should be expertly matched. The finish should be clean and clear, uniform in color, and pleasing to the eye. A well-rubbed, fine finish usually has a soft gleam; a high gloss or shiny finish is currently not very fashionable.

Rock the furniture to test for sturdy construction. There should be no wobble. Heavier pieces indicate thicker panels and greater strength.

Examine the backs of chests and cabinets. Higher grade furniture will have a sturdy back panel stained close to the front finish. Low priced case goods use backs of unfinished fiberboard.

Inside joints must be fitted tightly and perfectly, with no gaps. Look carefully at the drawers; they tell a great deal about quality. Interlocking dovetail joints indicate good construction. In superior furniture, drawer sides are dovetailed to front and back. In less expensive pieces, only the front may be dovetailed and the back fitted as tongue and groove. Drawers should have a single center guide with little side-to-side play, and should slide smoothly without hitting the case anywhere. To be dustproof, each drawer section should be separated from the adjacent drawer by a solid panel. Inside surfaces should be lacquered and smooth to the touch.

Open furniture doors to make sure they hang properly and do not drag on the frame.

Do not overlook hardware on furniture—handles, drawer pulls, and keyhole plates. They should be sturdy and well proportioned, and should harmonize with the furniture style.

Elegant furniture with fine details is usually more expensive. In buying a piece you should consider how much use it will receive, and how long you want it to last.

UPHOLSTERED FURNITURE

Be careful not to confuse size with comfort; a small, well-designed chair may fit the body better than a huge one. Test for comfort by sitting, and decide whether firmness or softness in cushions is best for you and your husband. Choose simple lines, not only for style but for ease of care. Avoid bulging curves, curlicues on the arms, and conspicuous, bumpy legs.

Good upholstered furniture is an investment you must make largely on faith, since you can't see construction details inside it. Go to a dealer you can trust. Choose first-class construction in a sofa you will keep for years. If it is necessary to economize, buy less expensive side chairs or accessories you will one day replace. Here are features to check:

The traditional overstuffed chair or sofa of better quality has a sturdy frame built of seasoned, kiln-dried hardwood. The parts are fitted together with tightly-doweled and glued joints, reinforced with triangular corner blocks which are glued and screwed to the frame. Interwoven across the seat area are strips of jute webbing three to four inches wide. In this webbing a coil-spring unit is placed. Sometimes coil springs are inserted individually, then carefully tied in place with twine. An alternative is the prefabricated spring unit in a metal frame. The depth of the springs is the key factor, determining how deeply and comfortably you can sink into the seat. Durability depends on how well the frame is made and how securely the springs are fastened.

In more modern styles, with their slimmer lines, shorter and firmer coil springs must be used. Medium and low priced lines often employ the convoluted (zigzag) springs or flexible steel bands instead. Springs must be made of high-carbon steel, tempered to maintain resilience. Convoluted spring construction is generally firmer and does not allow for that deep sinking-in produced by coil springs.

To prevent filler material working between the springs, tough, durable, insulator material is used. It may consist of, singly or in combination, burlap, steel wires, sisal (plain, loomed, or rubberized), or hair or felt pads. Next comes the filling to provide shape. Curled animal hair, long considered standard for filling, has lost ground to urethane and polyester fibers. Some makers use a heavy layer of felted cotton instead of the filling.

The padding, just under the covering fabric, furnishes final shape and surface resilience. Cotton felt or roll urethane are the usual choices today. Cotton padding can be made more resilient by chemically treating with resin. Another quality, durable construction utilizes molded sections of cored foam rubber. Urethane foam, unless properly formulated, tends to lose shape with time and use, particularly in seating applications.

Higher-priced, custom or decorator-upholstered pieces are often "double-covered"—first in muslin, then in upholstery fabric. Such pieces hold their shape better and are easier to re-cover. Sateen may be used in lieu of muslin and then slipcovered, providing seasonal changes.

QUALITY POINTS

Reversible cushions. Many have zippered covers so welt seams can be straightened to conform to the cushion shape whenever necessary. The fabric used to cover the seat deck—the area on which the cushion rests—should be, if not the same, at least as sturdy as the fabric used on visible parts. Cambric, which is lightweight, is used on lower-grade furniture.

Trim tailoring with straight, welted seams. Fabric should be smooth, without wrinkles or puckers. Note what happens to it when you sit. Fabric should be stretched taut, but not so tight that it won't give slightly when you sit on it. If the furniture has a skirt, it should be neatly hemmed and even all around.

Compare weight of similar pieces. Heavier pieces obviously have more inside them, and usually are of better quality.

Bounce up and down to check whether the seat thoroughly cushions you against the inner construction of the chair. Push against the back sprints too.

CUSHION TYPES

Latex foam made from natural and synthetic rubber is molded directly into final shape and stays in shape under constant use. It costs more than urethane foam but its wearing qualities are outstanding.

Urethane foam, made from chemicals, is often referred to as polyurethane or polyfoam. Avoid the very lightweight ones—they tend to "hollow out" and won't keep their shape.

Synthetic fiber-fills like Dacron, Kodel, Fortrel and Vycron (polyester fibers) have excellent resilience and are nonallergenic and mothproof. Sometimes wrapped around a core of urethane foam to give the cushion inner firmness and outer softness.

Feathers and down are generally comfortable. The more feathers, the firmer (and usually more desirable) the cushioning. All down is almost too soft. The 80 per cent feathers-20 per cent down combination and the 50/50 combinations are good. See PILLOWS in this book.

FABRIC FINISHES

Many upholstery fabrics are treated with a stain-resistant finish and are so labeled. Because so many stains, especially oily ones, are difficult to remove, you will find treated fabrics worth consideration. But remember that even finishes don't work miracles. All stains should be attended to immediately, even when there's a finish on the fabric. If you wait until the stain has set or changed chemically you'll find that many will never come out.

FABRIC FACTS

Fabrics that wear best are closely and firmly woven of tightly twisted yarns. Those made of fluffy, loosely-spun yarns (often shaggy on the surface) cannot be expected to give as good wear, though they can be decoratively interesting.

When you buy damask fabrics, avoid patterns with very long floating threads on the surface. These can easily catch, especially if your household includes small children or pets. To check firmness of fabric, tug on a corner in both lengthwise and crosswise directions to be certain the yarns don't shift easily.

As for fibers, cotton, rayon, acetate, and nylon are found extensively in upholstery fabrics. Many fabrics are blends of two or more fibers. At least 25 per cent nylon is needed in a blend to contribute appreciably to its strength. Some fabrics have one kind of fiber on the surface side and another on the back. For example, 100 per cent **nylon pile** means that the wearing surface of such fabrics as frieze or velvet is nylon, but the back could be a different fiber. **Nylon face** describes a flat fabric woven so that most of the wearing surface is nylon even though other fibers are used in the weave. In a **nylon warp,** the lengthwise yarns are nylon but those running crosswise are some other fiber.

Bright, intense colors such as turquoise and orange tend to show fading more and faster. Remember any color is apt to fade if exposed to continuous strong sunlight. Fabrics with solution-dyed fibers or exceptionally fast dyes are good choices.

Brocade. Has a raised pattern, usually floral, with background contrast in texture or color.

Matelasse. Also a raised pattern, more puffed than brocade. Pattern may be monocromatic or multicolored.

Damask. A flat-surfaced cloth on which weave variations form the pattern. Color effects on the reverse side are opposite from the ones on the wearing surface.

Frieze. A looped pile fabric. Pattern is varied by cut or uncut loops of different heights.

Tweed. A term describing a wide range of rough-textured fabrics with a mixed color effect.

Supported vinyl. Embossed or smooth plastic with a knit or woven backing to give it strength and durability.

Sateen. A strong lustrous fabric, usually all-cotton, plain or printed. The sheen is woven in.

DELAYED FURNITURE DELIVERY

A wait of six to eight weeks is understandable for custom furniture. But why the long wait for standard lines?

The tremendous variety of styles offered makes it impossible for any furniture or department store to keep large supplies of every line on hand. A few of the most popular styles—generally inexpensive ones—may be stocked in the warehouse, but most of them have to be ordered from the factory. The pieces aren't put together until a specific order is received. Why? Because so many choices of parts, such as fabrics and leg shapes, are offered that there may be more than a hundred variations on a single style. It would be costly and wasteful to make up all possible combinations; there's not enough space to store them.

A factory usually has facilities for cutting just a certain number of parts for one style at a time. If one of the items you order is out of stock, you may have to wait for the next cutting. This applies to case goods—wooden furniture, such as desks and dressers—as well as to upholstered pieces. However, you have a better chance of quick delivery of case goods, which are more likely to be stocked in quantity.

FURNITURE CARE |

REUPHOLSTERING

Reupholstering means more than just new fabric. When an upholsterer does a thorough job, he starts by stripping the furniture down to its wood frame. He tightens springs, reinforces and braces the frame, puts in new filling or padding if needed, and touches up the wood surfaces. After he's finished, you have an entirely new piece of furniture on the old frame.

The chair or couch may feel firmer and the cushions seem higher than before. Allow for some normal flattening and softening after you've used the piece for a while. A careless upholsterer might use too much filling, giving the piece a heavier look than you want, or skimp on the covering fabric so that it pulls at the seams. Specify the kind of cushion filling desired or the upholsterer might use his standard type—usually cotton felt.

WOOD FURNITURE

Wood furniture of all types needs regular dusting, periodic polishing, and an occasional special cleaning. Effective dusting may be done with a vacuum cleaner, since its soft brush picks up gritty particles which can scratch the surface when rubbed.

If you use dustcloths, select a soft, nonlinty, absorbent material such as flannel, cheesecloth, or even old diapers. There also are specially treated cloths which polish at the same time, and ones that attract and hold dust but contain no wax or polish. Do not use nylon or other synthetics, or any open-mesh, coarse, or "scratchy" fabric. Wash dustcloths after each use. A handy, aerosol product sprayed on your dustcloth or mop attracts dust like a magnet and keeps it from flying.

If furniture surfaces receive hard use—as on dining, cocktail, or end tables —polish at least once a month. Less used pieces need this protection two or three times a year. On high-luster woods the polish may be a liquid that is sprayed or wiped on, then wiped off with very little rubbing; a cream wax or polish; or one of the liquid and paste waxes that need to be buffed vigorously. All perform well to restore gloss and make furniture easier to clean (but see oiled finishes, below).

When the finish becomes sticky from fingermarks, etc., give it a light, quick sudsing—using very little water—and dry thoroughly. Then polish or wax it. Also see *hazing*, below.

Oiled furniture finishes, such as Danish teak and American walnut, have a subdued luster and require an oil polish containing little or no wax. Pour a little on a soft cloth (*not* on the furniture itself), apply it to a small area at a time, and rub just enough to loosen the dirt. Before the creamy film dries, polish with another soft, clean cloth.

To remove a hazy film, mix one tablespoonful of vegetable oil, one tablespoonful of pure turpentine, and one pint of warm water. Dampen a lintless cloth with this solution and rub a small area with the grain of the wood. Rub off immediately with a dry cloth, and buff.

When low-luster furniture becomes badly soiled, experts give it this more elaborate treatment: Mix boiled linseed oil (sold as such) and pure turpentine in equal parts, in a container you can cover and store for future use. Apply a thin film to a small area, then buff hard with a lintless cloth, until any feeling of an oily residue disappears. Repeat whenever routine dusting seems inadequate—every four to six months.

Hazing is a cloudy, smeary film which dulls a high luster. It may result from polishing too heavily or too often. To help prevent this, apply any furniture-care product lightly, and don't spare the buffing to distribute and harden the wax. Eventually, a build-up of wax may have to be removed. Use a special paste cleaner, sold in auto supply stores, and apply it as directed on the label. Then repolish the furniture.

Checking, a crisscross pattern of fine hairline cracks, may be brought on by exposure to sunlight or extremes of temperature. Refinishing is the only cure.

Yellowing of bleached wood also is accelerated by sunlight (not, as many suppose, by the color of a particular polish or wax). If the color change occurs evenly, it may not be displeasing; if it is patchy, consider refinishing.

Sticking of plastic film to wood may occur with tablecloths, doilies, or place mats under certain conditions of heat, humidity, and pressure. Plastic clings tenaciously, and if the finish is damaged, refinishing will be necessary. Try rubbing it off with a *dry* steel-wool soap pad, but very gently and only if the wood is well finished.

Pianos should be rubbed with the grain of the wood when cleaning or waxing. Wipe the keys (whether ivory or plastic) with a soft, slightly dampened cloth, adding a little mild soap or detergent to the water. Use a separate cloth for the black keys, rub gently backward and forward, not from side to side. Clean a few keys at a time, drying with a soft cloth. Ivory keys turn yellow in total darkness; to prevent this, leave the keyboard open to the light.

The delicate, complicated interior parts of the instrument are sensitive to heat, dampness, and sudden changes in temperature. Too much heat may cause the sounding board to dry and split, while moisture may cause wooden parts to warp and the keys to stick. Choose a location for the piano away from radiators or an open fireplace, and also away from open windows and doors where moist air or cold drafts may blow.

Since the strings are affected by these changes in climate, the piano needs regular tuning whether played or not—four times during its first year, twice a year thereafter. A neglected or very old piano may require regulating and voicing, two rather expensive expert jobs.

Curbing humidity in the home helps preserve fine wood furniture, as well as the piano and your TV set. An air conditioner condenses some of the moisture inside the house and disperses it to the outside air. In a dehumidifier the water drains off or collects in a tray. On hot, sticky days avoid *adding* moisture to the already humid air by following these practices:

Take tub baths instead of showers. Baths add less moisture to the air.

Choose menus that keep cooking to a minimum, and cook early in the day. Cover utensils while food is cooking and do not permit unnecessary boiling and steaming. A hood fan over your range, vented outside, will draw out moisture from cooking, as well as grease and odors. And a ceiling or wall exhaust fan will remove steam from the kitchen or bath.

If your clothes dryer is not vented, avoid running it on a humid day—a washer load of clothes sheds about one gallon of water in drying. If you must do a wash by hand, roll things out in towels before hanging. Towels then should be dried outdoors.

If your basement tends to be damp, open the windows in dry weather and close them on humid days. A dehumidifier can be helpful in the basement and in other moisture-gathering areas that can be closed off. Attic vents should be open to allow air to circulate.

LAMINATED PLASTIC

These materials, familiar on kitchen countertops, today are also used on dinette tables, coffee tables, children's furniture, and sometimes on decorative pieces in smooth or wood-grained patterns. The colors and patterns are sealed under hard, clear melamine and will not fade or come off. Merely wipe the surface clean with a damp or sudsy sponge and towel dry. But it is important to avoid cutting or roughening the smooth surface, as with a sharp knife or abrasive cleaners.

Do not set hot pans on plastic. Although it will shed most stains, certain dyes (such as grocery price stamps) may be transferred if the plastic is wet. If this happens, sparingly use scouring powder or a chlorine bleach to remove the stain, or make a paste of scouring powder and water, apply, let it sit for half an hour, then wipe off.

Laminates may be waxed or polished like wood furniture for a higher gloss. To avoid streakiness from light reflections, first wash the plastic with fairly hot water containing a little water softener (to remove old coats of wax). Wash and rinse a small area at a time and polish it dry. Then apply a thin coat of creamy polish or spray-on furniture wax, following label directions.

MARBLE

Marble is highly subject to food and drink stains, which leave a film. Remove stains with a special marble stain remover; or make a thick paste of hot water and scouring powder. Wet the marble with hot water, then spread the paste about a half inch deep over the stain. Let it stand a day or two until completely dry. Cover the paste with a damp cloth to remove it; then rinse marble and wipe dry.

OUTDOOR FURNITURE

Wood outdoor furniture will roughen and stain unless sanded and then sealed with exterior paint, or with wood sealer and/or varnish for a natural finish. Clean it periodically with thick soap or detergent suds and a brush, rinsing well. If rain water is not allowed to stand on it, yearly refinishing seldom is necessary.

Rattan, wicker, reed, or cane actually benefit from air dampness, but rain or direct sun are harmful and the furniture is best used under shelter. Refinish, if necessary, with enamel or varnish.

Aluminum furniture will not rust and usually needs only an occasional hosing or wiping off with a damp cloth. Rub any pitted surfaces with a damp steel-wool soap pad, and protect them from corrosion with a light waxing.

Steel outdoor furniture, also the tubular steel used in casual indoor furniture, will rust unless properly treated. However, the newer paints and baked-on coatings are extremely durable unless scratched or chipped (much like the body finish of an automobile). Clean off rust streaks with steel wool; repaint with a metal primer and outdoor enamel. To prevent rust stains on the floor from legs or bottom edges of steel furniture, either refinish the points of contact or cover them with plastic tape in matching color. (Some furniture already has a similar protection.)

Wrought iron of top quality can take dampness or rain for years without rusting. A light waxing will protect it. If rusty scratches do appear, touch up as described for steel.

Canvas duck may be scrubbed in place with brush and suds, or, if removed from frame for machine washing, replace it while still damp to allow drying in original shape. If faded, apply paintlike dyes, and brush on a sealing coat after the dye has dried.

Plastic, vinyl, and **cloth** coverings for outdoor furniture can often be wiped clean, or may be washed with household cleaner and sponge, then rinsed with a garden hose. Strips of webbing or cord may be purchased if needed for repair.

FURS | See also CLOTHING, WHAT TO WEAR

In one form or another, furs form an important part of almost every woman's wardrobe: a fur scarf, stole, bag, belt, beret, or—prized possession —a fur coat. Because of their cost and the relatively long life of a fur garment, buying furs is a form of investment to be made with care. Here is some sound counsel on this exciting subject:

Before you set out to shop, consider the color that will do the most for your wardrobe (and for you, too, of course)—beige, gray, deep brown, or black. Decide on the silhouette you want, as well. Box jackets or tunic-length coats, for instance, are fine with slim skirts but not with full ones. It's best to lean toward simple lines; they look right over more kinds of clothes, and your fur investment won't go out of style too quickly. On the other hand, you might be more venturesome with a casual, inexpensive fur you'll wear almost daily, to and from the market or the office.

For big or little fur investments, it's wise to shop around and compare, and to deal, always, with a reliable store or furrier. Look for thin spots in the fur. Examine the pelts to see that they match in color, texture, and depth. Make sure such hard-wear areas as sleeves, cuffs, collars, pockets, and hems are of thick, full fur. See that the pelts are soft and supple. Be sure to steer clear of unlikely bargains. Ask for advice. It's free, and many fur salesmen are very knowledgeable.

Study the hangtags for the plain and fancy facts about furs. The government requires that labels must give the true English name of the animal that produced the fur, and the name of the country of origin of all imported furs. The result may not be so glamorous as fur names in the old, happy-go-lucky days, but you'll know what you're getting.

If a fur product is composed in whole or in substantial part of paws, tails, bellies, sides, flanks, or gills, that too must be on the tag. If it is composed of or contains used or second-hand fur, these facts must be stated. If some or all of the fur is dyed, tip dyed, or bleached, the tag must say so.

FUR TERMINOLOGY

Here are terms used to describe furs:

Blending or tip dyeing. The process of applying dye to the tips of the guard hairs to produce more uniform color.

Bleaching. The process used to remove an off-color cast from white furs or lighten dark furs to dye them a lighter shade.

Letting out. An elaborate process used on mink, muskrat, or other skins—cutting and resewing the pelts to make them longer and narrower. The resulting long strips emphasize the darker color in the center of the back.

Glazing. A method of giving or restoring luster to furs.

Guard hairs. The long, lustrous top hairs which protect the soft, more perishable underfur.

Moiré. The wavy pattern in small rippled designs on lamb, kid, and pony skins.

Mutation. Some animals—mink and foxes primarily—are specially bred on ranches to produce various shades and colors. Some of the mink mutations made available by EMBA (a mink breeders association) are Aeolian, Arcturus, Argenta, Autumn Haze, Azurene, Diadem, Cerulean, Lunaraine, Jasmine, Lutetia, Morning Light, Rovalia, and Tourmaline.

Prime. The condition of peltries taken when both skin and fur are at their best development, which is usually in midwinter.

Rosettes. Petal-shaped marks on leopard, ocelot, jaguar, and cheetah skins.

Skin-on-skin describes the sewing together of pelts without changing their length or width.

Taping. Applying tape on the leather side of skin to maintain the shape of the seam and the contours of the garment.

A WHO'S WHO OF FURS

(Key to price categories: *Inexpensive*—less than $500 for a full-length coat; *inexpensive to moderate*—$500 to $1,000; *moderate to expensive*—$1,000 to $2,000; *expensive*—over $2,000.)

American Broadtail-processed Lamb. Smart; also used for accessories; fairly durable. Inexpensive to moderate.

Australian Opossum. Smart; good durability. Moderate to expensive.

Beaver. Versatile daytime fur; gives excellent wear. Moderate to expensive.

Broadtail Lamb. Very smart; also used in accessories; low to fair durability. Expensive.

Canadian Sable. Inexpensive for scarves, moderate for coats.

Cheetah. One of the smart spotted furs. Also used for accessories. Fairly durable. Moderate to expensive.

Chinchilla. A fur aristocrat. Fairly durable. Expensive.

Ermine. Glamorous evening fur. Fairly durable. Expensive.

Fox. Natural white fox, red fox (usually dyed), blue fox, and mutation foxes are much used for accessories and trimming. Fair durability, but shedding must be expected. Stoles are inexpensive.

Guanaco or **Guanaquito.** A long-haired, honey-toned fur. Fairly durable. Inexpensive.

Jaguar. A spotted favorite, also used for accessories. Fair to good durability. Moderate to expensive.

Leopard. Somali leopard, the most familiar kind, is smart; also used for accessories. Fair to good durability. Expensive. Long-haired snow leopard has fair to good durability and is expensive.

Marten. Rarely used for coats. Baum marten and stone marten give good wear; scarves and stoles are inexpensive to moderate.

Mink. The symbol of luxury. Also used for accessories. Has good durability. Expensive. Coats of mink paws, sides, or gills often have a smart, young look, and good durability. Inexpensive to moderate.

Mouton (processed lamb). Good durability. Inexpensive.

Muskrat. Versatile; has good durability. Costs more when skins are let out. Inexpensive to moderate.

Nutria. Smart; good durability. Moderate to expensive.

Ocelot. A spotted favorite. Also used for accessories. Fair to good durability. Moderate to expensive.

Otter. Attractive sports fur with good durability. Moderate to expensive.

Persian Lamb. Versatile; good durability. Inexpensive to moderate.

Rabbit. Fair durability. Inexpensive. Also used for linings and trimming accessories. In glamour treatments, resembles chinchilla and cost may rise to moderate.

Raccoon. Attractive sports fur, mainly let out nowadays, which places its price in "moderate" category. Good durability. Used for accessories and trimmings, too. Raccoon sheared in the manner of beaver and then dyed makes durable coats. Moderate.

Sable. Russian sable. The aristocrat. Good durability. Scarves are moderate in price; coats, expensive (very!).

Seal. Alaska sealskin is handsome, has good durability; moderate to expensive. Cape seal has fair durability; inexpensive to moderate. Hair seal, a smart sports fur, has fair to good durability; inexpensive to moderate.

Spotted cat. Smart; also used for accessories. Fair to good durability. Inexpensive to moderate.

FUR CARE

The care you give your furs is vital to protecting your investment. Even fragile furs will keep their looks and usefulness longer when they have tender care. Here are the most important rules:

Always hang a fur coat or jacket on a wide,well-made hanger that conforms to the shape of its collar and shoulders. A good hanger relieves strain on shoulder seams. Don't hang furs in garment bags. They need freely circulating air or they will dry out. And never hang furs on a hook.

When you're caught in rain or snow, always hang wet furs in a cool, well-ventilated room, away from heat. Excessive heat dries out the oils in the leather. If the fur has been soaked, it should be sent as soon as possible to a good furrier to be restored.

Avoid prolonged exposure to direct sunlight; this too may dry out the oils in the leather and fade the color.

Try not to carry your handbag or parcels in the same position day after day. Steady friction in one place will cause worn spots on a coat.

Remember not to slide in and out of automobile seats. This also causes worn spots, particularly in delicate furs.

Don't pin flowers or jewelry on your furs.

Never brush or comb furs.

Unfasten your coat and loosen it about the shoulders when you sit down, to prevent strain.

Inspect furs regularly for rips and tears, and have a furrier make repairs immediately to avoid further damage.

Never use cleaning fluids on fur; they dry out the leather.

Never douse furs with perfume or cologne. They dry the leather and stiffen the guard hairs.

Furs should be professionally cleaned once a year, to remove accumulated dust and soil and restore the leather, and they should be reglazed to bring back the luster.

In warm weather, furs should be stored in a modern cold-storage plant where temperature and humidity are kept at the proper level. Good fur storage provides that furs are hung so they have room to "breathe." Be sure you receive a statement of the insurance placed on the garment at your declared valuation. Keep the receipt in a safe place. The insurance should cover loss from fire, water, theft, moths, and any other damage to the fur while it is in storage.

GARBAGE DISPOSERS |

Food-waste disposers—units installed beneath the kitchen sink that shred garbage to a fine pulp and flush it down the drain—have come into wide use. Though a few cities forbid them on the grounds that the sewage system or water supply is inadequate, in some sixty communities they are now required in all new and extensively remodeled houses.

In the continuous-feed type, you turn on the switch and the cold-water tap and keep feeding the garbage into the disposer as long as you like. In the cover-switch or batch-feed type, you fill the disposer, lock the cover in place to start the grinding, and turn on the cold water.

The first type is faster and more convenient when there's lots of food to dispose of. The second offers extra safety, because nothing can be accidentally dropped into it once the cover is in place.

Disposers will handle almost any kind of food waste, including fruit rinds, vegetable tops, coffee grounds, etc. Most disposers will also take bones. They cannot handle hard sea-food shells, foil, cans or bottles, cardboard containers, or gum.

Average capacity for any one load is one to three quarts. They destroy it in a few seconds (for soft food) to five minutes (for fruit pits or large bones).

Disposers do make noise—from a low hum for soft foods to (in uninsulated types) a loud, almost frightening banging or grating for hard bones. De luxe models feature insulation that cuts the normal noise level in half.

Exercise some care in loading the disposer; forcing large amounts into it may cause it to jam. Big pieces, such as melon or citrus-fruit rinds or corncobs, should be first cut or broken into smaller sections. Fibrous materials, such as pea pods or corn husks, should be mixed with other waste.

Disposers are self-cleaning—just let the motor and cold water continue to run for 15 to 20 seconds after the waste disappears. (For fibrous waste, let them run for a full two minutes.) If onions or some other strong food leave an odor, grinding a lemon or orange rind or a tray of ice cubes should eliminate it. Once a week, flush the drain line by filling the sink with water, then removing the stopper. Never use drain-cleaning chemicals in a disposer; they may damage the mechanism.

Most properly installed disposers are perfectly safe so long as normal caution is observed. Don't let children play with the unit, and never reach inside while the motor is running. Watch for silver when scraping dishes as these pieces if accidentally dropped into the disposer can damage it.

A disposer can also be used with a septic tank. If the capacity of your present tank meets recommended standards for the size of your home (two bedrooms, 750 gallons; three bedrooms, 900 gallons, etc.), it will take the additional waste from a disposer without trouble. However, you should clean the tank a year or so earlier than you normally would, and you should not put collected grease or fats through the disposer.

The list price for disposers ranges from $50 to $160. The more expensive models feature harder cutting blades, larger capacity, faster operation, and noise insulation. Cost of installation varies from about $30 to $65. Because the installation must meet local plumbing and electrical codes, it's usually inadvisable to tackle the job yourself.

Disposers are not expensive to operate. Their water consumption averages 1½ to 2 gallons of water per person per day. (For comparison, one flushing of a toilet consumes 6 to 8 gallons.) Total annual operating cost of a disposer, in one West Coast city, is estimated not to exceed $1.50.

GASOLINE AND OIL |

Women who buy gasoline and oil for the family automobile are faced with a variety of products which they may find confusing. Automobile fuels are not just simply gasoline. They are a complicated mixture of gasoline with chemical compounds adjusted several times each year to seasonal and regional differences in driving conditions. Fuels also are adjusted to the engine designs of the different makes of car.

GRADES OF GASOLINE

Automobile manufacturers suggest in the owners' manual the grade of gasoline to use for the most efficient engine operation. A majority of cars, particularly the low-priced standards and compacts, are designed to use **regular-grade** gasoline. Bigger, more expensive cars may require **premium-grade** fuel; some with special engines use **super-premium.**

Gasoline prices can differ considerably from area to area depending on distribution costs, taxes, or competition among suppliers and dealers. The difference in price between grades depends on performance qualities built into the gasoline, including **octane number.** This number indicates the ability of a gasoline to burn properly in an engine without knocking (a series of sharp pings or clicks when you accelerate or climb a hill). Most regular grades have an octane number between 90 and 94. Premium grades average about 99 and super-premium, 100-102. Knocking can usually be eliminated by using a higher grade gasoline. You can determine your car's fuel requirements by this procedure:

Have the spark timing set to the manufacturer's recommendation.

When the gasoline tank is almost empty, fill it with regular.

If the engine knocks, on your next refill add one-half tank of premium to one-half regular, or go to a dealer who sells an in-between grade.

If there is still a ping or knock, try a full tank of premium.

In this way, you can find the grade of fuel that's best for your car at the lowest price. Premium grades of gasoline usually contain a wider variety of additives for prevention of corrosion, rust, and deposits. (They are usually a distinctive color, but this is due to identifying dyes and does not indicate the quality of the gasoline. By law, a dye must be added to any fuel containing lead, a principal antiknock compound.)

GRADES OF MOTOR OIL

Buying the proper motor oil also is important to the operation of your car. To make selection easier, automobile manufacturers recommend the types each car should use under different driving conditions. Service classifications set by the American Petroleum Institute, a trade association of oil companies, serve as a guide to buyers. All car manufacturers today, foreign and domestic, recommend using an oil certified by the supplier as satisfactory for *Service MS* (most severe). Types labeled *MM* (moderate service) or *ML* (light service) are still available for old-model cars, but their proper application to driving conditions requires a bit of know-how. Since modern cars use relatively little oil, any saving on cheaper grades rarely justifies taking the risk of impaired performance or durability of the engine.

In addition to type, oil is graded as to viscosity, or thickness, by standards set by the Society of Automotive Engineers. Commonly used are SAE 5W, 10W, 20W; 20 and 30; and a combination of these grades (for example, SAE 10-W30). The "W" indicates winter use. Lower numbers indicate thin oil; higher numbers, thicker oil. The multigrade oils, also called "all weather" (such as 10W-30), are designed to do the job of several SAE grades.

GOOD WAYS TO SAVE ON GASOLINE COSTS

Are you getting as much mileage as possible from the gasoline you buy? Most drivers do not. The American Automobile Association says that miles per gallon can vary as much as 50 per cent for identical cars using the same gasoline.

Three basic factors determine gas mileage: design of the car (engine, transmission, total weight, and powered accessories); driving methods; and car care.

The first, of course, is a one-time decision made when you purchase a car. If you buy a two-ton, eight-cylinder auto, you obviously plan to forego some gasoline economy for power and comfort.

Mileage drops and costs rise as speed increases. At 70 miles per hour, you use 25 per cent more fuel than at 45. Avoid fast starts. Accelerate smoothly with as light a foot on the gas pedal as possible. Try to drive at steady, constant speeds. The most economical range is from 25 to 40 mph.

As you drive, look and plan ahead. Slow gradually by easing off the accelerator when you see a stop sign in the next block. Try to get into high gear (the most economical) as quickly as possible. This is relatively simple with a manual shift. If you have an automatic transmission, a gentle, steady pressure on the gas pedal will get your car into high quickly. Do not idle your motor more than necessary. In cold weather, get moving quickly, but drive slowly until the motor warms.

MAINTENANCE TIPS

Although car care may be your husband's responsibility, you also should realize the need for regular maintenance. Oil should be changed periodically to assure good lubrication and preserve the engine from contaminants.

Owners' manuals today recommend oil-change intervals much longer than formerly (up to every 6,000 miles), made possible by improved oil filters. There are conditions requiring more frequent changes, however; and the American Petroleum Institute says it's safest to change oil at least every 60 days, regardless of mileage. Constant, short-distance, stop-and-go driving is hard on oil.

Not only to save fuel but for good performance, the motor should be tuned every 5,000 to 10,000 miles. Carburetor and ignition timing should be checked. Spark plugs must be cleaned, tested, and replaced when needed. It has been estimated that faulty spark plugs can waste one gallon of gas in every 10.

Most cars have automatic chokes which can stick and waste gas. The air filter should be cleaned or replaced as necessary. It should be checked with every oil change. Tires should be kept inflated at least to the pressures recommended by the car manufacturer. Underinflated tires increase fuel use and tire wear.

Poor wheel alignment also wastes gasoline and causes excessive tire wear, in addition to creating a steering hazard. If a front tire shows signs of uneven wear, have the alignment checked.

GLASSWARE | See also WINES AND LIQUORS

The expression "clear as glass" can't be applied to the subject of glassware itself. Whether you're shopping for tableware or decorative glass, you'll be confronted with a whole maze of terms. Some describe the process of manufacture or decoration; others refer to the substances added to the basic ingredient of glass (usually sand) to give it special qualities.

Crystal and **lead crystal** are popular names for glass to which lead oxide has been added. Real crystal is actually quartz, a mineral that is not used for glassware. Lead oxide gives glass a characteristic brilliance. It produces a long-ringing tone when tapped.

Milk glass gets its white, milky color from tin oxide or fluorspar added to the mix. It is used for decorative pieces and tableware. Today, opaque glass tinted aqua, pink, and other colors is also called milk glass.

Colored glass is made by adding small amounts of metal oxides to the molten glass. Copper may produce green; cobalt, blue; iron, amber. Almost any type of glass can be colored.

Heat-resistant glass, of the kind used for ovenware, contains a small portion of boric oxide. This prevents its cracking at high temperatures.

Hand-blown glass is made by skilled craftsmen, who take a blob of molten glass on the end of a blow pipe and form it into the desired shape. More imaginative designs are possible when glass is blown by hand. Today, most blown glass is produced by machine.

Top row, left to right: Dolphin; Hobnail.

Bottom row, left to right: Daisy and Button; Hobnail; Setting Hen; Lattice; Lacy Sandwich (the forerunner of pattern glass).

Pressed glass is produced by forcing molten glass into a mold. It can be made by hand or by machine. Complicated or delicate shapes are usually made by hand.

Pattern glass is pressed glass made in an elaborately decorated mold; the term refers particularly to that made during the late 1800s. Patterns include conventional tableware, as well as novelties such as log cabins and top hats. Some of the patterns prized by collectors of antique glass are being reproduced today, and a few are even cast from the original molds. Some popular patterns are illustrated; others include: Thumbprint, Lincoln Drape, Candlewick, Lord's Supper Plate, and King's Crown.

Cut glass describes a sculptured, textured look, produced, in the best grades, by hand. The object is held against small, revolving abrasive wheels. Glass can also be cut entirely by machine.

Engraved glass may have a frosted look. Though the process is similar to cutting, the designs are free-hand and are shallower and more delicate. Sometimes the design of a famous artist is used. Less expensive engraved glass is produced by scratching with a diamond chip.

Etched glass is sometimes confused with engraved glass because the surface is cut into. The design, however, is produced chemically; the glass is simply dipped in an acid bath. (Portions not to be etched are protected by a wax coating.)

Embossed glass has its design raised in relief, thus giving the opposite effect from that produced by engraved glass.

Tears are decorative, deliberately produced bubbles in the bowls and stems of glasses. Air-twist stems have elongated tears.

Crackled glass is described by its name. When the piece is still hot, it's plunged into cold water. This causes the outer surface to break into an intricate, crackled pattern.

Cased glass, sometimes called overlay, is made of two layers of glass, usually color laid over clear. For a two-color effect, the top layer is cut through to the level of the clear glass.

Enameled glass is painted by hand and baked on. Sometimes powdered colored glass combined with oil is used and fused into the glass by firing at high temperatures. Glass may also be decorated with decals, which are baked on; or a design may be printed on by machine.

HERBS AND SPICES | See SEASONINGS

HOLIDAY DINNER | See also CARVING GUIDE; MAIDS; TABLE SETTINGS

Giving a big dinner for Thanksgiving or Christmas may be a young housewife's first experience in large-scale entertaining. It is not necessary to approach the occasion in fear and trembling. Instead, give some thought to careful preparation and let joy be unconfined. Following is a schedule based on expert experience that can be invaluable. Begin about a week before the party.

First, plan the exact menu. On the chance that there may be a delay in serving, plan foods that can wait and also those that can be cooked in dishes that are nice enough to serve in, such as casseroles. Choose recipes that can be completely or partly cooked in advance to eliminate last-minute chores. Make a market list and order your turkey or roast. Order floral materials for a table centerpiece.

Start clearing the refrigerator (use up leftovers) to make room for party foods. Start freezing extra ice cubes; store them in plastic bags or cardboard boxes in a freezer.

Launder and press the table linens you plan to use. Decide what silver, china, and glassware is needed, and arrange to borrow items you may not have. Set aside enough ash trays and coasters. Decide how to serve the dinner—completely at the table or as a sit-down buffet. If all guests are at one table, will you need an extra leaf for the table? You may want several tables for seating at a buffet-style dinner, or a small table for children.

Clean your house thoroughly so that it requires relatively little brushing up before the party.

Six days before the party, buy staples for the menu. If dessert is a pie, prepare and assemble it, then freezer-wrap; freeze; and bake it on party day. Or make up ice-cream balls of various flavors, roll them in coconut or crushed sugared cereal, freeze firm, then freezer-wrap. These can be taken directly from the freezer to the table without last-minute fuss.

Three days before the party, sharpen paring and carving knives; clean the silver you intend to use. Gather and clean extra folding chairs and tables. Make seating place cards if they are to be used.

In case the weather is bad, make certain you have enough space and coat hangers for guests' wet coats, boots, and umbrellas. Closet extenders, which hang outside a closet door, are useful. If your closet space is inadequate and beds are to be used, get several yards of plastic to protect the bedspreads. Cover a cardboard suit-box cover with foil, or use plastic trays for boots and rubbers.

Is it time to thaw a frozen turkey? A twenty-to-twenty-four-pound bird requires about three or four days to thaw in a refrigerator. Allow two or three days for a twelve-to-twenty-pound turkey, and one or two days for a four-to-twelve-pound bird.

Two days before the party, check the menu carefully. Buy the needed perishable foods, fruits, and vegetables.

Get picture storybooks, coloring books, or quiet toys to entertain children on party day. If they sit at a separate table, plan special party favors or table decorations.

One day before the party, vacuum, dust, and get your house in order. Take out serving dishes and serving silver. Place dessert dishes, cups on saucers, cream pitcher, sugar bowl, and silver on a side table or buffet. Arrange cocktail glasses on a tray; nearby, set up your cheese board and a tray for crackers, spreads, and dips. Collect materials for your centerpiece; if they are not perishable, arrange it. Set the table *now*. (Serve breakfast from trays or a small table on party day.)

Make the spreads and dips for appetizers, and refrigerate them. Prepare raw vegetable relishes and garnishes; refrigerate them in containers of ice water. Refrigerate olives, cans of cranberry sauce, and juices.

Prepare your salad. Tear greens, quarter tomatoes, slice cucumbers, scallions, etc.; place them in a plastic bag in the refrigerator crisper. You can toss the salad ingredients in a salad bowl, with dressing, shortly before serving. (Don't put the dressing on a green salad till time to serve it.) Molded vegetable or fruit salads are perfect do-aheads. Coleslaw and Waldorf-type salads improve in flavor if prepared ahead.

If you plan to stuff poultry, prepare, measure, wrap, and refrigerate the stuffing ingredients; toss them together and use to stuff the bird *just before it goes into the oven.*

Your refrigerator may be jammed with food by now. To get additional refrigeration space, use an insulated picnic carrier with an inner container for ice cubes or dry ice, for overnight storage or less-perishable foods.

Carefully check the menu and organize tomorrow's cooking schedule. Schedule a starting time for each item.

On the day of the party, concentrate on last-minute food preparation. Don't waste time sewing up the bird. Poultry today has smaller openings so stuffing stays in without stitches. The bridge of skin now left on birds also holds the legs tight against the body and tucked in place, eliminating the need for trussing. Leave the wing tips on. Just fold them under the body.

If the bird is too big for the roasting pan, tear off a sheet of heavy-duty aluminum foil large enough to fit under the turkey and protrude about six inches on all sides. Center the bird on the foil, then carefully place it on the rack in the roaster. Turn up the edges of the foil to prevent drippings from running out—and to save scrubbing the pan. Cover the bird lightly with foil to keep it warm on top of the range while making gravy. Cook the gravy about fifteen minutes before dinner, then keep it hot in a double boiler or on a "keep-warm" setting.

To measure coffee faster, use a measuring cup (one-quarter cup equals four tablespoons, one-half cup is eight tablespoons). If your coffeepot is too small, make a pot ahead of time and keep it hot over very low heat. Or use a twelve-cup carafe of heat-resistant glass on a candle-warmer base.

Save serving steps. Keep a tiered tea wagon or small table at your right to hold the salad, dessert, and beverage things until serving time. The bottom tier can be used for collecting dishes and food from the main course before serving dessert. Or place a tray on the buffet before dinner to collect food and dishes.

Save energy by serving the first course in the living room. Nibblers, dips, even glasses of juice or mugs of soup can begin the party.

Make cleanup easier. Group soiled dishes, silver, and utensils as compactly as possible. Set a bag next to the sink and scrape food into this bag when you bring dishes into the kitchen. Don't put anything into the sink. You just have to unload it at dishwashing time. Leave pots and pans on the range, out of the way.

HOME BUYING | See also HOME BUYING COSTS; HOME SELLING;
MORTGAGES

Buying or building a home is usually the biggest single investment that most families ever make. Because of this, a family usually spends considerable time deciding whether a new home meets its requirements in every detail. (See Check List for a New House below.)

CHECK THE NEIGHBORHOOD

The neighborhood must also be carefully considered. Experts advise the following be kept in mind:

Convenience. Will your home be close enough to shopping facilities, schools, the church of your preference, and recreation areas for children's play? Are transportation facilities good? You may find that although your husband can get to work conveniently, his commuting expenses may be considerably higher.

Community services. Does the neighborhood have adequate police and fire protection? Good public utilities are essential. These include garbage removal, electricity, gas, telephone, water, and sewage disposal. (In some areas, private arrangements must be made for some services.) In new neighborhoods, if streets are not yet paved and sidewalks and curbs are unfinished, find out whether there are plans to complete them.

Planning. Aside from being physically attractive, a neighborhood, according to many authorities, should have the advantages of good planning. Streets should be curved where possible and they should intersect at approximate right angles. Dead-end streets are advantageous with young children, but they should be wide enough for trucks to maneuver in. Streets should be well lighted and neighborhoods should not be intersected by main arteries.

Zoning regulations. Check on how close factories, service stations, or other commercial buildings are to the home you want to buy. Find out whether it is possible for someone to build such a building on a vacant lot on your block. You will want to avoid the noise and, in some instances, smoke and smells of commercial areas. Property values frequently decrease when industry moves into residential neighborhoods.

Inspection. It will take time to check all the points that make a neighborhood a desirable one. But the time will be well spent. Don't just drive through; walk around the area. If possible, talk to residents about the points on this check list. This also gives you an opportunity to find out something about your future neighbors. For instance, are they cordial, and do they take good care of their own homes?

CHECK LIST FOR A NEW HOUSE

Little things count too. Making sure the house you buy will be trouble-free is not simply a matter of shunning major pitfalls—things like a wet basement, inadequate storage space, or insufficient electrical power. There are many less obvious defects that can also spoil your pleasure. Some you may have to put up with to get other features you want, but it's better to know about them in advance than to have regrets. Beware of:

No opening in the front door or alongside it (such as a window) that permits you to see who's at the door when the bell rings.

No port roof or roof overhang above the front door to protect you or your guests in rainy weather while you're fumbling for your key or while they're waiting for you to answer their ring.

No light or electrical outlet on the porch or terrace.

A hard-luck driveway—one, for example, that exits onto a blind curve or slopes up to the street, which means you may be hopelessly stuck some cold morning.

An accident-inviting door that opens directly over the basement stairs.

Inconveniently located gas, electric, or water meters in the kitchen or basement, instead of outside or in the garage, where they can be read without your being disturbed.

No light switches at the entrance to rooms or no two-way switches at strategic locations, such as both ends of a hall and the top and bottom of a stairway.

Bathrooms placed squarely in the public view—at the head of the stairs, facing the front of the house, overlooking a terrace, or in sight of the living room.

Walls cut up by windows and doors in such a way that it's difficult to place furniture effectively (a common fault in bedrooms).

"Fish-bowl" picture windows—those that expose you to the gaze of neighbors and passers-by. (Some are effectively screened in summer by plantings but in fall and winter, when leaves have dropped, are left unprotected.)

A hard-to-open window over the kitchen sink—for example, the double-hung type. A horizontal, sliding window in this location would be better; a casement window, opened by a crank, best.

Windows in a child's room too low for safety, too high for him to see out of.

Child-trap closets—those that can't be opened from the inside.

Judo closets—those with doors so narrow it's impossible to reach into the corners without gymnastics. (Remember, too, that the backs of sliding doors can't be fitted with mirrors, clothes hooks, or shoe bags.)

Closets with shelves too high to reach, clothes poles so low they permit long garments to touch the floor.

Walls so thin or a floor plan so open that privacy is difficult or impossible.

Noisy light switches, door latches, plumbing, etc. (It's true that you can replace or modify these. But why should you have to?)

No closet for cleaning materials on each level of a multistory or split-level house.

Easily spotted wallpaper or another nonwaterproof finish around the bathroom washbasin or within splashing distance of it. (Wallpaper used anywhere in a bathroom will also tend to peel, if you like hot showers that create a great deal of steam.)

An in-the-way refrigerator door—one that opens toward the adjacent counter, which means you will have to carry food around the door.

No doors leading directly from outside to kitchen and basement, to prevent needless tracking through the house by deliverymen, or children with muddy feet.

Too few electrical outlets for lamps and appliances. (A plus to look for in new houses is built-in telephone outlets in all major living areas.)

An "icehouse" bedroom—one above an unheated area, such as a garage or terrace. Unless you have separate thermostatic controls for your heating system, you'll never be able to keep this room comfortably warm without overheating others.

HOME BUYING COSTS | See also MORTGAGES

Tom and Jane Wilson, who had saved enough money to make a down payment on a house, were startled to find that they had to pay more than $800 in additional expense before the purchase was completed. Although these expenses vary, there are almost always some fees to pay.

The Wilsons had selected a $20,000 suburban home in the northeastern part of the United States. They paid $5,000 down and carried a $15,000 conventional mortgage. Here are the additional costs they paid:

Land survey	$ 30
Home inspection	30
Title search and insurance	182
Mortgage tax	75
Bank charges for its attorney, appraiser, and mortgage processing fees	150
Fees for recording the deed, registering the title, recording the mortgage, and notary charges	20
Advance payments for taxes, fire and comprehensive insurance, and other items	190
Buyers' attorney fees	200
Total	$877

Most families will need expert advice in buying a home. Many authorities say that a buyer should be represented by an attorney familiar with the real estate laws of the community. A lawyer, they say, is essential in dealing with the legalities of deeds, and complications which might be revealed in a survey or in a title search (the examination of records and documents concerning previous ownership). In many communities, the attorney's fee is 1 per cent of the purchase price, but often it is less.

Home inspection. Before signing a sales agreement, it is wise to have a licensed engineer or architect inspect the home for structural defects, and the condition of plumbing and heating equipment, electric wiring, and drainage. In some communities, this is done by home-inspection firms. You should receive a written report, including whether there is evidence of termites. Fees range from $30 to $75 depending on the cost of the house. (This inspection is *not* an appraisal, and a value is not usually placed on the house. An appraiser can set a value on a house and give a good idea of its condition. His fee varies, but in some areas, it is one-tenth of 1 per cent of the sale price.)

If an inspection uncovers any evidence of termites or you want to make sure they are not present, an exterminating company usually will make a free inspection. If exterminating or repair costs are necessary, they may amount to several hundred dollars, but they are usually paid by the seller.

Survey. A land surveyor checks the boundary lines of the property to make sure they coincide with the description on the deed. He also determines whether the buildings are set back from the street and property lines to conform with the distance required by community law. (Again, it is essential to know of any violations *before* signing a sales contract.) Most survey fees range from $30 to $75.

Title insurance. This insurance protects you against loss from title flaws or claims against the property. The cost varies with the purchase price, but it can be several hundred dollars. Lending agencies require title insurance, when available, in the amount of the mortgage. Additional title insurance to cover the buyer's equity can be less expensive if taken out with the same company.

In some states, title insurance is either not available or not customarily used, but a title search is necessary. This can cost from $50 to $100. (With title insurance, these fees are included in the premium.)

Service charges. The mortgage lender charges fees for processing the mortgage and for other services. These cost from ½ to 3 per cent of the mortgage. Included are a credit check, a fee for an appraiser to determine for the lender if the mortgage value is covered by the market value of the house, and the lender's attorney fee.

Closing costs. The actual closing costs—for recording the deed, registering the title, and recording the mortgage—are comparatively low. But at the closing any required state mortgage tax or real estate transfer tax must be paid. The lender may also require prepayment of real estate taxes or insurance premiums which might fall due within the first year. After that, they often are covered in the monthly payments to the lender. The buyer also pays the seller a prorated share of any prepaid taxes and other items.

HOME NURSING |

When least expected, you may be called on to provide nursing care for a member of your family. At one time or another, most families have had such experiences. Much can be done to make them easier, and at the same time, to promote the general well-being of the patient.

The sickroom may be made comfortable and pleasant with flowers, house plants, attractive curtains, or a colorful picture. Furnishings that will not be useful can be removed to make the room easier to clean. Good ventilation and lighting are important. Disturbing noises should be minimized, and if possible, eliminated.

Sickroom equipment can often be improvised to save the expense of buying or renting it. For example, a simple orange crate, with an added shelf, makes a practical bedside table. Special equipment such as hospital beds can sometimes be borrowed from local health and welfare agencies.

In order to cope with the extra work with a minimum of effort, organize a *regular* routine. Careful planning based on common sense is necessary. Decide what you must do, when to do it, and what the patient can do for himself. Other family members should share in the nursing responsibility. If you need outside help or advice, the doctor may suggest the services of a visiting nurse, or other aid.

If requested by the doctor, keep a daily *written record* of the patient. This prevents mistakes or confusion if others are helping in the care. Such information as temperature, pulse, food intake, and administration of any medications or treatments may be noted daily on a chart (a lined notebook can be used for this purpose). Record or check each duty as it is carried out. Be sure you have the doctor's instructions in writing with the record.

Meals. Illness generally curbs a person's appetite. Although a sick person should not be forced to eat, nourishment is essential. A patient's appetite can be stimulated by food that is well prepared and attractively served. A colorful tray with small food portions and a flower or a little surprise gift or food item can encourage a patient to eat. If visitors are allowed, a relative or a friend may be invited to join him for an occasional meal.

A patient's progress may depend a good deal on his **mental outlook.** Try to keep up his spirits by being cheerful and understanding. Check with the doctor on the types of activities allowed. Reading, knitting, sewing, letter writing, radio, television, puzzles, and crafts are some ways for the bedridden to occupy the time. A patient may be able to perform small jobs such as helping with mending, sorting, and mounting photographs in an album, or arranging and filing recipes.

A free course in home nursing, offered by many Red Cross chapters, is a practical way of preparing for this type of emergency. The "Home Nursing Textbook" by the American Red Cross (paperbound, $1.25; and clothbound, $1.75) is a good reference for any home, available at bookstores or local Red Cross chapters.

HOME REMODELING LOANS |

Once you have planned to remodel the kitchen or other parts of your home, you must decide on how to finance it. Most banks, savings and loan associations, and credit unions will lend money for home remodeling and usually do not require a down payment to be made on the work.

You should approach a remodeling loan on the same basis that you do any loan. First, determine how much you can afford to spend in monthly payments. Then it is advisable to discuss the planned remodeling with the lender. He can objectively evaluate the cost of remodeling with the worth of your house. It may be that the work you plan is far too expensive compared to what you would receive from selling the house.

Although contractors or dealers usually will arrange remodeling loans, you have the choice of the type of loan and the lending institution. You give the lender or the contractor information about your mortgage and other outstanding debts. Be sure you know, as separate amounts, the cost of the job and the interest charges.

On Federal Housing Administration-insured loans for major home improvement and sometimes for other large remodeling projects, the FHA or the lenders inspect the work as it progresses. On Title I loans (see chart) the lender pays the contractor only when the borrower has signed a completion certificate stating that the work is complete and satisfactory.

If you apply for a loan yourself, you may have to present the plans, drawings, and estimates to the lender, with credit information. If the loan is approved, the lender gives the money to buy materials or pay the contractor.

The Home Remodeling Guide chart outlines the most common types of home-remodeling loans. Not all are available from all lending institutions. Eligibility requirements also vary. The first four listed have shorter repayment time limits and are for smaller amounts. The last four allow longer repayment time limits and larger amounts.

With discount loans, the interest charges are paid at the time the loan is made. This means that the true interest is considerably higher than the announced discount rate. If the loan is repaid in installments, the true interest rate may be almost double.

HOME REMODELING GUIDE

Type	Maximum Amount	Cost	Maximum Repayment Time	Comments
FHA Title I	$3,500	$5 per $100 discounted for year up to $2,500; $4 per $100 discounted on remainder.	5 years	FHA insures 90 per cent of the loan in the event the borrower fails to repay. Cannot be used for luxury items such as swimming pools, patios, etc.
Home-improvement plans of banks, savings and loan associations, etc.	About $5,000	Usually $6 per $100 discounted per year.	5 to 7 years	Life of borrower may be insured. In the event of his death, the loan is paid off. Can be used for luxury alterations.
Personal loan	Up to $5,000	Banks and credit unions from $4 to $6 per $100 discounted per year.	Usually 2 to 5 years	May need collateral, such as stocks and bonds, for some personal loans.
Contractor's installment loan	Cost of the job	Carrying charges, which may be higher than interest rates on regular loans.	1 to 5 years	Such plans are offered as part of a "package" home-remodeling project.

	Amount	Interest	Term	Remarks
Open-end mortgage (also called mortgage readvance)	Amount of the mortgage already paid off	Prevailing interest rates.	Usually to original maturity time of the mortgage	Open-end provision must have been part of original mortgage. Repayment time may be extended, but monthly payments will still usually be more than you have been paying on mortgage.
FHA Title II, section 203 (k)	Up to $10,000	6 per cent true interest per year on outstanding balance, plus ½ per cent on outstanding balance for insurance premium.	20 years	Difficult to get because many lenders say interest rate is not favorable to them.
FHA refinanced mortgage, Title II, section 203 (b)	$30,000	5¼ per cent true interest on outstanding balance, plus ½ per cent for insurance premium.	30 years	Monthly payments may be about the same as an original mortgage. You have to pay bank fees and charges.
Conventional mortgage or refinancing	Up to 75 or 90 per cent of the value of the property	Prevailing interest rates.	20 to 30 years	Same as FHA refinanced mortgage (above).

HOME SAFETY | See also POISONING

Know the danger spots in your home. Accidents occur more frequently at home than anywhere else. Room by room, here are potential hazards to guard against:

Kitchen. One of the most hazardous rooms in the house. Chief danger point is the range. Watch out for grease fires. (Use generous amounts of baking soda or salt to put out grease fires—never water. Better yet, keep a carbon dioxide or dry-chemical fire extinguisher handy.)

Mop up slippery floors immediately to prevent falls; do not overwax or overpolish them.

Avoid overloading electrical circuits.

Store household cleaners, polishes, and insecticides out of children's reach —under the sink is a poor place unless you use a locked cabinet.

Living room. Arrange your furniture to leave normal traffic paths clear. Make sure scatter rugs are secured. The fireplace should be screened when in use and screen should cover the entire opening. Ash trays should be large, deep, and solid to prevent spilling.

Bedroom. Fires caused by careless smoking, and falls by elderly people are among the greatest dangers.

Provide a straight, clear path from bed to door, with light control at both places. Avoid use of flame-type room heaters that may use up oxygen. Electric blankets and heating pads should have the Underwriters' Laboratories (UL) label.

Basement. Many home fires start here. Oily dust rags, paints and paint cloths, many insecticides, and kerosene are potentially dangerous. Do not bunch or wad oily rags. Best practice is to destroy such rags after using, or to wash and dry them thoroughly. Avoid accumulation of rubbish.

Bathroom. Falls, scalds, electric shock, and poisonings are most frequent bathroom accidents. Use nonslip pads in shower and tub. Provide securely anchored grab bars above tub; angle them so they will not be used for towels. Do not keep electrical appliances or leave plugged-in cords where they can be touched simultaneously with water or water fixtures. Keep all medicines out of reach of children.

Halls and stairways. Avoid projections such as wall fixtures and shelving in hallways. Keep closet doors closed. Halls and stairways should be well lighted. Provide handrails on stairways, and make sure all carpeting is tacked securely.

Attic. Stored materials are likely to be dry and highly combustible. Do not store old clothes, broken toys, old magazines, etc.

Outdoors. Do not leave insecticides, ant paste, lye, weed killers, or other poisons lying around the garage. Do not use gasoline for cleaning. Never leave the car motor running in a closed garage. Keep walks, driveways, and pavement well lighted and in good repair.

ELECTRICAL SAFETY CHECK LIST

Electricity is the servant of the housewife, but it must be used correctly. Electrical accidents can result from carelessness or misuse; and danger signals should be heeded. For example, there is a need for corrective measures if fuses blow frequently, if lights grow dim or the radio fades when appliances are turned on, if the television picture shrinks, if cooking appliances heat slowly, or if shocks are received from appliances.

Weakening current is usually caused by an overload on the electrical wiring system. It may help temporarily to cut down on the number of lamps and appliances on the circuit. Experts advise, however, that any work on the wiring system itself be left to a qualified electrician. Repairs of fixtures and switches should also be done by an electrician. See that frayed or cracked cords and broken plugs or sockets are repaired or replaced. Have noisy motors in fans, vacuums, etc., checked by a serviceman.

If any electrical shock—regardless of how small—is received from an appliance or light socket, repairs should be made before further use. Avoid these shock dangers:

Do not turn on electrical switches while hands are wet, while standing in the bathtub, or while in contact with any wet surface, water pipe, or radiator. *Never* touch a radio, hair dryer, etc., under these circumstances.

Do not yank electric cords out of sockets or pry out with a tool. Grasp the plug, not the cord, and if it sticks, rock it gently back and forth.

Do not run extension cords under rugs or over pipes, where abrasion or heat could cause a short circuit. Never pinch a cord in a door or window jamb, or drive tacks through it. Use extension cords of light wire for lamps only, not for appliances.

Look for the Underwriters' Laboratories (UL) label on the appliance or tool itself—not just on the cord. In the latter case, it covers the cord or plug only. The UL label signifies adherence to a strict safety code.

Do not tinker with a television set even if it is turned off. High voltage can remain in the set.

Put safety guards on wall outlets if you have children who might stick hairpins or nails into them.

Many appliances are supplied with a three-prong plug on a three-wire cord. The third wire grounds the appliance to protect against shock. There are adapters for a two-slot wall outlet for three-prong plugs. The appliance will not be grounded, however, unless there is a wire connection from the adapter to the grounded metal case of an outlet, usually through the cover screw.

Be sure you have adequate circuits for heavy-duty appliances (ranges, air conditioners, washing machines, etc.). Your electric company may check this for you.

FIRE SAFETY CHECKUP

Every day there are fires in more than 1,000 homes in the United States. According to fire-protection authorities, carelessness is the chief cause. To avoid them, the national Fire Protection Association and the National Board of Fire Underwriters recommend that these points be checked regularly.

Smoking. Provide plenty of large ash trays. Be sure matches and cigarettes are out before disposing of them. Do not smoke in bed. Keep matches out of children's reach. Check rooms for lighted cigarettes before going out or to bed.

Cooking and heating. Be prepared to douse small grease fires in the kitchen with a large, flat lid. Keep stove and utensils free of grease. Do not hang curtains near stoves, fireplaces, or heaters. Use a metal fire screen in front of a fireplace. Have a serviceman check and clean your furnace, flue pipes, and chimney regularly. If walls or ceiling around a furnace, stove, boiler, or heating pipes are hot, have equipment checked—it may be defective or improperly installed. Basement doors at the head of the stairs should fit properly and be closed at night.

Housekeeping. Do not store rubbish. Keep paint cans tightly closed and stored in a cool place. Use only nonflammable cleaning fluids. Do not burn leaves on a windy day or near a building or fence. Douse the last ashes with water.

Emergency precautions. Every member of your family should know two escape routes from each room of your home. Occasionally rehearse escape plans. Keep the number of your local fire department by each telephone. If you suspect a fire, even if you just smell smoke, get everyone out of the house immediately and call the fire department. Never leave children at home alone—even for a few minutes. Instruct baby sitters on what to do in case of a fire. If your fire department has a free home-inspection service, use it and follow the inspector's advice. The International Association of Fire Chiefs reports that in some cities there was a substantial reduction of home fires the year after the home fire-inspection program had begun.

Ash trays. The National Fire Protection Association says that small, shallow ash trays are responsible for about a third of the 95,000 annual fires in United States homes attributed to careless smoking.

A cigarette butt that falls from an ash tray may smolder for hours in a rug, on a desk, in upholstery, etc. This smoldering fire is doubly dangerous: it may burst into flame hours after the family has gone to bed, or it may exhaust the oxygen and suffocate people in their sleep long before there is a flame to indicate a fire.

A safe ash tray is shaped to prevent cigarettes (regular and king-size) from falling or flipping out. It is big enough to hold at least ten cigarette butts, yet not so big that it becomes a catchall. It should have holding grooves and a wide outside rim, or a device to hold or snuff out cigarettes within the bowl, or deep sides to fence in the smokes. It should be made of material that will not burn, melt, or transmit heat.

Never use plastic coasters, wooden shelves, or paper plates as ash trays. Finally, be sure to empty ash trays into safe, nonflammable containers.

DISCARDED REFRIGERATORS

Young children are irresistibly attracted to abandoned refrigerators and old ice boxes or freezers. These "playhouses"—airtight and virtually sound-proof—can prove to be fatal traps. According to the National Safety Council, forty-four children died in refrigerators in 1964, the worst year to date. Since 1958, refrigerators shipped interstate have been required by federal law to have doors that can be released from inside. The greatest danger comes from older units now being discarded or those temporarily out of use. And even the new law will not fully eliminate hazards.

The danger season for refrigerator accidents begins in March, reaches a peak in June, and continues through the fall. Three out of four victims are from three to six years old.

The best way to render an abandoned refrigerator or icebox harmless is to remove the door. This can sometimes be accomplished in a few minutes with a screw driver. If you cannot remove the door, call a serviceman. Members of the Refrigerator Service Engineers Society will remove the door without charge.

It is illegal in many states and cities to discard a refrigerator or similar unit in a hazardous condition. Report dangerous units to the police, or ask a city sanitation department how to dispose of them safely.

GLASS-DOOR DANGERS

Glass doors are modern and attractive; they permit more light to enter the home, and offer good views of outdoor scenery. For these reasons, many new homes have sliding glass doors leading into the yard or patio. But case histories indicate that glass doors can be dangerous. They often do their job too well: many people simply do not see the doors, and walk or run into them. Serious and sometimes fatal accidents, particularly among children, can result if unsafe glass is used.

Plate or sheet glass is ordinary glass, the kind windowpanes are made of (though thicker). It usually shatters or explodes into long, dangerous slivers when broken.

Laminated glass, better known as "safety glass," is made of two sheets of glass separated by a layer of tough plastic. It is used in automobile wind-shields. When it breaks, laminated glass does not shatter, but clings to the plastic. It is safer than plain sheet glass, but it can be broken easily.

Tempered glass, also a safety glass, is the strongest of the three kinds. It is usually used in the side and rear windows of automobiles. A rock thrown forcefully at tempered glass can break it, but the glass distintegrates into small particles that usually do not cut.

To avoid accidents involving glass doors, the Division of Accident Prevention of the U.S. Public Health Service suggests:

If you are building a new house or remodeling an old one, be sure that glass doors and large glass panels are made of safety glass, either laminated or tempered.

Decorate doors with decals, painted initials, scrolls, or other markings. Use fluorescent paint that can be seen in the dark. Remember, though, these decorations are meant to supplement safe glass, not to substitute for it.

MOTH BALLS

Keep moth balls out of reach of children. To some children, moth balls—in spite of their odor and taste—appear to be candy. And when winter clothes are being stored and summer clothes are being taken out, the chances increase that young children may find some moth balls and eat them. Certain types can cause illness.

Many moth balls are made from naphthalene. In extreme instances, naphthalene poisoning has even caused death. (Some children seem less susceptible than others. A number who have eaten moth balls, it must be noted, do not become ill.)

Naphthalene poisoning can cause abdominal pain, headache, nausea, and fever. In severe cases, the red blood cells may be affected, causing anemia. If your child swallows mothballs, call your doctor. He probably will advise that you induce vomiting.

Some mothballs are made from paradichlorobenzene, which is not as toxic as naphthalene. The label on the box should be saved, so that in an emergency, you will know what your child has swallowed.

Do not store diapers or baby underclothing in naphthalene mothballs.

HOME SELLING | See also HOME BUYING

House for sale? This can help. Every year, more than two million American families sell their homes. Some sales are faster, easier, more profitable than others because the owners take time to learn something about the art of selling a house.

Most homeowners use real estate brokers when they sell their homes. (A realtor is a real estate broker who is a member of the National Association of Real Estate Boards.) A reputable broker will help you to determine a realistic asking price and will provide expert guidance and counsel throughout negotiations. He will help you with the sometimes complicated arrangements when you are ready to sell. In addition, he can help you avoid the inconvenience of unannounced visitors by making appointments to show your house to prospects; and he will arrange for necessary advertising. Many homeowners feel that the broker who performs these services conscientiously is well worth his commission (usually 5 or 6 per cent of the selling price).

Nevertheless, you may prefer to sell your house on your own to avoid paying the commission. This works out best when you already know of one or more prospective buyers, when you are in no particular hurry to sell, and when you feel competent to handle the financial arrangements. In any case, you would still need an attorney for the legal details involved in closing the sale.

Should you make improvements before you sell? Most real estate brokers will encourage you to do so in order to make your house more attractive. Painting should be done if it is badly needed, and the house should be in good repair. Authorities say women are strongly attracted to such features as tiled bathrooms and modern kitchens with ample cabinet space. And, say the experts, the woman's vote is usually the critical one in the decision to buy the house. However, it is up to you to decide whether it will be worthwhile to make improvements that will involve considerable expense.

Keep the lawn trimmed and edged, hedges cut, and flower beds cultivated. Keep the yard tidy.

Bright, clean windows will help the sale.

Obvious defects, such as dripping faucets, loose steps and doorknobs, sticking drawers, and warped cabinet doors, should be fixed.

Display the full value of storage and utility spaces by removing all unnecessary articles from the basement and attic. Neatly arranged closets look larger.

Turn on all lights for evening inspections.

Bathrooms should be clean.

If you have already bought another house, try to leave as much furniture as possible in your old house until it is sold. Most people find it hard to visualize what an empty house will look like with furnishings.

Keep children and pets out of the way. If you use a broker, try to be away when the house is shown.

Eliminate unpleasant cooking odors as much as possible.

Keep stairways free of objects that give a cluttered appearance.

If you have a fireplace and the weather is cold, a good fire will be an inviting feature.

Some real estate experts say the house need not be immaculate at all times. They feel that a comfortable, lived-in atmosphere is desirable.

HONEY |

Many near-miracle properties have been claimed for honey—from curing heart ailments to adding sparkle to the eyes. Such claims are usually baseless in fact. Unfortunately, they may cause the real and valuable uses of honey to be overlooked.

Basically, honey is a sweetener—one with a special flavor. It can be used on fruits or cereals; as a spread; in beverages, salad dressings, marinades, glazes, canning, and preserving; and to flavor vegetables. Because it tends to retain moisture, it is often used in baked goods to preserve freshness.

Bees make honey from nectar, a "sweet water," which they gather from flowers and take back to a hive. They fan the nectar with their wings to evaporate much of the water. After the nectar is processed into honey, the bees seal it into wax combs. The finished product is made principally of sugar (about 77 per cent) and water (about 18 per cent). It contains only traces of vitamins and minerals.

The flavor of honey is determined by the type of flower the bees visit while gathering nectar. Flavor varies from very bland, as in **clover honey**, to a stronger, more flavorful honey like **buckwheat**. As a rule, the darker the honey, the more distinct its flavor. The most widely used honey in the United States is clover honey. Other fairly common types are **orange, sage,** and **alfalfa.** A number of honeys enjoy regional popularity such as **Tupelo** in Florida, **Thistle** and **Mesquite** in the Southwest.

Honey should be stored at room temperature. It can be bought in a comb, liquid, liquid and comb combined, and creamed spread.

HOUSE CLEANING | See also FLOOR CARE; VACUUM CLEANERS; WINDOW WASHING

At one time the housewife's principal equipment for cleaning house consisted of a broom, a mop, a pail, soap and water, some brushes, rags—and a strong back. There was constant temptation to let the job go until annual "spring cleaning" of accumulated dirt. Today, ingenuity in labor-saving machinery, materials, and supplies has made it easy to maintain a clean and sparkling house without turmoil or arduous toil.

The more complete your equipment and supplies, the easier it is to stay ahead of the dirt. So today, house cleaning begins with a list of the things you need.

EQUIPMENT

Vacuum cleaner and attachments—for floors, rugs, and dusting.
Carpet sweeper—for quick, convenient brush-ups.
Rug shampooer—may also be rented.
Floor polisher and scrubber—for scrubbing, polishing, buffing all floors; may also be rented.
Floor wax applier.
Mops—wet and dry.
Broom—for bare floors and outdoors.

Dustpan—with long handle to save bending.
Brushes—for radiators, bathtub, toilet bowl, scrubbing.
Sponges—cellulose or plastic; much handier than rags.
Pail—plastic ones are lightweight, rustproof.
Paper towels.
Steel wool—plain and in soap pads.
Household gloves—for protection of hands.
Cloths—for cleaning, dusting, polishing. Soft, knitted, absorbent, for heavy duty; treated, for furniture.

SUPPLIES

Detergent or general purpose cleaner.
Household ammonia.
Window and glass cleaners.
Chlorine (household) bleach.
Silver and metal cleaners.
Household cleanser.
Floor and wall cleaners.
Furniture polish or wax—including scratch-concealing type.
Disinfectant.
Cleaning fluid and spot remover.
Floor wax—self-polishing and polishing types as specified.
Wax remover.
Upholstery and rug cleaners.
Oven cleaner.
Toilet-bowl cleaner.
Drain cleaner.
Rust remover.

In addition, the market offers polishes, cleaners, etc., in unlimited variety for practically every special purpose or problem. Many come in aerosol containers, easier to use. Ask questions at the store; investigate materials for their advantages. See also related items in alphabetical place in this Guide.

SPECIFIC JOBS

Here's how to handle some of the dirtiest jobs in the house:

Cleaning the oven can be postponed by wiping up splatters as they occur. Low roasting temperatures (not over 325°F.) and taking care not to overfill casseroles help avoid spills; and leaving the oven door open to cool helps prevent baking them in. Put a small cookie sheet covered with foil on the bottom rack as a drip catcher.

A recent boon is a protective spray which, applied to the interior of a clean oven, keeps food from sticking; soil is easily washed off. Use chemical oven cleaners carefully (read directions and wear gloves). Ammonia also loosens grease; equip the bottle with a sprayer top and the night before cleaning, spray the oven thoroughly. Next day, add a little ammonia to sudsy water and finish the job with a steel-wool soap pad.

Cleaning Venetian blinds is easy only if you do it often. Using the small vacuum-cleaner brush, tilt the blind so the slats lie flat, and vacuum down or across as you prefer. When slats need washing, dunk the blind in a bathtub of sudsy, warm water. Sponge off if necessary, but don't let the blind soak. Blot to stop dripping; then replace it at the window, and towel it dry. Unless the blind is extremely soiled or the water too sudsy, no rinsing is needed. Wood blinds must be handled quickly to avoid warping.

Cleaning the fireplace. Start by shoveling the ashes down the trap, or dampen them slightly before shoveling them into a bucket. Vacuum all around with the dusting brush of the cleaner (it can be rinsed later). To remove smoke stains from brick, use a strong solution of trisodium phosphate (sold in paint stores) and a scrub brush, and wear household gloves. Rinse well with clear water. Polish brass with a good metal cleaner, using a fine steel-wool pad if necessary.

Cleaning trash cans, whether metal or plastic, is easiest outdoors, with a long-handled brush and the garden hose. Or pour in a pailful of warm, sudsy water, swish it around with the brush, and empty it either outdoors or in the toilet bowl. Smaller kitchen cans and plastic or metal wastebaskets should be washed and dried often. To make the can or basket fresh and thoroughly clean, add a dose of household disinfectant, bleach, or ammonia to the suds.

Cleaning the toilet bowl takes some special equipment. Liquid or granular bowl cleansers are merely poured into or sprinkled on the water. They go to work immediately, loosening stains and hard-water deposits. A few whisks with a nylon bowl brush, and the bowl is clean. Keep the brush nearby in a metal or plastic holder made for its storage.

Cleaning a stall shower is quite a task in hard-water homes, because the tile acquires water spots that won't budge unless handled right. Use warm water with enough Calgon water conditioner to make water feel slippery, and a sponge or plastic pan scourer. Brighten a white tile shower floor with cleanser.

To clean a scummy rubber shower mat, go over both sides with a damp steel-wool soap pad and wash in the automatic washer on delicate cycle. Then rinse the stall by turning on the shower and directing the spray. For real sparkle, dry the walls with a towel.

Wallpaper cleaning. Finger marks and smudges on wallpaper can cause an otherwise spotless room to look messy. Although almost all wallpaper can be washed, it is wise to first test a small, inconspicuous section by rubbing with a damp cloth or sponge dipped in cool, sudsy water. The paper is washable if it dries with a good appearance and the colors do not run. For cleaning nonwashable wallpapers (these are usually imported or screen-printed), there is a commercial puttylike product on the market.

Plastic-coated or treated wall coverings of materials other than paper can be washed or scrubbed frequently without damage.

To wash wallpaper not treated with plastic but known to be washable, start by dusting the entire surface with a vacuum-cleaner attachment. Then make a sudsy solution of detergent and cool water. Gently wash a small area of wall (about two feet by two feet) with a damp cloth or sponge. Work from baseboard to ceiling without scrubbing or soaking. Rinse each section with clean, cool water before beginning the next. Continue washing and rinsing small areas, always overlapping the previously cleaned part.

Spot cleaning is simpler. Finger marks can be cleaned with an art-gum eraser. Grease or oil spots can be removed in two ways. Make a thick paste of fuller's earth and a nontetrachloride-type cleaning fluid. Apply it to the spot, and when dry, brush it off. Or press a piece of white blotter on the spot with a hot iron for a minute or two. Wallpaper often gets especially grimy over radiators; it is best to go over these areas lightly with a dry rubber sponge or an artist's kneaded rubber eraser before washing. Ink eradicator will remove small ink stains, however, it may also remove some of the paper's color. You can sometimes correct this by filling in the design with colored pencils.

HOUSE PLANTS |

House plants are not only decorative but fun to grow, and increasingly prominent in contemporary furnishing. Besides the traditional window box, a planter may be used as a room divider, often to set off an entrance hall or dining area from a living room.

A window with southern exposure (direct sunlight) will grow a wide variety of flowering plants, and such spring bulbs as tulip, hyacinth, and lily of the valley may be forced. Northern exposure restricts the choice to foliage plants such as ivies and ferns, and to a few flowers such as African violets and begonias. Interior locations with only dim daylight or artificial light are tolerated by philodendron, sansevieria, Chinese evergreen, rubber plant, and a few others.

Temperature, generally somewhat cooler than central heating provides; humidity; air circulation; watering and drainage; and proper plant foods are as important as exposure. (For a booklet on the care of house plants, send 15 cents in coin to the Superintendent of Documents, U.S. Government Printing Office, Washington, D.C. 20025, asking for Farmers' Bulletin No. 1872. Your state agricultural extension station may also issue a booklet on house plants.)

Over- (or under) watering house plants is one of the commonest errors. Here is a simple test: Each morning, tap the pot with your knuckle. If it makes a hollow, ringing sound, the plant needs water. If it makes a dull, thick sound, the soil is still moist.

HOUSE PLANTS MOST LIKELY TO SUCCEED

Good Housekeeping's *The Better Way* surveyed twenty state agricultural extension stations to find out which plants are most easily and successfully grown in their areas. Here are the plants mentioned most frequently (popular names appear after the Latin name):

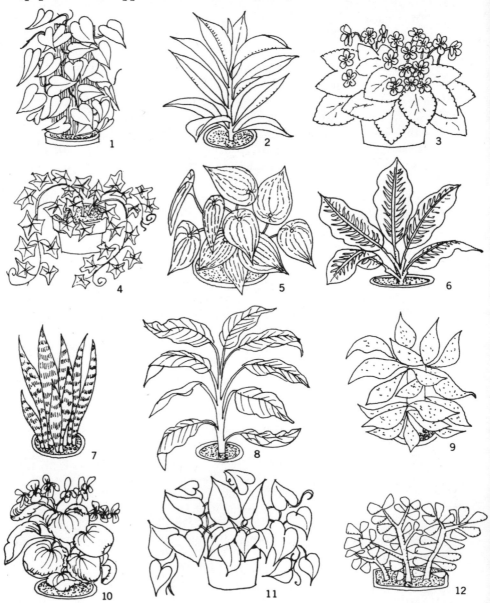

1. **Philodendron cordatum**—heart-leaf philodendron.
2. **Ficus elastica**—rubber plant.
3. **Saintpaulia ionantha**—African violet.
4. **Hedera helix**—English Ivy.
5. **Peperomia sandersi**—watermelon leaf begonia (although it is not a begonia).
6. **Dieffenbachia amoena**—dumb cane, tuft root.
7. **Sansevieria zeylanica**—snake plant, leopard lily, bowstring hemp, mother-in-law's tongue, golden stripe, sword plant.
8. **Aglaonema simplex**—Chinese evergreen, Chinese water plant, Japanese leaf.
9. **Dracaena godseffiana**—spotted dracaena.
10. **Begonia semperflorens**—wax begonia, perpetual or ever-flowering begonia.
11. **Scindapsus aureus**—pothos, devil's ivy, hunter's robe, Colombo agent, marble queen, golden pothos, silver marble.
12. **Crassula arborescens**—jade plant.

Some of these plants, such as the philodendron, ficus, hedera, dieffenbachia, and sansevieria, have several species that grow equally well outdoors.

TIPS ON POTTING A PLANT

Plants purchased from florists generally come properly potted, but the health of the plant will be affected by where you place it and the care you give to it. Also, if the plant outgrows its pot (becomes "pot-bound") you will need to know how to repot it successfully. See illustration 13 for pointers.

FIRST AID FOR AILING HOUSE PLANTS

A change in care may turn a sick plant into a healthy one. Here are problems which frequently occur, as illustrated on page 189.

14. **Loss of foliage** is probably the result of the plant's not getting enough water, having too much fertilizer, or being subjected to a sudden change in temperature. However, it can also be caused by overwatering, a change in light intensity, keeping the plant in too small a pot, or the shock of being transplanted.

15. **A tall, spindly plant.** The most likely reason is lack of light, but it can result from too much or too little fertilizer, improper ventilation, and too high temperature. Most house plants require temperatures from 65° F. to 75° F. during the day and about 55° F. to 65° F. (10° cooler) at night.

16. **Lack of growth.** A plant stops growing if it does not receive enough light, fertilizer, and water. Some plants go through a dormant period—usually during winter—when it is not advisable to fertilize or water heavily.

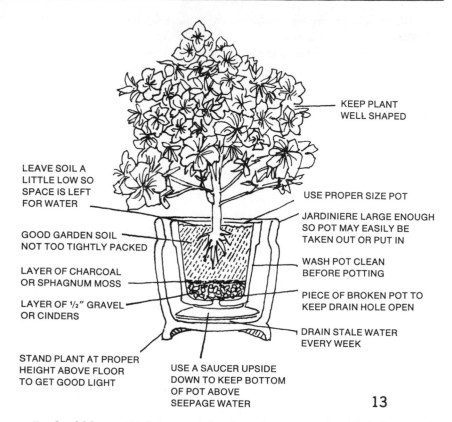

KEEP PLANT
WELL SHAPED

LEAVE SOIL A
LITTLE LOW SO
SPACE IS LEFT
FOR WATER

USE PROPER SIZE POT

JARDINIERE LARGE ENOUGH
SO POT MAY EASILY BE
TAKEN OUT OR PUT IN

GOOD GARDEN SOIL
NOT TOO TIGHTLY PACKED

WASH POT CLEAN
BEFORE POTTING

LAYER OF CHARCOAL
OR SPHAGNUM MOSS

PIECE OF BROKEN POT TO
KEEP DRAIN HOLE OPEN

LAYER OF ½" GRAVEL
OR CINDERS

DRAIN STALE WATER
EVERY WEEK

STAND PLANT AT PROPER
HEIGHT ABOVE FLOOR
TO GET GOOD LIGHT

USE A SAUCER UPSIDE
DOWN TO KEEP BOTTOM
OF POT ABOVE
SEEPAGE WATER

13

17. **Lack of bloom.** Lighting and fertilizer have considerable effect on the bloom of a flowering plant. Some plants, like poinsettia and chrysanthemum, will not bloom properly if exposed to artificial light at night during the late fall, winter, and early spring. A poinsettia can even be affected by the light from a small night lamp.

18. **Yellow or drooping leaves.** Wet roots are the most common offender. Do not water too heavily or too often. Be sure the plant container has a drainage hole and that the plant is allowed to stand in water not more than ten minutes after watering. Another cause of yellowing is that the soil lacks nitrogen. Other causes can be too little or too much light; or too high or low temperature.

19. **Sudden collapse.** A fine, healthy plant that seems to collapse overnight has probably been fertilized too much or watered excessively. Or someone may have emptied an alcoholic drink into the pot.

20. **Brown leaf tops** may indicate excess fertilization or exposure to cold drafts. They also can develop if plants are improperly watered. Be careful not to wash the soil away from the crown (where the stem and root join). Also avoid getting water into the crown.

21. Black foliage. Freezing or burning will kill the leaf tissue instantly and cause leaves to blacken. This may also happen if there is not enough fertilizer or light, or if the plant is overwatered or attacked by insects.

Spotted foliage. Too much or too little water causes this reaction. Plants with fuzzy leaves, like African violets, spot if hot or cold water is splashed on their leaves. Another cause of spotted foliage is exposure to direct sunlight.

Rotted stem. If the plant is overwatered or allowed to get wet roots, the stem may rot. This can also happen if the stem rubs against the edge of the pot. A bruised or rotted stem should be cut off below the injured section.

White crust on soil or pot. This is a symptom of trouble to come if not corrected. It indicates there is an excess of salts in the soil. The crust should be washed off the pot and the layer of soil removed and replaced with fresh soil. To avoid this condition, water occasionally from the top of the pot and throw away any water that drains from the bottom. Authorities suggest that twice a year you leach salts from the soil by pouring water equal to five times the capacity of the pot through the soil. If this much water will not pass through the pot within two or three hours, the drainage is not adequate, and the plant should be repotted.

ICE CREAM |

Ice cream has become virtually a staple of the American family diet, since it combines a flavor treat with wholesome food values. Quality varies widely, and unlike some other sweets, ice cream does not keep indefinitely. Finding your favorite brand is largely a matter of taste testing, but here are other points to consider.

Stabilizers and emulsifiers are added to ice cream for texture, to keep ice crystals small. An amount of air, called overrun, incorporated in the body increases volume and lightness. Good-quality ice cream should be firm, but not solid or rubbery; also, when melted, it will have a creamy, rather than a watery appearance. A high percentage of butterfat will make it especially creamy.

Price is an index of richness—the higher the butterfat content, the more expensive the ice cream. Also in fruit flavors, the higher priced ones will be labeled fresh fruit. Artificial flavors are permitted by law. Generally you will save money if you buy half-gallon or gallon containers for your home freezer.

Ice milk, sold like ice cream, contains less fat, more protein and other nonfat solids, and fewer calories. **Diabetic ice cream,** made with artificial sweeteners, is not necessarily lower in calories than regular ice cream.

STORAGE

The freezer is the place to keep ice cream in quantity—a month's supply if you wish. Store unopened containers in the coldest part of freezer. Reseal opened containers tightly to prevent loss of flavor and formation of ice crystals. Store away from the freezing surface to keep it nearer serving consistency. In a refrigerator-freezer combination, the freezer temperature will be close to 0° F. when the control is at the normal setting. Pints, quarts, or even half gallons may be stored up to a month, tightly covered.

In conventional refrigerators, ice cream stays firmer when it is removed from the carton and stored in an ice-cube tray. But be sure it's a tray you keep just for the ice cream, or you may spoil the tray for ice-cube use. Cover the tray with wax paper or foil; place it where it is in contact with the freezing surface. If necessary, turn control to a colder setting, but return it to normal as soon as possible, or other fresh food may freeze. Use the ice cream within a few hours.

Remember, too, that it is preferable to freeze homemade ice cream mixtures in a freezer or a refrigerator-freezer combination, rather than in a conventional refrigerator.

INSURANCE CHECKLIST | See also LIFE INSURANCE

Every family's insurance needs a regular checkup. One of the best ways to get the most out of an insurance policy is to know what it covers at all times. Family situations change, and a policy should be kept up-to-date to cover new developments. For example, your home may now be worth more than you realize. According to a government guide on construction costs, a house built for $7,000 in 1945 would cost $14,000 to replace today. Your insurance may need changing to cover this.

Insurance experts advise policyholders to check their insurance annually, if possible, or at least every two years. Such checking with your broker or agent costs nothing. You are entitled to this service.

The following checklist on questions to ask about your various policies is based on interviews with the Institute of Life Insurance, the Insurance Information Institute, and the Health Insurance Institute:

FIRE, THEFT, AND CASUALTY

Is your home insured for its full value?

Is damage to your home covered on an actual cash value, or on a replacement basis?

Are valuable furs, jewelry, and art objects individually insured for their full value?

Do you have an expensive glass picture window in your home? This requires special coverage in addition to regular fire insurance.

Are you insured against jet plane sonic-boom damage?

Have you bought a second car? If it's insured under the same policy as the first, you may save on premiums.

Have members of your family had clear driving records in the past three years? If they have not been found at fault in an accident and have committed no serious traffic violations, you may get a discount.

Do you hire gardeners or household help? If so, you may need both liability insurance and workman's compensation coverage.

Package insurance policies for homeowners usually cover these points at reduced cost. Similar package policies are available for driving and auto coverage.

LIFE INSURANCE

Have family protection needs changed? Are there more children or dependents?

Are beneficiary provisions correctly stated?

Have family financial plans been revised? You may want to start a college plan or a retirement plan.

Have property or indebtedness conditions changed? Is coverage needed for a mortgage or a loan you may have recently made?

Will policy benefits be paid as you want them to be? Your husband may want the policy to pay a lump sum while it now provides monthly payments, or vice versa.

Can you save on costs by changing premium payments from a monthly basis to quarterly, semiannually, or annually?

Are there policy features that might be added without cost to improve coverage?

Is there any change in income or employment conditions which affects your family's life insurance? Does your husband have group coverage at work, or is there any change in the occupational risks of his job?

Does the insurance company have your current address?

In most cases, your present life insurance can be adjusted to cover needed changes. It usually is advantageous to add to an old policy rather than to take out a new one.

HEALTH INSURANCE

Are all members of your family covered?

Do you know the policy's waiting periods, exclusions, limits, etc.?

To what age are children insured under your policy?

How do you apply for benefits, and how soon must you apply?

Do you have coverage for mental conditions?

If you have an individual policy, is it noncancellable no matter how many times you use it?

Does the insurance pay for hospitalization and operations?

What coverage is provided for expenses outside a hospital?

In many cases, families are covered by a group policy provided by employers. Its terms should be understood. Additional coverage may then be obtained from individual major-medical policies. Some individual policies help replace income lost because of disability.

INTERIOR DECORATORS | See also FURNISHING A HOME

The services of a professional interior decorator, or interior designer, as many prefer to be called, offer a practical solution to many problems of furnishing a home, and need not be expensive. However, not everyone who calls himself an interior decorator may be fully qualified by training. Those who belong to either the American Institute of Interior Designers (A.I.D.) or the National Society of Interior Designers (N.S.I.D.) use these initials after their names. In addition to the members, there are other qualified decorators who may be judged by examples of their work.

WHAT DOES A DECORATOR DO?

He (or she) is a trained designer. He knows perspective and proportion, color harmonies, architecture, and furniture by types and periods. He keeps up with what's available in fabrics, and in floor and wall coverings. He knows where to shop, including places that you might never discover without him. (Many decorators have studios where clients can select fabrics, furnishings, and carpeting from samples.) He can help to decide the best way to make installations, such as cabinets, and to supervise workers in many crafts and trades.

If a decorator knows his business, he doesn't try to make his work reflect only what he likes, but what his client desires and finds most comfortable and attractive to live with.

HOW MUCH DOES HE CHARGE?

If you want only advice in solving a decorating problem, whether major or minor, payment is on an hourly basis, ranging from ten to twenty-five dollars an hour. A decorator may supply you with rough layouts indicating where furniture should be positioned, list places where you should shop, and give specific ideas about effecting the changes you have in mind. But if you want to buy all or most of your furnishings from or through the decorator, you ordinarily pay no more than you would by shopping at customary retail sources. The decorator makes his profit by buying the furnishings at wholesale costs from the dealer or manufacturer and then selling them to you at regular, or occasionally less than regular retail prices.

There may be other charges if you want renderings (such as sketches) of what the decorator plans to do, or if you authorize travel to other cities to shop. In any case, a contract should state clearly what services you have been promised, how much money you agree to spend, etc.

The A.I.D. and N.S.I.D. say most of their members are available for virtually any assignment, whether it involves spending $300 or $30,000. Too, you can engage in long-range planning with a decorator. Say that you want to do over your entire house and have only $500 immediately available, but you know that you'll be able to spend equal, if not higher, amounts in each of the next few years. Most decorators would be willing to handle the over-all planning, mapping out what eventually is to be done, and shopping for the items as money become available.

HOW DO YOU SELECT A DECORATOR?

Before hiring anyone, talk to him. Discuss what you have in mind. Perhaps your taste and preferences are so dissimilar that it would be difficult to work together. Most large department stores now offer professional decorating advice. In using their services, you usually are obligated or urged to buy most, if not all, of the merchandise at the one store. It's usually possible to buy on time payments at these stores, and this is not generally true if you use an individual decorator.

If you're at a loss about whom to consult, you can write to either the A.I.D. (673 Fifth Avenue, New York, New York 10022) or the N.S.I.D. (157 West 57th Street, New York, New York 10019).

IRONING | See also STAINS

Despite modern wrinkle-resistant fabrics, it is still necessary to iron or press most articles of outer clothing for best appearance, or at least to touch up collars and cuffs. New products and techniques make skillful ironing easier, cut time and backaches. These include a heat-controlled dry iron, a steam iron, a firm and well-padded ironing board with cover, and a lint-free pressing cloth.

IRONS

Dry irons containing a 1,000- to 1,500-watt electric heating element are used on articles that require dampening, heavy linens, and handkerchiefs.

Steam irons, containing water to provide moisture while ironing proceeds, are suited to synthetic fabrics used in sport shirts, women's and children's clothes, and other items.

Basically, dry ironing is hotter, since it is heat that smooths wrinkles. Cooler steam ironing is better adapted to special weaves such as corduroy, cottons with a wrinkle-resistant finish, knit goods, underwear, pajamas, or lingerie. It may also be used for pressing. A spray feature permits spot-moistening of very rough or wrinkled places.

The best irons, both dry and steam, provide a wide range of temperature settings, for less worry over scorching filmy synthetics, and smoother results in heavier fabrics. Weight of a well-designed iron should not exceed three or four pounds, and it should feel well balanced. Poor balance can tire your wrist and arm muscles. It should have a comfortable handle, a temperature-fabric dial that is easy to read and adjust, and a good-size soleplate (small ones cover less area per sweep). Combination steam-dry irons generally are most convenient.

Care of an iron. Don't drop it! Such an accident may put the iron out of commission. Be sure the ironing board is level and not too heavily padded, so the iron won't topple off. Also, put the iron in a safe place to cool.

Try to avoid excessive scratching of the soleplate by ironing around, not over, hooks, snaps, slide fasteners, etc.

A good steam iron holds about a cupful of water, and the kind of water used is important. Check the instruction booklet, and always measure the water. Some manufacturers specify tap water; however, very hard tap water will build up mineral deposits which gradually clog the steam passages. For this reason, other manufacturers specify distilled water, purchased at a hardware or drug store; or deionized water, which is made at home by running tap water through a small demineralizing accessory. Refrigerator defrost water, rain water, or boiled water will *not* take the place of dis-tilled water. In an emergency, you can get by with tap water, since it takes considerable time for the deposits to accumulate.

When a steam iron is clogged, there is no satisfactory way to "boil" it out. The iron must be disassembled and cleaned by a service man. Always empty the water after use while the iron is still hot, to evaporate remaining drops inside; and store the iron on its heel rest.

Avoid bringing a hot iron in contact with nylon or Dacron, which can take only a very low temperature setting. The heat may melt the fabric, leaving a sticky deposit on the soleplate. To remove it, heat the iron until it is only slightly warm to the touch, and rub the soleplate lightly with a steel wool soap pad dipped in acetone (an ingredient of nail-polish re-movers). Wipe clean with a damp cloth or paper towels.

IRONING-BOARD COVERS

The right kind of cover saves time and produces better results. Consider these points when shopping:

Size. Covers come in three lengths—48″, 54″ (standard), and 60″—and have drawstrings, elastic bands, or metal fasteners to insure a wrinkle-free, drum-tight fit. Measure your board to make sure of the size. (Manufacturers of specialty boards—those with an unusual shape—also make special covers to fit them.)

Material. The least expensive covers are of plain cotton drill. If you want a scorch-resistant cover, look for one that has been treated with an aluminized, silicone finish, or Teflon, or one that contains asbestos. Treated covers have other advantages: they do not absorb moisture; they reflect heat, thus saving time and ironing effort; and they create less friction, hence last longer.

Washability. Cotton covers can be washed, but look for a label indicating shrink resistance. For best results, put the cover back on the board while damp, smoothing and stretching it gently into place. Treated covers should be wiped clean with a damp cloth or sponge; washing may remove some of the finish.

SEVEN STEPS TO EASIER IRONING

1. Organize your ironing area by keeping aids nearby: distilled or demineralized water and a measuring cup with a pouring spout (for steam irons); a sponge and dish for water to dampen spots; a plastic sheet or piece of fabric to cover the floor and protect large articles from soil; hangers; a pressing cloth; and a can of spray starch.

2. An adjustable ironing table used alternately in standing and sitting positions will ease strain on your back. Do large, flat pieces while standing so your arm can make a full swing the length of the board. You can sit while doing smaller pieces and detail work.

3. Fabric softeners added during the final rinse help to cut ironing time by preventing deep creases and allowing the iron to glide more easily.

4. Clothes taken from the dryer or line while slightly damp will not need much sprinkling. If you are not ready to iron dampened clothes, place them in the refrigerator in plastic bags. They will keep without mildewing or souring for several days.

5. When clothes are dampened, use warm water and fold rather than roll to aid the water penetration. Then let them "season" for an hour or two.

6. Children's and men's trousers can be dried on a pants stretcher. Then they will need only touch-up ironing.

7. Iron low-heat fabrics (silks and synthetics) first, then work up to higher cotton and linen temperatures. This eliminates waiting for the iron to cool and avoids accidental scorching.

STARCH

If you miss the crispness in some wearables, try a light starch or fabric-finish treatment, either instant starch in the washer or a spray-on starch applied as you iron. Most such sprays contain silicone or similar "slippery" ingredients which significantly speed up ironing. For light stiffness, spray-starch one section of the fabric at a time with a fine, even spray and use a dry iron. For lighter body, a steam iron is best. For heavier body, spray and iron, then spray and iron again. Do not spray too heavily at any time; the starch may flake off and adhere to the iron, making the job more difficult.

IRONING PROCEDURE

First iron the parts of a garment that hang over the edge of the board (cuffs, collars, and sleeves). This avoids double work in retouching wrinkles if the body of the garment is ironed first.

Put three **handkerchiefs** on the board at once. Fold women's handkerchiefs in a square, men's handkerchiefs in thirds, lengthwise and crosswise.

Iron all **clothing** absolutely dry as you go, especially double thicknesses and heavy seams. This keeps the fabric from wrinkling or from dampening adjacent areas and forcing you to reiron. Judge dryness by touch; some acetates, for example, may look dry before they really are.

Press lightly over **buttonholes**, to prevent sagging. Heat may harm some buttons; to avoid this, turn button side down on a thick bath towel and iron over it. Do not iron directly over a zipper, but use the nose of the iron to smooth out wrinkles in the tape.

Shirts. Today's durable press and wash and wear shirts require little or no ironing. If you must iron plain cotton, before ironing lightly dampen the shirt, beginning with its front and collar. Then fold the shirt in thirds, sprinkling as you go.

Wherever there are double thicknesses—collar, cuffs, buttonhole bands, yoke—iron on both sides and use a firm pressure for better finish. Start by ironing the collar on the wrong side partly dry, then thoroughly dry on the right side. Pull the material taut and iron slowly from points in. Iron the neckband, then fold and shape collar. Next fold the yoke flat and iron dry.

Iron each cuff exactly like the collar. Nose the iron well up into the gathers so that both cuff and sleeve will be dry. Iron along the underarm seam. Finally iron the body of the shirt, first the back and then the fronts. Hold the front pleat taut so it will be free from tiny wrinkles.

To fold the shirt neatly, lay it flat and button the top, middle, and lowest buttons. Fold under each side lengthwise, about one-fourth of the width. Lay sleeves lengthwise. Turn shirt over and fold.

Skirts. Iron pleats (other than permanent pleats) by arranging several pleats in a group. Space them evenly and pin for pressing. If the material shows shine, use a pressing cloth. A gored skirt, cut on the bias, should be ironed with the weave of the goods. At the hem, iron with the straight of the goods. This prevents wrinkling or bulging at the seams.

PRESSING

Use a steam iron, or a pressing cloth with a dry iron, and the "wool" temperature setting. Brush clothes well, including pockets, trouser cuffs, and under collars. Use a treated pressing cloth, which permits higher temperatures than untreated cloths, dampened lightly with a sponge or sprayer. Press by lifting the iron up and down rather than sliding it back and forth as in regular ironing. On pockets, lapels, and other double thicknesses that must be pressed on the right side, use a light pressure to avoid shine.

Don't let the pressing cloth become completely dry. Lift it while still steaming and beat the fabric being pressed with a clothesbrush to bring up the nap. Use a shoulder mitt (a rolled bath towel will serve) to slip into upper parts of sleeves and shoulders; then you can press without ironing creases into the fullness. To press trouser legs, be guided by the original creases. Move iron with a circular motion over the inside of each leg in turn, then press the outside.

With a steam iron, wool skirts and many dresses may be pressed on the wrong side without a pressing cloth. On the right side, use a double thickness of cheesecloth, which protects the fabric while permitting the steam to get through. Press with the nap, not against it; on smooth fabrics, press with the grain. Let pressed clothes hang freely for a while before storing, to get rid of any residual dampness.

IRONING PROBLEMS

Cure for shine. Attempt this only with wool, and with great caution to avoid damaging a worn spot in the fabric. Sponge the area thoroughly, then go over it gently with fine steel wool, over a six-to-eight-inch area. Let dry, and press.

Scorching may occur when the iron is too hot or if you leave it on one spot too long. It also occurs if the detergent has not been thoroughly rinsed out of the fabric. With starched articles, it may be wise to drop the heat of the iron one notch from the normal setting for the fabric.

Scorch stains may be removed from *washable* fabrics by a good laundering or by bleaching, if the stain is not too severe.

Nonwashable fabrics must be sent to a dry cleaner for removal of scorch stains. In any case, the scorching must be expected to weaken the fabric even if the stain completely disappears.

Ties. Without precautions, pressed neckties may get shiny and flattened. Cut a cardboard insert to slip inside each half of the cravat. Press with a steam iron over cheesecloth.

JEWELRY CLEANING |

Whether it is an inexpensive piece of costume jewelry or a diamond ring, jewelry requires care to highlight its beauty and to prevent needless damage. Keep each piece in a separate compartment of a jewelry box, or wrap them individually in tissues to prevent pieces from scratching each other. (Appearance can also be dulled by contact with cosmetics, body oils and acids, dust and dirt.)

Except for watches, which should be cleaned only by experts, most jewelry can be cleaned safely at home. Here are some tips on good care:

Diamonds, other precious stones, gold, platinum. Soak for a few minutes in warm water to which a little detergent and a few drops of household ammonia have been added. Brush gently with a soft brush. Do not scrub or use a pin to remove dirt from a stone, as this may loosen the setting. Rinse in warm water and dry with a soft, lint-free cloth. Commercial jewelry cleaning solutions are also available.

Silver. Polish tarnished silver jewelry as you would table silver, using a good silver polish and a soft brush, if necessary, on patterns with tiny crevices.

Costume jewelry. When stones are glued or cemented, rather than held with prongs as in precious jewelry, do not put in water (the settings may loosen). Instead, wipe with a soft, damp cloth, using a few drops of ammonia in the water.

Pearls. Whether real pearls (natural or cultured), simulated, or artificial pearls, frequently wipe clean with a soft cloth. Cosmetics, including hair spray, dirt, and other substances can discolor or damage pearls if not removed. If film or marks persist, slightly moisten the cloth. Keep artificial pearls out of water. Real and cultured pearls, however, may be dipped into warm sudsy water. Rub them gently with a soft cloth; rinse in clear warm water; dry thoroughly. Have a necklace restrung whenever the string begins to stretch or soil. Valuable pearls should receive professional cleaning by a jeweler once a year.

Opal and turquoise. Treat these less hardy gems gently and do not expose them to excessive heat. Clean them in the same way as pearls.

KITCHEN RANGES |

Whether gas or electric, kitchen ranges combining top-stove cooking with an oven and broiler come in widths from 20 inches (apartment-size) to the standard 38 to 40 inches. You can get one oven/broiler plus storage space for utensils; two oven/broiler units; or one oven plus a separate, side broiler.

On top, gas ranges have four to six heating units, electric ranges usually four. Generally they are grouped so as to provide working space to one side, in the center, or in front. Some women choose a staggered arrangement which leaves more room between pots when several burners are in use at one time, but sacrifices some work space.

In standard electric ranges, broiling is done at the *top* of the oven under the top heating element; in gas ranges, usually *below* the oven in a separate compartment. If you want to bake and broil at the same time, you need two ovens or one oven plus a separate broiler. Electric broiling is radiant-type, the so-called "charcoal" effect; but the same effect is built into some gas ranges by having the flame heat a metal or ceramic radiant surface.

Built-in ranges, slide-in or high-oven, have become popular for the custom look they give a kitchen. Tri-level ranges also give the advantage of two ovens in thirty inches of space. In shopping for a range, the quality of basic construction, including tight-fitting doors, easy-sliding broiler trays, sturdy parts and exterior finish, is as important as the choice of fuel.

Since both gas and electric ranges do a first-rate job on all types of cooking, and offer many of the same optional features, which you choose will depend on personal preference and the cost of installation and operation. Bear in mind that utility rates go down as you use more of a single fuel, so it may be economical to have most of your major appliances, especially the range, water-heater, and dryer, powered by the same fuel. Remember, though, that an electric range will require its own heavy-duty circuit.

Best buy for you depends on the features you find most useful. Extras, naturally, raise a range's price, so weigh the value of each in terms of time, convenience, and better meals, and then balance these long-term benefits against your budget.

Automatic oven clock controls, for instance, are often bought at extra cost and never used at all—a shame, when they offer such advantages. You simply set the clock control for cooking time, the oven for temperature, and the rest is done automatically, the control turning the oven on and off at the designated times. Various ranges may accomplish this automatic timing in slightly different ways—some requiring the selection of start-and-stop cooking times, others geared to the length of cooking time.

Another oven innovation: "keep-warm" ovens that let you cook ahead, then keep food at serving temperature. Just set two dials, one for timing, the other for temperature. These automatically turn the oven down to a keep-warm temperature (170° F.) at the end of the cooking time, and keep food at this low temperature for hours without overcooking. The low temperature permits putting your best china serving platters or a basket of napkin-wrapped rolls in the oven until serving time. Other oven features include automatic meat thermometers and rotisseries.

Top-stove units have cook-and-keep-warm settings, too, that not only let you keep mashed potatoes warm—without sticking—but eliminate the need for a double boiler. A thermostat control gives you uniform temperature at any setting you select, just like the oven.

Large griddles, built into the range surface, are available on some models. They're convenient for a large number of hamburgers, chops, eggs, etc. Some may be converted to a fifth unit.

Finally, don't forget service. If discount buying means no guaranty, or taking a brand for which parts and service will be hard to obtain, it may prove to be no bargain.

EASIER RANGE CLEANING

Tremendous strides have been taken in the direction of easy care of ranges. To guide you as you shop, here's a run-down of the features you'll find.

First thing to look for is an acid-resistant cook-top that's rimmed or recessed (to protect the floor from spills) and has a back-splash of sufficient size to protect the area behind the range. If the cook-top can be removed, tilted, or propped up to simplify cleaning underneath, so much the better.

Next area to examine is the surface units. Electric units lift up or unplug; all units, electric or gas, should have wash-at-the-sink reflector or drip pans. Unit-control dials (but not push buttons) should be removable.

Several new ranges have a self-cleaning oven which cleans itself automatically and more thoroughly than it is possible to do by hand. Although the process used requires an extremely high temperature, double controls and thicker insulation insure safety to the user.

For no-stretch oven cleaning, doors may lift off, drop down out of the way, swing to the right or left, swing up and tilt forward, or open out from the center like French doors. To conceal oven interiors, many glass doors are patterned with "etched" designs. Others are mirrored, tinted, or made of black glass. Some glass is even removable. Oven interiors are lined with porcelain enamel or chrome (so you can safely use chemical oven cleaners).

Construction of some ovens is one piece. All should have rounded corners. To make care easier, bottoms may lift out, bake and broil units lift up or unplug. One range features throwaway oven linings, of standard 18-inch foil, which do away with all heavy cleaning of sides, top, bottom, and back. In another, oven linings roll out like drawers for cleaning. The removable oven panels of still another are coated with Teflon (nonstick) finish, which you wash as you would a nonstick frying pan. If there's a storage drawer below the oven, check to see if it lifts out for easy cleaning (and for sweeping under the range).

Broiler pans of porcelain enamel (sometimes with chrome broiler racks) should be sink size, with rounded corners and no rough edges. Two special constructions—one, a broiler unit under glass; the other, an extra-deep broiler pan cooled by water in a pan beneath—help to keep broiler spatters off oven walls. Some broilers also have removable doors.

TIPS ON USING A RANGE

Some thermostatically controlled surface units (these are the ones that take the temperature of the pan during cooking) are marked "low" or "warm" instead of 150° F. Use this setting when recipes or instructions call for temperatures of 150° to 190° F.

For continuous accuracy, keep the sensing device in the center of your thermostatically controlled unit clean, using either a damp cloth or fine, dry steel wool.

If a gas range controlled burner gives a choice of flame heights as well as temperatures, take into account the material your utensils are made of as well as their size. For aluminum pans, set the flame about the same diameter as the pan bottom. A more reduced flame height is desirable for utensils of other materials.

Surface elements on some electric ranges offer a choice of heat patterns to match the size of your cooking utensil.

For most top-range cooking, start on high heat, then turn to medium or low, whichever continues the cooking gently.

Medium heat is preferable to high for browning and cooking in stainless steel utensils, except when you are bringing water to a boil.

When using your rotisserie, it's important to balance and center the meat on the rod. If the meat has a bone (for example, a leg of lamb), insert the spit parallel and close to the bone. Use your broiler pan under the meat to catch any drippings (you'll probably be surprised how few drippings there are).

A meat thermometer is the easiest and most accurate way to gauge when a roast in a rotisserie is done. In using a meat thermometer, insert it almost parallel, but at a slight angle, to the rotisserie rod, not perpendicular to the rod. Be sure it does not contact bone or rod. If it does, the internal temperature reading of the meat will not be accurate.

KITCHEN TOOLS | See also KNIVES; POTS AND PANS; WORKSAVERS

Fully equipping your kitchen could take a lifetime, as your food and party-giving habits change or new needs arise. The best plan for a beginner is to start with a basic set of *good quality* utensils, even if some must do double duty (a frying pan as a griddle, a saucepan as a teakettle, etc.).

Whichever cooking ware you prefer, always choose sturdy, well-made, evenly balanced utensils with tight-fitting covers and heat-resistant handles. Poor-quality pans will warp, dent, and become wobbly; poorly balanced ones may tip over when empty or nearly empty; skimpy covers won't keep their shape; even an inferior can opener or egg beater is an economy you will regret.

Consider not only the quality of each item but how often you will use it. Economize, if you must, by postponing less essential purchases. For top-stove cooking, choose ware that fits your range. Bottoms should be the right sizes for the heating units. The following list will serve as a general guide for early needs:

1 large covered pan (kettle, saucepan, or Dutch oven), 5- to 10-qt. size. Use it for meats, soups, stews, spaghetti.

1 double boiler, 2- to 3-qt. bottom. Units may be used separately as saucepans, or depending on design, as a casserole.

2 saucepans, 1-qt. and 2-qt., with covers.

2 skillets (frying pans): 10-in. with cover for large-quantity frying, braising, vegetables, one-dish meals; 7-in. for other frying. Both may be used as griddles. Teflon coatings are a plus in cleaning.

1 pressure saucepan, 4-qt. size. Permits quick cooking of pot roast, stews, vegetables; a favorite of working wives.

1 roasting pan with rack, uncovered, 12 to 15 in. long, 10 to 12 in. wide, 2 or 3 in. deep.

1 casserole, 2-qt. size—but plan soon to add 1 or 2 more of other sizes.

1 loaf pan, 2-qt. size. For meat loaf, etc., as well as for breads.

2 round layer-cake pans, 8 or 9 in.; 1 square cake pan, 8 or 9 × 2 in. deep; and 2 pie pans, 8 or 9 in. Aluminum or glass give best results.

1 muffin pan, 6- or 12-muffin size.

1 teakettle, 2- or 3-qt., either enclosed or with lid (which is easier to clean inside.) It frees a saucepan otherwise used for boiling water.

1 or 2 cookie sheets, large size. They are handy for warming up breads and rolls.

1 or 2 measuring cups (liquid), and 1 set of graduated measuring cups (dry).

1 set of mixing bowls, from 2 cups to 4 qts. They may double as ovenware (if so labeled), and for refrigerator storage.

1 starter knife set: French knife, carving knife, slicer, medium-size utility knife, and 2 paring knives.

2 flour sifters, 1-cup and 5-cup. (These depend on how much "start-from-scratch" baking you'll do.)

1 grater, or set of graters, for cheese, chocolate, vegetables, etc.

2 strainers—1 small for tea, 1 colander.

1 canister set with scoops for storing staples.

2 cutting boards, 1 large for meats, 1 small for cheese, vegetables, breads.

1 rolling pin. For pastry baking or for crushing crumbs, etc.

1 portable electric mixer, 1 hand beater with heavy-duty gear construction.

1 food grinder (new types need no clamping down).

1 reamer for lemon juice. Also 1 large juicer for oranges if you do not have an electric one (and prefer fresh juice to frozen).

1 metal spatula, long and narrow. Teflon pans may require a plastic spatula.

1 ladle.

1 cooking fork.

1 can opener, electric or wall type.
1 pastry blender.
1 pancake turner, short and broad.
1 large spoon, solid or perforated.
1 potato masher (optional).
1 kitchen shears.
1 set of wooden spoons.
1 set of refrigerator dishes.

SIMPLE TOOLS TO MAKE COOKING EASIER

In the past twenty-five years, all sorts of marvelous gadgets and appliances have been developed to make life in the kitchen easier for homemakers. However, even in this time of automatic mixers, coffee-makers, dishwashers, and disposers, some of the best cooking aids are simple, inexpensive tools.

1. A quick twist of the wrist with a notched-tooth opener loosens screw tops and twist-off caps. This opener bites into a variety of sizes, from very narrow (as in Tabasco bottles) to those four inches in diameter.

2. There is no need to fight vacuum-sealed jars and bottles. Use this simple one-piece key opener to flip open lids.

3. When you buy measuring spoons, choose a set with long handles which dig deep into large as well as small cans, jars, and packages. Stainless-steel spoons are marked with accurate measures of one tablespoon, one teaspoon, one-half teaspoon, and one-quarter teaspoon. Extra sets for permanent storage in canisters—salt, coffee, sugar, etc.—save spoon-washing time.

4. A vegetable-and-fruit-parer (with a bean-slicing feature) produces paper-thin parings from potatoes, carrots, cucumbers, apples, pears, etc.; cleans brown spots or other blemishes from celery or cauliflower; makes neat curls from bar chocolate, and slivers for flavoring from lemon or orange rind; scoops the eyes out of potatoes. In sum, it is a culinary must.

5. A stainless wire beater will do many things. It whips, beats, stirs, blends, mixes—all on a light-duty basis. An excellent aid in ridding gravy or sauces of lumps.

6. Kitchen shears have many uses, from cutting poultry with large ones to cutting herbs with small ones. The notches inside the pair shown are handy in removing can or bottle tops.

7. It is old-fashioned and wasteful of precious juices to turn steaks and chops with a fork. Instead, use kitchen tongs, which do not puncture the meat. They also are a boon in handling hot corn on the cob and baked potatoes, and in dispensing ice cubes.

8. You do not have to be a clock watcher if you have a minute timer. Whether you have a cake in the oven, a steak in the broiler, or a stew on the stove, just set the timer for any interval within a 60-minute period, and

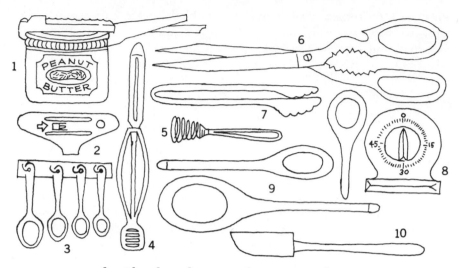

you can proceed with other chores until it rings. When you are going to work outside the kitchen, carry the timer with you.

9. Assortments of wooden spoons are convenient and help keep the insides of your pans smooth and unscratched.

10. A rubber bottle scraper with a narrow blade and long plastic handle helps to get the last bit out of the mayonnaise, mustard, chili sauce, or honey jar. Equally useful for scraping out double boilers and electric blender containers.

A pegboard for hanging tools is a good way to increase kitchen efficiency.

KNIVES | See also CARVING GUIDE

A well-equipped kitchen needs a set of basic knives, as illustrated, not only to prepare food well, but to save time. Having the right knife at hand for any particular cutting job remarkably improves efficiency. Your own experience may suggest various specialty knives as well; for example, if your family likes hard-crusted breads, consider a saw-toothed bread knife as well as the scalloped type shown.

For kitchen use, the best knives have hollow-ground (slightly concave) blades of stainless steel that take and hold a keen edge and don't rust. It is no longer any problem to sharpen a stainless knife; some special-bladed types stay keen indefinitely. Electric home sharpeners, through which you merely draw the blade a few times, produce an excellent edge. Some manual, wall- or counter-mounted sharpeners make honing easy without any special skills. Sharpen your knives frequently or have them honed professionally.

Don't abuse knives to open cans, bottles, or jars; and don't carve on glass, metal, or tile surfaces. This both dulls the blade and scratches the surface; use your wooden cutting board. Store knives in a holster or rack to protect the edges and prevent cut fingers; also hand-wash individually for safety's sake, and dry immediately. Knives with Pakkawood or other melamine handles may be washed in the automatic dishwasher; other handles may warp or roughen if soaked in water.

1. **Knife sizes** refer to the length of the blade. Other parts are named in the diagram. The number of rivets reveals the length of the tang; in full-tang construction it runs entirely through the handle for extra strength. Styles and names may vary slightly among manufacturers.

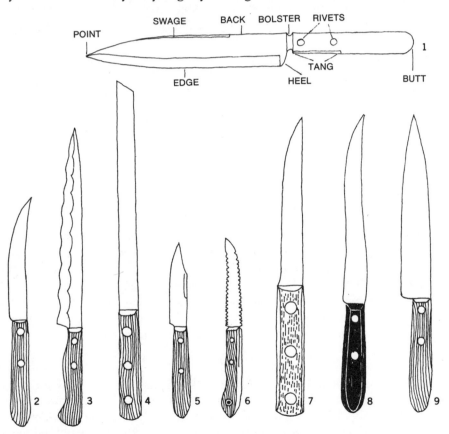

2. **Utility knife,** 6 or 7 inches. Use when paring knife is too small. Edge also made scalloped or serrated.

3. **Bread knife,** 8 inches. The scalloped edge won't crush even such very soft foods as sponge or angel-food cake.

4. **Cold slicer,** 10 inches; sometimes called a ham slicer. Its long, narrow blade cuts easily through cold fat.

5. **Paring knife,** 3 or 3½ inches. Indispensable for dozens of kitchen chores: peeling, seeding, pitting, etc.

6. **Grapefruit knife.** 3½ inches, with curved blade, usually has at least one serrated or scalloped edge.

7. **Boner,** 6 inches; also called a trimmer. Special tapered edge for boning ham or leg of lamb, fileting fish, etc.

8. **Hot slicer,** 8 or 12 inches. Most commonly used for carving roasts and other hot meats and poultry.

9. **Cook's knife,** 8 inches, or French or chef's knife, 10–12 inches. Handle's position gives knuckle space for chopping. (See below).

When buying knives, the quality of the steel used in the blade is the most important feature. Generally, the higher the price of the cutlery, the better the blade.

A basic carving set consists of a knife, fork, and sharpening steel. The carving knife has a curved edge, 8 or 9 inches long. Carving forks should have a guard above the tines to protect the hand when the knife cuts toward the fork. Cutlery handles should feel comfortable and balanced. Flat handles, usually made of plastic-impregnated wood or bone, should be fastened with three rivets. Rounded stag handles need a secure cap and bolster.

More elaborate carving sets may include a 5- or 6-inch carving knife for boning, and a 10- or 12-inch knife for heavier cutting. A slicing knife, which has a long, flexible blade and usually a rounded tip, is useful for cutting thin slices of ham or fowl.

Electric slicing knives are an aid to quick, neat, and professional carving or slicing. They consist of a power handle with hardened steel, serrated blades that snap out of the handle for cleaning. When the handle is held in natural fashion, a slight pressure of the fingers actuates the knife. The blades move in a reciprocal motion, back and forth up to 2,400 times a minute. This gives very precise control. You merely place the blade where you want to cut and hold it there while it does the work.

HOW TO USE THE FRENCH KNIFE

The growing vogue for Continental and Oriental cooking calls for much chopping and slicing of raw foods. The design of the French knife makes it an efficient tool, the standby of famous chefs. The blade is wider than the handle, allowing room for your fingers when the knife cuts through the food to the cutting board. Its tapered point permits rocking the blade back and forth.

To slice celery, for example, place two or three stalks together on the board in parallel rows. Place a wide pan or plate alongside, lower than the board. Grasp the celery firmly with one hand, with fingers well back from the blade. Holding the knife in your other hand with its point on the board, bring the blade down through all the stalks of celery, cutting to desired length. Raise the handle, leaving knife point on the board as a pivot, and feed more celery under the blade. Continue cutting with this rocking motion, pushing the cut pieces into the pan with a sidewise motion.

To chop with a French knife, hold the handle in one hand and press down on the back of the blade, near the point, with two fingers of the other hand. Use the same rocking motion as in slicing, but hold the point in one position and pivot from side to side through whatever you're chopping.

LAMPS, TABLE | See also LIGHTING

1. **Column.** The classic motif conveys a feeling of the dignity appropriate for the English eighteenth century, Regency, and Directoire furnishings. Simple versions also harmonize well with contemporary. Another lamp often used in the same room with the column is the urn. Its rounded form contrasts effectively with the classic style of the column lamp, and it is available in both metal and china.

2. **Jar.** Most styles have a charming informality especially suitable in early-American and provincial settings. Others may be Oriental.

3. **Cylinder.** This is the simplest of all lamp shapes and it lends itself to varied materials, patterns, and textures. The base shown here is a wallpaper roller.

4. **Vase.** Everyone is familiar with the Far Eastern design with its fluid curves and perfectly balanced proportions. The one shown is a reproduction of a Chinese vase. Others may be of classical origin.

5. **Candelabra.** The ornamental branches of the candelabra lamp add a

note of elegance to formal traditional interiors, such as Regency and Empire. The four-arm style with intricate scrollwork holds four light bulbs. (The candlestick lamp is so familiar it needs no description. It is available in many sizes and materials.)

6. **Figure.** Sculpture ranging from classic busts to French court figures is often incorporated into lamps. The subject determines the period.

7. **Baluster.** Borrowed from architecture, the molded support of this lamp with its rhythmic curves is readily adaptable to both traditional and contemporary rooms. It is seen most often in wood or plaster.

8. **Globe.** In Victorian days, the glass bowl and chimney shielded an open flame. Now purely decorative, the motif is retained in simplified styles. It is frequently hand painted.

9. **Bottle.** Popular in elongated, slender, contemporary designs.

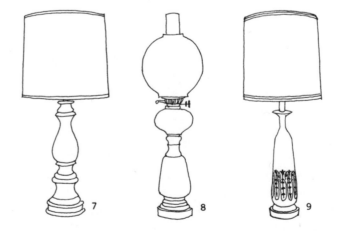

10. **Twin**. Also called "student" because it gave better reading light than other lamps used from 1875 to 1900. This harmonizes with colonial furniture, despite later origin. It also comes in single-globe versions.

11. **Oil**. Fuel reservoir and key for turning up the wick are typical. Usually seen in china or glass.

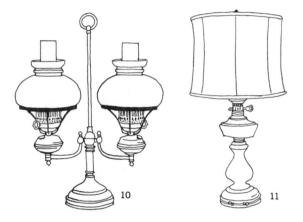

10   11

LAUNDERING | See also IRONING; LAUNDERING PROBLEMS; LAUNDRY PRODUCTS; STAINS; WASHERS AND DRYERS

Automatic machines for washing, drying, and ironing clothes greatly ease the once dreaded "washday" chore. Good planning will also save time and work. Try to arrange laundry facilities compactly and in the order of the four major tasks: preparation, washing, drying, and finishing. Many homes provide a first-floor utility room; otherwise a space of about 9′ × 9′, in or preferably near the bedrooms or kitchen, is better than a basement location.

PREPARATION

Here clothes are sorted and mended and stains are removed. A counter or table top is needed, with a deep-bowled sink desirable. Provide storage space for detergents, starches, bleaches, fabric softeners, etc. A folding, wheeled laundry or shopping cart may be used as a temporary hamper.

WASHING

Carefully study the directions that apply to your washing machine for proper use of automatic features or special settings. These may be indispensable for certain items such as woolens.

Do your laundry frequently and don't overload the washer. Unless you have a large-capacity washer (fourteen to sixteen pounds), a typical load should weigh eight or nine pounds and contain no more than two large pieces (sheets or tablecloths) which may weigh about two pounds each, with the remainder made up of smaller pieces. Separately wash large, bulky items such as spreads and blankets. In a properly loaded agitator washer, the clothes should disappear under the water and reappear within a few minutes. In a tumbler, the clothes should fall freely to the bottom as the basket revolves.

Group clothes for washing according to the degree of soiling, time, and water temperature required. Sort them into separate loads: white and pastel, colorfast cottons, and colored synthetic materials or blends; non-colorfast clothes; white nylon and other synthetics; and gentle or hand-washables. Watch out for bright or deep colors; when brand new, wash these articles separately to remove any excess dye. Search pockets for lint-makers such as tissues and for stain-makers such as crayons.

Pretreat shirt collars and cuffs, knees of children's trousers, and under-arms of shirts and blouses. With a small, soft brush, apply a liquid detergent to these areas, or a concentrated solution of dry detergent and water. Then use the same detergent for washing the entire load.

BASIC WASHING METHODS

The timing and water temperature of the wash cycle depends on the amount of soil in the clothes. The time may range between 4 and 15 minutes —don't wash more than 15 minutes. Overwashing will let soil re-enter fabrics and produce extra wear and lint. One rinse is good, two are better.

Lightly soiled clothes, wash and wear, durable press, and delicate fabrics require 4 to 6 minutes wash time. The gentle or short wash cycle is usually sufficient to get the clothes clean. Medium to cold water is adequate for light soil and for most wash and wear or durable press garments. It helps maintain the color of non-colorfast fabrics. The cold water rinse, followed by a short or slow spin, makes ironing of wrinkle-resistant synthetics easier.

Heavily soiled clothes may require the full 12 to 15 minutes wash time with normal agitation and spin. Hot water wash should be followed by a warm or cold water rinse.

Soaking or a pre-wash cycle may be needed for clothes having heavy, ground-in soil such as work and garden clothes. Use the "soak" cycle of the automatic washer if such a cycle is available; otherwise, set to "warm rinse" for the preliminary wash. After the spin cycle, reset the time dial to start at the wash cycle. Set to "hot" (140° to 160°) with the full washing time.

Hand washing is for such items as nylon stockings, sweaters, fragile blouses or lingerie, silk scarves, blouses or dresses trimmed with rhinestones or sequins; or colored articles that must be washed alone to prevent dis-coloring others. These items may be washed in the machine if you have a very gentle cycle. (See your instruction booklet). Putting such items in a nylon mesh bag helps to protect them. If you do not have a very gentle cycle, then hand-wash in the following manner:

Use warm water (90° to 110°) and mild soap or detergent; squeeze suds through the article until clean; rinse thoroughly. To get the water out, press the article between clean bath towels; or hang it up to drip dry (particularly synthetic fibers which need no ironing, and all permanently pleated skirts). Lay sweaters flat.

OTHER LAUNDERING TECHNIQUES

To save money and avoid damage to clothes, measure the amount of cleaning products with care. Keep a measuring cup and a quart measuring pitcher handy. Premeasured detergent tablets help eliminate much guess-work.

Bleaching. A chlorine bleach is traditional for whitening soiled cottons and linens and for removing stains, but can be damaging to silk, wool, acetate, and spandex. Labels on some garments of specially treated cotton warn not to use a chlorine bleach. If you make a mistake causing yellowing, try this remedy: soak the garment in a solution of two tablespoonfuls of sodium thiosulfite to one gallon of very hot water; rinse well. Or use packaged color remover.

One cup of liquid chlorine bleach in a top-loading washer, and one-half cup in a front-loading washer, are ample for occasional bleaching. Be sure to dilute the bleach in one quart of water before adding to wash water. One-quarter to one-half cup of powdered chlorine bleach usually is recommended for agitator washers, one-eighth to one-quarter cup for tumbler washers. (Bleach in soluble packets eliminates measuring.) Mix the powder with wash water before adding clothes.

Non-chlorine (fine-fabric or all-fabric) bleaches are designed for materials requiring a gentler action, including most washable colors, silk, spandex, acetate, and wool. Follow directions on the label.

Bluing makes white clothes appear whiter by giving them a slight bluish cast. If you use liquid bluing, avoid streaks by mixing it thoroughly with the water before adding clothes.

Starch may be added to the final rinse in an automatic washer; follow directions in the instruction book. Or do this in a separate bowl. After an item is starched, allow it to dry completely, then sprinkle well and allow it to season about an hour before ironing. Liquid plastic and spray starches may be used on synthetics and blends as well as on cotton. Liquid plastic starch lasts through several washings. Spray starches save time since they are applied on damp or dry fabrics as you iron.

TIPS FOR BETTER LAUNDERING

If the wash comes out gray and harsh, some lapse in proper procedure usually is at fault, rather than the washer itself. Be sure to use enough detergent or soap, up to the maximum amount recommended on the package. Use a water conditioner with soap if the water is hard enough to form a ring around the bathtub. Bleaches or bluing improve whiteness, and fabric softeners avoid harshness. To whiten cottons and linens and remove stains, add a chlorine bleach (or an all-fabric bleach for fabrics labeled "do not bleach").

In tumbler machines, some laundry products build up so much foam as to hinder washing action. A low-sudsing detergent will correct this. If your washer won't spin when it should, chances are you have oversudsed it. Stop the machine and rinse the interior several times with cold water and at least one cup of vinegar or 2 capfuls of fabric softener, then rewash. If thumping occurs with spinning, the load is unbalanced (and some washers will shut themselves off). Redistribute the clothes or reduce the load.

Washable fabrics require careful label reading; the question is *how* to wash them. Some may be washable only by hand, especially silks, woolens, and some synthetic fibers. Some white synthetics have a tendency to absorb dyes from other fabrics, and should be washed separately. Study the basic washing methods above, before assuming that a washable fabric may be machine-washed without special precautions.

Fast colors. The term "colorfast" refers to the degree of a dye's resistance to cleaning and to sunlight. The label "vat-dyed" assures excellent colorfastness, recommended for articles that require frequent washing or are exposed to the sun. Colorfast fabrics can be washed in the machine with other clothes. However, bright colors should not be hung in the sun to dry, as this may cause fading. Most fabric manufacturers give washing directions, or may specify dry cleaning.

Shrinkage. Look for labels giving the percentage of "residual shrinkage," which means the shrinkage you can expect from repeated washing or dry cleaning. Federal Trade Commission rules require that this percentage be specified when words like "shrunk" or "preshrunk" are used. One per cent is hardly noticeable; 2 or 3 per cent is satisfactory. Higher shrinkage may be tolerable depending upon the use of the article. A bed sheet or blanket may be too short after washing if residual shrinkage exceeds 6 per cent. A 72" drapery may lose well over 2 inches with 3 per cent shrinkage.

Mend first, then wash. Mending tape saves sewing; simply press it over rips or tears with a hot iron. Match the tape with the color of the article.

DRYING

Hanging clothes on a line outdoors or in the basement is one way of drying, but machine-drying is easier. However, avoid overdrying in the machine, as this causes wrinkles and shrinkage. If you use the right technique, work clothes, sheets, pajamas, shorts, etc., should dry soft and require no ironing. Follow the drying-time chart in the instruction book, and experiment with sorting clothes into washing loads that will require the same time to dry. Dry only one load at a time.

With a mixed load, set the time dial for the lightest-weight fabrics, or for those you want to remove while slightly damp for ironing. Then continue to reset the dial as needed, keeping heavy Turkish towels for the last. Leave T-shirts and knit underwear with the wet towels to prevent shrinkage; remove after twenty minutes while the towels continue to tumble. With an "automatic" cycle or "sensing" device it's much easier.

Be sure to empty the dryer's lint trap after each use, and occasionally brush out the air intake and floor of the cabinet. A surprising amount of lint accumulates (because it can't blow away as in outdoor drying), and it can cause overheating.

Hanging clothes on a line, in view of the present-day popularity of the dryer, may be a vanishing art. Here are suggestions to avoid marking with pins or stretching the material out of shape:

Fold sheets double, hem to hem; then turn about 4 inches over the line and use four clean, smooth clothespins. Straighten by running your fingers down the selvage at the sides. The sheet dries evenly and will be easier to iron.

Hang men's shirts by the tail, first folding double by bringing the two shirt fronts together. Fold the tail three or four inches over the line and pin at the ends.

Never hang your towels by one corner, but always over the line. Shake towels vigorously before hanging, to restore fluffiness.

Hang clothes when possible so the prevailing breeze will billow out sleeves and pajama legs. But cotton dresses, trousers, knitted goods, in fact most garments you want to keep in original shape should be hung on hangers rather than on the line.

LAUNDERING PROBLEMS |

Pillows. Examine ticking of feather, down, or urethane-foam pillows; mend weak or open seams and tears. Place in a pillowcase and baste the open end to allow water circulation.

Wash two pillows at a time for a balanced load, or if washing just one, add towels to balance. Fill the automatic washer with warm water and push pillows down to saturate them completely before agitation begins. Use the "regular" wash cycle. Stop the washer and turn pillows over halfway through washing.

To dry, put the pillows in your automatic dryer and set it at a low heat. Allow about one-and-a-half hours. Be sure they are completely dry; dampness can cause a musty odor and mildew in feather and down pillows.

Synthetic-fiber filled pillows should be washed by hand. Squeeze them gently in warm water with detergent added to make medium suds. Do not twist or wring. The ticking may be cleaned by scrubbing it with a soft brush. Rinse thoroughly in warm water and squeeze to remove water, or spin the pillow in the final cycle of an automatic washer. Dry in an automatic dryer on the "regular" setting until both the ticking and stuffing are dry.

If latex foam-rubber pillows have washable zippered covers, remove and wash them like pillowcases. Wash the pillows by hand, squeezing in warm suds until clean. Rinse several times in the same way. Latex foam-rubber is fragile when wet, so place the pillow in a loose pillowcase and fasten the open end with safety pins. Then put one pillow and two heavy towels for balance in the automatic washer and set for the spin cycle.

Finish drying at room temperature (never in the sun). If most of the water is spun out by the washer, pillows should dry in about a day.

Blankets. Use a cellulose sponge and liquid detergent to spot-clean stains and soil, particularly along bindings.

Fill washer with warm water (or cold water), add detergent. When the detergent is dissolved, immerse one large or two small blankets and soak for about 10 minutes. Use the "soak" cycle if washer is equipped with one, or stop the washer after filling. Then wash the blankets for one minute; keep agitation at a minimum. Spin water from the washer on a "normal" spin cycle for about three minutes. Rinse twice for one minute, first in clear warm water, then with fabric softener added. Spin blankets for another three minutes.

To dry wool, wool-blend, and rayon blankets in an automatic dryer, preheat the dryer at the highest temperature for ten minutes. Put blanket in the dryer with three or four terry towels to act as buffers. Tumble for about fifteen minutes. Remove the blanket while damp and hang on two parallel lines in shade. Shape by gently stretching it in both directions.

Blankets made of acrylic fibers can be dried at the regular wash and wear setting. Check after twenty minutes and remove them as soon as they are dry to prevent wrinkling.

Brush blankets gently with a soft brush. To press bindings, use a steam iron at "synthetic" setting.

Comforters. To be washable, comforters should be well stitched in an all-over pattern. Check the label to be sure they are washable. (Some must be dry-cleaned.) Wash comforters like blankets, and dry them in the same way as acrylic blankets.

Bedspreads. Wash one double or two twin-size bedspreads at a time. Select water temperature according to fiber content—hot for cottons, warm or cold for synthetics. Use the "regular" cycle and laundry detergent. Add fabric softener to the last rinse.

For line drying, stretch and smooth the spread, and if possible, dry in a breeze. In an automatic dryer, use the "regular" setting for cottons, low heat for synthetics. Remove the spread as soon as it is dry to prevent wrinkling.

How to fold fitted sheets:

1. Fold sheet lengthwise once by bringing corners of both ends to hang loose. Pockets should be right side out.

2. Place sheet on ironing board with selvage edges towards you. With left hand, pick up extreme left end of sheet; and with right hand, push top pocket down into bottom pocket. Bring extreme left end of sheet over toward selvage edges (as indicated).

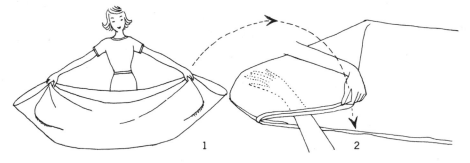

3. Left end of sheet now looks like this. To accomplish similar fold at other end of sheet, push top pocket into bottom pocket, fold, and smooth out as you did on left end of sheet.

4. Sheet now looks like this. (If you wish to iron your fitted sheets, press all flat surfaces.)

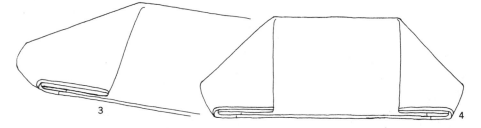

5. Fold sheet in half by bringing center fold over to selvage edges, as shown.

6. Fold both ends to middle and fold in half again, as many times as you wish. If you've been careful to buy your fitted sheets labeled Sanforized, they will always fold to the same exact dimensions.

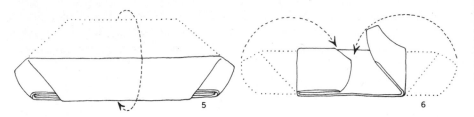

5   6

Electric blankets come in a variety of synthetic fabrics, some are blends, others are 100 per cent acrylic. With just a little care, shrinkage is no problem. Rayon blends, however, are more subject than others to shrinkage, particularly if exposed too long to the high heat of a clothes dryer. All modern electric blankets are washable. Never have them dry-cleaned. This can harm the electrical system in the blanket by damaging wire insulation.

Before washing, protect the plug by tying a cloth around it, then basting the cloth to the blanket. Spot-clean stains and soil by rubbing them lightly with liquid detergent on a sponge.

All blankets require the soaking room of a full washer tub of warm water. After one-third cup of detergent has been added, set the washer control for a one minute-and-a-half wash on gentle-agitation. Then stop the machine and allow blankets to soak for ten to fifteen minutes. Follow this with a fast spin and two thorough rinses. Add fabric softener to the final rinse; spin dry.

Dry your blanket in the shade over two parallel clotheslines, or in a dryer by setting the control on its high-heat setting. Put the blanket in the dryer with four to six dry bath towels for buffers for fifteen to twenty minutes. Remove it just before it is completely dry. Straighten and smooth, then brush the surface lightly to raise the nap. Press the binding with a steam iron at "synthetic" setting. Check the instructions with the blanket.

Diapers. If you have a washer and dryer, and from four to five dozen diapers, washing every other day will keep the supply going. To care for diapers after use, you'll need a large covered pail. After you remove diapers or soiled sleeping togs, flush away any soil: hold them by one corner in the toilet bowl and swish them around. Then half fill the pail with cold water, deodorize it with one-half cup of activated borax, and place the diapers in the pail to soak.

When ready to wash the diapers, drain and put them in your clothes washer. Add a fabric softener to the final rinse. Use the hot-water cycle and enough soap or detergent and chlorine bleach to make a lively suds. Wash about ten minutes and rinse thoroughly. Rinsing is important.

If you do not have a clothes dryer, hang each diaper by two corners, in the sun whenever possible. When they are dry, fold and put them away. Do not iron. Ironing wastes time and makes the diapers less absorbent.

Other baby clothes. Such articles as bibs, shirts, wrappers, nighties, and crib sheets collect so fast that you'll have enough for a washer load every day or so. Wash in hot suds for three or four minutes, and rinse thoroughly.

But if the clothes are stained from spinach, carrots, fruit and meat juices, etc., first let them soak in cool or lukewarm water, as hot water sets the stains. If stains from these foods are set, use a chlorine bleach treatment.

Curtains. Consider, before you leap too quickly into the job, what kind of curtains they are and how they should be handled. Check the original hang-tags or labels for fiber content and washing instructions. If these have been misplaced, keep these pointers in mind:

Dust is likely to accumulate on curtains of any fabric, so give them a short ten- or fifteen-minute soak in clear, cool water before washing.

Cotton curtains can be washed in pairs by hand, or in window lots in an automatic washer. If they are fairly new, use the "cotton" setting; if old and a little fragile, the "fine-fabric" setting. Wash and dry them in the usual way, except if "easy care" (resin finished). With these do not use a chlorine bleach unless you have the original label stating they are bleachable. If curtains are wrinkled, you may want to spray-starch them as you iron.

Fiber glass. This is a hand-washing job. Use any good laundering detergent, squeeze the curtains through the suds twice, and rinse them well. Put chlorine bleach in the wash water if they are white. But do not scrub, wring, or twist them—the glass fibers can be easily damaged. After rinsing, simply hang the curtains to drip-dry. A shower rod is handy. Or roll them in a towel and rehang them at the window. Fiber-glass curtains not only never need, but never should be touched by, an iron.

Nylon and other synthetics. Use gentle wash cycle and dry in dryer, or handwash as follows:

Drop curtains into a warm to hot water and detergent bath, swirl them around a bit, and let soak 5 minutes. A chlorine bleach may be used for extra whiteness. Drain off wash water and rinse in cool water, refilling the tub several times. When thoroughly rinsed, either blot (don't wring) the curtains with heavy towels and hang to dry, or drip-dry. The barest minimum of steam ironing should take care of washing wrinkles. Drip-dried curtains should need little or no ironing.

Table linens. Before washing, examine them for greasy stains from cream, salad dressings, and the like. Washing does not always remove such stains, and ironing may set them. Give any suspicious spots a preliminary treatment. Gather the sections surrounding the stains and soak them in cleaning fluid for ten minutes. Then wash and rinse them.

Gloves. Washable leather gloves should not be washed if previously dry-cleaned. If washable (not chamois or doeskin), wash on the hands. Work in a little extra suds on soiled fingertips and cuffs; roll them off the hands; then turn the gloves right side out. Rinse thoroughly; press out excess water with a clean bath towel. Shape and puff out the fingers by blowing into them. Lay gloves flat on a towel to dry, and when almost dry, soften them by gently working with the hands.

Wash white fabric gloves in an automatic washer with regular white load;

or hand wash by squeezing in warm suds, then rinse thoroughly. Dark colors may bleed and cause streaks, so wash separately by hand. Press out excess water as described for leather gloves, until dry enough to prevent settling of dye. Shake out, straighten seams, hang to dry in a warm place with clip clothespins.

Before washing wool gloves, draw an outline of them on paper. Squeeze through a cold-water wool wash solution, without hard rubbing, and rinse well. Press out moisture with a towel. Shape gloves to your outline drawing, and allow them to dry away from heat. To restore fluffiness, brush gloves when dry with a medium-stiff brush.

LAUNDRY PRODUCTS | See also LAUNDERING

The many soaps, detergents, bleaches, starches, and other kinds of special cleaners on a supermarket's shelves are each designed to meet a specific need.

Soap is an effective means of removing dirt—if soft water is available. Used with hard water, it forms a scum that penetrates fabric and dulls it.

Detergent can be used in soft or hard water. There are two types of heavy-duty detergent—normal-suds detergent for agitator washers, and the controlled-suds kind for either tumbler or agitator washers. Some cold water detergents are also classified as heavy-duty. The mild detergents designed for dishwashing by hand are also recommended for hand washing of lightly soiled or delicate fabrics.

Water conditioner or **softener,** added to hard water, makes soap or detergent more effective, and prevents soap scum, rings, or rust stains.

Fabric softener, added to the final rinse water, gives garments a soft, fluffy finish, leaves them more wrinkle-free, and reduces static electricity in synthetics. Special products for diapers and baby's clothing have both softening and deodorizing properties.

Bleach, for removing stains from and brightening white and colorfast fabrics, is available in two forms: the chlorine kind (liquid or powder) for use on linens, cottons, and synthetics; and powdered, nonchlorine (fine-fabric or all-fabric) bleach for silk, wool, and other unbleachables. The nonchlorine bleach can be used on all fabrics. Read labels carefully.

Ammonia can be added in small amounts to wash water to help cut grease and brighten white or colored garments. *Do not add with chlorine bleach.*

Bluing gives a frosty, immaculate look to white fabrics, and can be added to wash water (one type is a combination detergent-bluing) or to final rinse water.

Starch gives a crisp finish to cottons, and is available in several forms: instant cold-water starch; powdered, for use with hot or cold water; liquid spray; and liquid "plastic" starch that adheres to the material and usually lasts through several launderings.

Coldwater compounds clean and soften woolens, elastic garments such as girdles and bras, and lingerie; and cut down matting and shrinking.

LEARNING TO DRIVE | See also DRIVING TIPS

Everywhere except in cities well served by rapid transit, the automobile has become America's major mode of passenger transportation. Many of today's homes and communities are so located or laid out that a housewife virtually cannot function or complete her duties without a car. If you do not know how to drive, but intend to learn, take a tip from the experts: Learn to drive from professional instructors. *Do not* ask your husband, brother, or even your best friend to teach you.

Experts emphasize thorough professional driving instruction for four reasons: Experience has shown that friends or relatives seldom make good teachers unless trained in that calling; they may actually teach *bad* driving habits they have unconsciously acquired themselves; ever-increasing traffic requires greater skill; and professionally trained drivers have fewer accidents.

Many automobile clubs (members of AAA) offer a professional driving course for the wives and families of members. In addition, there are commercial driving schools in most cities and major towns. Since the latter may vary in standards all the way from very good to inadequate, it is a sound idea to check with a Better Business Bureau, auto club, or local safety council before signing up for the course.

One way to evaluate a course is to compare it with driver education in a public high school. Also read books that give you some advance preparation for learning to drive (a good one in paperback is *The Feel of the Road*, by William Laas). A good course will feature a dual-control vehicle. The instructor, sitting beside the student, can steer or stop the car himself if necessary.

A standard "driver ed" course approved by state education departments consists of at least thirty hours of classroom study and six hours of actual driving, spread over a semester. The time spread is important, to permit the ideas presented to sink in. These courses teach more than how to start, steer, and stop a car; they take students beyond mere mechanical knowledge into good road judgment, good citizenship, self-discipline, respect for rights and privileges of others, and understanding and respect for laws.

Most studies indicate that school-trained drivers have substantially fewer accidents and violations than drivers of comparable age who lack such training. While the statistics may be debatable and the program has its critics, leading safety authorities enthusiastically support driver education, and the insurance companies set a money value on it.

Most auto insurers offer a discount to all male drivers and unmarried female drivers under 21 who were trained in an approved high school course. In most cases, this may amount to as much as 15 per cent off the rate they would otherwise pay. Every man under twenty-five, and any unmarried man under thirty, who is the principal driver of a car pays an *extra* premium.

Why do young people have to pay more for automobile insurance? About 20 per cent of the nation's drivers are under twenty-five years of age. Yet this group is involved in 31 per cent of all motor vehicle accidents—that is, in half again as many as would be expected in proportion to their number. Just why this is true cannot be said with certainty; but a principal problem with young drivers unquestionably is *inexperience*.

Regardless of age, any new driver faces the same problem. Professional training provides the equivalent of experience *before* one takes the wheel of a car. Manipulation of the controls is simple (almost too simple). But the multitude of situations that can arise in today's busy, fast-moving traffic calls not only for skill, but for deeply ingrained, good safety habits and sound judgment. Learning to drive should never be approached lightly. There is no question that the new driver needs all the education, training, and experience that he (or she) can get.

Even if you have driven a car for years, a refresher course might be advisable, or at the very least, you should have some continued self-training in technique.

LEATHER CARE |

Leathers generally are named for the animal they come from, such as calf, kid, cowhide, etc. Although a number of these animals are rare or extinct, their names are still used. Antelope is actually lambskin, goatskin, or calfskin finished to resemble antelope; chamois is now sheepskin; doeskin is almost always made from sheep and lambskins. Following are other descriptive terms:

Grain. Refers to the hair or wool side of animal skin, which is usually smooth when used as leather.

Top grain. The top layer of the grain side. It has natural grain markings, left by hair follicles, and is used in quality leather goods.

Suede. This is usually the flesh side of the skin, buffed to give it a soft nap.

Rawhide. Leather that is dehaired, deodorized, and preserved but not tanned.

Patent leather. Leather coated by layers of varnish to produce a high gloss.

CLEANING

No leather should be permitted to become badly soiled. When a garment needs more than spot-cleaning, it should be professionally cleaned. Suede stored with grease spots may be attacked by moths, carpet beetles, ants, and other insects.

Professional leather cleaning and refinishing are quite different from regular dry cleaning, and require special equipment. Because leather can be ruined if improperly handled, it is a good idea to use leather processors or only dry cleaners you know are experienced in handling leather. For home care, the following can be helpful:

Suede and brushed leathers. Suede garments can be freshened by rubbing soiled areas with a dry sponge or gum rubber. Suede should never be placed in water, and home cleaning fluids should not be used. Worn nap can be roughened with a very fine sandpaper. Suede shoes may be brushed with a special wire brush. This brush, though, should not be used on other suede garments because they do not have a hard backing, and the wire may tear them.

Smooth and grain leathers. Dust, wipe with a damp cloth wrung out in a mild soap-and-water solution or a mild detergent, and dry with a soft cloth. Upholstery needs no other care. Shoes can also be polished with a commercial shoe polish to add luster, or with a liquid polish to cover scuff marks. Handbags can have the added touch of neutral leather cream buffed off with a clean cloth. Saddle soap or neutral cream adds a shine to luggage. Leather tabletops should not be washed. They can be dusted regularly and occasionally given a light paste (not liquid) wax application and buffing.

Reptile. Alligator, snake, lizard, and other reptile leathers need only dusting with a soft cloth.

Patent. Smudges can be removed by sponging with a damp cloth.

Gloves. Unless the gloves are guaranteed washable or if they have been dry cleaned previously, it's best to send them to a professional cleaner. If there are washing directions, follow them exactly. See LAUNDERING PROBLEMS in this Guide.

When pressing leather, cover it with heavy brown paper and press one panel at a time. The iron should be set at a low setting and steam should never be used. Alterations should be undertaken only by an expert.

STORING

Leather should be stored where it is neither too hot, too damp, nor too dry. (This rules out most basement and attic storage areas). It needs air, and should be wrapped in a soft cloth or paper.

Luggage keeps best when raised slightly off the floor or shelf so air can circulate under it. Handbags should be emptied and hung. Fill, but do not stuff them, with crumpled paper to retain shape. If left standing for long periods, they may buckle.

LEAVENING AGENTS |

Baking powders are classified according to the acid ingredients they contain. There are three types, as listed below, and double-acting baking powder is likely to be most widely available. The kind to use depends on the recipe; don't freely substitute, since baking actions are quite different.

Double-acting baking powder reacts very slowly, releasing about one-fifth to one-third of its leavening in the cold mixture, the rest in the heat of the oven.

Phosphate baking powder reacts slowly and requires heat to liberate about one-third of its leavening.

Tartrate baking powder reacts rapidly and begins its action at room temperature as soon as liquid is added.

Baking soda is used alone or with baking powder to raise cakes made with buttermilk, sour milk, chocolate, molasses, fruit juices, etc. The acid from these ingredients reacts with the soda to release leavening bubbles. When using soda, don't delay mixing or baking, since the gas will escape.

Active dry yeast. This modern dry yeast, which comes in quarter-ounce packages and in four-ounce jars, stays fresh for several months on a cool, dry shelf and gives uniformly fine results if used before the expiration date on the package. When dissolved in warm water, one package of active dry yeast works the same as a three-fifths-ounce cake of compressed yeast; use it as you would use dissolved cake yeast in any favorite recipe.

Cake yeast (compressed) is perishable and so must be kept in the refrigerator, and for not longer than a week or two. It can be frozen for as long as six months, but after thawing (at room temperature) it should be used immediately. Crumble yeast between your fingers to determine whether it's usable; if it crumbles easily, even though the edges are slightly brown from drying, it is still good.

LIFE INSURANCE | See also INSURANCE CHECKLIST

How much and which kind of life insurance should your family have? More and more families have found that insurance requirements can best be met by programming coverage to meet certain well-defined objectives, not by simply buying a new policy from time to time. For instance, a twenty-five-year-old man can pay anywhere from $60 to $500 a year for a $10,000 policy. A qualified underwriter can help you tailor an insurance program to meet the specifications you set.

How is this done? Using a check list or form, you and your husband estimate how much money you and your children would require for various needs if he died. Include these major considerations:

Immediate expenses. The ones that dependents face—funeral and medical costs, taxes, debts, etc.

Income provisions. Many experts consider this the most important element: arranging for dependents to receive an adequate regular income. Three periods should be planned for. The first is while your children are under eighteen years of age, when as a widow, you might receive Social

Security benefits of as much as $254 a month. The second is after your children are eighteen and these Social Security payments end. Finally, when you are sixty-two, you may again be eligible for Social Security payments, but they will be smaller than when you had dependent children to support.

Readjustment fund. If your husband died, your family might have to reduce its standard of living. This scaling down can't be done overnight. Consequently, you would need more money than is provided by the income protection to help bridge the gap—for only a few months or maybe much longer.

Mortgage. If you are buying a home, you and your husband should decide whether you would want to pay off the mortgage in the event of his death. To do so, the mortgage holder should be insured with reducing term insurance.

Special funds. Some families believe planning should also include funds to guarantee a college education for children, to cope with emergencies, or to provide retirement income.

This itemizing suggests how much money you will need for future security. Some of this may be supplied by your husband's employers through group insurance. There are also Social Security benefits to be considered. You may have savings, investments, and other sources of income, or you may be in line for an inheritance. Or your skills and circumstances may be such that if your husband died, you yourself could return to work.

Nevertheless, the amount of insurance needed is almost always considerably more than most young families can afford at one swoop. Say, for example, that your family can afford $250 a year, about a third of what the entire coverage you outlined would cost. The problem is simple: which needs must be taken care of first? In subsequent years, as money becomes available, other needs can be met.

Insurance underwriters agree that, for young families with children, cleanup expenses and guaranteed income should have top priority. After those, mortgage protection seems to rank the highest.

You hear a great deal about the "living benefits" possible from permanent life insurance, the kind that builds cash values as you pay premiums. These benefits might include money to use for retirement funds or as a source for loans. However, for most young families, the emphasis should be on *protection*—against loss of income, loss of your home, and so on. This frequently is best achieved through a combination of *permanent* life insurance and *term* policies (which provide coverage for a specific period only).

For a young couple, term insurance is much cheaper. But be sure you understand that it builds *no* cash values; that its rates will be higher each time it is renewed; and that you will rarely be able to renew it after the age of 60 or 65. Generally speaking, though, people need less insurance protection as they grow older, because dependent children grow into self-supporting adults. Term coverage can fit into your program while your needs are greatest and your available funds most limited.

Child insurance is admittedly one of the least pressing of a young family's insurance needs. Even when insurance is used to save for a child's college education, underwriters frequently advise that it be written as a policy in the father's name.

Wife insurance, though, is another matter. In addition to the obvious tragedy in such a loss, the death of a wife may create a severe financial hardship for her family. Many wives carry policies for $1,000 or so to cover funeral and medical costs. A bigger consideration, however, is the cost of duplicating a wife's work in maintaining a home and in taking care of the children.

Estimates for these services when two children are involved have ranged as high as $6,000 a year. It may be that relatives can care for young children, but if there are no relatives and no money to employ help, a mother's death might result in placement of children in foster homes.

Ways to approach the question can be demonstrated by the following three plans for a twenty-five-year-old wife: One, for a $25,000 ordinary life-insurance policy, costs about $310 a year. Another, for a $25,000 term policy, renewable every five years, costs about $115 a year to start, increasing in cost each time it is renewed. By age forty, the premium would be about $168. (Unlike the first, this policy builds no cash values.) A third is a family-income policy that provides a lump-sum payment of $10,000 and $200 a month income if death occurs within a 15-year period. The income continues from the time of death to the end of the term. The cost is $200 a year.

Many people have been using family-plan policies to cover husband, wife, and children in one package. These plans usually distribute coverage so that the husband has four or five times as much insurance as either his wife or children. In general, young marrieds without children have no pressing need for wife insurance.

LIGHTING | See also LAMPS, TABLE

One generally inherits the electric wiring of a house or apartment, and must take the location of outlets into account when furnishing each room.

Long electric cords lying loose are both dangerous and unsightly, while major changes in circuitry call for the services of an electrician. But most decorating problems involving light can be solved by judicious choices among the wide variety of modern lighting fixtures.

Light sources are of two basic kinds: incandescent bulbs and fluorescent tubes. Each has advantages. Bulbs, the commonest type, cost less initially and are more flexible in use. They fit all standard lamp sockets; the light may be focused over a limited area; and it may be increased or decreased within limits by changing the wattage of the bulb, or by use of a dimmer switch. Fluorescent tubes provide a line of light that eliminates shadows, ideal for a work area. They provide three or four times as much light as bulbs of the same wattage, a saving in current; and they produce less heat, often important in ceiling and wall fixtures. Some fluorescent tubes (labeled "preheat") do not light instantly at the turn of the switch; if the slight lag is undesirable, look for such labels as "Slimline," "Instant Start," "rapid-start," or "trigger-start."

In the decorating scheme, lighting may be direct, indirect, or diffused. A spotlight, for example, casts direct light upon the area where aimed. The same light becomes indirect if "bounced" off the ceiling to light the rest of the room; or diffused if enclosed in a translucent lamp shade or bowl. Incandescent bulb designs provide various combinations:

Clear glass for a sharp, intense light which must be shaded or diffused to protect the eye; frosted glass for partial diffusion, although shading is still required; decorator bulb for white indirect light in lamps without a diffusing bowl; reflector bulb, silver coated except at the open end, for spotlighting or floodlighting; tubular bulbs, like those used in store showcases, to provide a line of light similar to that of a fluorescent tube.

Fluorescent light may be warm- or cool-white, or colored. Sometimes a pink tube and blue tube are combined in one fixture (such as an artist's studio lamp) to give a lighted object its true coloring. Softer and warmer incandescent light, being somewhat yellow, makes a color look different indoors than out.

Table lamps are of two principal types: one with a diffusing bowl pointing upward, often taking a 3-way bulb (50-100-150 watts or 100-200-300 watts); the other with a harp of bent metal to which the lampshade is attached by a screw at the top. A reading lamp should be not less than 100 watts for casual reading, 150 watts for prolonged reading (in floor lamps, 150 and 300 watts). Some light should penetrate the lamp shade, which should be open at the top to throw light upward for diffusion.

Ceiling fixtures for general lighting of a kitchen or bedroom should be shielded, if incandescent, with shallow diffusing glass, and with enough sockets to provide 150 to 200 watts in the kitchen, 200 watts in the bedroom. Fluorescent fixtures should be side-shielded. In the dining room, a central down light of 75 to 100 watts has a dramatic effect, supplemented by 200 watts in a surrounding glass-shaded fixture. It may be suspended from the ceiling. A more elaborate chandelier, hung relatively low, adds a striking note to furnishings without loss of floor space.

Wall lighting, combined with upward lighting of portable lamps, provides a glamorous environment in the living room. Valances may be used at windows with draperies of light color, to provide indirect lighting on the ceiling and down lighting on the wall. On other wall spaces, and mounted somewhat lower than the valance, consider wall brackets—for example, to illuminate a picture, as a reading light for a bed, or over work counters and range in the kitchen.

Lighted cornices may run the full length of a wall or large window, making a low-ceilinged room look higher. Fluorescent tubes are shielded behind faceboards from four to sixteen feet in length, which direct the light downward. Incandescent tubular bulbs may be preferred for their warmer light, flattering to complexions and to food. The faceboards are shaped, papered, painted, or upholstered to suit the decoration of the room.

Television lighting. Watching television in darkness is hard on the eyes, and does not improve the TV picture. Position a portable lamp to one side of the set, where it will not be reflected in the TV screen, or back-light the set by means of a wall bracket. One simple solution is to attach an adjustable wall lamp to the back of the set itself, where it will be invisible, and point it upward.

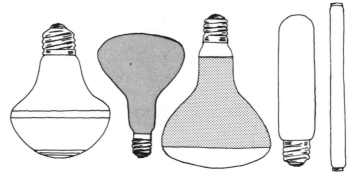

New developments in incandescent bulbs include the decorator bulb for use in unshaded fixtures designed for bare bulbs; the white indirect-light bulb for table and floor lamps without diffusing bowls; reflector bulbs, coated with an opaque silver finish to make them useful as spotlights or floodlights; and tubular bulbs, some with standard screw-type base, others (called "Lumiline") requiring special sockets, used mostly for decorating purposes in the home. Lumiline lamps are much softer and warmer than fluorescents. See illustration.

LIQUORS | See WINES AND LIQUORS

MACARONI, NOODLES, AND SPAGHETTI |

Macaroni, spaghetti, and noodles, all members of the macaroni family, are no mere "starchy fillers." Even small additions of meat, fish, cheese, eggs, or milk give their cereal proteins a big lift in nutritive value. Tomatoes and other vegetables in the sauce add vitamins and minerals. A fine prop for a shaky budget, macaroni also offers a pleasant change from potatoes or bread, and a base for scores of interesting dishes.

Since *pasta*—the Italian name for this family of foods—has a long life on the pantry shelf, it can be stocked as a staple. It comes in a fascinating number of shapes and sizes, as illustrated. Don't let the names bewilder you; they merely describe about a hundred and fifty forms of essentially the same thing. The main differences are these:

Macaroni is of tubular shape with a hole down the middle that facilitates thorough cooking. Often the tubes are cut into short, bite-size pieces, or the dough is formed into decorative shapes, such as seashells, without the hole. **Lasagne** is macaroni rolled into broad, noodlelike strips. The larger size of these members of the family gives them a "toothy" consistency when cooked.

Spaghetti is of solid rodlike shape (no hole) stretched thinner than macaroni; *vermicelli* is the thinnest. *Linguine* is flattened spaghetti, like a slender noodle.

Egg noodles are ribbonlike lengths made with an egg dough, in fine, medium, and broad styles, or in fanciful bow ties, alphabets, etc.

Best quality macaroni and spaghetti are made from durum (hard) wheat semolina (the medium-size particles sifted out in milling) mixed with water. This gives them a distinctive flavor and consistency compared to doughs made of soft wheats or a finer flour. Egg noodles consist of durum flour, water, and at least 5½ per cent egg solids, as required by law. Most manufacturers also enrich macaroni products with vitamins B_1 and B_2, niacin, and iron, as shown on their labels.

COOKING TIPS

Eight ounces of packaged macaroni or egg noodles make about four and a half cups when cooked. Eight ounces of packaged spaghetti make about five cups. Each variety yields enough for four to six servings.

Never overcook macaroni, spaghetti, or noodles. In following label directions, remember that the correct number of minutes (for you) will depend upon how well done your family likes macaroni—from *al dente*, which is just barely tender, to any degree of softness. Test by biting a piece. If it's firm all the way through but not hard in the center, it has reached the *al dente* stage. From then on, each additional minute of boiling will soften it rapidly. Drain and serve as soon as right; don't let it stand in the hot water.

Don't rinse macaroni products unless they are to be chilled and used in a salad; then use cold water.

Grocery shelves today contain expertly cooked, fix-and-serve macaroni dishes in cans or jars, packaged or frozen. Among them, you will also find *ravioli,* a dumpling made of macaroni dough and a meat or cheese filling.

HOW TO EAT SPAGHETTI

There are two schools of thought on just how spaghetti should be transferred from plate to mouth. You can, of course, beg the question by breaking or cutting it into short lengths. But if you must do as the Romans do, try one of these methods:

With fork in right hand, spear three or four strands. Hold the tines against the plate. Twist spaghetti into a ball. Lift slowly to release the longest strand, wind it up, and lift to your mouth.

Or pick up strands with the fork. Twist against a spoon, held on the plate with the left hand. Lift with the fork. Support the spaghetti with the spoon part way. And tuck a napkin into collar or bodice—or wear a bib!

OTHER PASTA (Some Illustrated)

Alphabets (1); Pastina (Stellini). Letters of the alphabet are macaroni, chiefly in soups. Pastina consists of tiny macaroni pieces, sometimes star-shaped. It often comes in vegetable flavors. Used in soups and soft-diet dishes.

Creste di Gallo; Riccini. Creste di gallo is macaroni shaped like a cockscomb; ideal for serving with any sauce (the shape holds gravy well). Riccini is macaroni with a curl shape; good with most sauces.

Gnocchi; Spaghetti; Spaghettini; Vermicelli. Gnocchi is dumpling-shaped macaroni, good in soups. Spaghettini is thin spaghetti; and vermicelli is extra-thin. Both are good with sauce and in soups.

Cut spaghetti; Linguine. Use cut spaghetti as you would elbow macaroni. Try linguine (flat spaghetti) with tomato sauce, parsleyed garlic-and-olive-oil sauce, or various sea-food sauces.

Fusilli; Folded fine egg noodles. Fusilli are spindle-like spaghetti, good with sauces—particularly tomato. Folded fine egg noodles are used frequently in clear soups. Try them deep-fried for snacks or in chop suey.

Folded medium egg noodles (2); Folded wide egg noodles. Use with any sauce, or try them buttered and sprinkled with parsley or chives,

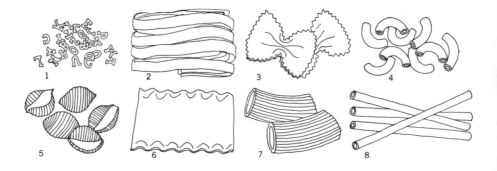

chopped almonds, poppy or caraway seeds. They're nice with sauerbraten, pot roast, curries, or stews.

Egg noodles; Green noodles. Egg noodles are ribbon-like lengths, and come in three widths—fine, medium, and wide. They may be vegetable-flavored, with spinach, carrots, or tomatoes.

Bows (3); Small bows are egg-noodle products, shaped like bow ties or butterflies. Good topped with cheese, meat, vegetable, or sea-food sauce. They may be used in casseroles, and are nice in salads with vegetables.

Elbow macaroni (4); Macaroni (8). Elbow-macaroni-and-cheese is a casserole favorite. Serve elbow macaroni also with sauces and in salads. Long macaroni is good with most sauces; try cheese sauce sparked with a pinch of powdered ginger.

Shells (5); Lasagne (6). Shell-shaped macaroni is ideal with sea food or combined with peas or broccoli. Lasagne—broad, flat or curly macaroni—is used mostly in the Italian meat-and-cheese dish of the same name.

Ziti; Mezzani. Ziti—macaroni cut in lengths—is good in casseroles or with most sauces. Mezzani is cut macaroni, sometimes grooved. Particularly good with tomato-meat or tomato-vegetable sauce.

Mezzani rigati; Mostaccioli rigati. Mezzani rigati is cut, grooved macaroni. Mostaccioli rigati is cut on the diagonal. Bake with tomato sauce; serve with most sauces.

Rigatoni (7); Tufoli. Rigatoni is large, grooved macaroni. Tufoli is extra-large. Stuff with meat or cheese mixture, and bake in a tomato sauce.

Ditali; Manicotti rigati. Ditali are short lengths of macaroni, especially good in salads. Manicotti rigati is extra-large, grooved macaroni. Try stuffing with meat or Italian cheese and baking.

MAIDS | See also TABLE SETTINGS; WINES AND LIQUORS

In our servantless society, an experienced and competent maid often is hard to find. If you hire a maid to serve guests, either full-time or part-time for a party, you may have to train her yourself. Since she can make or break the occasion, much depends on her knowing exactly what is expected of her.

Have the maid in beforehand to practice, since it's easier to demonstrate than to explain in words. (See the article on table settings for proper placement of dishes and silver.) Write out the menu together with detailed instructions or reminders. Those that follow are equally helpful to the hostess who does her own serving—the basic procedures remain the same.

Stand at left of each person when placing or removing dishes and offering food from a server. But stand at right (to avoid reaching in front of the guest) when placing beverages or dessert silver. Pick up a used plate with the left hand; place a new one with the right hand in exchange. Do not "stack" plates for removal; take one or at most two at a time to the kitchen or a side table.

Serve the hostess first, then the guest to her right, and so on around the table, skipping the host. Return to serve the host last.

To offer a platter of food, support it on the palm of your left hand with a side of the platter toward the guest, steadying with your right hand if necessary. Hold it low enough for easy serving. Have handles of serving implements pointed toward the guest, fork at his left, spoon or knife at his right. Do not touch the guest.

Use a napkin folded into a square under the serving dish, to protect the hand from heat or cold. Serve small dishes from a tray with a napkin under it. Do not use a napkin when carrying or exchanging plates separately. But hold one in the left hand to catch stray drops when refilling water goblets from a pitcher.

Move quietly and unobtrusively. If uncertain, do whatever would least disturb a guest. Avoid the appearance of handling dishes: do not extend your thumb over the rim of a plate; pick up goblets by the lower part only.

Before serving any course, have everything ready to avoid a second trip or the appearance of haste. Have heated plates ready for hot food, chilled dishes for cold food.

After each course, remove dishes only when all persons have finished. Take serving dishes and platters first, then used plates, glasses, and silver; finally unused silver, salt shakers, etc.,—all in the manner described above.

As dinner time approaches, fill goblets three-quarters full of water, place butter pats on butter plates, light candles, arrange chairs. Put the first course (if cold) on service plates on the table. If hot soup is the first course, delay until guests are seated. Stand in the doorway, address the hostess, and say in soft tones, "Dinner is served."

After exchanging first course and service plates for warm dinner plates, serve the main course in this order: meat, vegetables, gravy, bread, relishes. If the host carves the meat, place implements before him leaving space for the platter; then bring in the platter. As he carves and arranges meat on dinner plates in front of him, stand at his left with an extra plate in your right hand. Pick up a filled plate with the left hand and replace with the extra. Serve meat to the hostess, exchanging plates in the same manner, and return to the host for the next serving. Repeat for all guests before serving vegetables, etc. Then return the platter and other serving dishes to the kitchen to prepare for offering guests a second helping.

Serve salad in one of three ways: Bring individual salads as part of main course, placing one to left of each guest. Or place empty salad plates first, then offer salad to each guest from a bowl. Or the hostess may fill salad plates from the bowl at her place just as the host carves the meat, for serving to each guest in turn.

Clear the table for dessert, at each place picking up the used dinner plate in your right hand, salad plate in left; then butter plates and unused silver. Crumb the table if necessary and refill water goblets.

Individual desserts may be served from the kitchen with silver on each plate. Or first place the silver on the table, then serve the dessert in plates. Or if dessert is to be passed in a manner similar to the salad bowl, put a plate before each guest with silver on it (he removes fork and spoon to the table). A fingerbowl may be served on a doily on the same plate, for the guest to remove to his left.

Coffee or tea may be served from the kitchen on a tray, in cups with spoon on saucer. Place to the right of each guest. Or the hostess may pour coffee for each guest at her place in the same manner as serving salad, adding sugar and cream as each requests. Or the coffee may be served in the living room, sometimes with a dessert that may be eaten with the fingers. Pass cups to the guests on a tray with the sugar and cream. In the same manner, offer a second cup to those who want it.

Between courses, the maid may make things easier for herself if you instruct her where to place the used dishes and silver—to avoid clutter in the kitchen and to prepare for cleaning up later.

MAIL |

That amazing system of communication, the United States Post Office, can be an important household aid. Most families take the mails for granted, but there are ways of putting Uncle Sam more efficiently to work. Even in this telephone age, the written word still is the effortless and businesslike way of handling many matters that concern a housewife every day. Here are some pointers on using the post office to advantage, including its less familiar services:

First, stock postage stamps just as you do other household staples. The 5-cent stamp used for most letters comes in a handy roll of 100; in a purse-size booklet of 20; and on stamped envelopes. Air mails (8 cents) come in booklets of 25 and on envelopes. An assortment of 1-, 2-, and 10-cent stamps will be handy for combining into any required amount of postage. Keep loose stamps in an envelope between sheets of wax paper to prevent sticking.

Note that you can use basic stamps in proper amount to pay any postal fee, but not special-purpose stamps. That is, a special-purpose stamp such as air mail or special delivery is not valid for ordinary postage.

Stock 4-cent postcards and make them a habit. They're ideal for conveying the kind of brief, explicit information that so often gets lost or garbled, and wastes telephone time: for example, to send someone a correct name and address, a change in subscription or billing, an hour of arrival, a reminder of a date. Carried on the person, postcards enable you to write a quick message wherever you are, drop it in a mailbox, and be reasonably sure it will reach the individual or department intended.

Copy the time schedule of mail pickups posted on your corner mailbox and keep it with the stamps for reference. Just catching rather than missing a pickup can mean a difference in speed of delivery of one day to one weekend. If you set up a special place near the door, the family may make a habit of picking up outgoing mail for posting whenever leaving the house.

A post office leaflet on rates and a small postal scale can save trips to the post office, especially before Christmas. Remember that weights are figured exactly; a tiny fraction over one ounce will require postage for two ounces. However, a letter can get pretty bulky before exceeding one ounce. You gain nothing in service by adding unnecessary stamps.

First-class mail (five cents per ounce) includes most of your letters and is so called because the post office gives it first priority in handling. It also enjoys the unique privilege of privacy. Postal employees may not open a first-class letter for inspection; the secrecy of your sealed communication is protected by law. Also, an undeliverable first-class letter will be returned free if you put your return address on it. Before that happens, the post office will follow your addressee from one place to another if so directed. If you receive a letter for someone who is away from home, you may forward it merely by crossing out the address, writing in the new address, and dropping it unopened in a mailbox (no stamp needed).

Postcards (four cents), whether the post office kind, souvenir, or private mailing cards, travel as first-class mail. But they are not secret, of course; and not returnable unless return postage is guaranteed.

Air mail (eight cents per ounce), a kind of super first-class mail, is an immense time-saver over long distances. For the extra pennies, it shrinks days en route into mere hours. Air mail is not automatically faster, though, at distances less than about five hundred miles or to points remote from a commercial airport. Sometimes the transfers between air and ground can actually delay delivery.

Air-mail postcards (six cents) will often save the cost of a telegram or long-distance phone call—a must for a traveling husband or student away at school. You may convert a four-cent card to air mail by adding a two-cent stamp and writing "Air mail" next to the address. If you correspond overseas, latch onto another bargain: the **air letter** (or **aerogramme**) that flies anywhere in the world for only eleven cents.

Special delivery (fee thirty cents and up, by weight) is widely misunderstood. The fee, added to regular or air-mail postage, assures immediate delivery *after* the letter reaches its destination post office. En route to that point, it travels no faster than other mail. What's saved is the normal wait for the regular letter carrier, who might not be scheduled to go out on his route again until the next day. Instead, a special carrier will deliver the letter if it arrives before 11 P.M. on weekdays in cities, before 9 P.M. in smaller places, or before 6 P.M. on Sundays and holidays.

Within your own postal area, you can use special delivery like a messenger service. That is, mail a letter in the morning and have it delivered within the same day. At a greater distance, it's helpful if you think your letter might arrive at night or on a nonworking day.

Registered mail (seventy-five cents and up, by value) provides proof of delivery, which is sometimes important for legal reasons or to protect valuable contents. Always send currency, bonds, and stock certificates by registered mail. When sending documents of no intrinsic money value, such as a contract or lease, you may use cheaper certified mail (thirty cents). For higher fees you may request a receipt of delivery to a specified person only. The post office keeps a record in any case.

You're not apt to use **second-class mail** unless you publish a periodical. But **third-class mail** is a service to business that individuals may use on occasion. Basically it carries printed matter or merchandise weighing less than one pound at a low rate (two cents per ounce, minimum four cents). It takes longer than first-class mail and must be open (unsealed) for postal inspection.

Third-class may *not* be used for personal letters, signed or unsigned, although some people do send unsealed, imprinted Christmas cards this way. (This is not recommended, since there is no assurance of delivery on time, and no return.) Third-class mail is mainly for a large club or committee mailing of a circular or announcement, and for sending things like magazines, paperback books, and small packages of minor value.

Book rates are another bargain, actually a postal subsidy to education. Did you know that you can mail a one-pound book anywhere in the country for a dime, plus five cents per additional pound? Mark the package "Special Fourth-Class Rate—Books." If returning books to a library, pay only four cents the first pound, one cent each additional, and mark the package "Library Rate." The same ten-and-five or four-and-one rates apply to other materials considered educational: 16-mm. movie film, music, recordings, teaching aids, and manuscripts if no covering letter is included.

Fourth-class mail (parcel post) must weigh one pound or more. Rates increase per pound and with distance, measured in eight zones; or if you want the parcel to go by air. You may stamp and post packages from home, but for **insurance** (twenty cents and up, by value) or **registry,** you must take them to the post office.

Special handling (fee twenty-five cents and up, by weight) gives a package the same priority service as first-class mail. It is obligatory for certain fussy items, such as baby chicks or a live alligator. Don't confuse it with special delivery, though. For both services you'd have to pay both fees.

The post office limits parcel weight to forty pounds locally, to twenty pounds beyond the second zone, to seventy pounds if addressed to rural or military areas. The rates no longer are insignificant in figuring the cost of anything you send or order by mail. For large parcels or long-distance shipments, also check the rates of privately operated railway and air express agencies. Be sure to include *all* charges for comparable service, such as insurance. On C.O.D. shipments, express companies sometimes charge extra if a delivery must be made more than once to find the recipient at home.

For information about postal rates, regulations, etc., don't hesitate to phone the post office. In a large office, ask for "Inquiry." They're glad to oblige. Rates are subject to change from time to time.

The *zip code* number in an address positively identifies the state, town, and post office within that town. It helps eliminate errors (for example, "Mo." for Missouri could be mistaken for "Me." for Maine) and thus speeds up delivery. Eventually it will permit machine sorting of mail. Always use the zip code, placing it *after* the name of the state, like this:

Harper & Row, Publishers, Inc.
49 East 33rd Street
New York, N.Y. 10016

MANTELS |

Starting with flat hearthstones around which primitive dwellings were built, the fireplace has always been the center of warmth and family life. Even with central heating, the fireplace continues to be an important part of interior architectural design. The mantel, an integral part of all fireplaces, has a number of present-day versions which derive from the basic types shown.

1. **The Medieval mantel** is the oldest of mantels, dating from their introduction in the Middle Ages. It is usually deep and high, and often attached, as here, to a metal or masonry chimney hood. Of wood and tile, this mantel often displays plates, pewter tankards, or trophies.

2. **The Greek Revival mantel** stems from the eighteenth century revival of classic architecture. The style is simple, and any ornamentation is in the classic tradition. An appropriate painting often hangs over the mantel.

3. **The Adam mantel** reflects the eighteenth century and is a combination of simple lines with refined classic ornamentation. Usually it is of painted wood and is carved with figures, garlands, and urns. Sometimes a Wedgwood plaque is set into the facing. Accessories may include a mirror frame ornamented with the same type of figures and urns that appear in the carving, and small vases of flowers.

4. **The Georgian mantel** is English, usually a little higher than other

mantels to emphasize height rather than width. It can be either wood or marble, often with carved wood paneling above, and is generally accessorized with classic objects—bust, little covered jars, or classic urns.

5. **The Victorian mantel,** in one of the most popular versions, is French inspired but much more elaborately ornamented than the French mantel. It may be of marble or black cast iron and decorated with flower and fruit motifs, often interspersed with scrolls. The fireplace usually has a coal-

burning grate. Typically Victorian accessories such as epergnes, flowers in glass bells, and Staffordshire pieces are appropriate.

6. **The French mantel** is recognizable by its curving outline. The example shown, a Louis XV mantel, is usually of marble, but can be of wood and is often built into a paneled wall. Suitable accessories may be an ormolu clock and branched candlesticks as shown. This is a relatively simple French mantel. Those popular during the reign of Louis XVI were considerably more elaborate.

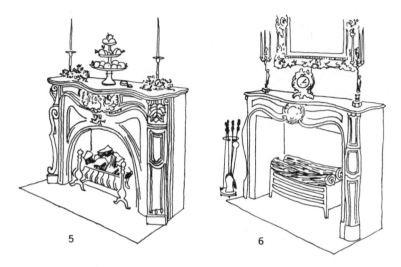

5   6

7. **The Early American mantel—informal** version was originally part of a kitchen fireplace used for cooking. Often the mantel runs the full length of a wall, and frequently there are cupboards above it. Accessories may be soup tureens, pitchers, etc., and cooking implements may hang from it.

8. **The Early American mantel—formal** derives from the versions used in colonial living rooms and bedrooms. It has a simple molding and is nearly always of wood in natural tones or painted white. It usually has little or no ornamentation. A portrait often hangs above it, and pewter or silver candlesticks and small figurines make appropriate accessories.

9. **The Williamsburg mantel** is typically rather shallow and simple. Often it is painted a characteristic "Williamsburg blue" to match the walls. Appropriate accessories may be plates, tureens, vases, or figurines. Since the mantel is narrow, accessories are usually either small or tall and slender.

10. **This contemporary mantel** is a modern version of a colonial mantel, often framed with a simple bolection molding, as pictured. In keeping with other contemporary decor, the arrangement of accessories is most effective if it is asymmetrical, usually comprised of an odd number of pieces. These may be ceramics, sculpture, apothecary jars, or the like.

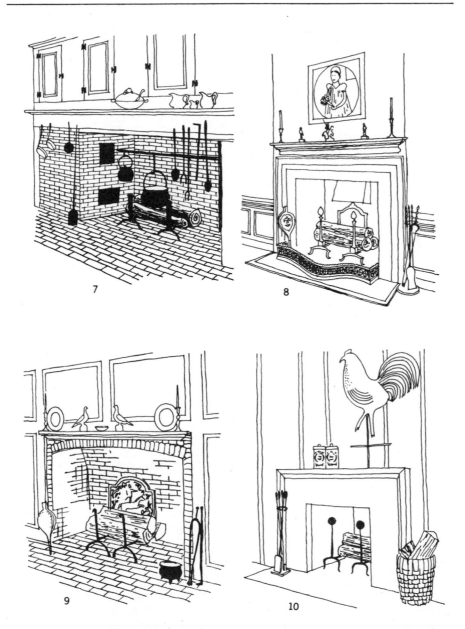

11. This contemporary mantel is not a real mantel in the formal sense. It is placed below instead of above the fireplace, is relatively deep, and serves as a bench as well as a shelf. Accessories should be asymmetrical, perhaps with large tropical plants or driftwood, and some bright cushions for seating.

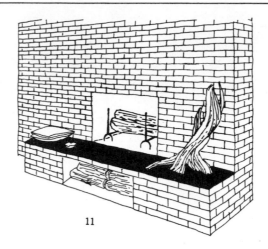

11

MEAT | See also FRANKFURTERS; SAUSAGES; STEAKS; VARIETY MEATS

The American custom of serving lots of meat is a fine one. Few foods are a richer source of important food values, with flavor and good appetite satisfaction at the same time. These things are true of any meat if it's properly prepared, regardless of cut and grade—or whether it's cut to order, prepackaged fresh, quick-frozen, cured, "cured and smoked," or canned.

It takes an expert to judge quality just by looking at the color, the fat, and the bone. So, for most of us, it's safer to rely on a meat packer's brand or a federal grade, to be sure of getting the quality we pay for.

BUYING MEATS

First check for wholesomeness. All meat shipped in interstate commerce is federally inspected. The round, purple U.S. "Inspected and Passed" stamp, illustrated, guarantees that the meat came from an animal judged wholesome by a federal inspector and that the plant where it was processed passed sanitary regulations. The stamp's purple dye is not harmful and need not be cut off the meat before cooking.

Then look for the packer's brand name. Several well-known meat packers stamp or burn their own brands on better quality beef, veal, lamb, and cured meats. Fresh pork is seldom branded because there is less variation in the tenderness of this meat. Once you find the brand you like, stick to it. The packer's brand on packaged and canned meats (bacon, ham, sausage, franks, etc.) indicates the quality, too.

Or look for a federal grade. Some beef, veal, and lamb cuts carry a U.S.D.A. grade stamp to indicate quality. This shield-shaped stamp runs

FEDERAL
INSPECTION
STAMP

FEDERAL
GRADE
STAMP

MEAT PACKER'S STAMP

like a purple ribbon along the entire length of the carcass. The U.S.D.A. grades of beef are:

Prime. Highest grade. The supply is relatively limited.

Choice. Highest grade of beef commonly found and sold in volume in retail stores. The lean is usually bright red, firm, and velvety to the touch. It is well streaked (marbled) with little veins of fat, and has a thick, white or creamy white, firm fat covering. The meat is especially flavorsome and tender. (If aged or ripened by hanging in cold storage, the exterior lean turns a darker red and the meat becomes even juicier and more tender.)

Good. Still of excellent quality. Meat is a slightly darker red, has less fat and marbling, and somewhat thinner fat covering than that found in Choice.

Standard. Meat with very little marbling. These meats are better for braising (pot roast, Swiss steaks, etc.) and cooking in liquid (stews), than for roasting.

Commercial and **Utility.** The lowest passable grades, with a thin or very thin fat covering. These low-priced meats have cooking limitations similar to Standard, are often sold as ground meat, or in frankfurters, bologna, etc.

Recently a new kind of *tendered beef* has been developed through the introduction of a food enzyme (papain) into the circulatory system of the beef animal. This assures tenderness throughout all the beef roasts and steaks when cooked. Tendered cuts such as top and bottom round, rump, blade, chuck, etc., which we usually think of only for pot roasting or braising, can be broiled, grilled, rotisseried, or oven roasted if desired.

Charts on the following pages identify the various cuts of meat.

TO STORE MEATS

If meat is wrapped in market paper, unwrap it. Separate different kinds. Do not wash meat; it keeps better if the surface is not damp.

See that steaks, chops, cold cuts, and large pieces lie flat, not curled.

Then, with wax paper, foil, plastic, or the inner wrapping used by the meat dealer, loosely rewrap each kind, leaving ends open. Keep pre-

CUTS OF MEAT

(Charts courtesy of National Livestock and Meat Board)

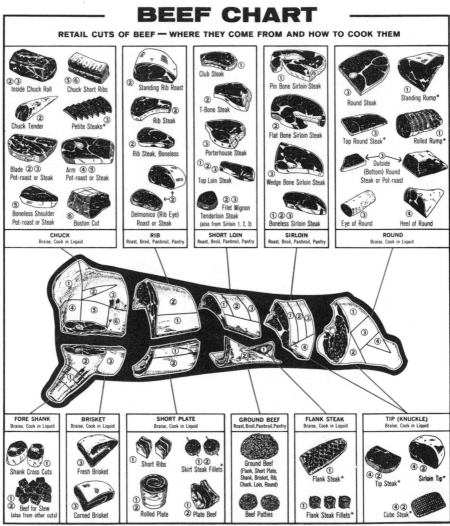

BEEF CHART

RETAIL CUTS OF BEEF — WHERE THEY COME FROM AND HOW TO COOK THEM

* May be Roasted, Broiled, Panbroiled or Panfried from high quality beef.

(Charts courtesy of National Livestock and Meat Board)

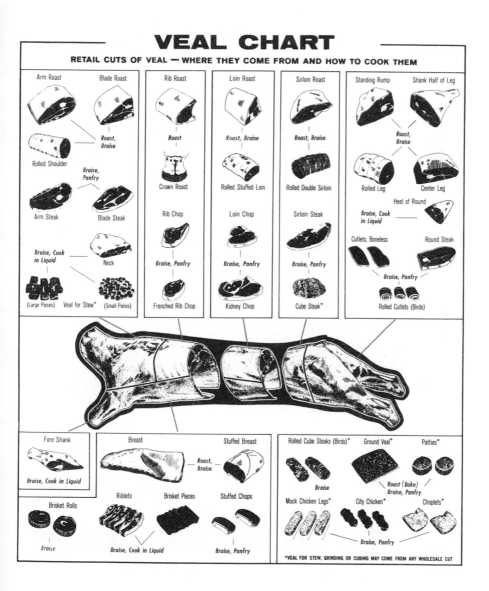

VEAL CHART

RETAIL CUTS OF VEAL — WHERE THEY COME FROM AND HOW TO COOK THEM

Arm Roast · Blade Roast — *Roast, Braise*

Rolled Shoulder · *Braise, Panfry*

Arm Steak · Blade Steak · Neck

Braise, Cook in Liquid

(Large Pieces) Veal for Stew* (Small Pieces)

Rib Roast — *Roast* · Crown Roast

Rib Chop · *Braise, Panfry* · Frenched Rib Chop

Loin Roast — *Roast, Braise* · Rolled Stuffed Loin

Loin Chop · *Braise, Panfry* · Kidney Chop

Sirloin Roast — *Roast, Braise* · Rolled Double Sirloin

Sirloin Steak · *Braise, Panfry* · Cube Steak*

Standing Rump · Shank Half of Leg — *Roast, Braise*

Rolled Leg · Center Leg

Heel of Round · *Braise, Cook in Liquid*

Cutlets, Boneless · Round Steak · *Braise, Panfry* · Rolled Cutlets (Birds)

Fore Shank · *Braise, Cook in Liquid*

Breast · Stuffed Breast — *Roast, Braise*

Brisket Rolls · *Braise*

Riblets · Brisket Pieces · *Braise, Cook in Liquid* · Stuffed Chops · *Braise, Panfry*

Rolled Cube Steaks (Birds)* · Ground Veal* · Patties* · *Braise* · *Roast (Bake) / Braise, Panfry*

Mock Chicken Legs* · City Chicken* · Choplets* · *Braise, Panfry*

*VEAL FOR STEW, GRINDING OR CUBING MAY COME FROM ANY WHOLESALE CUT

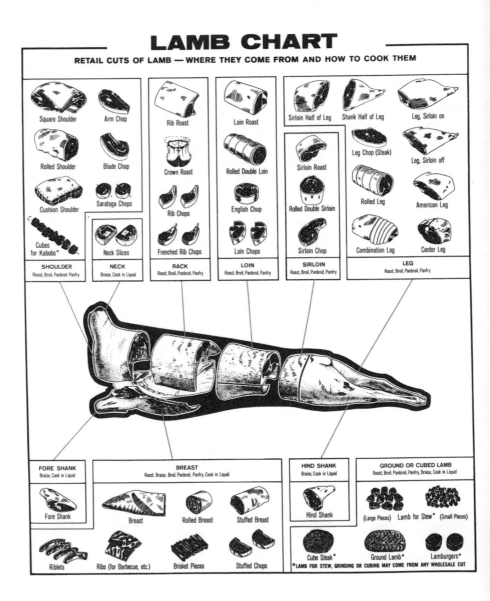

LAMB CHART

RETAIL CUTS OF LAMB — WHERE THEY COME FROM AND HOW TO COOK THEM

Square Shoulder — Arm Chop — Rib Roast — Loin Roast — Sirloin Half of Leg — Shank Half of Leg — Leg, Sirloin on

Rolled Shoulder — Blade Chop — Crown Roast — Rolled Double Loin — Leg Chop (Steak) — Leg, Sirloin off

Cushion Shoulder — Saratoga Chops — Rib Chops — English Chop — Sirloin Roast — Rolled Leg — American Leg

Cubes for Kabobs* — Neck Slices — Frenched Rib Chops — Loin Chops — Rolled Double Sirloin — Sirloin Chop — Combination Leg — Center Leg

SHOULDER Roast, Broil, Panbroil, Panfry

NECK Braise, Cook in Liquid

RACK Roast, Broil, Panbroil, Panfry

LOIN Roast, Broil, Panbroil, Panfry

SIRLOIN Roast, Broil, Panbroil, Panfry

LEG Roast, Broil, Panbroil, Panfry

FORE SHANK Braise, Cook in Liquid

BREAST Roast, Braise, Broil, Panbroil, Panfry, Cook in Liquid

HIND SHANK Braise, Cook in Liquid

GROUND OR CUBED LAMB Roast, Broil, Panbroil, Panfry, Braise, Cook in Liquid

Fore Shank — Breast — Rolled Breast — Stuffed Breast — Hind Shank — (Large Pieces) Lamb for Stew* (Small Pieces)

Riblets — Ribs (for Barbecue, etc.) — Brisket Pieces — Stuffed Chops — Cube Steak* — Ground Lamb* — Lamburgers*

*LAMB FOR STEW, GRINDING OR CUBING MAY COME FROM ANY WHOLESALE CUT

(Charts courtesy of National Livestock and Meat Board)

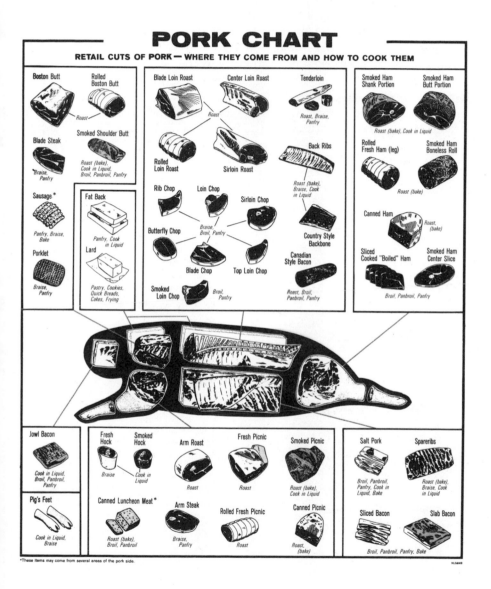

packaged fresh meat in the original wrapper, but loosen it to allow circulation of air. Or follow label directions.

Store all fresh meats at once in the coldest part of your refrigerator food compartment, or in the compartment specifically designed for meat storage. In the latter, the meat may be stored unwrapped.

If you are unable to cook meat for the meal for which it was planned and you have a home freezer or refrigerator-freezer combination, freezer-wrap and freeze meat; then use within the recommended time. If you have no freezer, just the frozen-food compartment of a conventional refrigerator, you can keep freezer-wrapped meat in it for one or two weeks.

Refer to the storage time guide below for the maximum time meat may be

STORAGE TIME GUIDE FOR MEAT
(kept in cold refrigerator at 36° F. to 40° F.)

MEAT (Uncooked, loosely covered)	STORAGE LIMIT FOR MAXIMUM QUALITY	MEAT (Uncooked, loosely covered)	STORAGE LIMIT FOR MAXIMUM QUALITY
BEEF		**VEAL**	
Corned beef	7 days	Chops and steak	4 days
Hamburger	2 days	Roast	5 to 6 days
Pot roast	5 to 6 days	Stew meat	2 days
Short ribs	2 days	**VARIETY MEATS**	
Standing rib roast	5 to 8 days		
Standing and rolled rump and sirloin tip	5 to 6 days	Brains	1 day
		Heart	2 days
Steak	3 to 5 days	Kidney	1 day
Stew meat	2 days	Liver, sliced	2 days
Tenderloin	3 to 5 days	Sweetbreads, cooked	2 days
		Tongue, fresh	2 days
		Tongue, smoked	7 days
PORK (fresh)		**COOKED, LOOSELY COVERED**	
Chops	3 days	Franks	4 to 5 days
Pork sausage	2 to 3 days	Ham or Picnic	7 days
Roast	5 to 6 days	Leftover meat	4 days
Spareribs	3 days	**SLICED READY-COOKED**	
Knuckles or hocks	3 days		
		Dry sausage	1 to 2 weeks
		Liver sausage	2 to 3 days
HAM, BACON (cured pork)		Luncheon meat	3 days
Bacon	6 to 7 days	Meat loaves	3 to 4 days
Half ham	7 days	Semidry sausage	7 to 8 days
Whole ham	1 to 2 weeks	**UNSLICED READY-COOKED**	
Sliced ham	3 days		
Picnic	1 to 2 weeks	Bologna	4 to 6 days
		Dry and semidry sausage	2 to 3 weeks
		Shank	2 days
LAMB		Stew meat	2 days
Chops	3 days	Liver sausage	4 to 6 days
Roast	5 days	Meat loaves	4 to 6 days

kept in the food compartment of a refrigerator for maximum flavor and eating pleasure. This chart is a general guide; but many factors influence the length of time a meat can be kept satisfactorily. So use the meat you buy as *promptly as possible*; or freeze it as described above.

Cured and smoked meats. Today's prepackaged ham, bacon, and sausage should be refrigerated at once in their original wrappers. When removing some of the meat, return the unused portion to the refrigerator at once.

Canned full-size hams must be refrigerated as the label very prominently directs. **Canned small 1½ lb. ham pieces** may be stored on pantry shelf. **Other canned meats**, if not labeled "Keep in Refrigerator," may also be kept on the pantry shelf.

Frozen meats must be kept frozen at 0° F. or lower until ready to use.

COOKED MEATS

Cooked meats are a boon to menu planners—and not just for sandwiches or short-order occasions. They may be baked, sautéed, or served as hot or cold main dishes.

Fully cooked ham. This wrapped, cooked ham comes with bone in (8 to 22 lbs.) or rolled and boned (11 to 12 lbs.). You can buy it whole, by the piece, or in slices. It may be served as is, or baked, pan-fried, or broiled. Check wrapper information carefully. **Skinless, shankless ham** comes fully cooked. Serve cold, just as it comes from the wrapper; or serve it hot, following the directions on the label. **Boiled ham** is cooked, boned ham which is sold sliced.

Cooked smoked picnic (shoulder) (3 to 9 lbs.) comes all ready to serve sliced cold, quickly heated, or glazed.

Cooked Smithfield-style ham. This bone-in ham (8 to 12 lbs.), with its distinctive flavor, is sold at specialty shops only.

Prosciutto (Italian-style ham). A lean whole ham (12 to 20 lbs.) pressed and aged in spices to achieve a concentrated, rich, mellow flavor. It is ready to serve, without further cooking, and should be sliced paper-thin.

Liver cheese (liver loaf) is for those who want sandwich-shaped slices of liver sausage. It's made in a loaf shape, and covered with fresh white pork fat to keep it moist. Use it hot or cold.

Luncheon loaf comes in a square, round, or loaf shape. It has a hamlike flavor. Serve it cold, sautéed, or baked.

Meat loaf is a combination of the same meats and seasonings that are used in homemade meat loaf. Buy it sliced for sandwiches and cold plates, or as a whole or half loaf to bake as a main dish.

Specialty loaves include meat, with cubes of cheese throughout; pickle-and-pimento loaves; pepper loaves of many varieties, etc.

Tongues (beef, lamb, and pork) also come fully cooked, ready to serve.

AMOUNT TO BUY

For a cold-meat platter, allow about two or three ounces of meat per serving. For salads and sandwiches, allow one to two ounces per serving. To store, make sure meat slices lie flat; keep prepackaged meats in wrapper. Wrap sliced meat in wax paper, plastic, or foil and refrigerate. To enjoy the fine flavor, use unsliced dry or semidry sausage within two or three weeks.

CARE OF MEATS

Refrigerate at once. Don't make the mistake of letting hot cooked, roasted, or leftover cooked meats stand until cold before refrigerating them. This is a risky practice, which only invites food poisoning. Either refrigerate the meat at once (this does not impair its flavor, despite old wives' tales), or cool the meat quickly, then refrigerate at once. To hasten cooling of meat in broth, lift meat from broth to a wire rack; then cool the kettle of broth in cold water in the sink, changing water and stirring broth often. At the end of a half hour, no longer, refrigerate both meat and broth.

In any case, *never* let cooked meat stand out of the refrigerator longer than two hours. And plan to use it up within four days.

MEAT TENDERIZER

A relatively new product derived from the papaya juice used by South American Indians for the same purpose, powdered instant meat tenderizer permits cooking the less tender cuts of meat as you would cook the more expensive, tender cuts.

The powder comes in shaker-top jars, with or without added seasoning. It may be used on steaks, chops, roasts, pot roast, and ground meats; in stews; on fish, variety meats, game birds, and poultry. It helps seal in juices, cuts down shrinkage, and reduces cooking time not only for meats but in cooking dried beans, peas, and limas. Follow label directions carefully.

MEDICINE CHEST CARE |

There are two good reasons for paying special attention to the contents of the medicine chest. Today so many specialized drugs are in use that it's impossible to remember which is which; and some are dangerous, especially to children, if improperly used. The cluttered, untidy medicine chest no longer is a joke. It pays the housewife to observe these do's and don'ts:

Do follow a regular schedule for inspecting and rearranging the medicine chest. A card posted inside the door of the cabinet, with dates for checking, is a good idea. This will insure discarding half-evaporated bottles of antiseptic, etc., which may have become unfit for use or even dangerous;

and loose razor blades, shelf-worn gauze bandage, and other useless odds and ends.

Don't allow your supplies of essential items to run out. Check for this on your regular inspection.

Do discard any half-used prescription medicine (expensive though it was), unless you consult your doctor on its keeping properties, and the advisability of *ever* using it again.

Don't keep anything except staple articles such as toothpaste and mouthwash in a medicine chest that is accessible to children—and realize that as toddlers grow, they learn to climb. Store all drugs or antiseptics in a closet or a special box which can be locked. Many commonplace items, including iodine, boric acid, and aspirin, are potentially poisonous. To be absolutely sure, set aside a special storage place for such items, clearly labeled as poisonous.

Do be especially careful about pleasant-tasting cough syrups, laxatives, etc., which children are apt to swallow like candy.

Don't keep any unlabeled or illegibly labeled box or bottle in the medicine cabinet. If you're not absolutely sure of the contents so you can relabel, discard it.

Be sure to screw the caps of bottles tightly; the contents will keep better, and children will be less likely to open them.

Don't use *any* medicine or antiseptic until you have read the label twice. Make a habit of this sensible safety precaution.

MENU PLANNING | See also DIET FOR YOUNG CHILDREN; FIGURE CARE; FOOD PLANNING IN QUANTITY

Nothing is more important to any family's healthy and happy life than breakfasts, lunches, and dinners that combine good eating with a wise selection of food and still stay within budget limitations. In this weight-conscious age, everyone knows about calories, and most people own a chart for counting them. But calories are by no means the whole story. It is possible to eat 1,500 calories a day and feel marvelous, or to "starve" on 2,000.

Women who plan meals should understand food values—which foods provide necessary proteins, minerals, vitamins, and other diet essentials. Americans have little excuse for not eating well and wisely. Cost is seldom any real hindrance to food enjoyment or to a sound diet. A well-seasoned, tasty meat loaf provides as high-quality protein as prime ribs of beef. Sauces and desserts made with nonfat dry milk need make no apology for either flavor or food value.

Following are the basic building blocks of sound daily menu planning: what foods you should eat, how much, how often, and why. The first four are the most essential, the *protective* foods.

1. **Meat, poultry, and fish.** At least one serving each day. **Eggs.** At least four every week. For high-quality protein, B vitamins, vitamin A, and iron.

2. **Milk (liquid, evaporated, dried, or as cheese).** One quart per day for children, three cups per day for adults, or equivalents. Provides calcium, high-quality protein, riboflavin, vitamin A, and alkaline residue.

3. **Citrus fruits (oranges, lemons, etc.), and tomatoes.** At least one serving each day. For vitamins A and C, minerals, and alkaline residue.

4. **Leafy green and yellow vegetables.** At least one, preferably two, servings every day. For vitamins A and C, minerals, bulk, and alkaline residue.

5. **Breads and cereals,** including macaroni and flour products, enriched or whole grain. Three or more servings every day. For supplementary proteins, B vitamins, iron, calcium, and energy (carbohydrates).

6. **Dried beans, peas, lentils, etc., and nuts.** Three or four servings every week. For supplementary proteins (complete proteins in many nuts), energy, and alkaline residue.

7. **Potatoes.** One or two servings every day. For minerals, vitamin C, and alkaline residue.

8. **Vegetables and fruits** (in addition to those in blocks 3 and 4). Two or more servings every day. For vitamins A and C, minerals, bulk, and alkaline residue.

9. **Butter or margarine.** Two or three tablespoons every day. For vitamin A, and energy. Other fats and oils (use a variety), amount as required in food preparation. For essential fatty acids, and energy.

10. **Sugar.** As needed for flavor, and consistent with energy requirements. See blocks 5, 6, and 9 for other energy-supplying foods.

APPROXIMATE DAILY CALORIE REQUIREMENTS FOR NORMALLY ACTIVE PEOPLE

Men (154 lbs.)	Calories	Children up to 10 years	Calories
		Under 1 year	52 per lb.
25 yrs.	2,900	1 to 3 (29 lbs.)	1,600
45 yrs.	2,600	3 to 6 (40 lbs.)	1,300
65 yrs.	2,200	6 to 9 (53 lbs.)	2,100
Women (128 lbs.)		Children over 10 years	
		GIRLS	
25 yrs.	2,100	9 to 12 (72 lbs.)	2,200
45 yrs.	1,900	12 to 15 (103 lbs.)	2,500
65 yrs.	1,600	15 to 18 (117 lbs.)	2,300
		BOYS	
		9 to 12 (72 lbs.)	2,400
		12 to 15 (98 lbs.)	3,000
		15 to 18 (134 lbs.)	3,400

What is a calorie? It is a unit of energy—the energy needed to stoke the engines of our bodily processes and provide the fuel for our physical activities. Some foods, such as pure fat and pure sugar, supply energy calories principally. Others contribute vitamins, minerals, proteins, and other values vital to health and well-being. These are the protective foods listed in Nos. 1 to 4 of the "building blocks" above.

The calorie table, compiled by the National Research Council, shows the number of energy units that average people need daily for their physical activities. If your food supplies the number you need, you neither gain nor lose weight. If you need to lose weight, reduce the number of calories you are now taking daily—but not too drastically and *never* at the expense of protective foods. (Most of these are not high in energy units, anyway.)

Don't reduce your calories below 1,200 to 1,300. *Don't* try to lose more than two pounds a week. *Always* consult your doctor about weight reduction.

The following family menu patterns have been designed to help you plan well-balanced meals in two situations: first, a maintenance diet for a man and woman twenty-five to thirty-five years old and now at their ideal weights; and second, a reducing diet.

Younger children, who may not need quite 1,800 calories, will usually set their own pace on quantity. But be sure they eat some of everything, and that they get that extra pint of milk. Teen-agers, underweights, and active men can add calories via larger servings, seconds, and snacks.

DAILY MAINTENANCE DIETS

Woman's (2,100 calories)
BREAKFAST
1 cup citrus fruit or fruit juice
2 soft- or hard-cooked, poached, or baked eggs
2 slices buttered and jellied toast

or

½ cup cooked cereal or 1 cup ready-to-eat cereal with 1 glass milk
1 soft- or hard-cooked, poached, or baked egg
1 slice buttered toast

or

½ cup cottage cheese
1½ slices lightly buttered or jellied toast
1 glass milk

and

coffee or tea (a simple way to avoid unwanted calories is to cut down
on the sugar and cream).

LUNCH OR SUPPER
3 thin slices meat or poultry or 1 generous serving fish or seafood
2 servings of these vegetables: asparagus, broccoli, Brussels sprouts, cabbage,

carrots, cauliflower, celery, green beans, greens, Italian beans, okra, sauerkraut, spinach, tomatoes.

Serve them hot, or as salads, using a small amount of dressing.

or

2 sandwiches (each filled with 1 sliced egg or 1 slice poultry, lean beef, ham, or cheese) with mustard, catsup, or greens, as desired

or

¾ cup seafood, poultry, or egg salad
2 tablespoons salad dressing; greens
½ slice buttered bread

or

2-egg western, mushroom, or plain omelet, cooked in 1 tablespoon fat
1 slice jellied or buttered toast

and

a small serving of gelatin dessert or pudding; or a thin slice of angel-food or sponge cake; or a serving of fresh or canned fruit; or a small serving of sherbet

and

a glass of milk.

DINNER

4 thin slices lean meat or poultry or a generous serving fish
2 servings vegetables—one from luncheon list and one of the following
½ cup beans, corn, rice, macaroni family, or potatoes, or 1 slice bread

or

1 serving of a casserole or 1½ servings of a low-calorie main dish
1 or 2 servings vegetables—see luncheon list

or

any main course from luncheon list
1 slice buttered or jellied toast or bread
a generous serving gelatin dessert with whipped cream; or a pudding; or fruit with crackers; or a small serving of pie, cake, or ice cream
a glass of milk.

Man's (2,900 calories)

BREAKFAST

1 cup citrus fruit or fruit juice
2 soft- or hard-cooked, poached, or baked eggs
2 slices buttered and jellied toast

or

½ cup cooked cereal or 1 cup read-to-eat cereal with 1 glass milk
1 soft- or hard-cooked, poached, or baked egg
1 slice buttered toast

or

½ cup cottage cheese
1½ slices lightly buttered or jellied toast
1 glass milk

and

coffee or tea.

LUNCH OR SUPPER

3 slices meat or poultry or 1 generous serving fish or seafood
one serving from each of the following:

a) asparagus, broccoli, Brussels sprouts, cabbage, carrots, cauliflower, celery, green beans, greens, Italian beans, okra, sauerkraut, spinach, or tomatoes;

b) potatoes, macaroni family, rice, corn, beans, peas; or 1 slice buttered bread or a roll

or

2 sandwiches (each filled with 2 sliced eggs or 2 slices poultry, lean beef, ham, or cheese) with mustard, catsup, or a bit of salad dressing; greens as desired

or

1 cup seafood, poultry, or egg salad
2 tablespoons salad dressing; greens
buttered bread or a roll

or

3-egg western, mushroom, or plain omelet, cooked in 1 tablespoon fat
2 slices buttered toast
a serving of gelatin dessert or pudding; or a slice of angle-food or sponge cake; or a generous serving of fresh or canned fruit; or a serving of sherbet
a glass of milk.

DINNER

4 slices lean meat or poultry or a generous serving fish;
2 servings vegetables—see the two luncheon lists

or

1½ servings of a favorite casserole; or 2 servings of a low-calorie main dish
2 servings vegetables—see two luncheon lists

or

any main course from luncheon list
1 slice buttered toast or bread
a generous serving gelatin dessert with whipped cream; or pudding;
or fruit with crackers; or a small serving of pie, cake, or ice cream
a glass of milk.

SNACKS

300 calories are allowed for your snacks.

BASIC REDUCING DIETS

Woman's (1,200 calories)

BREAKFAST

½ cup citrus fruit or fruit juice
1 soft- or hard-cooked, poached, or baked egg
1 slice lightly buttered toast

or

½ cup cooked or 1 cup ready-to-eat cereal
(flaked or puffed cereals are best choices) with 1 glass skim milk

or

⅓ cup cottage cheese; and 1 slice lightly buttered or jellied toast
coffee or tea, black or with a bit of skim milk and no more than 1 teaspoon sugar.

LUNCH OR SUPPER
3 thin slices lean meat or poultry or 1 medium serving fish or seafood,
2 servings of these vegetables: asparagus, broccoli, Brussels sprouts, cabbage,
carrots, cauliflower, celery, green beans, greens, Italian beans, okra, sauerkraut,
spinach, tomatoes.
Serve them hot (unbuttered), or as salads, using low-calorie dressing
or
1 sandwich (2 sliced eggs or 2 slices poultry, lean beef, ham, or cheese)
with mustard, catsup, low-calorie salad dressing; or greens as desired
or
½ cup seafood, poultry, or egg salad prepared with
3 tablespoons dressing; seasonings, greens as desired
or
2-egg western, mushroom, or plain omelet, cooked in 1 teaspoon fat
1 slice jellied or buttered toast
1 fresh peach, pear, apple, or small banana; or 2 fresh apricots or plums; or
1 cup fresh grapes, cherries, berries (all kinds), or cubed melon
(if you wish, substitute dietetic-pack fruit)
½ glass skim milk or buttermilk.

DINNER
3 thin slices lean meat or poultry or a medium serving fish
2 servings vegetables—one from luncheon list and one of the following:
½-cup serving of beans, corn, rice, macaroni family, or potatoes; or
1 slice lightly buttered bread
or
1 serving low-calorie main dish; 2 servings vegetables—
one from luncheon list and one from dinner list
or
any main course from luncheon list
1 slice lightly buttered or jellied bread or toast
½-cup serving gelatin dessert or pudding made with skim milk; or 1 thin slice
angle-food or sponge cake; or 1 serving fruit from luncheon dessert list
1 glass skim milk or buttermilk.

Man's or teen-age girl's (1,800 calories)
BREAKFAST
1 cup citrus fruit or fruit juice
2 soft- or hard-cooked, poached, or baked eggs
2 slices lightly buttered toast
or
½ cup cooked cereal or 1 cup ready-to-eat cereal with ½ glass skim milk
1 soft- or hard-cooked, poached, or baked egg
1½ slices lightly buttered toast
or
½ cup cottage cheese
1½ slices lightly buttered or jellied toast
1 glass skim milk
coffee or tea, black or with a bit of skim milk and no more than 1 teaspoon sugar

LUNCH OR SUPPER
4 thin slices meat or poultry or 1 generous serving fish or seafood
2 servings of these vegetables: asparagus, broccoli, Brussels sprouts, cabbage,
carrots, cauliflower, celery, green beans, greens, Italian beans, okra, sauerkraut,
spinach, tomatoes.
Serve them hot, or as salads, using a small amount of dressing

or

2 sandwiches (each filled with 1 sliced egg or 1 slice poultry, lean beef, ham,
or cheese) with mustard, catsup, low-calorie salad dressing; or greens,
as desired

or

¾ cup seafood, poultry, or egg salad
2 tablespoons salad dressing; greens;
½ slice buttered bread

or

3-egg western, mushroom, or plain omelet, cooked in 1 tablespoon fat
1 slice jellied or buttered toast
1 fresh peach, pear, apple, or small banana; or 2 fresh apricots or plums; or
1 cup fresh grapes, cherries, berries (all kinds), or cubed melon
(if you wish, substitute dietetic-pack fruit)
1 glass skim milk or buttermilk.

DINNER
4 thin slices lean meat or poultry or a generous serving fish
2 servings vegetables—one from luncheon list and one of the following:
½ cup serving of beans, rice, corn, macaroni family, or potatoes; or
1 slice bread

or

1 serving low-calorie main dish
2 servings vegetables—see luncheon list;
1 slice buttered bread

or

any main course from luncheon list
½ slice buttered or jellied toast or bread
1 cup serving gelatin dessert or pudding made with skim milk; or 1 thin slice
angle-food or sponge cake and 1 serving fruit from luncheon dessert list
1 glass skim milk or buttermilk.

HOW TO CALCULATE THE NUMBER
OF CALORIES IN A RECIPE

1. Select your recipe and write down the individual ingredients and the
amount of each.

2. Look up each item in a calorie table, noting particularly the calorie
count *per unit*. For example, if the table gives the number of calories per
ounce of cheese, and your recipe uses eight ounces, then you would multiply
this number by eight.

3. Put down these figures opposite each item in the recipe and add them up. This gives the total calorie count of the dish.

4. Divide by the number of servings that the recipe makes. This gives the calorie count per serving.

5. P.S. Don't cheat!

Example. Baked Macaroni and Cheese. Serves four.

½ pound processed American Cheddar cheese (2 cups, grated)	840
2 cups raw macaroni, in 2-inch pieces	650
4 teaspoons minced onion	5
2 tablespoons butter or margarine	200
1 tablespoon flour	25
¼ teaspoon dry mustard	—
¾ teaspoon salt	—
Speck pepper	—
2 cups milk	330
4 teaspoons butter or margarine	135
¾ cup soft bread crumbs	60
	4)2,245
Each serving 560 calories (approx.)	561

METAL CLEANING |

Copper or brass objects may be cleaned with metal polish, some of which are specifically for these metals. Apply the polish to smooth surfaces with a soft cloth or sponge, and to embossed or wrought patterns with a brush. Wash in hot sudsy water, rinse in hot water, and dry with a clean, soft towel. Some metal polishes help retard the formation of tarnish.

Lacquered copper or brass may tarnish when the lacquer begins to wear off. Some lacquers may be removed with acetone. Then you may either have the piece relacquered, or polish the exposed metal and apply furniture wax or copper cleaner with tarnish-retarding properties.

Chromium does not tarnish, but may become dulled with film. If washing fails to restore its gleam, clean with silver polish.

Pewter is susceptible to abrasive cleansers. Instead, use two tablespoons of ammonia per quart of very hot, sudsy water; wash thoroughly; rinse in hot water; and buff with a soft cloth. If tarnished, clean with silver polish or brass polish.

Aluminum used decoratively usually has a special soil-resistant finish. Wash in sudsy water like aluminum pots and pans, but do not use soap-filled steel wool pads.

Sterling or plated silver will need less frequent polishing if you use and wash often. Some silver polishes contain tarnish preventives. Clean with silver paste or polish, using a soft brush on chased or embossed patterns.

Stored showpiece silver, such as formal table settings, will stay shiny if wrapped in anti-tarnish treated cloth bags. These bags may be reused when the pieces are put away again after your party. Regular dusting with specially treated cloth now on the market helps prevent tarnish.

Stainless steel or Monel metal, for the most part, is restored by daily washing. Where necessary, however, make a paste of fine scouring powder and a few drops of ammonia; polish with this; rinse and dry thoroughly. Buff any scratches with very fine stainless steel wool (ooo or finer).

Enameled metal cabinets, refrigerators, etc., should not be scrubbed with harsh abrasives; use a mild solution of general-purpose liquid cleaner, or one of the aerosol spray cleaners for this purpose. Polish with kitchen wax, a creamy emulsion which leaves a dirt-resistant film. On ranges, cool before cleaning to avoid crazing of the porcelain enamel.

MILDEW |

Generally, it's much easier to prevent mildew than to remove it. If let go too long, mildew—a mold or fungus that usually shows itself as furry blotches of gray, green, or black—can discolor or rot clothes so badly that they can't be reclaimed. Here are some precautions to take:

Keep all storage places dry. Burning a small electric light continuously in a closet will help prevent moisture from accumulating. You might also try leaving closet doors and dresser drawers open occasionally, especially on a cool night. A portable electric fan can help, too. Hanging clothes loosely, not too close together, will enable air to circulate more freely. In some areas, where the weather is unusually humid, an electric dehumidifier or even central air conditioning may be the only answer.

Keep garments and storage places clean. Wash or dry-clean clothes and polish shoes before storing them. (Incidentally, be sure to wash out any starch in fabrics to be stored for long periods. Starch attracts mildew.) Use a good paste wax on shoes, including the soles. If you place clothing in tight plastic garment bags it helps to keep them clean and dry. Aerosol spray disinfectants now available give antimildew protection to sprayed closets, hampers, etc. if used weekly.

Use moth crystals (paradichlorobenzene) in tightly closed clothing containers, such as suitcases, cardboard boxes, etc. Don't skimp on the crystals; follow the directions on the package carefully. *Warning:* "para" can harm plastic, so use wooden or metal hangers instead of plastic ones, remove all plastic buttons and ornaments, and never use "para" in plastic garment bags unless they're specifically made for the purpose.

Air, sun, and brush stored garments frequently. If possible, take them out into the sunshine and brush them well every ten days or so during humid weather.

Don't put damp clothes into a closed container. Dry soiled clothes, towels, and washcloths before putting them into a hamper. If you have a steam iron, many articles to be ironed won't need dampening. In any case, try not to dampen more things than you can iron in one day. If you have to keep dampened clothes overnight, store them in a plastic bag in the refrigerator.

Spread out your shower curtain along the rod to dry after you take a shower.

MILDEW STAINS

The sooner you find them, the easier it is to get rid of them. Surface growths on fabrics can be brushed off with a whisk broom. It's a good idea to do the brushing outdoors and to air the garments thoroughly afterward. At the first sign of mildew on shoes, brush or wipe off the spots; then polish the shoes. If mildew is more deeply entrenched, try one of these methods:

Fabrics. Wash thoroughly; if the spots don't disappear, use a good bleach.

If soiled dishcloths or washcloths smell sour and musty—a sign of mildewing—either boil them a few minutes in water to which baking soda has been added (two tablespoons to a quart of water), or wash them in very hot water and then use a chlorine bleach.

Shoes. Wash with thick soapsuds or saddle soap. Wipe with a damp cloth, and dry in an airy place. Polish.

Shower curtains. Soak in the bathtub, using warm water and a detergent. Then scrub with a stiff brush, rinse in clear water, and hang over the shower rod.

Nonwashable suits, dresses, coats, etc. Except for giving them a good brushing, don't try to treat them yourself. Send them to a good dry cleaner.

MILK AND CREAM |

Grocers' shelves contain such a wide variety of milk products that many people have difficulty learning which is which. This simple glossary may help.

Raw milk is fresh whole milk, just as it is taken from the cow.

Pasteurized "Grade A" milk has been heated, then cooled rapidly, to destroy harmful bacteria. It usually contains from 3.5 to 3.8 per cent butterfat (the natural fat in whole milk).

Certified milk, raw milk which has an extremely low percentage of bacteria, is produced under sanitary controls established by the American Association of Medical Milk Commissions, Inc. It may sometimes be pasteurized.

Homogenized milk has been forced through a machine that breaks up the butterfat into very small particles. The cream is thus evenly distributed throughout the whole milk.

Premium "extra-rich" milk, which has an unusually high butterfat content —generally from 4 to 5 per cent—is drawn from certain breeds of cows, particularly the Guernsey and Jersey.

Skim milk, the portion remaining after almost all butterfat is removed, retains all the nutritional values of whole milk except vitamin A and the calories found in the cream.

Low-sodium milk is whole milk from which the natural sodium has been extracted.

Cream is the part of the milk containing the butterfat. Light or coffee cream normally contains not less than 18 per cent butterfat; heavy or whipping cream, about 30 to 40 per cent.

Half and half, a mixture of light cream and whole milk, contains about 10 to 12 per cent butterfat.

Pressurized cream, "instant whipped cream" in an aerosol can, may be mostly cream, or a mixture of cream, nonfat milk solids, and other ingredients. Be sure to read the label carefully.

Sour cream, which actually tastes fresh and tangy rather than sour, is light cream to which harmless bacteria have been added to break down the sugar content. It is sometimes called salad cream.

Buttermilk is skim milk "soured" in much the same way as sour cream.

Yogurt, which has a naturally tart taste and a custardlike consistency, is produced by adding a particular strain of bacteria to whole or partially skimmed milk. It is available plain or flavored.

Chocolate dairy drink is skim milk with chocolate flavoring; **chocolate milk** is made with whole instead of skim milk.

Malted milk, available in powder form, is a mixture of whole milk, malt (made from ground barley malt and wheat flour), sugar, and various flavorings.

Evaporated milk is canned after about 60 per cent of the water is removed from the whole milk.

Sweetened condensed milk is similar except that sugar is added before the water content is removed.

Instant powdered cream. A 100 per cent pure dairy product—all fresh cream and other milk products—in instant powdered form, that stays fresh and never needs refrigeration. It not only dissolves instantly in hot coffee, tea, or cocoa, but can replace cream or milk in many recipes if the manufacturer's directions are followed.

Coffee lightener is a nondairy product with a fresh natural flavor, that lightens the color and flavor of a cup of coffee.

MIRRORS |

Besides their obvious usefulness, mirrors can be decorative. They can add a spacious feeling to a small room, reflect a view, and direct light into dark corners.

Mirrors may be framed or unframed, but the current trend is toward frames in such finishes as metal leaf, antique gold, burnished bronze, mahogany, maple, walnut, and a revival of sparkling "Venetian" glass.

Mirrors with the best, or truest, reflections are made of polished plate glass rather than window or sheet glass. The reflective coating of most mirrors is silver, but gold, lead, and other materials may be used. Some leading mirror manufacturers offer a ten-year guaranty on the silvering under conditions of normal use.

Streaking and clouding of mirrors are hastened under exposure to direct sunlight, extreme humidity, and sea air, and can be corrected only by resilvering. The process calls for equipment, chemicals, and know-how of a very technical kind. Resilvering by a plate-glass dealer costs about $1.25 a square foot.

HOW TO RECOGNIZE THE 11 BASIC MIRRORS

Although many antique mirrors are available with their original glass, practically all the styles are being authentically reproduced, more reasonably, by manufacturers. Here are the most popular styles of hanging mirrors.

1. **Sheraton.** Frequently gold-leaf, occasionally natural-wood finish. Painted-glass panel, spiral columns, molded ball top are typical.

1   2   3

2. **Federal.** Also called convex, bull's-eye, or girandole. The attached eagle and candle sconces are typical.

3. **Chinese Chippendale.** Usually in gilt or lacquer. English eighteenth century versions of Chinese motifs identify this style. Another Oriental mirror is frequently found in a square or oblong shape framed in red or black lacquer with rounded corners. It is sometimes seen in natural wood too.

4. **Adam.** Usually done in gold leaf in a light version of classic design. Figures, urns, or other Greek motifs are identifying marks.

5. **The Venetian** mirror is usually framed in glass, elaborately etched and scrolled. Extra glass motifs are frequently applied.

6. **French.** Louis XV style with shells and lacy scrolls. Often gilt-finished but also done in fruit woods.

4   5   6

7. **Biedermeier.** The oblong shape often combines contrasting woods. Gold or painted insets are typical.

8. **Chippendale.** Nearly always seen in either mahogany or walnut. The thin, flat cutout scrolls surrounding outside frame are typical.

9. **The pier or cheval glass,** widely used in the Victorian age, is not often seen in contemporary rooms.

10. **The triple-view** mirror is in common use on dressing tables. It comes in a wide variety of styles, both framed and unframed.

11. **The shaving** mirror is often seen on top of a man's chest of drawers, particularly if the chest is a mahogany antique.

Contemporary mirrors (not illustrated) are available in several styles— simple wood frames at top and bottom only, sides unframed; others may be unframed and have touches of brass or glass studs.

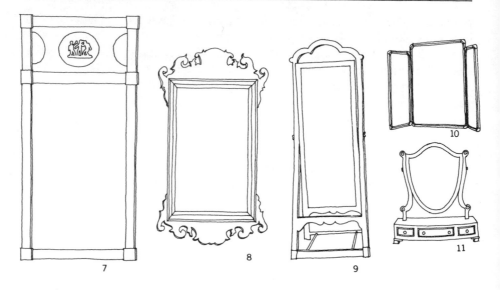

7   8   9   10   11

MORTGAGES | See also CREDIT AND DEBT; HOME BUYING; HOME REMODELING LOANS

A mortgage loan that you take out to pay for a home consists of two major documents—a *note* promising repayment of the loan within a certain number of years on a specified schedule; and the *mortgage* itself, pledging your home as security for the loan. Each monthly payment consists in part of an installment on the loan (known as the *principal*); and in part, of *interest*. If you cannot pay, the mortgage entitles the lender to take possession of the property in settlement of your debt.

Mortgages, it should be understood, cost money. The reason for them is to permit a buyer to enjoy possession of a home years before he has the cash to pay for it in toto. Spreading the payment over many months lets him budget his housing costs much like paying rent. However, the way a mortgage is arranged can save or add thousands of dollars in the ultimate cost of a house. Early in the term of the loan, and often for ten or fifteen years, the major part of each monthly payment is the interest.

Most home mortgages are obtained from savings and loan associations and banks. They can either be conventional loans or those that are government-insured by the Veterans Administration (VA or "GI" loans) or the Federal Housing Administration. In VA and FHA loans the government assumes a large part of the risk, as an inducement to lenders to make mortgage money available with a smaller down payment, for a longer term, and at a lower interest rate than conventional loans.

VA and FHA loans are limited to a maximum interest rate, recently 5¾ per cent, plus a ½ per cent insurance premium on FHA loans. Conventional loan rates have ranged in recent years from 5¼ to 7 per cent. In both cases rates are subject to change, up or down, depending upon the "money market" or upon conditions in your area. A fraction of a percentage point makes a big difference. If you bought a $15,000 home on a 20-year mortgage, paying $5,000 down and leaving $10,000 to repay, your interest would amount to $6,510 at 5½ per cent; $7,194 at 6 per cent; and $8,607 at 7 per cent.

Each year of the loan also adds to ultimate cost. Taking a $15,000 loan this time, at 6 per cent, the monthly payments would total $25,812 in 20 years; $29,025 in 25 years; and $32,400 in 30 years. That is why the size of your down payment is a key factor. First, it reduces the amount of money remaining to be borrowed. Second, lenders often will grant a lower *rate* of interest for a smaller mortgage—because it leaves the loan well secured by the market value of the house.

For instance, if a family puts 10 per cent ($2,000) down on a $20,000 house, the interest rate may be 6 per cent. Paid off at $108 a month for 30 years, the total cost for the house would be $40,880. But if the family made a 25 per cent ($5,000) down payment and got an interest rate of 5½ per cent, *the same monthly payment of $108* would buy the house in 18½ years at a total cost of $28,976. The additional $3,000 down payment cuts costs almost $12,000, and brings full title (unencumbered ownership) 11½ years closer.

Most families approach home financing with a monthly payment in mind, based on income, which they feel they can afford. Long-term mortgages do appear to reduce the monthly payment necessary to carry the loan. But in the long run, much more money is paid for the house. Experts point out that a term longer than 30 years does *not* reduce monthly payments enough to justify the greater total cost. From this point of view, a long-term, low-down-payment mortgage may not be your best buy even though it permits a smaller monthly outlay.

In most cases, you cannot get a mortgage of more than 70 to 75 per cent of the purchase price of a house twenty years old or more. Mortgages covering more of the purchase price (up to 97 per cent with certain FHA-insured loans) are usually limited to new houses. The lender appraises each house and sets a value on which the maximum mortgage will be based. In times of "tight" money, the terms both as to down payment and interest rate tend to stiffen.

At such times, many lenders feel they cannot make a fair profit on a VA or FHA mortgage without "discounting." This in effect charges the builder a premium that will increase the lender's return on the loan. Although the practice is legal, financial institutions are frequently reluctant to discount and may simply decline to grant you a VA or FHA loan.

You will generally find lenders charging a uniform rate on mortgages of a given type in your community, but there are other points to check. A conventional mortgage usually takes less paper work and may be obtained faster than VA or FHA mortgages. *Closing costs* are another factor, especially the service charge for processing and appraisals. This fee is 1 per cent on VA and FHA loans; other lenders may charge 2 per cent. Highest charges are usual where the lender assumes a greater risk, such as accepting a small down payment and a long repayment period.

A *prepayment clause* allows you to pay off the mortgage (or any part of it) in advance whenever you have the cash, thereby saving very considerable amounts of interest. An *open-end clause* allows reborrowing on a mortgage after part has been paid off. This is like getting a new mortgage and usually entails some new closing costs.

Other forms of home financing are available in some states, under such names as *land contract* or *conditional sales contract*. Generally they are not as favorable to the borrower as a mortgage. Interest rates are higher (7 to 10 per cent or more), and the penalty for missing a payment may be total loss of all money previously paid. (With a mortgage, the buyer retains his paid-in equity even if the house is repossessed.) Such contracts are resorted to by people who cannot raise a sufficient down payment or otherwise qualify for mortgage financing.

IF YOU NEED HELP

Here are some things you can do if you have trouble getting the kind of mortgage you want—or any mortgage at all.

You can ask a *mortgage banker* to locate a VA-guaranteed or FHA-insured loan for you. There are about 1,500 such bankers in the United States. They try to arrange for a mortgage with a lender in another part of the country. You pay the banker a fee for his services, usually about 1 per cent (for example, on a $10,000 loan, the fee would be $100). A mortgage banker can also locate a conventional loan.

Your husband may be eligible for the *Direct Loan Program for Veterans.* Former servicemen living in designated rural areas, where private financing is not available, are eligible for these loans. The qualifications are the same as those for a regular VA mortgage. Direct loans can be used to build, purchase, or improve a home, to purchase a farm with a home on it, or to improve a farm residence. Application can be made at any regional VA office.

You can apply for a VA or FHA mortgage through the *Voluntary Home Mortgage Credit Program,* sponsored jointly by the government and private lenders, such as banks and insurance companies. Regional committees of the VHMCP will locate mortgage money for rural home buyers in towns with less than 25,000 population. The VHMCP also assists members of minority groups who have been refused mortgages because of discrimination (the population requirement does not apply in this case). More information may be obtained by writing to the Voluntary Home Mortgage Credit Program, Washington, D.C. 20025.

If you own a farm or a tract of land in a rural area, you may be able to get a mortgage through the *Farmers Home Administration.* This program is for people who have not been able to establish credit from a private lender. Money is lent for constructing or improving homes on farms (which must produce at least $400 worth of commodities a year) and for homes on rural building sites. The interest rate is low (4 per cent) and up to 33 years can be taken to repay. Arrangements can be made at county offices of the Farmers Home Administration or by writing to the national headquarters, care of the U. S. Department of Agriculture, Washington, D.C. 20025.

MOVING |

Most Americans move several times during their lives—some as often as every five years. At its best, household moving is a chore and an expense. But the move can be orderly, instead of confusing and tiring, if you give yourself plenty of time. If possible, begin preparations at least four to six weeks in advance. This check list can be useful in making your changes of location smoother and easier.

BEFORE YOU MOVE

1. Get price estimates from several movers before you contract for the job and set a moving date. Watch out for unusually low prices; an estimate gives you approximate cost, but if actual costs are higher, you must pay. Reputable firms give honest estimates based on years of experience. Look for good service, too. Make inquiries among friends and business associates, or check with the local Better Business Bureau on any mover you plan to use. Also make sure the moving man who makes the estimate sees *everything* you plan to take.

2. Know whether the charge will be based on the *weight* of the load (usual in interstate or other long-distance moves) or on the *time* the move takes (customary when moving within the same city or local area). Then see tips, below, on saving either weight or time.

3. Go through your house systematically, and get rid of everything you don't need. Be merciless. That old piano, for example, may cost more to move than it's worth. Check bureaus, desks, closets, attic, and basement for things to be discarded. Remember that books and papers are surprisingly heavy.

4. Prepare a complete written inventory, room by room, of your household goods. Most movers provide inventory forms.

5. Ask the mover if he supplies packing labels and tags. If not, buy them or make them up yourself well in advance. Get free change-of-address cards from the post office.

6. Some appliances will need special servicing for moving. Find out about your washing machine, dryer, freezer, stereo, TV set, etc., from local appliance dealers.

7. Arrange to have your TV antenna and draperies taken down in advance. Take up tacked carpets yourself, or have your carpet company do it.

8. Include your children in moving preparations by letting them help wherever possible. For example, they might enjoy sending away to the Chamber of Commerce for maps and information about the new area.

9. Get medical and dental records, including vaccination data and prescriptions for eyeglasses and medications.

10. Notify utility companies to discontinue gas and electric, water, and telephone services.

11. Notify insurance agencies, post office, and regular delivery services (dairy, bakery, newspaper, etc.).

12. Discontinue or transfer charge accounts and bank accounts. Ask your bank to supply credit recommendations for use in your new community. Transfer items from your safe-deposit box.

13. Send out change-of-address cards to friends, relatives, stores, and publications. Most magazines require four to six weeks notice.

14. Return library books and other borrowed items.

15. Get copies of your children's school records.

16. If you have pets, you will have to take them with you or ship them by Railway Express. The mover is not allowed to take them.

17. Give away house plants unless you plan to take them with you in the car. Movers will not take them on the van. (Some state laws prohibit entry of certain plants.)

18. Inflammable liquids and items that may be explosive, such as cleaning fluid, kerosene, turpentine, lighter fluid, etc., cannot be shipped on the moving van.

19. Insure household goods for their full estimated value. The mover's liability for loss or damage is limited to 30 cents per pound per article.

Compare insurance rates. For moves of less than 700 miles, a cargo- or transit-insurance policy, available from a local broker, can give you the same protection at lower cost than coverage purchased from the mover. For longer hauls, one of the "protection plans" offered by movers will probably be a better buy. Do not overlook the importance of insurance.

PACKING

Many professional movers will do the entire job, even to packing and unpacking your belongings. Although you can save money by doing the packing yourself, you probably won't be able to pack as well or as quickly. If you are inexperienced, professional packing of valuable china, glass, pictures, and mirrors may be worth its cost. Remember that movers can disclaim responsibility for breakage of fragile goods you pack yourself.

Most people favor a combination: the movers pack the difficult things; you do the rest. Here are tips for the self-packer:

1. **Stock up in advance on sturdy cartons and crates** from grocery, hardware, and appliance stores. Movers usually charge for containers they supply. Get how-to-do-it advice in advance from your mover (often available in printed form).

2. **Label everything.** Gummed labels may come off in wet or humid weather; marking crayons or waterproof marking ink are best. Tag furniture and cartons with different-colored labels that signify the room they're to go in at the new location.

3. **Glasses and dishes.** Wrap each piece separately in two sheets of newspaper, and stuff additional shredded paper or excelsior around each. Pack glasses with the drinking edge down; dishes on edge, not flat. Place the most fragile pieces toward the top of the container, and mark it FRAGILE.

4. **Books and phonograph albums.** Small cartons are best, since heavy ones may break open when carried. Pack on edge, not flat, with pieces of cardboard between layers to prevent them from rubbing or sliding into one another.

5. **Lamp shades** are easily crushed. Wrap them in paper (not newspaper, though; the print may rub off) and pack one to a carton, bottom side down. Stuff the carton with crumpled tissue paper to keep the shade from shifting.

7. **Do not pack cartons above the top edge**; seal with heavy gummed tape. Moisten tape with *warm* water (a sponge works well) and press firmly in place.

8. Pack lightweight, unbreakable things—**linens and clothing**—in bureau drawers, to save both space and time. Remove from drawers all bottles or jars that could spill or break.

9. **Liquids** should be discarded as a general rule, except for expensive items such as medicines, perfume, and liquor. Tape down the tops of bottles you do take, wrap in newspapers, and pack in a strong carton or hamper.

10. **Do not pack jewelry or other valuables.** Send them ahead by registered mail or take them with you.

11. If you pack **electric appliances** with shredded paper or excelsior, wrap them first with newspaper to keep the shreds from getting into the mechanism. Tape down the arm of a record player before packing it.

12. If moving within the same town or area, don't pack anything that needs cleaning—**draperies, rugs, or extra clothing.** Send them out to the cleaner, who will deliver them to the new address at no extra cost.

13. **Tie together loose objects** such as mops and brooms, and consolidate

as many belongings as possible near the entrance the movers will use (to save moving time).

14. At the last hour, **unscrew attached fixtures** such as curtain rods, can openers, wall bookcases, etc. Disassemble beds; roll up rugs and tie them securely. Movers often charge extra for these jobs.

15. **Group together** any belongings you plan to throw or give away, or to take with you in the car, and mark each item DO NOT MOVE. A cardinal rule is *don't* trust your memory or expect to "take care of things" during the confusion of moving day. Keep careful lists.

NEEDLES |

Needles come in a variety of types to suit every purpose from stitching delicate embroidery to sewing heavy upholstery fabric. The size of a needle refers to its thickness; generally, the smaller the number, the thicker the needle. Packages marked "1/5" would include needles in assorted sizes 1 to 5. Always choose a needle a little thicker than the thread you are using so the thread will pass through the fabric easily. Here are the nine basic types of needle:

Sharp. Most widely used needle for dressmaking and common sewing jobs. About 1½″ long.

Between. Short (about 1″) version of sharp. Good to use on heavy fabrics.

Darners (cotton, wool, yarn). These are 2¼″ to 3″ long and have elongated eyes to accommodate darning cotton, wool thread, or yarn.

Embroidery. About the same length as sharp, but it has an extra-long eye for embroidery floss.

Chenille. Similar to embroidery type, but has an even larger, wider eye.

Tapestry. Also similar to embroidery needle, but it has a blunt point for working needle-point and other tapestry stitches on canvas.

Straight mattress. Long (6″ to 8″), heavy needle used on thick articles such as pads, pillows, and mattresses.

Curved mattress. Ranges in length from 2½″ to 5″; the curve enables it to get into hard-to-reach places. Good for sewing lamp shades, hat frames, handbags, etc.

Bodkin. Blunt, sometimes flat needle, about 2½″ long, with large eye. Used to thread tape, elastic, ribbon, etc., through casing and hem.

NURSERY SCHOOLS |

At one time a nursery school was merely a place where three- and four-year-olds could be left to play together. Today, the good nursery school can be a valuable educational experience for preschool children. Many women wonder, though, whether it is right to send very young children away from home, and if so, how to determine whether a nursery school is good.

Why send your child to nursery school? It can provide something often lacking in small families: experiences with other children and adults under the supervision of trained personnel. Through nursery school, a child can learn to live with and to get along with children his own age. Nursery school is a child-size world—with low toilets, tables, and chairs—and in good ones, the child can develop independence and self-confidence by doing things himself.

The school promotes a child's physical development by providing space and equipment not usually available in homes. Through such activities as painting, climbing, pushing wheelbarrows, and modeling clay, a child can develop talent, strength, stamina, and coordination.

Although the child does not learn reading and arithmetic, he does learn many skills basic to later learning. For instance, in deciding how many chairs to put around the table, he develops number concepts. He is encouraged to use and to enlarge his vocabulary. Through trips and stories, he develops curiosity and a positive attitude toward learning.

Mothers also can benefit from sending children to nursery school. It allows them some time to themselves to pursue adult interests, and through teacher conferences, etc., can help them understand a child better.

Is nursery school right for your child? This depends mainly on your own judgment. At three, some children are not ready to be away from home, even for a short period each day. If nursery school is used simply as a way to get rid of a child (or if there is a new baby in the house), it may be difficult for him to accept the school. However, if the child feels secure and knows you will be home when he returns, he is probably ready for the new experience.

CHOOSING THE SCHOOL

How can you choose a good nursery school? Visit the school in session, observing these points:

Staff. The teachers are the most important consideration. A teacher should be warm, relaxed, and patient with the children, and they should like her. She should be trained and certified in early childhood education. Make sure there are at least two adults for each group (of no more than twenty children).

Safety. Rooms should be well lighted and ventilated, clean, and comfortably warm. Find out whether the school is certified for safety by local health and fire authorities. Dangerous items, such as appliance wires or cleaning materials, should be out of reach. Unused wall outlets should be plugged. There should be at least one toilet and washbasin for every fifteen children.

Health. Teachers should be aware of a child's daily health status, and a doctor should be on call at all times. Also, the school should have a health record for each child. Check for an isolation area for children who become ill during school hours. Is there good balance between vigorous play and quiet activity or rest periods? If it is a full-day program, make sure children nap and have well-balanced meals.

Space. There should be enough room for the children to play freely without getting in each other's way.

Equipment. Look for variety and for materials that encourage physical development and creative play. This includes large unstructured pieces, such as boards and packing boxes for climbing and arranging; wagons and other wheel toys; building blocks; clay, paints, and large crayons; books and simple musical instruments; growing things (plants and pets).

Program. Activities should be well-planned without being rigid. For example, in periods for quiet activity, all children should not be forced to do the same thing. Instead of being told what to do with materials, children should be encouraged to explore the possibilities themselves. Some routine is necessary to make the children feel secure, yet there should be enough new experiences (short trips, new pets, etc.) to stimulate growth and interest.

Parents. A good nursery school, say authorities, schedules at least two parent-teacher conferences yearly, as well as group meetings. Mothers should cooperate with the school by keeping sick children home, and by informing teachers of problems that may affect the child's behavior.

Where can you find nursery schools? Some are privately owned, a few are in public schools, and a growing number are cooperatives, run by parents. There are also nursery schools run by colleges for child-study departments; those sponsored by religious groups or by health organizations (usually for the handicapped children); and others operated by social agencies for children from homes where both parents work. Sources of additional information are your local board of education, college or university, council of social agencies, and health or welfare departments.

How much will it cost? This depends on the school's location, who sponsors it, whether it is a half-day or full-day program, etc. Private schools seldom charge less than forty dollars a month for a half day.

NUTS |

Let the brand name on the nut shell or package be your guide in buying plump, meaty, fresh, sweet nut kernels. Varieties that come in-the-shell (in bags or bulk) include:

Almonds	Pecans
Black walnuts	Pistachio nuts
Brazil nuts	California walnuts
Chestnuts	(top-quality, large ones likely to carry
Filberts	red brand stamp on shell; medium
Peanuts	ones, blue brand stamp)

Shelled nuts (in clear bags, vacuum cans, or jars) include:

Almonds	Coconut chips
Blanched, whole or sliced	Dry toasted nuts, several varieties
Roasted, diced	Filberts
Toasted, blanched, slivered	Macadamias
Smokehouse cocktail	Pecans
Unblanched, whole or sliced	Salted pecans, peanuts, mixed nuts, etc.
Black walnuts	California walnuts
Cashews	

Store nuts in the shell, except for prolonged periods. Keep them in a nut bowl, or in a cool, dry place—preferably the main section of your refrigerator. For best protection, freeze kernels you shell yourself.

Store *unopened bags* or *cans* of kernels in the main section of the refrigerator, or in a freezer. After opening, keep unused kernels in the refrigerator, or in the freezer. In freezing nut kernels, put them in a tightly covered freezer container or plastic bag. Before using or refreezing, thaw them and allow moisture to dry out.

Almonds. *To blanch.* Cover shelled almonds with cold water. Bring to a boil; then remove from heat at once and drain. Slip off skins by pressing each almond between thumb and forefinger. Then dry blanched almonds on paper towels. *To toast.* Use 300° F. oven for twenty to twenty-five minutes for whole almonds, less time for slivers. Remove nuts before they are quite as dark as desired (they continue to brown after removal from oven). *To roast.* Toss nuts in a shallow pan with one teaspoonful salad oil per cup of nuts. Roast at 300° F., stirring occasionally, until evenly browned.

Brazil nuts. *To shell.* Freeze a few hours or overnight; then use a nutcracker to shell. Or boil them in water to cover for three minutes; drain. Then let them stand in cold water one minute; drain. Now they'll crack easily. *To slice.* Cover shelled Brazil nuts with water; simmer two to three minutes; drain. Now they'll slice easily. Or use a vegetable parer to make curls.

Walnuts or pecans. *To crack.* If you haven't a nutcracker, place each nut on end, holding it by the seam. Strike with a hammer on the pointed top of the nut. *To chop.* Spread nuts on a wooden board. Hold the tip of a long, sharp knife close to the surface of the board with one hand; then with other hand, move the knife handle up and down, and around in a semicircle, so the blade goes through uncut nuts. Today's nut choppers do a good job, too. So does the electric blender, especially when you have a large quantity. Or you can place kernels inside a plastic bag; roll lightly with a rolling pin. *To toast walnuts.* Boil kernels in rapidly boiling water three minutes, then drain; spread them in a shallow pan. Bake at 350° F. ten to twenty minutes, or until lightly toasted, stirring often. While hot, brush with butter and sprinkle generously with seasoned, or garlic, or regular, salt. Cool, then refrigerate.

BUYING QUANTITIES

In shell:

Almonds	1¼ lbs.	= 1 to 1¾ cups nut meats
Brazil nuts	1 lb.	= 1½ cups nut meats
Peanuts	1 lb.	= 2 cups nut meats
Pecans	1 lb.	= 2¼ cups nut meats
Walnuts	1 lb.	= 1¾ cups, chopped

Shelled:

Almonds	1 lb. 2 oz.	= 4 cups
Brazil-nut meats	1 lb.	= 3 cups
Pecan meats	1 lb.	= 4 cups
Walnut meats	1 lb.	= 4 cups

COCONUT

Flaked coconut is in thin, short flakes, slightly sweetened, and needs neither cutting nor chopping when used as an ingredient in recipes. It is available in a 3½-oz. can or carton (about 1⅓ cups), 7-oz. tray pack (about 2⅔ cups), and 14-oz. polyethelene bag (about 6⅓ cups).

Fine grated coconut is also slightly sweetened. It's available in a 7-oz. tray pack (about 2 cups). One cup of packaged fine grated coconut equals 1⅓ cups of flaked coconut; so adjust recipes accordingly when using.

All packaged coconut, once opened, should be stored in an airtight container in either the refrigerator or the freezer until used up—it's perishable fruit!

Fresh coconut. It's easy to open a fresh coconut this way: with a long nail, puncture the three indentations at the end. Drain the milk out of these holes. Then, in a shallow pan, bake whole coconut at 350° F. fifteen minutes; this will crack the shell. Complete cracking with a hammer; then pry out the white meat in as large pieces as possible. With knife or vegetable parer, cut the brown skin from the white meat; then grate the meat, rubbing each piece the full length of the grater.

PARTIES | See CHILDREN'S PARTIES

PERFUME AND PERFUME FRAUDS |

Perfume, toilet water, and cologne all usually have an alcohol base. But perfume is the costliest—it has the highest concentration of the fragrance-giving substance (usually a compound of floral oils and a carrier material). The difference between the other two is less clear-cut.

Originally, toilet water, though less concentrated than perfume, was stronger than cologne, which was essentially a light scented tonic with a citrus base used to stimulate the skin after a bath. Today, however, there is sometimes little difference in strength between the cologne offered by one firm and the toilet water of another. If one firm offers both, the toilet water is likely to be the stronger fragrance and more expensive.

Some promoters make many thousands of dollars selling diluted or mislabeled perfumes by representing them as bargains in imported scents. The Perfumery Importers Association has warned: ". . . there are no bargains in high-class perfumes, which are as stable (in value) as diamonds."

The best French and domestic perfumes are always expensive. If you are offered a perfume at $5 an ounce and the seller claims it usually costs $30 an ounce, it most likely is an imitation of one brand or another. One of the main targets for such perfume is the man who buys a present for his wife, or business executives who buy gifts in quantity at Christmas for their associates and employees.

Most famous manufacturers produce a cologne to match their perfume products. One fraud is to buy this cologne, perhaps dilute it, and then rebottle it in small containers with the name of the well-known manufacturer prominently displayed. A purse-size container sells for about one dollar as "perfume." It may contain only sixteen cents' worth of the original cologne.

Spray containers sometimes are sold that carry no brand name—just unitials, such as "A," "C," or "M.S." Salesmen may tell customers that "A" stands for Arpege, "C" for Chanel No. 5, and "M.S." for My Sin. Makers of these famous French perfumes say they never use such labeling. These initial-brand products, on investigation, have contained none of the imports.

One of the most fraudulent schemes is to label imitations with the name of a famous perfume and to offer them at extremely low prices. Such sales are made on sidewalks, in hotels, and in offices. Sellers explain the low price is possible because the perfumes have been smuggled or acquired by other dishonest means.

Another fraudulent sales technique is to label a domestic perfume "Made in France." Also, beware of a price on a container which is far higher than the perfume ever sold for. For instance, a package could have a twenty-dollar price printed on it. Then, salesmen sell this perfume at what ostensibly is a bargain price of two to five dollars. The perfume, in fact, was never sold for twenty dollars.

PEST CONTROL | See also FIRST AID

This list includes the most common insects and animal pests that infest homes in the United States. They have been divided into groups according to the type of damage or annoyance they cause. Some pests are definite menaces to health and property; see illustration on page 274. All of them can be controlled if the recommendations are followed carefully.

The list includes no mention of such wood-destroying insects as termites. Their control can be adequately handled only by professionals. If you have any suspicion that your home is infested with termites, seek professional counsel promptly. For any type of insect control, excellent services are available in all parts of the United States.

Remember: Most effective pesticides are also poisonous to human beings and other warm-blooded animals. So use them and store them with care. Follow the detailed instructions on the label of the insecticide you buy. Take particular care that hands, food, and food-handling surfaces are well protected from any contamination by insecticides, no matter in what form these are used.

It has been possible to list here only the basic formulas effective for insect control—5 per cent DDT, 2 per cent chlordane, 0.5 per cent lindane, etc. Many insecticides available today are combinations of ingredients that, together, may do an even more efficient job than DDT, chlordane, lindane, etc. alone in higher concentrations. Study the label carefully to make sure that the specific use to which you wish to put the insecticide is listed.

FOOD-VISITING INSECTS

1. **Housefly.** Disease carrier (typhoid, dysentery, etc.); annoyance.
Eliminate breeding places when possible. Clean stables, barns, etc. thor-

oughly at regular intervals. Keep garbage and other refuse tightly covered, and dispose of it frequently. Provide adequate screening, tight-fitting door- and window frames. Paint screens, window sills, doorsills, and other areas where flies alight or congregate with 2 per cent chlordane, 0.5 per cent lindane, 5 per cent DDT, terpene polychlorinates, or a special formula including one of these. (Some fly strains have become "DDT resistant," so DDT may be ineffective.) Use 5 per cent DDT or 0.1 per cent lindane as space sprays to kill flies that do get in.

2. **Cockroach.** Disease carrier; contaminates food; destroys book bindings, paper, and even starched clothing.

Use dieldrin or chlordane, the most effective insecticide for roach control, in liquid form (2 per cent) along baseboards and around pipes, risers, and surfaces where roaches nest, run, or hide; in powder form in cracks and crevices. Do not use chlordane as a space spray. Insecticide-treated paper may be used in drawers and cabinets.

3. **Ant.** Mainly annoyance and contaminator of food. Some species sting or bite.

Outside the house, use 5 per cent chlordane dust directly on ant hills. Inside the house, where there is no danger of contaminating foodstuffs, use 2 per cent chlordane liquid or 5 per cent chlordane dust. In proximity to foods, use a pyrethrum spray. "Ant traps," containing highly poisonous thallium salts, may be used if constructed so that children and pets cannot get at the contents. Insecticide-treated paper may be used in drawers and cabinets.

4. **Flour beetle, meal moth, cereal weevil.** Cause waste of otherwise edible foods. (None of these insects are disease carriers or are harmful in any way.) Practice scrupulous cleanliness in the kitchen and pantry. When infestation occurs:

Discard all packages of infested food.

Transfer contents of open uninfested packages to screw-top jars.

Scrub storage shelves thoroughly and spray with 5 per cent DDT or a special formula containing it.

BITING AND SUCKING INSECTS

5. **Mosquito.** Some species are disease carriers (malaria, yellow fever). Others are harmless, but cause great discomfort.

Provide adequate 16-mesh screening, tightly fitting door- and window frames. Paint screens, window sills, and doorsills with 2 per cent chlordane, 0.5 per cent lindane, 5 per cent DDT, terpene polychlorinates, or a special formula containing one of these ingredients. Five per cent DDT or 0.1 per cent lindane (or a special formula containing one of these) may be used as a space spray to destroy mosquitoes that do get in.

6. **Bedbug.** May be a disease carrier; its bite is highly annoying.

Spray mattresses and bedframes thoroughly with 5 per cent DDT. Treat wall cracks and baseboards in infested rooms with 5 per cent DDT in oil, or 10 per cent DDT dust. Terpene polychlorinates may also be used.

7. **Flea.** Disease carrier; in one stage of development, it is host of tapeworm. The bite is highly annoying.

PESTS

(See text for identification)

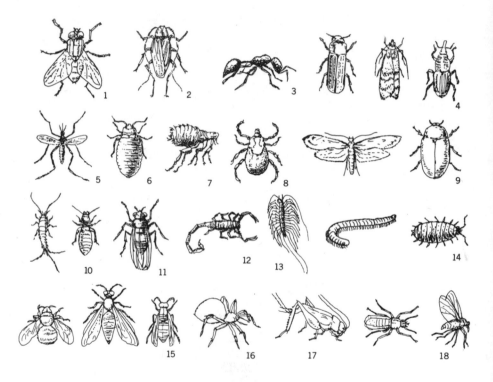

Spray floors of infested houses with 5 per cent DDT. Treat infested dogs and their sleeping quarters with 10 per cent DDT dust, special lindane dust prepared for dogs, or special aerosol containing lindane. Treat cats and their sleeping quarters with rotenone or pyrethrum dust.

8. **Tick.** Carrier of spotted fever; annoyance to pets and people.

Remove with forceps, being careful not to crush. (This is important! The fluid is dangerous. Also the head of the tick may remain embedded even though the body is removed.) Holding a match flame or lighted cigarette close to the tick may force it to emerge. Or anesthetize the tick with acetone (nail polish remover) before extracting. Treat dogs with 10 per cent DDT dust, kennels with 10 per cent DDT dust or 5 per cent DDT in oil.

FABRIC-DAMAGING INSECTS

9. **Clothes moth, carpet beetle.** Destroy clothing and upholstery materials of animal origin—wool, silk, fur, hair, etc. (Damage is caused by larvae, not by adult moths.)

Clean clothing, blankets, etc. thoroughly before storing. Use paradichlorbenzene (one pound fine crystals per hundred cubic feet) in storage containers. Keep containers tightly sealed; otherwise vapor will escape and moth-killing powers will be lost. Paradichlorbenzene may also be used in closets if periodically renewed. *Note:* Do not let paradichlorbenzene come in contact with vinyl plastics.

On clothes, use mothproofing sprays containing DDT, methoxychlor, a fluosilicate, perthane, or terpene polychlorinates. Follow label instructions closely for method of application and amount to use. (Remember that laundering and/or dry cleaning may remove mothproofing.) Closets, etc. may also be sprayed with DDT, methoxychlor, perthane, or terpene polychlorinates.

10. **Silverfish, book louse.** Damage wallpaper, book bindings, and clothing. Apply 5 per cent DDT in oil or 10 per cent DDT dust or terpene polychlorinates (or a special formula containing one of these) to cracks and crevices. Repeat in two weeks if necessary. Insecticide-treated paper may be used in drawers and cabinets.

MISCELLANEOUS INSECTS

11. **Pomace fly** (fruit fly). Annoyance. Discard fruits promptly. Use a pyrethrum spray in infested areas.

12. **Scorpion.** Has extremely painful, even lethal sting. Search premises thoroughly, and destroy by mashing any scorpions found. Close all possible entrance holes from ground. Get rid of possible breeding places near the house, such as rocks, decayed wood, etc. Use DDT spray (5 per cent) directly on insect. Check shoes and clothes before putting them on.

13. **Centipede.** Bite may cause severe pain (rare). Otherwise, it is a beneficial insect, since it destroys other insects. If destruction is desired, mash with a foot or use a pyrethrum dust or spray directly on the insect. Keep the house free of moist places.

14. **Millepede, sow bug.** Mainly annoyance. Both may attack house plants, sow bugs may damage stored potatoes.

Use 5 per cent DDT in oil or 10 per cent DDT dust in infested areas. (Do not use DDT in oil where it may contact house plants.)

15. **Bee, wasp, hornet.** Have painful stings. Some people have a violent allergic response to venom. Screen ventilators leading to cellars and attic. Spray wasps' and hornets' nests with 5 per cent DDT in oil, or dust with

10 per cent DDT powder. Spray attic screens, window frames, and walls with 5 per cent DDT in oil.

16. **Spider.** Bite of the black widow is poisonous; other species, only annoying. Crush egg sacs as well as adult spider. Or use 2 per cent chlordane in oil. Brush away cobwebs.

17. **Cricket.** Damages any soiled fabric, as well as clean silk and rayon. To infested places (usually warm and dark) apply 2 per cent chlordane in oil, 5 per cent DDT in oil, 2 per cent chlordane dust, or 10 per cent DDT dust.

18. **Sard fly, gnat.** Annoying bite. Paint screens and surfaces near light fixtures with 5 per cent DDT in oil.

19. **Cluster fly, elm leaf beetle.** Annoyance. Spray window frames, doorsills, or other points of entrance with 5 per cent DDT in oil (being careful not to let it touch house plants). Spray congregations of insects on porches or sides of house with 5 per cent DDT. These insects are very difficult to control, particularly if trees are in close proximity to the house. If necessary, seek professional advice.

ANIMALS INFESTING HOUSES

20. **Mouse, rat.** Disease carriers. Rat's bite is dangerous and painful. When possible, seek professional advice on rat-proofing buildings. Use bait containing warfarin. Follow label directions carefully.

21. **Bat.** Makes annoying night noises, has very objectionable odor. Block all entrance holes. Scatter flake naphthalene liberally in infested areas. Repeat as necessary. If this fails, secure the services of a professional exterminator. If bitten by a bat (rare) suspect rabies and call a doctor at once.

PET CARE | See also PEST CONTROL

Just as people require a balanced diet, so do dogs and cats. Pets would be fed properly if they ate—or would eat—the same food prepared for a well-balanced family meal. Basically, both dogs and cats require a combination of proteins, fats, carbohydrates, minerals, and vitamins.

A diet consisting solely of filet mignon would not be good nutrition for a dog. Similarly, only filet of sole would be a poor diet for a cat. Wild animals which feed on other animals obtain an adequate diet by eating heart, intestines, kidneys, and liver in addition to muscle meat. Internal organs contain nutrients—such as vitamins—that muscle meat does not have in significant amounts.

Just like people, individual animals of the same breed may assimilate food differently. One may become overweight on a particular diet while a second remains lean. Dogs, and especially cats, develop food preferences.

Often it can be a matter of trial and error to find a balanced diet which is palatable. Too, a pet may tire of one diet, may need a change in taste or consistency.

Considerable research has been done on the nutritional requirements of dogs. A summary of these studies, made by the Animal Nutrition Committee of the National Academy of Science-National Research Council, is used as a guide by major pet-food manufacturers. Dog foods designed to furnish a balanced diet are labeled a complete food. The Pet Food Institute, a trade organization, says a "complete" pet food is "one which provides the normal nutritional requirements of the animal." For example, chemical analysis (as listed on the label) of one commercial dry-type complete dog food shows it contains: 24 per cent crude protein, 7 per cent fat, 4.5 per cent crude fiber, and 10 per cent ash (minerals). It also has added vitamins and other minerals.

Most cat nutritionists favor a diet higher in both protein and fat than that usually used for dogs. The Pet Food Institute says even though many cat requirements are not yet known specifically, "complete cat foods are available which have been tested on generations of cats of different breeds."

Not all pet foods are designed to furnish a balanced diet, nor do manufacturers claim they are. Straight pack foods contain one primary ingredient, such as meat, fish, or chicken. Variety products include stews, chowders, and meat or chicken in broth or gravy. Biscuits and cookies for dogs and cats can be used for meals or for rewards. Supplemental foods may either be mixed with a complete food or fed separately to add variety and high protein nutrition to the diet.

Pet owners customarily feed pets table scraps as a supplement, rather than as a total diet. Veterinarians agree with this practice. Fresh foods—meat, fish, milk, and cooked eggs—can overcome diet deficiencies. But it is also recommended that these fresh foods be mixed with the pet's usual diet so that the animal does not wait for leftovers and refuse to eat his own food.

Veterinarians should be consulted on diets for pregnant animals and for those that are nursing their young. Fresh water is necessary for both cats and dogs. Bones which splinter should not be given to either animal. Bones are not essential to diet, and many owners prefer to substitute a biscuit-type or fake bone to satisfy the animal's normal urge to chew.

For proper nutrition, pets also need a human response. This is especially true of cats, who should be petted. It is also important to set a feeding routine for animals and stick to it.

YOUNG KITTENS

A baby kitten should not be taken away from the mother cat before he has been weaned and has a full set of teeth, which is usually six weeks of age. Kittens are not ideal pets for small children, who often literally love them to death with hugs and squeezes. A kitten should be handled with care. His whole body should be supported when he is picked up.

From the kitten's first meal, establish a regular schedule of four or five meals a day of raw beef (chopped into fine pieces) or baby food or cereals and milk. Water should always be available.

Cats can eat practically anything humans do. So as the kitten grows, he can be fed vegetables and cooked meats from your meals (but not pork, or chicken or fish containing bones), eggs, cereals, and commercial pet foods. At three months, the number of meals should be reduced.

Like any baby, a kitten needs lots of sleep. Set aside a warm, cozy spot out of drafts for a box lined with wool or cotton. The kitten may eventually select a chair in the living room or other center of activity as his own. A pillow or cushion for him elsewhere in the room may curb this practice.

Place a metal or plastic pan with sand, shredded newspaper, sawdust, or commercial litter material in a secluded spot for housebreaking. Some mother cats "toilet-train" their kittens so they need only be shown the pan. If a kitten is not housebroken, put him in the pan immediately after feeding and upon awakening. Keep the pan clean, or he will seek another spot.

A kitten will soon start scratching, but a catnip-scented scratching post or square yard of old carpet can usually divert him from the furniture. When he starts to scratch furniture, make a noise by clapping hands and take him to the scratching post.

A veterinarian should check the kitten's health early and give him a series of two vaccinations for enteritis (cat distemper). Inoculation against pneumonitis, a respiratory viral infection, is usually given at about eight weeks and repeated at six- to twelve-month intervals. The U.S. Public Health Service urges inoculation of all cats against rabies at six months of age and annually thereafter. Seven or eight months is a good time to have your kitten spayed or altered if you do not want it to have kittens or to have the disagreeable manifestations of the heat period. Males, when altered, usually are more home-loving and gentle.

If the kitten gets fleas, use only powder especially labeled for cats. If he scratches his ears and they look dirty, have a veterinarian check him for ear mites. Cats can carry skin disorders which are contagious to humans, so any skin irregularity should be checked.

While kittens are clean and fastidious, a daily combing or brushing prevents knots in his coat, and shedding. This grooming helps prevent hair balls, caused by licking his coat, from forming in his stomach.

BOARDING KENNELS

Pet owners who are planning a trip away from home, even just a weekend, are often faced with the question of what to do with their pets. Because leaving a dog with a relative or friend can impose an unfair responsibility, a good boarding kennel can be the answer.

Metropolitan areas usually have neighborhood boarding kennels. But if you are planning to be away for more than a week or two, a kennel in the suburbs or country may be a better choice because it frequently has more outdoor exercise space. The best way to choose a kennel is to visit it yourself. Here is what to check (cat facilities are similar to those for dogs):

A well-run kennel does not have an overpowering odor. Look for signs that the kennel is kept clean—tidy cages, washed floors, and clean animals. If you are not allowed to view the boarding area or there is a strong odor, you can be concerned about the kennel's sanitary condition.

Each dog should have his own cage or stall. An attached run or outside exercise area should be available. If the cage is for sleeping only, it should be big enough for the dog to stand erect and to lie down without being cramped. If the dog stays in the same stall day and night, except for exercise periods, the cage should be bigger. (A dog the size of a fox terrier should have at least four by four feet of floor space and a Great Dane, at least six by eight feet.)

Fresh drinking water should always be available. Find out whether the kennel will supply the food your dog normally eats. Note whether the ventilation is good but draft-free, and whether there is heat or air conditioning.

The most careful kennels do not accept dogs without assurance or proof that they have been inoculated against infectious diseases such as distemper, canine hepatitis, and rabies. The kennel may require these vaccinations before the dog is boarded. This may cost from ten to fifteen dollars.

If the kennel is not operated by a veterinarian, it should have a veterinarian on call for emergencies. Some kennels reserve the right to have a sick dog treated without permission from the owner, who may be asked to sign a waiver of immunity. Read carefully any papers you are asked to sign.

Boarding prices usually are based on the size of the animal—small, medium, or large. Prices vary from area to area, but range mostly from $1.25 to $4 a day. Grooming charges are usually extra.

When you leave your dog, be sure you clearly specify the length of stay, and that you know how to extend the stay if you cannot return at the agreed time. This is to keep the kennel operators from thinking the dog has been abandoned.

PHONOGRAPH RECORD CARE |

Proper care of phonograph records can keep them in good condition almost indefinitely. Dust and lint are major causes of damage. Particles are readily attracted by the magnetism caused by static electricity that is usually present on any record surface. The static charge can be removed temporarily with a damp cloth, or with commercial antistatic cloths and fluids.

Unless the record, needle, and turntable are cleaned frequently, loose dust is ground into the grooves (where sound is recorded) whenever records are played, stacked, or rubbed against something. The abrasive action of a needle on embedded dust rapidly wears the grooves.

Wash your records with warm water, a mild detergent, and a soft sponge to remove impacted dust. Rinse under a tap and dry with a soft, lint-free cloth. Record companies generally recommend wiping off superficial dust gently with a soft, damp cloth. Always follow the path of the grooves. Too, there are several types of record cleaners available—fluids, cloths, brushes, and devices for mounting on the arm or alongside the turntable. Remove dust from the needle with a soft brush.

Use both hands to hold records. Handle only by the rim and label and do not touch the playing surface. When records are not being played, keep them in their jackets. Spread the jacket apart when sliding a record in or out to avoid scratching. It is best to store records vertically in a bookshelf or cabinet, away from extreme heat, cold, and dampness.

Follow the phonograph manufacturers' instructions to avoid undue stress and wear on a record. A worn or chipped needle quickly ruins sound reproduction and permanently damages the grooves. Have your needle examined regularly under a microscope (many record stores provide free inspection service), and replace a defective needle immediately.

PICTURES AND SCULPTURES | See also WALL DECORATIONS

Once a hobby of the very rich, art collecting is now for everyone. Galleries in cities and resort towns, in stores and at county fairs, cater to art lovers in every income bracket. Three basic types of picture are the **original,** the **print,** and the **reproduction.** Sculptures may be either original or reproduced.

Original oils, watercolor paintings, drawings, and sculptures, as one-of-a-kind works of art, naturally are more expensive. An art print, such as an etching or lithograph, is pressed by hand in limited quantity from the artist's original plate; often each copy is numbered. A reproduction is least expensive since it is a mass-produced copy of the original work; the cost varies with the quality of manufacture. Museums and art shops today offer faithful reproductions of old masters and fine contemporary works, including paintings, prints, and sculptures, for very little money.

Colorful posters (some available free from foreign government tourist offices), maps, tapestries, Navajo rugs, African wood carvings, and Eskimo statuettes are among the many other art objects to consider.

Choosing art is strictly a matter of taste; there are no rules. However, a cultivated taste instantly recognizes bad art, and it does not hurt to seek expert advice or consult books if you are unsure. Otherwise, if you like a picture or sculpture and feel it belongs in your home, it's not necessary to explain why.

Basic rules of decorating apply to picture placement and framing. Above all, colors and moods should be in harmony. For example, vivid but harsh color might clash with a formal dining room. In framing a print, a mat enhances the picture by adding a blank area between print and frame. It may be a neutral tone, or a color "picked up" from a matching color in the picture. Simple frames generally are best; neither mat nor frame should compete with the print for attention or cause you to tire of it.

HOW TO HANG A PICTURE

The usual rule is to hang pictures below eye level of a person standing in the room, but the rule is flexible. The top of a piece of furniture should not cover any part of the frame—a point often overlooked when a lamp is placed below a picture. Also, a lamp should light the whole picture, not just part of it.

If possible, relate pictures to furniture. Keep picture and furniture sizes to scale. That is, don't hang a large grouping of pictures over a small piece of furniture; or a small, single picture over a large piece.

When large pictures or groupings are hung over a couch or sofa, the bottom of the frame should be about eight or ten inches above the top of the furniture.

Pairs of pictures gain in importance when they are hung side by side or one over the other.

Picture groupings usually look best when the outside edges of the frames form a square or rectangle. Keep the bottom edges straight when pictures in pairs or groupings are placed over a long, straight object, such as a couch, sofa, or buffet. If the furniture varies in height, keep the top edges of the frames straight.

Larger, more important pictures gain interest when they are centered over a mantel or big piece of furniture. This is particularly true in a formal setting. In a more casual room, it is often pleasing to hang a large, single picture off-center over a piece of furniture. This may help to lengthen a wall, or balance a heavier object in the room.

Tall pictures usually look best on a narrow wall; broad pictures, on a wide wall.

Before putting a nail or hanger into the wall, place a small strip of cellophane tape on the wall at the hanger point. This may help to keep the plaster from chipping. Picture nails or hangers should be hammered into the wall at an angle. Small, lightweight pictures may often be hung from a carpet tack. The hanging device should not show.

Finally, don't be afraid to experiment. You can occasionally break the "rules" and still achieve a tasteful wall decoration.

PLANTS | See HOUSE PLANTS

POISONING | See also FIRST AID

Scores of products used for everyday household jobs can be poisonous if swallowed, and in some cases if inhaled or spilled on the skin. The risk cannot be entirely avoided, since some danger is latent in virtually every useful material, including medicines and even foods. A cupful of common salt, for example, or a pint of brandy, might be fatal if quickly gulped down. Cases of accidental poisoning of children constitute the commonest type of emergency call that pediatricians receive.

To protect her home against such emergencies, a housewife should take these advance precautions:

1. In the phone book look up the number of the nearest **Poison Control Center** (sometimes called Poison Information Center). Or ask your doctor or hospital for it. *Post the number prominently with other emergency numbers such as the doctor's, police, fire department,* etc.

These centers were established some years ago specifically to help doctors in an emergency to identify the poison involved. Correct treatment depends on this information. Given the brand name or other description of a product over the phone, a Poison Control Center can quickly pinpoint the lethal ingredient and specify the antidote. Or it might reassure you that the product swallowed is *not* poisonous.

2. Acquaint yourself with the first-aid treatment for poisoning. This is important because the first few minutes may be vital. However, *every* poisoning case requires calling a doctor at once.

3. Keep a bottle of **ipecac syrup** in the medicine chest—the standard emetic. The first emergency step in *most* cases of a swallowed poison is to induce the patient to vomit. (But see important exceptions below.) **Alternate homemade emetics:** two tablespoons of salt in a glass of water; or two teaspoons of dry mustard dissolved in a glass of water.

4. Keep a supply of the dry ingredients for the following **basic antidote.** It is given to a victim who cannot or should not vomit, or when you're not sure what poison has been swallowed. It is also specific for certain of the most virulent poisons. A doctor may direct you to give this antidote pending his arrival.

BASIC ANTIDOTE FOR POISONING

2 parts activated charcoal	1 part magnesium oxide
1 part tannic acid (powder)	Mix with water

Alternate: Two pieces thoroughly charred toast, finely crushed; mix with one-half cup strong tea, one-half cup milk of magnesia, and water.

5. Learn some of the key **symptoms** that should make you suspect poisoning when you are not sure what has gone wrong. Usually the victim's skin becomes pale, then blue. Drowsiness, difficult or rapid breathing, loss of muscular coordination, incoherent speech, cramps, headache, blurred vision, deafness or ringing in the ears, sweating, vomiting, and diarrhea are other danger signs. With such symptoms, your cue as a general rule is to make the patient vomit.

Different symptoms distinguish poisoning by one of the *acids, alkalis,* etc., listed separately below. Burns on lips and mouth and burning pain in mouth, throat, and stomach are typical. *Here vomiting should be avoided.*

In **asphyxiation** by carbon monoxide and other noxious gases, the skin usually turns pink rather than pale, then red. This calls for fast action to restore breathing, similar to a rescue from drowning.

6. Make a safety habit of storing, handling, or using any of the household materials and devices in the accompanying lists with special care.

INHALED POISONS

Carbon monoxide is odorless; it can overcome a victim before he is aware of its presence. The gas comes not only from automobile exhausts, but also from anything that burns fuel, such as coal, oil, and gas furnaces or stoves. It is dangerous in any closed space, and the preventive is ventilation. All space heaters (other than electric) must be properly vented to the outside air. A window should be kept open at all times.

Poisonous inhalations may also occur from *hydrogen sulphide,* the "rotten egg" smell of sewers, cesspools; or from a massive intake of *petroleum* vapors, *ammonia, carbon tetrachloride, naphthalene, acetone, DDT,* and *mercury.* See below for sources of these. The treatment for asphyxiation is always the same:

Give the victim *no* emetics or stimulants. Do not let him walk. Carry the victim into the fresh air immediately and administer artificial respiration. Keep it up even after breathing is restored. Send someone to call for help— the doctor, and a police/fire emergency squad equipped with oxygen tank. Loosen the victim's clothing but keep him warm, lying on his back, till help arrives.

CHEMICALS ON SKIN

Caustic alkalis and acids can cause severe, painful, or disfiguring damage to skin. The emergency treatment is *water,* applied copiously and promptly. Rip away clothing touched by the poison. Pour water over the skin from a hose, faucet, or shower continuously for ten or fifteen minutes. Cover burns with a loose bandage but *do not* apply ointment or other remedies. Take the victim to a doctor.

If an eye has been splashed, hold the eyelid open and wash out with a gentle stream of tepid water from a kettle or syringe for ten or fifteen minutes. Take the victim to a doctor.

SWALLOWED HOUSEHOLD PRODUCTS

The first list that follows consists of *exceptions* to the general rule stated in the discussion above. These victims should *not* be made to vomit. Some of the corrosive material might get into windpipe and lungs, causing pneumonia. If the victim vomits, hold his head lower than his hips. Avoid giving more of the antidote than the victim can keep down.

Acids—hydrochloric, sulphuric, nitric, etc., used by plumbers, mechanics; also carbolic, oxalic, etc., in cleaners, polishes, stain removers; laundry bleach; disinfectants; deodorizers. Give one cup milk of magnesia, or milk, or water. Wash burned area with same. Then give one-quarter to one cup olive or mineral oil, melted butter, or starch and water.

Alkalis—caustic soda, lye, potash, oxides, peroxides, carbonates, drain cleaner, paint remover, strong washing powders and cleaners. Give one cup to one quart citrus fruit juice or diluted vinegar; otherwise, water or milk. Wash burned area with same.

Ammonia—in cleaning products. Give one cup to one quart fruit juice or diluted vinegar. Then give one-quarter to one cup milk or olive oil.

Ammonium, sodium, or potassium thioglycollate—in home permanent wave solutions. Same as for alkalis, above.

Chlorine—laundry bleach; disinfectants; deodorizers. Give one-quarter to one cup milk, starch and water, or milk of magnesia.

Petroleum—gasoline, kerosene, fuel oil; cleaning and lighter fluids; polishes; paint thinner; insect and garden sprays. Give water only.

OTHER HOUSEHOLD PRODUCTS

In all the following cases of swallowed poison from household products, follow the general rule to *induce vomiting* as the first immediate step. If a child refuses ipecac syrup or other emetics, give him water or milk and tickle the back of his throat with your finger in his mouth. Continue giving liquid between retchings, until vomited matter looks clear.

Arsenic—in dyes. See among pesticides below.

Camphor—in mothballs, flakes. Give water only.

Carbon tetrachloride—dry cleaning fluid; spot and grease removers; in fire extinguishers, some polishing waxes. Give one teaspoon salt in a glass of water; repeat after vomiting stops. Do *not* give milk (or any fats or oils).

Cyanide—in metal polish. See among pesticides below.

Ethylene glycol—so-called "permanent" antifreeze. Induce vomiting only.

Naphthalene—in mothballs, flakes, crystals. Give one-quarter to one cup milk, egg whites, or liquid gelatin. Do *not* give any fats or oils.

Turpentine—paint thinner; in waxes, polishes, deodorizers. Give two ounces mineral oil; then one cup milk, followed by plenty of water.

Wood alcohol—methanol or methyl alcohol; in paints, varnish, paint remover; canned heat; nonpermanent antifreeze. Symptoms may resemble drunkenness. Give one teaspoon baking soda in a glass of water.

PESTICIDES

Arsenic—insect and rat poisons; weed killers; also in certain dyes. Give baking soda and water; or just water.

Cyanide—insect and rat poisons; fumigants; also in metal polish. Induce vomiting only.

DDT—universal insecticide. Give one teaspoon salt in a glass of water (no milk or fats).

Fluoride—in ant and roach powders. Give one cup milk and two egg whites.

Mercury—fungicide for molds, mildew, garden rust; also in antiseptics, disinfectants. Give basic antidote (recipe above); or one cup milk, or one-half cup egg whites. Repeat after vomiting stops.

Strychnine—potent rat poison. Give basic antidote (recipe above). Keep the victim quiet in a darkened room.

Thallium—in ant and rat poisons; also in cream hair removers. Give milk, or starch and water.

MEDICINES

Antihistamines—for allergies, motion sickness, colds. Give strong tea or coffee; keep the victim quiet in a dark room.

Barbiturates—sleeping pills. Give strong tea or coffee. Keep the victim awake; force him to walk and get him talking.

Boric acid—external antiseptic. Induce vomiting only.

Bromides and tranquilizers—for relief of tension, nervousness. Give water; specific treatment depends on the specific drug.

Camphor—in liniments, camphorated oil. See among household products, above.

Iodine—external antiseptic. Give starch or flour in water; or milk; or egg white.

Iron—in tonics, and medicines for anemia. Give milk or milk of magnesia.

Opium derivatives—morphine, codeine, laudanum, etc., in cough medicines, pain and tension relievers, sleeping draughts. Give basic antidote (recipe above).

Salicylates—aspirin, oil of wintergreen, pain relievers. Symptoms may not appear immediately; induce vomiting anyway. Give milk; sponge feverish face or body with cool water.

Strychnine—in laxatives, tonics. See among pesticides, above.

COSMETICS

Acetone—fingernail polishes and polish removers. Induce vomiting only.

Alcohol—either ethyl or isopropryl; in rubbing alcohol, perfumes, cologne, deodorants, skin lotions, hair tonic; disinfectants. Symptoms resemble drunkenness. Give strong coffee.

Thallium—in cream depilatories. See among pesticides, above.

Thioglycollates—in home permanent wave solutions. See under *alkalis* in swallowed household products, above.

POSTAL RATES | See MAIL

POTS AND PANS |

When you're shopping for pots and pans, you may decide that a matched set is exactly what you want. But you will usually do better to buy assorted wares whose different characteristics suit various needs.

Aluminum is practically unbeatable for all-round use, but it does require care to keep it clean and shiny. Its even heat distribution is valuable in frying. There is no truth whatever to the old story that harm may result from cooking or storing certain foods in aluminum. Repeated research has proved the metal entirely safe.

Stainless steel, somewhat more expensive, is easy to clean and practically indestructible. If you select stainless-steel pans, be sure they have copper, aluminum, or laminated steel bottoms, to give an even distribution of heat and to prevent the appearance of dark heat spots. The second metal may not be visible, so check tags and labels regarding construction.

Bonded metals such as Duranel (an aluminum exterior, stainless-steel interior) combine the best features of two metals.

Copper utensils are handsome but not popular for cooking. They should be tin-plated inside for easier cleaning, but eventually the tin will wear through and the pan must be replated.

Enamelware is glass fused on metal, so careful handling is necessary to avoid cracking, chipping, or discoloring. Use is generally limited to teakettles, double boilers, and saucepans because the heat distribution is not even.

Cast iron is sturdy ware for skillet or Dutch-oven use. It must be kept seasoned to prevent rust.

To season cast iron, spread melted shortening or salad oil on the inside of utensil and cover. Do not use any fat containing salt. Place the utensil in a warm oven or over low heat for several hours, swabbing the sides and covering occasionally with more fat. Wipe off excess fat or oil with paper towels. Seasoning is retained longer by washing with soap rather than detergent.

Porcelain enameled ware handsomely combines the bright color of porcelain with the sturdiness of cast iron or aluminum. Porcelain is applied on cast iron both inside and out, producing a heavy utensil. The porcelain is put on only the outside of cast aluminum, so the inside surface requires the same care as other aluminum utensils. It is lighter weight than cast iron. Although the finish eliminates the need for seasoning, abrasives should be kept away from the shiny surface to avoid scratching.

Teflon is a useful, safe coating applied to the cooking surface of utensils and to glass and aluminum ovenware. The coating makes it possible to cook with less fat, with no sticking and surprisingly easy cleanup. But the Teflon surface is easily damaged and must be protected against scratching. Use no metal tools, only a wooden spatula or a special Teflon or nylon turner. Nylon spoons, forks, and other implements are also available.

Glass ceramic ware can take extreme temperature changes, may be stored in the freezer or refrigerator, go directly to the range and then to the table. It may be washed in an electric dishwasher or by hand.

POULTRY |

Time was when turkey appeared on the table only at holiday time, and fried chicken only in summer. These days, however, production and marketing methods make it possible to serve fine poultry of all kinds at all seasons of the year. Like meat, poultry is a rich source of important food values. It is low in calories, low in fat, and reasonable in price.

CHICKEN

You will want to select just the right bird for the dish you plan to prepare. In most markets, you'll find chicken available in the following styles:

Ready-to-cook chicken. These meaty, tender, top-quality birds come either fresh, ice-chilled, with a tag identifying the brand, or quick-frozen in a branded package. They have been fully drawn, pinfeathered, cleaned inside and out—all ready for the oven or pan. You can buy them whole, with the cleaned giblets and neck wrapped separately, in the body. Or you can buy them cut up—split in halves, quartered, or disjointed and cut up for frying.

Ready-to-cook birds have another plus. Their tag, wrapper, or package carries the packer's name, the bird's weight, the price, as well as the U.S. grade and inspection mark. The wrapper of quick-frozen chicken also carries cooking directions.

For small families and those preferring only light or dark meat or a special part, chicken is now marketed in fresh, ready-to-cook pieces—breasts, drumsticks, thighs (or legs), wings, etc.—more than thirty-one different packs. Chicken parts also come packaged fresh-frozen—usually broiler-fryers, but similar stewing chicken parts are available in some markets.

AMOUNTS OF CHICKEN TO BUY PER SERVING

[Per serving, not per person. Some persons take more than one serving.]

For sautéing or frying	¾ to 1 lb.*
For roasting	¾ to 1 lb.
For stewing	¾ to 1 lb.
For broiling	¼ to ½ bird
Rock-Cornish hen	1 bird per serving (1 to 1¼ lb.)

* Buy smaller amount if serving with rice, macaroni, or biscuits.

Five varieties of chicken are available; they differ in size, tenderness, and age.

Rock-Cornish hens, the smallest, youngest members of the chicken family, are at their peak when 6 weeks old. They average 16 oz. to 1¼ lbs., seldom more than 2 lbs. ready-to-cook weight. The bird is a cross between a Cornish chicken and another breed; the word "hen" does not imply female. This is usually a one-per-serving bird which may be roasted, barbecued, or rotisseried whole. Cut in half it may be broiled, fried, or baked. The larger size will serve two.

Broiler-fryer chickens are small, tender, usually 9 weeks old, of 1½ to 4 lbs. ready-to-cook weight. A 2- to 2½-lb. bird should make 4 servings. If it is cut up, you may sauté, oven-fry, bake, or broil it. Roast, simmer, barbecue, or rotisserie whole birds.

Roasting chickens are a little older and larger, 3½ to 6 lbs. ready-to-cook weight. Roast, barbecue, or rotisserie these sweet, tender-meated birds; or for a crowd, cut them up to fry or oven-fry.

Hen, stewing chicken, or fowl is a mature, less tender 2½- to 5-lb. female, with more fat than other kinds of chicken. Heavier, meatier birds, weighing 5 to 8 lbs., are called bro-hens; they come from flocks used to produce broiler-fryer chickens. Bro-hens may take less time to cook than other stewing chickens of the same size. They are excellent for soup or leisurely stewing, and provide ample tender meat for dishes such as chicken fricassee, chicken pie, à la king or creamed chicken.

Capons are young desexed male chickens of 6 to 8 lbs. ready-to-cook weight. They have exceptional tenderness and flavor and a large amount of white meat. They are usually roasted.

STORING AND COOKING CHICKEN

Fresh-frozen, ready-to-cook chicken should go into the freezer as quickly as possible. Stored at 0°F. or less, for maximum quality, frozen chicken may be held for several months if properly wrapped. Completely thaw chicken before cooking, following label directions. Once thawed, remove giblets and neck from the body, if whole, then cook the bird at once exactly as if fresh.

Buy **fresh ready-to-cook chicken** only from a market that keeps birds refrigerated. Once home, quickly remove the wrapper. Remove giblets and neck from body, if it is a whole bird. Then wrap the bird loosely, with ends open, in wax paper, foil, or plastic sheet. Store in the coldest part of your refrigerator food compartment. Use within twenty-four hours.

For safety's sake, always put leftover roast chicken in the refrigerator *at once*. But first remove stuffing from the body and neck cavities. Also, if most of the bird has been carved, remove the rest of the meat from bones. (Broth made from bones will have fuller flavor now than if you wait until the carcass is bare.) Immediately refrigerate meat, stuffing, and gravy in separate containers. When reheating the stuffing or gravy, heat only as much as is needed, leaving the rest in the refrigerator. Both spoil quickly if kept warm very long. Plan to use up stuffing within two days, gravy within three days; cooked chicken within three days.

TURKEY

Turkeys, like chickens, are now found in most markets wrapped, cleaned, and ready-to-cook. Many have a band of skin near the tail under which you can tuck the legs, eliminating the need for trussing or lacing after stuffing. Follow cooking directions on the wrapper closely. Fresh ice-chilled and quick-frozen birds weigh as follows: small turkeys, 4 to 9 lbs.; medium to large turkeys, 10 to 24 lbs.

When buying ready-to-cook turkeys under 12 lbs., allow ¾ to 1 lb. *per serving*. When buying birds of 12 lbs. and over, allow ½ to ¾ lb. *per serving*. Or follow the chart below:

SERVINGS FROM TURKEYS

Ready-to-Cook Turkey (pounds)	Number of Servings
6 to 8	6 to 10
8 to 12	10 to 20
12 to 16	20 to 32
16 to 20	32 to 40
20 to 24	40 to 50

Frozen stuffed turkeys come in weights of about six to sixteen pounds. They're a help if you're pressed for preparation time. But be sure to follow label directions *exactly*. These frozen, prestuffed birds are an exception to the thaw-before-roasting rule. They're to be roasted while still frozen, and unless covered while roasting, will take considerably more time than is normally required.

You can now buy fresh turkeys cut up into breasts, drumsticks, etc.; also, there are packaged frozen turkey parts. Frozen rolled turkey roasts, since they are boned, are especially convenient to slice after roasting. Handle as the label directs. Some are ready-sliced, with gravy.

Smoked turkey. Some come ready to eat; some require further cooking. So check the label and follow its directions. For maximum flavor enjoyment, plan to use any refrigerated leftovers within ten to fourteen days.

To store turkeys, follow the same procedure as for chickens. Plan to roast fresh turkey within two days. All frozen unstuffed turkeys should be thawed slowly and *never* at room temperature or in warm water. In thawing, follow label directions, or use either of these methods:

Place the bird, still in its original body wrap, under running cold water. Allow two to six hours for thawing. Or leave the bird in its original body wrap. Place it on a tray in the refrigerator. Allow one to three days for thawing. Prompt cooking of a fresh or thawed turkey is preferable.

DUCKLING

Packaged ready-to-cook Long Island and other specially raised, brand-named ducklings come to market frozen whole with giblets and neck, as well as in parts; or you can buy them fresh, ice-chilled. Allow at least three-quarters to one pound of duckling per serving. A four- to-five-pound bird makes four servings.

Store in the same manner as chicken or turkey, or as the label directs. To thaw, place the frozen bird in the refrigerator in its original wrapper, *without* puncturing the wrapper, then allow one to one and a half days for thawing. Use promptly. Cut duckling up for cooking after thawing. With heavy scissors, halve each duckling lengthwise, first along the backbone, then along the breastbone on the other side; then cut the two halves crosswise, just above the thigh, making four pieces. Next, if desired, cut away extra skin and fat.

OTHER POULTRY

Geese come packaged quick-frozen, and ready-to-cook. Market sizes vary from four to fourteen pounds. Allow about one to one and a half pounds of ready-to-cook goose per serving.

Squabs are very young pigeons, averaging about one pound apiece. Allow one squab per person.

Guinea hens have a gamey flavor and are tenderer, but drier, than chicken. They average about one and a half to two and a quarter pounds each, after cleaning. The choice meat is on the breast; it is white, thick, tender. One hen makes two or three servings.

PRIVATE SCHOOLS | See also NURSERY SCHOOLS

With today's increased emphasis upon education, choice of the proper school for a child often becomes an important problem long before he reaches college age. The growing competition for college entrance, especially to the more famous universities, reaches far down the educational ladder to high school and even to grade school where a child first demonstrates his ability to learn. Certain towns have become favored places to live because of a superior public school system. Or parents look for a private school to give their children the best in education. These guiding principles will make their search more productive.

One great advantage of private schools is that, being independent, they can be individual in their programs and general atmosphere. The school that is best for one child is not necessarily so for another. A school that the parents attended may have changed in character, or in any case may be unsuitable for their child's personality and interests. Even within the same family, a school that proved perfect for the older child may be completely wrong for the younger. Parents with the best intentions often make the mistake of forcing a child to adapt himself to a school; far better to find a school that fits the child. There are many different types to choose from:

ELEMENTARY (THROUGH 8TH GRADE)

In most large cities and their suburbs **private day schools** enroll boys and girls of all ages from sub-kindergarten through high school. Less common, but more suitable when the parents work or travel, are **coeducational boarding schools.** The groups are small, and the children live the life of a large family, as if having their school work as well as their play at home. These and **elementary boarding schools,** which separate boys and girls and cover the elementary grades only, often are operated year-round to meet the needs of absent parents or of broken homes. Also, some private secondary schools have **junior divisions** for children above the age of eight or nine.

SECONDARY (4 YEARS OF HIGH SCHOOL)

Whether private boarding or day schools, these offer two main types of study: college preparatory and general. Today the majority are keyed exclusively to meeting college entrance requirements. Others offer the general course only, and less commonly, some offer both.

General courses, though primarily academic, are designed for students who do not plan to go to college. They may include such subjects as business administration, accounting, and manual training, for boys; secretarial training and home economics, for girls. Actual vocational training, however, is seldom offered; true trade-preparation courses are found in public technical high schools.

College preparatory, the traditional "prep school" curriculum, basically consists of sixteen credit units (or more) of college-required academic work, including English, mathematics, and a foreign language. If a boy or girl definitely plans to enter college, select a school specializing in this course or one that gives it to a majority of its students. A student who is not sure about college might well take the basic preparatory work, but some general courses should also be elective, such as typing or shop. In a strictly "prep" school, he might find himself out of step with the college-oriented student body.

In evaluating a preparatory school, ask for its student record. What percentage of graduates went to college, and to what colleges? How many were admitted to the college of their first choice? How well did they do in college? A good school will be glad to give you the answers. Also, write for the catalogue of any specific college your son or daughter has in mind, so as to plan a school program to meet all requirements.

Most secondary schools, public and private, give students the College Entrance Examination Board Scholastic Aptitude Tests (SAT) now required by most universities. Note also any special achievement tests in languages or the sciences required by your selected college.

Military schools for boys are academically the same as other private secondary schools, and should be judged by the same standards. In their military (or naval or aviation) training, emphasis is on the development of physique and qualities of obedience, self-control, initiative, and executive ability. Students wear uniforms, and live in barracks or in simply furnished dormitories. Schools classed as "essentially military" have a Reserve Officers Training Corps (ROTC) directed by officers assigned by the Army, Navy, or Air Force Departments. Those designated Honor Schools may recommend graduates for entrance to West Point, Annapolis, or the Air Force Academy.

Country day schools in metropolitan suburbs are similar to private boarding schools except that the students go home at night. Some will board children during the week and send them home each weekend. Typically, they enroll students of all school ages, including the secondary level.

Ranch schools, particularly in the Southwest, offer an extra-curricular emphasis on riding and life outdoors in a healthful climate. Only small numbers of students are enrolled, and rates are above average.

Parochial or church schools include religious training as part of the curriculum. Since they are sponsored, supported, or staffed by church denominations, their rates often are lower than average for private schools.

Tutoring schools, for those who need individual help in college preparation, sometimes offer a year-round program, usually at higher rates than average. Some specialize in preparation for the military colleges.

Summer schools and camps, or summer sessions of regular schools, are helpful when students need additional credits, makeup courses, or tutoring. Some specialize in music and the arts. If credit is desired, make sure the student's regular high school or intended college will accept the summer courses.

Special schools is the accepted term for those that teach children who are mentally, physically, or emotionally unable to hold a place in normal school life, either permanently or temporarily. Since the training is individualized, rates are higher than normal—often on a sliding scale according to the degree of personal attention required. Most states have publicly supported special schools, either free of charge or with moderate fees when a family can afford it. The parents of a child in need of assistance should consult their family physician, and in contacts with the selected school should be completely frank about the child's condition. Only in this way can the school honestly determine whether it is suitable.

ACCREDITING

Much as parents might desire it, there is no single agency by which one may ascertain the "rating" or comparative standing of a specified school. Any school chartered or licensed by the state education department is "accredited" only in the sense that it conforms to standards set by the state —which vary widely throughout the country. Responsibility still rests with the parent to make the proper inquiries about each institution.

A number of accrediting associations have been formed by groups of schools to set up minimum standards for all schools that would be members. Some are regional, some functional (as for medical schools). They have no legal status or power of compulsion, but are recognized by educators as authoritative. While standards differ, there is considerable uniformity on minimum endowment required, library and laboratory facilities, ratio of faculty to students, and similar technical measures of an accredited school. The associations do *not* attempt comparative ratings within the group.

For secondary schools, regional accrediting agencies include the Middle States Association of Colleges and Secondary Schools; also the Southern; North Central; Northwest; and New England associations of similar title.

Other groups, which do *not* have an accrediting function, are: California Association of Independent Secondary Schools; Association of Military Colleges and Schools; Secondary Education Board; and National Association of Independent Schools.

Information helpful in selecting a private school may be secured from books available in most libraries or at the high school guidance office, and also from the directories appearing in reputable magazines. There are a few professional advisory services as well, some of which charge a fee.

CHOOSING A BOARDING SCHOOL

Here are important points to consider:

Location may be influenced by cost. Ideally, the child should be far enough away from home to center his interests at the school. Although it is natural for parents to wish to keep a child close by, frequent visits home could pull his attention in two contrary directions.

Rates vary with living costs in different sections of the country. They are highest at Eastern and Pacific Coast schools, lowest in the South, median in the Middle West, and higher in urban than in rural areas. When comparing costs, make sure to include all charges listed in each school's catalogue, such as laundry, medical and athletic fees, laboratory breakage, optional instruction in music or sports, uniforms, etc. Some schools charge an all-inclusive fee, but this is uncommon.

Also keep in mind that schools most in demand are likely to charge higher fees. However, through scholarships and by other means, the best schools today endeavor to establish a democratic atmosphere by enrolling students from all income groups.

Size of the school is important in fitting a child's needs. For example, a shy child might be lost amid a large enrollment, and would gain more from the environment of a small group and personal contact with instructors. But a well-poised, aggressive one might benefit from the competitive stimulus of a big school. To compare size, check not merely the total enrollments but the number of students in your child's age group.

Coeducational or not is another moot point. The parents' own preference should be subordinated to the emotional character of the adolescent. Besides individual temperament, such factors as the size of family and a child's previous social experience help determine whether mingling, or separation, of the sexes creates the better environmnt.

Progressive versus **conservative** education is no longer a clear-cut distinction, since most modern schools practice both methods to some degree. The differences are most marked in the early grades in teaching the fundamental reading and mathematical skills. Basically, progressive education allows a child considerable freedom of choice in developing his own creative abilities; while the conservative method stresses established educational procedures, disciplines, and class routine. Even a "conservative" school today, however, may use such elements of the "progressive" approach as group projects and field trips.

Social activities at a private school are almost as important as its type of education, and again should be related to the individual. Study the back pages of the catalogue for the description of extra-curricular activities. Don't send a singer, for example, to a school which has no chorus or glee club. One of the advantages of private schooling is the integration of academic work with your child's own interests. Sometimes a hobby such as photography or tinkering with radios can lead to serious interest in a professional career.

RECIPES, HOW TO FOLLOW |

Your cookbook, your magazines and newspapers provide an endless choice of recipes—but do you know how to follow one? There are at least twenty-one ways to ruin a good recipe. When a recipe from a reliable source turns out to be a disappointment, the usual explanation is that the cook did not follow instructions exactly. Even seemingly insignificant details, if neglected, can add to this list of some of the most common cooking mistakes:

INGREDIENTS

Do you substitute ingredients? This is always risky—don't do it! For example, sifted flour is not interchangeable with unsifted.

Doubling or dividing a new recipe also is dangerous. Ingredients in a good recipe are in exact proportion. In smaller or larger amounts the proportions may vary. The pan size, cooking time, and temperature also will need altering.

Adding a little more "to make it better" can upset the careful balance of ingredients.

Carefully read the label on a package or can. You may not be using the right ingredient or amount.

Use the baking powder called for. Different types of baking powder cannot be substituted for each other without changing the amount.

Ingredients which are not top quality or fresh cannot give you a high-quality product and may even cause complete failure.

PREPARATION

If you start preparing a recipe without reading it through, you are bound for trouble. Have the necessary ingredients, utensils, *and* time before you begin.

Follow the beating directions exactly. A good recipe states how to mix ingredients and how much to beat. For example, overbeating a muffin batter will result in large tunnels and a peaked top. Each term—fold, stir, or beat—has a different meaning.

Failure to preheat the oven or broiler means that food starts to cook at too low a temperature, and baked goods may turn out heavy.

Preparing the baking dish properly is important, and should be done before combining ingredients. A sponge, angel, or chiffon cake will not rise well in a greased pan; butter-type cakes, on the other hand, will be difficult to remove intact if directions are not followed exactly.

Not completely dissolving gelatin before combining it with other ingredients will not give you the texture or consistency you want. Too, it may not jell.

The water used with yeast must be *warm*—105° F. to 115° F. Water that is too hot will kill the yeast action.

Letting yeast dough rise too long, or rushing the rising period of the dough, will lead to a small loaf or cake with a coarse texture, and rolls may be flat. It is best to place the covered bowl of dough in a warm corner of the kitchen away from drafts—never on top of a hot range. An unheated oven with a pan or bowl of boiling water on the rack below is another good resting place for yeast dough. In either case, be sure to check for rising occasionally, noting the time guide suggested in the recipe.

UTENSILS

Failure to use a pan or baking dish of recommended size can ruin an otherwise good recipe. Too small a pan causes a mixture to run over; too large a pan produces an underbrowned, skimpy, or flat-looking dish. If you are not sure of a pan's size, measure it. To find out how much a pan holds, fill it with measuring cupfuls of water.

Perhaps one of the most common mistakes made by cooks is guess measuring. Always use a standard measure and be sure to level it. For instance, if a recipe calls for three-quarters of a cup of flour, use a one-half cup measure and a one-quarter cup measure leveled, rather than three-quarters of a full cup measure. Liquids should be measured in a glass measure at eye level.

When a recipe specifies cooking to a particular temperature, use a roast-meat thermometer for roasts or a candy deep-fry thermometer for frostings, candy, jellies, and deep-fried foods.

Using mixing bowls and beaters that are not clean and dry can produce baffling results. Egg whites, for instance, will not whip up well unless bowls and beaters are both clean and dry, and free of any bit of egg yolk.

COOKING TIME

Guess timing, like guess measuring, is sure to lead to trouble. Always note the time, or, better yet, set a timer so you will know when something needs attention.

Baking on either the highest or lowest oven-rack position or crowding the oven may cause uneven cooking. Edges may burn while the center is underdone. For best results, have your rack at the center of the oven and leave at least two inches around each side of the pan.

Do not increase the heat to speed up cooking. Cooking can't be rushed.

Opening the oven door during baking causes a draft and lowers the oven temperature. A temperature drop of even a few degrees can ruin some baked goods.

REFRIGERATORS | See also FOOD STORAGE; FREEZERS

In selecting a refrigerator, make a distinction between *refrigerating* food for temporary storage, and *freezing* it for long-period preservation. Cost varies from $120 to $700, depending in part upon whether the appliance has a large "zero zone" for freezing. A combination refrigerator-freezer is really two appliances enclosed in one cabinet. In the freezer part, the temperature drops to or below zero, and there is no exchange of air with the refrigerator part. Therefore you can keep the freezer as cold as needed without freezing fresh food elsewhere in the cabinet.

In a conventional refrigerator, the temperature in the freezing or ice-cube compartment may run from 10° F. to 20° F. and the compartment is not sealed off. Natural circulation of air cools the entire refrigerator. You can store frozen food with the ice cubes for two or three weeks, but in a true freezer combination it will keep for months. Defrosting also is necessary more often in a refrigerator (every two or three weeks) than in a freezer combination (every two to six months). This is because the sealed-off freezer section does not pick up as much moisture from circulating air.

REFRIGERATOR FEATURES

Before deciding on which refrigerator or refrigerator-freezer combination you should buy, here are points to check:

Size ranges from eight to twenty-eight cubic feet internally; external bulkiness has been greatly slimmed in recent years. Self-defrosting or ice-making features are usually available only on the higher priced models. If you own a separate home freezer, you can get "all-refrigerator" models of ten to eighteen cubic feet with only ice-tray space at the top or bottom.

Defrosting by hand is eliminated in many models. These models are called by various trade names: Frostproof, No-Frost, Frost Guard, etc. Frost that forms behind the scenes is melted and evaporated automatically. You never see it or have to do anything about it. Other models have a heat cycle to speed defrosting, though you must still remove the drip water. Or you can buy a separate electric defroster for any refrigerator.

Forced air refrigerators have a fan that directs the coldest air to certain areas. This principle assures even temperature throughout the box, especially in enclosed or partially enclosed compartments, and on the door. The older principle of natural air circulation works well in an interior space designed for it, and has less tendency to dry foods.

Ice-cube trays of easy-release type are now standard. In some models, you merely slide the inverted tray over a storage container and the cubes drop out. You can keep an extra supply while freezing additional cubes, and they won't stick together. Automatic ice-makers, connected to a water supply, will automatically fill trays, freeze cubes, and drop them into a container with no attention from you.

Doors are now required by law to be openable from inside; hence many today use magnetic closing (no latch). Right-hand hinging is standard, but you can order a left-hand model if your kitchen plan requires it. A wide variety of roll-out, swing-out, or adjustable shelves are offered. Points to check in choosing the most agreeable arrangement are whether it provides adequate tall-bottle storage, a vegetable crisper, and a fresh-meat storage compartment.

FACTS ON REFRIGERATION

For general food storage, a temperature of 35° to 40° is maintained by the average setting of the refrigerator dial under *normal* conditions. But if the weather is exceptionally hot and humid, if you open and close the door constantly, if you have loaded up the refrigerator or put hot food in it, the temperature may gain several degrees. You will notice butter softening, moisture collecting, and other signs. Turn the control to a colder setting for a short period. But turn it back after a while or you may find iced milk and frozen oranges.

Keep all frozen foods in the freezer section, if any; otherwise, in the ice-cube compartment. They will thaw out on the ordinary shelves, and must then be used immediately or discarded.

Keep vegetables in the covered crisper, or buy one to place on the bottom shelf. Potatoes and other root vegetables, and onions, are best kept out of the refrigerator. Clean vegetables before storing, and drain salad greens well to prevent "rusting." Keep all leftovers tightly covered in appropriate, preferably see-through containers; also fruit juices, iced tea, etc. Virtually all foods except fruits with skins (oranges, apples, berries) should be wrapped or covered. Usually there is a special section for eggs; if not, store them in their box. Keep milk, cream, butter, and cheese well chilled, or in the compartments provided for them.

The best policy with fresh meats is to cook and serve them as soon after purchase as possible. Even smoked or cured meats, such as bacon, ham, and sausages, will lose flavor rapidly after five to seven days. Store meat in the coldest part of the refrigerator or in the meat keeper, wrapping fish well to prevent odors.

Cleanliness is a principal consideration in refrigerator care. Moisture collecting on humid days is normal; simply wipe it up. But be careful of the gasket around the door; it must make a tight seal, and any grease will cause older types of rubber gaskets to deteriorate. Occasionally clean the interior with lukewarm water and a little baking soda. Wipe up any spills at once. Defrost when a half-inch of frost collects on the freezer unit.

To defrost a refrigerator quickly and easily, follow these steps: 1. Turn off the current. 2. Remove the ice-cube trays, and replace with flat pans of warm, not boiling, water; or use an electric defroster. 3. Keep the drip tray in place, and spread clean paper on the shelf below to catch stray meltings. 4. Empty the tray before it gets too full, two or three times if necessary. 5. Discard the paper, clean the refrigerator inside and out, and turn it on.

RICE |

Here are the varieties of packaged white and brown rice you are likely to find on your grocer's shelf. No longer do they need rinsing or draining.

Regular white rice, packaged in long-, medium-, and short-grain types, has the entire outer coating of bran removed. It may come polished or unpolished. Some brands are enriched by partial restoration of vitamins and minerals lost in milling. Check the label. Medium- or short-grain rice is popular for rice pudding, croquettes, molded rings, and other dishes in which creaminess is desired.

Processed white rice (also known as parboiled or converted) is a long-grain white rice that has been processed to retain a large percentage of the natural vitamins and minerals present in the bran of the whole grain.

Precooked or "quick" enriched white rice is made of long-grain white rice. It's completely cooked, then dehydrated. You get fluffy white rice in a jiffy.

Regular brown rice is the whole unpolished grain of rice, with just the outer husk removed. It retains all natural vitamins and minerals. Its nutty flavor is excellent as stuffing for game, as a vegetable, in main dishes, etc. Cook as the label directs.

Rice mixes. A number of flavored rice mixes are on grocers' shelves today, including Spanish rice, saffron rice, herb rice, curried rice, Cheddar and onion rice, beef and onion rice, herb and onion rice for sea food, rice with vermicelli—rich in chicken flavor—and several main dinner dishes.

Wild rice, a food of North American Indians, is a totally different plant from cultivated rice. Its flavor is highly prized as accompaniment for duck or game dishes. Difficult to grow and harvest, wild rice is also expensive— priced in dollars rather than cents.

RUG CLEANING | See also FLOOR CARE; STAIN REMOVAL

All rugs need a thorough commercial cleaning every two years or so, and costly Oriental rugs should be cleaned *only* by experts. Since currently this costs from seven to ten cents per square foot (eight to ten dollars for a nine-by-twelve domestic rug), in-between cleanings at home can save money and add to the life and looks of your rugs. Two modern products make this possible, while appliances eliminate much of the work.

Rug shampoos mixed with water clean all except high-pile cotton rugs— but check for the effect on color and texture, as directed on the label.

Apply the suds to the rug and brush back and forth or in circular motion. Repeat for even removal of soil; take up soiled suds with old toweling. A special manual device available for shampooing rugs consists of a long-handled shampoo dispenser which rolls suds onto the rug as it brushes. Dry the rug thoroughly; then vacuum to remove suspended dirt.

Rug-cleaning powder is particularly useful for removing food spills, etc., from small areas. To clean an entire rug, sprinkle the moist powder over an area about three feet square, then rub it in with a brush or dry rug cleaner applicator. Dry for an hour, or as recommended on the label, then vacuum up the powder. Protect bare floors with newspapers, and open windows wide for good ventilation.

Many electric floor polishers and some vacuum cleaners have special attachments for shampooing rugs. If liquid shampoo is used, a dispenser on the machine feeds it to the rug and brushes or discs work it into the pile. Follow these steps:

1. Vacuum the rug to remove loose dirt.

2. Test for colorfastness by applying some suds to a small area and rubbing with a clean dry cloth.

3. Test the shampooing device for its effect on the rug's surface; the brushing may fuzz the surface of some loop- or twist-type rugs.

4. Remove furniture from the rug or place waxed paper or foil under the legs of pieces that can't be moved.

5. Scrub with a back-and-forth motion in the direction of the rug pile, overlapping cleaned areas. Don't bear down; let the machine do the work.

6. Dry the rug for at least half an hour; then vacuum it.

RUGS AND CARPETS | See also RUG CLEANING

The choice of carpeting fabric to cover a floor depends not only on its good looks but on its function as insulation against cold and noise, and on the care you are willing to give it. Some types of carpeting will resist heavy traffic, others take hard wear less successfully. Light shades show soil more quickly than dark shades. A cut-nap rug of solid color in the dining room will show food stains more than a figured, patterned, twist-type or pebbly rug. Wall-to-wall carpeting looks luxurious, is a good insulator and sound deadener, but may not fit if you move to a new home. Also, it must be cleaned on the floor, which is not as satisfactory as sending a rug out.

Here are some hints, followed by definitions of terms you should know in shopping for rugs.

DECORATING HINTS

Decide on the rug color and pattern best suited to your room, and choose one that will go with future changes in walls, draperies, or upholstery.

For informal rooms, modern or traditional, use textured effects, tweeds, or heathery mixtures.

For formal rooms, modern or traditional, use plain or carved effects, or formal repeat designs.

Dark colors make a room seem smaller; light colors give a feeling of space to a small room.

Use a plain or textured carpet with patterned upholstery or wallpaper.

Use carved carpeting for an appearance of depth and richness.

Choose a rug size to fit the room with a space of from six to fifteen inches between rug and wall, fairly evenly divided on all four sides.

BUYING HINTS

Measure the area you want to cover, and have ready the figures on exactly how much you need.

Go to a reputable store where you can get dependable advice.

Beware of bargains, and don't buy a carpet that doesn't bear the manufacturer's name. With carpets perhaps more than with other furnishings, you get what you pay for.

Compare carpets of different quality and price. The best carpets have thickly packed surface yarns. If possible, take a sample home and live with it awhile.

For rooms in constant use, choose one of the major rug fibers (see chart, page 302f). Consider the more economical, but less resilient fibers, such as cotton or rayon, for areas not subjected to constant crushing, especially if the pile of the carpet is high.

Select a good padding. Ask your dealer to recommend the best pad for your carpet. The "give" or softness is not necessarily a key to quality.

A good carpet has a closely packed pile on a firm backing. Though the height of the pile is important, the density or closeness of the surface yarns is more important for long wear. Check pile density by bending a corner of the carpet back upon itself. Don't buy a skimpy pile. It may have a luxurious feel when new, but will crush noticeably within a short time. When a carpet is made of rayon or cotton fibers, which do not recover from crush as readily as the major fibers, you'll find that a short, dense loop pile with high-twist yarns will best disguise crush marks.

The backing is usually made of jute, or of man-made materials. Grasp and knead the backing between your fingers to make sure it is firm. If sleazy or lacking in bulk, the carpet is poor quality.

On their backs, tufted carpets always have a latex coating, which helps secure the tufts or surface yarns. Some poorly made tufted carpets tend to buckle or wrinkle in humid climates. To minimize this problem, good-quality tufted carpets have a secondary backing over the main backing.

MODERN CARPET FIBERS

Fiber Names & Manufacturers	Abrasion Resistance	Crush Resistance	Soil Resistance	Cleanability	Price Range for Good Quality
ACRYLIC: Acrilan (Chemstrand) Creslan (American Cyanamid) Orlon (DuPont) Zefkrome (Dow Chemical) MODACRYLICS (used in blends): Dynel (Union Carbide) Verel (Eastman Chemical)	Good to very good	Very good	Good	Good	$9 to $15 per square yard
NYLON: Caprolan (Allied Chemical) Celanese Nylon (Celanese) Cumuloft (Chemstrand) DuPont Nylon (DuPont) Enkaloft (American Enka) Nyloft (Firestone) Tycora (Textured Yarn)	Excellent	Very good	Good (Carpets with shiny appearance show soil more than duller textures)	Very good	$7 to $15 per square yard

POLYPROPYLENE: Herculon (Hercules) Marvess (Alamo) Polycrest (U.S. Rubber) Vectra (National Plastics)	Very good	Good	Good	Excellent (outstanding stain resistance)	$7 to $10 per square yard
WOOL	Good (varies greatly with quality of fiber)	Excellent	Very good	Very good	$10 to $25 per square yard
COMMENTS: Polyester fiber is new in carpets and most promising, but not yet in wide distribution. Its crush-resistance is excellent.	Most abrasive resistant is nylon. In blends, at least 20 per cent nylon is needed to increase abrasion resistance.	How much crushing shows will depend on construction. Short, closely packed pile surfaces show crushing less than high piles.	Dull and dark shades hide soil best. Yellows and oranges show soil more than blues and greens. Brown-beiges look better longer than rose-beiges.	Rate of resoiling is high if detergent is left in pile, so rinse well when removing stains.	

Today, many woven carpets also have a latex-coated backing, which gives a better looking, cleaner appearance.

CARPETING TERMS

Velvet construction is the simplest of the major carpet weaves. When closely woven, it is long wearing and rich looking. Velvets are usually solid colors, sometimes tweed. They have a plush appearance with a cut pile, a pebbly texture with uncut or loop pile.

Wilton carpets are woven on Jacquard looms, making possible a variety of textured or sculptured patterns, in multicolor designs and solid colors.

Axminster carpets come in unlimited combinations of design and color. Most are level-cut pile, although the pile may be looped and multilevel to form a carved effect. You can recognize an Axminster by the ridged backing, which permits the carpet to be rolled only lengthwise.

Chenille is the aristocrat of woven carpets. Most are custom made. Since more yarn is used in weaving them, they wear exceptionally well. Usually they are made in a solid color, though an infinite number of designs is possible.

In **knit**, as well as **woven** carpets, the backing and surface are interwoven simultaneously on a loom or knitting machine.

Tufted carpets are made by inserting tufts of yarn into a woven backing of jute or man-made material. The more tufts per inch, the better the carpet. Most carpets today are made by the tufting method.

Broadloom means simply a carpet fabric made on a wide loom, does not refer to any particular weave, and may be of any color or pattern.

Fibers. The *quality* of fiber is as important as the *kind*. There are many grades of wool, for example, and the phrase "all-wool" does not necessarily connote a good carpet.

Shooting or sprouting in a rug refers to a loop that extends above the pile. It should be snipped off level with the rest. Pulling it out can cause damage.

Fluffing, the shedding of yarn cut off the pile in manufacturing and left imbedded in it, occurs naturally in new rugs and is no cause for alarm. Fluffs may show up in the vacuum cleaner for months. It is a more frequent problem in plush cut piles.

Shading is an apparent change in color tone, caused by the nap being brushed or pressed in different directions. Particularly noticeable in solid colors, it usually may be corrected by vacuuming in one direction.

Matting is flattened pile in areas of excess traffic or under heavy objects such as a piano leg. Brush the pile vigorously to raise the nap, or rearrange your furniture occasionally to relieve pressure on a particular area.

SUMMER RUGS

Manila-hemp rugs are the most durable type. Hemp is hand woven into squares and then sewn together. The material usually comes in a natural beige, but can be bleached to off-white. A good choice for outdoors—rain won't hurt it.

Sisal is similar to hemp, but can be dyed. It is often made in two-color designs in a checkerboard pattern. Sisal has more sheen than hemp and sheds less. Though rain won't affect it, sunshine will, so it's a good choice for outdoors only if area is covered.

Grass rugs are reasonably durable but won't last as long as hemp or sisal. Seagrass has a slight sheen, rush does not. Seagrass is stronger and sheds less than rush. Rugs are made in their natural color—tan to yellowish-green. They take to rain and sunshine.

Kraftfiber or Kraftcord is not grown but is manufactured from wood pulp. The tighter the twist and the heavier the rug, the better the wear. The rugs should be finished for water repellency. They can be dyed many colors and are made in a variety of patterns. They usually will fade in direct sunlight so are better indoors or in covered areas.

SAUSAGES | See also FRANKFURTERS

Sausage was probably one of the first attempts at food preservation. It is still an appetizing and nourishing type of meat. Here are six main sausage classifications and some well-known variations:

Fresh sausage is made of uncured meat (curing is the salting of meat for preservation). The most perishable sausage, it must be refrigerated, and cooked thoroughly before serving.

Bratwurst, a German sausage of pork, beef, and sometimes veal, comes in links about 4 inches long by 1⅜ inches in diameter.

Pork sausage is made of finely ground selected fresh pork. When the meat is ground more coarsely, it is *country-style* pork sausage, shaped in a continuous "rope" about 1½ inches in diameter.

Weisswurst, made of veal and pork, is almost white. Links are about 4 inches long, 1¾ inches in diameter.

Uncooked, smoked sausage is usually made of cured meats, smoked to produce a distinctive color and flavor. It must be refrigerated, and cooked before serving.

Kielbasa is coarsely ground pork and beef, highly seasoned with garlic. Links are 4 to 5 or 8 to 10 inches long and 1½ inches in diameter. Smoked *country-style* sausage, made of coarsely ground pork and beef or plain pork, comes in links.

Cooked, smoked sausage is the most popular variety in the United States.

Usually made of cured meats which are smoked and cooked, this sausage must be refrigerated for storage.

Berliner sausage is pork and beef with no seasoning.

Bologna is cured beef and pork and mild seasoning. It comes in sizes from 1 inch to 5 inches in diameter.

Frankfurters, wieners, or hot dogs are usually made of 60 per cent beef and 40 per cent pork and veal which is finely ground.

Knackwurst or *knoblauch* is made like frankfurters, but contains garlic and the links are slightly larger in diameter.

Cooked sausage is made of cured or uncured meats which are thoroughly cooked. These require refrigeration but no preparation before serving.

Blood sausage or *blutwurst* is diced, cooked pork fat, finely ground meat, and gelatin materials which are mixed with spice and beef blood. It is 4 inches in diameter.

Liver sausage or *liverwurst* is finely ground pork fat, livers, and gelatin material.

Braunschweiger is smoked liver sausage which is soft and light in color.

Cooked meat specialties are combinations of meat products which require refrigeration and are ready to serve.

Head cheese is made from cured hog-head meat and other pork cuts. It is 4 inches in diameter.

Dry sausage is cured meat and spice which has been air-dried for long periods. It will keep for a long time under refrigeration and needs no cooking before serving.

Cervelats are mildly seasoned and may be soft (summer sausage) or hard. They are usually made of pork and beef, and vary in spices, shape, smoking, grinding, and drying.

Pepperoni is pork and beef seasoned with red pepper and other spices. About 1½ inches in diameter.

Salamis are made of pork and beef highly seasoned with garlic and other spices, and may be soft (cooked, semi-dry) or hard.

SEASONINGS |

Seasoned salt, celery salt, garlic salt, onion salt, salt, paprika, grated cheese, seasoned pepper, cinnamon-sugar mixture, and others are available for your use in convenient shakers. They are quick and very good seasoners for meat dishes, vegetables, sauces, salads, etc. They also add glamor when sprinkled on crackers, breads, and rolls before heating.

Seasoned or seasoning salt. A flavorful blend of many spices with salt; each brand has its own distinctive blend. Perfect for many everyday foods.

Celery salt. Mixture of ground celery seeds with salt. Gives zest to such dishes as:

Fish	Salad dressings
Oyster stew	Soups
Potato salads	Tomato juice, etc.

Garlic salt. Mixture of garlic powder with salt. Use with, or instead of, salt for a garlic flavor in:

Ground meats	Soups
Salads	Steaks or chops
Salad dressings	Tomato juice
Sauces, such as spaghetti sauce	

Onion salt. A blend of dehydrated onion and salt. Adds a delicate onion flavor to:

| Meats | Spaghetti sauce |
| Salad dressings | Vegetables (add to cooking water) |

Seasoned pepper. A blend of imported and domestic pepper with rare spices—slightly mild, mellow in flavor. Excellent with:

Meats	Fish
Eggs	Vegetables
Salads	Soups
Poultry	Gravies

Monosodium glutamate. Not a seasoning in itself, this modern invention has done much for cookery by bringing out the natural flavors of many foods. Especially effective for meats, poultry, vegetables, fish, gravy, soup, and salads. Add it from the shaker before or during cooking, along with other seasonings, in these approximate amounts:

1 teasp. per lb. of ground beef
½ teasp. per lb. of roasts
½ teasp. over each side of individual steaks
¾ teasp. per 4 servings of vegetables
1 teasp. per chicken

HERBS AND SPICES

Here are tips on using the dried herbs and spices that add so much to modern, distinctive cooking:

Buy only in small containers; a little dried herb or spice goes a long way. Also, they lose flavor with time. Store away from heat and sunlight.

Note date of buying on label; then renew at least once a year, even if not used up. Don't make antiques of spices and herbs. Smell them occasionally —once the scent is gone, they're worthless.

If you aren't following a specific recipe, start with a little herb or spice;

taste to decide whether to add more. A good rule of thumb: add one-quarter teaspoonful to a dish that makes four servings.

If it's a stew or soup you're making, add herb or spice during the last hour of cooking. If the soup is canned or frozen, add as you heat the soup.

For a roast, add herb or spice toward the end of roasting. For a steak or chops, sprinkle with herb during broiling. Or, about one hour ahead, brush with salad oil, sprinkle with herbs, then refrigerate until needed.

For meat loaf, hamburgers, stuffings, etc., add herb when mixing. If it's a vegetable or sauce, add herb or spice while cooking.

In a dish that calls for no cooking, like vegetable or tomato juice, salad dressing, a dip, dunk, or spread, let herb or spice stand in it a while. Soaking dried herbs for a few minutes in a little French (dry) vermouth gives them a flavor very close to fresh herbs.

HERB AND SPICE DICTIONARY

ALLSPICE
(resembles blend of cinnamon, nutmeg, and cloves)

Use whole in: Pickling, gravies, meats, fish dishes.

Use ground in or on: Cakes, cookies, puddings, relishes, preserves, tomato sauce, steak.

ANISEED
(licoricelike flavor)

Sprinkle on: Coffeecakes, sweet rolls, fruit.
Use ground in: Cookies, sweet pickles, candies.

BASIL
(an herb of west Europe)

Sprinkle on: Green beans, lamb chops, meats, peas, potatoes, sauces, soups; or on egg, poultry, salad, and tomato dishes.

BAY LEAVES
(from a laurel tree grown in eastern Mediterranean countries)

Use whole in: Fish dishes, pickling, sauces; and gravies, stews, and soups.

CARAWAY SEEDS
(from Holland)

Sprinkle (whole or ground) over, or use in: Sauerkraut, cabbage, asparagus, noodles, French fries, soups, cookies, breads and rolls, cheese spreads, pork, liver, kidneys, loaf cake.

CARDAMOM SEEDS
(small pod of brown seeds)

Use whole in: Demitasse, pickling, curries.
Use ground in: Cookies, coffeecakes, grape jelly, melon.

CAYENNE PEPPER
(blend of most pungent chili peppers)

Use in: Sauces, meat and egg dishes, sea food, curries.

CELERY FLAKES
  (dried green leaves of celery stalks; may be home-made)   Sprinkle on: Same dishes as parsley flakes.

CELERY SEEDS
  (tiny seedlike fruit)   Use whole or ground in: Cheese dishes, fish dishes, salad dressings, sauces, soups, stews; tomato, egg, or potato dishes; vegetables.

CHERVIL
  (resembles parsley; herb is slightly peppery)   Delicious in: Egg, fish, poultry, tomato dishes. Or in peas and carrots, salads, summer squash, and salad dressing.

CHILI POWDER
  (blend of chilis and spices)   Use in: Chili con carne, cocktail sauces, egg dishes, gravies, sea food, stews.

CINNAMON
  (spicy bark of Oriental trees)   Use whole in: Pickling, preserving, canned or stewed fruits, mashed sweet potatoes, toast, blueberries, apple or pineapple dishes, broiled grapefruit, bananas, cakes, ice cream, cookies, puddings, hot biscuits.

CLOVES
  (nail-shaped flower bud of clove tree)   Use whole in or on: Pork and ham roasts, pickling, peaches, pineapple, etc.
    Use ground in: Baked dishes, stews, chocolate puddings, vegetables (beets), broiled grapefruit, potato soup.

CORIANDER SEED
  (dried, ripe fruit of an herb of the parsley family; tastes like combination of lemon peel and sage)   Use ground in: Buns, pastry, cookies, cakes.

CUMIN
  (a seed with distinctive salty-sweet flavor, ingredient of chili powder)   Use whole in: Cream, cottage, or Cheddar cheese; cabbage.
    Use ground in: Deviled eggs, meat loaf, hamburgers, chili con carne, rice, sauerkraut, fish.

HERB AND SPICE DICTIONARY (Continued)

CURRY POWDER
(blend of spices)

Use in:

Sauce for eggs, fish, meats, poultry, vegetables; in tomato juice, etc.

DILL SEEDS
(small seeds of dill plant, imported from India)

Use whole or ground in:

Pickling, gravies, apple pie, soups (borsch), potato salad, any cheese spread or dunk, salads, sauerkraut, cabbage, turnips, cauliflower, spaghetti, and tomato dishes, cream- or cottage-cheese mixtures.

DILL WEED
(dried fine leaves of dill)

Use in:

Fish dishes; mixed with mayonnaise, salad dressings.

GINGER
(root of Oriental plant)

Use cracked in:

Chutneys, conserves, pickling, stewed dried fruits, applesauce.

Use ground in:

Gingerbread, pumpkin pie, Indian pudding, summer squash, melon, canned fruit, chicken dishes.

MACE
(dried pulp around nutmeg kernel; flavor similar to nutmeg)

Use whole or ground in, or on:

Cherries, chocolate dishes, whipped cream, jellies, canned fruit, gingerbread, poundcake, broiled grapefruit, fish sauces.

MARJORAM
(herb of the mint family from France or Chile)

Use sparingly in or on:

Roast lamb, meat pies, hash, stews, stuffings, asparagus, carrots, greens, limas, squash, cheese and egg dishes, fish or vegetable sauces.

MUSTARD SEED
(from European varieties of common plant)

Use whole in:
Use ground in:

Pickling mixtures.
Mustards; mixed with water for "hot" mustard; in other dishes replacing pepper.

NUTMEG
(kernel of nutmeg fruit)

Use ground in:

Cakes, breads, cabbage, cauliflower, broiled fruit, green beans, greens, puddings, sauces.

Use as topping for:

Eggnog, custards, whipped cream, sauces.

OREGANO (herb imported from Italy and Mexico)	Good in or on:	Pork, hamburgers, chili con carne, pizzas, omelets, stews, spaghetti sauce, vegetables, cheese dishes. Or in melted butter served with sea food.
PAPRIKA (mild member of pepper family; adds color, flavor)	Sprinkle on or use in:	Canapes, fish, gravies, meats, salad dressings, shellfish, vegetables.
PARSLEY FLAKES (green herb, distinctive mild flavor)	Sprinkle on:	Soups, salads, stews, sauces, all vegetables, omelets, potatoes.
PEPPER (world's most popular spice, from East Indies)	Use whole peppercorns in: Use ground (black or white) or coarsely ground or cracked black pepper in:	Pickling, soups, pepper grinders. Eggs, gravies, meats, salads, sauces, soups, many vegetables—in fact, most foods.
POPPY SEEDS (fragrant seeds from Holland)	Sprinkle on: Use in:	Breads, rolls, cookies, etc. Salads, noodles.
POULTRY SEASONING (fragrant herbs combined with sage)	Delicious in:	Biscuit dough, stuffings.
ROSEMARY (an herb—looks like a pine needle)	Delectable in, with, or on:	Biscuit dough, boiled potatoes, roasts, stews, vegetables, lamb or poultry dishes, sauces for meat or fish, or tossed in vegetable, orange, pear, grapefruit, or peach salad.
SAGE (a favorite herb with distinctive, positive flavor)	Use lightly in or on:	Cheese, fish, pork, veal, ham, poultry, poultry dressing, sausage, or tomato dishes, salads.
SAFFRON (hand-picked dried stigmas of a plant of crocus family; it takes 225,000 to make a pound. World's most expensive spice; a little goes a long way.)	Use whole stigmas. Rub, and use in:	Baked goods, Spanish rice, etc.

SAVORY
(herb of the mint family   Use in or on: Baked beans, green limas,
from France and Spain)   vegetable soup, meat loaf,
                                                         roasts, hamburger, egg or
                                                         rice dishes, potato or
                                                         squash dishes.

TARRAGON
(leaf with anise flavor)   Good in: Salads, sauces, sea food, beets,
                                                          greens, mushrooms, peas,
                                                          egg and poultry dishes,
                                                          tomato dishes.

THYME
(many varieties of this   Use sparingly in or   Veal, pork, carrots, eggplant,
herb)   with: peas, tomatoes, breads,
                                                          stews, chowders, stuffings,
                                                          cheese or fish dishes.

TURMERIC
(mild, slightly bitter flavor)   Use ground in: Mustards, curries, pickling
                                                          mixtures, chicken, eggs, fish.

SHELLFISH |

Thanks to improved transportation and freezing methods, most varieties
of shellfish, once a rare delicacy except where they're caught, are available
and reasonable everywhere today. To keep shellfish at its best, from market
to table, don't overlook these important pointers:

If raw fresh, plan to use within a day or two after you buy it. Refrigerate
at once, either wrapped in plastic sheet or foil, or in a tightly covered dish;
keep there until used. (If shellfish needs cleaning, dip into cold salted water,
then wipe with a damp cloth.)

If cooked fresh, you'll want to refrigerate and then use as soon after
buying as possible. Cooked shellfish is highly perishable and deteriorates
quickly if not refrigerated.

If frozen, whether frozen raw or cooked, store in your freezer as soon
after purchase as possible. When time to use, transfer in original package
to refrigerator to thaw or not, as recipe or label directs.

If canned, store in a cool dry place. Once can has been opened, refrigerate, covered, and use promptly.

CLAMS

Soft-shell clams are very popular for steaming, Boston clam chowder,
fried clams, clam fritters, clam broth, etc. There are two sizes, the smaller
ones known as "steamers," the larger ones as "in shells." If your recipe calls

for shucked clams, order them by the pint or quart. If serving them in the shell, buy by the dozen, peck, quart, or pound. Always make sure the shells are tightly closed, but for the protruding neck, and that they close quickly when touched. Reject all broken ones, and *never* eat one that won't close.

Hard-shell clams are called "quahogs" in New England, "clams" in much of the East, and "round clams" or "little-necks" in the South. Dealers call the large ones "chowder clams," medium ones "cherry stones," and smaller ones "little-necks." They're purchased shucked or in the shell. Large-size hard-shells are popular in Manhattan clam chowder, and for broth. Medium and smaller ones are famous in a clam cocktail, or as clams on half shell. For opening directions, see *Oysters* below.

Pacific coast clams include the butter, little-neck, razor, and 1½ lb. pismos up to giant 6-lb. geoducks.

Canned clams, either whole or minced, come in 10- to 10½-oz. cans (about 1¼ cups). Either pack makes a delicious speedy chowder. Minced clams are popular for spaghetti sauce.

CRABS

Blue crabs are the most familiar kind in Eastern markets, from the Atlantic and the Gulf of Mexico. In both hard-shell and soft-shell states, and alive or cooked, they may be sold in the shell individually, by the dozen, or by the pound. Soft-shell blue crabs are also marketed frozen.

Hard-shell crabs are available throughout the year, but are more plentiful in the summer. They should be alive and usually weigh from one-quarter to one pound.

Soft-shell crabs. When a hard-shell crab sheds its shell and the new one has not yet hardened, it is called soft-shell crab. It is a great delicacy, available in the spring and summer. Each weighs one-seventh to one-third pound. Frozen soft-shell crabs are available the year round.

Rock crabs. Most abundant off the New England coast, this crab is said to have more meat than blue crabs. Each weighs about one-third pound, and the flavorsome meat is brownish white.

Dungeness or **Pacific crabs.** This crab weighs from 1¾ to 3½ pounds and is usually sold by the pound. The meat is pinkish white.

Cooked fresh crab meat. From both the Atlantic and Pacific coasts and the Gulf of Mexico, this meat of the crab comes, by the pound, in pry-open cans—about three cups per pound—in ice, under refrigeration. The meat is graded, the top grade being lump white meat, also know as "special" or backfin lump.

Frozen King crab meat. From the icy waters of Alaska, King crabs supply large, luscious crab meat chunks for salads, casseroles, etc., in each six-ounce package. Completely drain the thawed frozen crab meat before using. This liquid may replace an equal amount of the liquid called for in the recipe.

Remove any membrane. Canned King crab (unfrozen) from Alaska or Japan should be completely drained before using.

Frozen Alaska King crab legs. Split leg sections in the shell, cut into serving portions, come frozen in twelve-ounce packages. Nice for broiling, barbecuing, etc.

LOBSTER

Live northern or Maine lobsters, so named, come from East Coast waters and are available the year round. Peak production in Maine is the early fall, often carrying through into December.

The live lobster shell varies from a bluish green, with touches of red, to a brownish color. During cooking, it turns bright red. Most of its meat is in the two large claws and tail section. The most desirable live lobsters weigh one to two pounds each, the one-pounders being called "chicken lobsters." The female, preferred by many, is recognized by the softness of its two uppermost appendages.

When buying live lobsters to cook at home, check their tails to be sure they're alive. The tail of a live lobster should curl under the body when the lobster is picked up—a sign of freshness. If its tail is limp and extended out straight, the lobster is probably dead. Since you have no way of knowing how long ago this happened, don't use it.

Always refrigerate live lobsters until ready to cook. But never place them in water or in fresh-water ice—they'll smother.

When buying a cooked-live lobster, make sure its tail curls toward body and springs back into place after being straightened. Refrigerate cooked meat as soon as possible.

Live lobsters may be shipped directly to your home. The Public Relations Office of the Department of Sea and Shore Fisheries, Augusta, Maine, will provide the latest information on these shipments. Cook the lobsters as soon as possible after arrival, following label directions closely.

Rock-lobster tails come quick-frozen and have the country of origin clearly marked on the package. The meat resembles lobster but comes from a different shellfish. Especially desirable are those fished in the icy waters of the Benguela current, which comes up from the Antarctic along the coast of South Africa. These are labeled South African and have a rough-looking reddish-brown shell. Cold-water tails from Australia and New Zealand are also available.

Frozen rock-lobster tails also come from the warm waters of the Caribbean and other areas. The warm-water variety has a smooth, spotted, light-colored shell. The meat in the tail section is tender, white, and delicious.

Frozen South African rock-lobster tails are sold in nine-ounce and one-and-a-half-pound cartons. Each tail in the carton weighs about three to four ounces; larger sizes can be bought in tray packs in supermarkets or "loose" in fish markets. Rock-lobster meat also comes canned.

In rock-lobster dishes, four ounces of the meat is an ample portion. When served broiled, allow two four-ounce tails per person.

Frozen Langostinos are the frozen, bite-size tails of tiny Chilean lobsters, somewhat resembling shrimp. They are cooked, shelled, then sold in rose-pink blocks of six and twelve ounces. May be used in place of cooked shrimp, lobster, or crab.

OYSTERS

Oysters from Eastern waters come extra large, large, medium, small, and very small. Western Olympia oysters are small. Pacific oysters are larger than Eastern oysters. All these fresh varieties are sold raw, shucked by the dozen, or in half-pint, one-pint, and one-quart containers. They should be a natural gray in color, plump, with clear liquor, and free from shell particles. Or they may be purchased in the shell by the dozen. Oysters on the half shell are prepared to order, to be served like clams on half shell.

To open oysters. Scrub shells well; rinse in cold water. Insert point of sharp thin knife into hinged end of oyster; push blade between shells until muscle at center is cut and valves begin to separate. Run knife around shell; separate valves; loosen oyster from shell. Put shucked oysters in sieve to drain; pick over oysters, taking each between finger tips, to remove bits of shell.

SCALLOPS

Scallops, one of the tastiest gifts of the sea, come in two varieties in this country—sea scallops and bay scallops. Allow about one pound of scallops for three or four servings.

Sea scallops are harvested in deep waters off the New England coast and are available the year round in fresh and frozen form. Their meat is sweet, nutlike, and firm, and there's no waste to pay for. They're larger than bay scallops—one to one and a half inches across.

Bay scallops are tiny—one-half to three-quarters inch across—and luscious. They come from tidal inlets and bays and are not distributed as widely as sea scallops. Usually found as a local winter delicacy. A rich dish, one pound will serve three.

Frozen French-fried scallops come breaded and fried, ready to heat as label directs; or breaded, uncooked, ready for frying.

SHRIMP

Shrimp has become perhaps the most popular of shellfish nationwide, in areas distant from the seacoast. Here are kinds to look for:

Fresh raw shrimp in shell are sometimes shipped to market between layers of ice. Many more are frozen before shipping and then thawed by the dealer before he sells them. They are neither cleaned nor shelled.

In some markets you will find freshly cooked shrimp—usually by the pound—which have been shelled and deveined. Make sure they've been kept refrigerated or packed in ice.

Frozen shrimp comes to market in several packs: raw, in the shell; raw, in shells, but deveined; raw, shelled, and deveined; cooked, in shells; cooked, shelled, and deveined.

Frozen breaded shrimp come either "round" or fantail (sometimes called "butterflies"), either cleaned and breaded, but uncooked; or cleaned, breaded, and cooked—all ready to heat as the label directs.

One pound of frozen or fresh uncooked shrimp, after cooking and shelling, yields 1⅓ to 1⅔ cups (or ½ lb.), or two or three servings.

Canned shrimp come deveined or nondeveined in 4½- and 5-oz. cans (1 cup), either "wet pack" (in brine) or "dry pack" (in a vacuum without liquid). Always drain them, then rinse under tap water before using.

MUSSELS

Mussels, a neglected yet delicious shellfish, have one advantage—they are in season when oysters are out of season. They can be bought the year round, but are at their best in the winter.

Mussels should be bought alive. If the shells gape and do not stay closed when squeezed shut, the mussels are either dead or weak, and should not be used. Keep them covered with a wet cloth, in a cool dark place, until used.

Mussel shells should be washed very well before cooking. The little tuft of black hair (the byssus) is easily removed after cooking. Cook the mussels just as you would oysters or clams. Sometimes you'll find little sandcrabs inside the mussels; discard these. Also beware of "pearls" or tiny white stones, if you eat mussels steamed in the shell. One-half peck of mussels, steamed, makes five servings.

SHORTENINGS |

When "shortening" is called for in a recipe, the reference is to those shortenings which come in one-pound and three-pound cans. Whether these are all-vegetable, or a combination of meat fats and vegetable oils, they are specifically adapted for quick-method cakes, as most labels indicate. They're used, too, for pastry and other forms of baking, sautéing, frying, etc. Creamy in texture, bland in odor and flavor, they are light, workable, and easy to blend with other ingredients. They require no refrigeration. Some well-known brands are now processed to retain more of the original values of the basic oils.

OTHER SHORTENINGS

Butter has always been a favorite shortening because of its rich flavor and its ability to enhance the texture and taste of so many of our everyday dishes. It gives us important amounts of vitamin A, as well as a high energy value of 100 calories per tablespoonful. Refrigerate, covered, or in a butter conditioner.

Margarine. Most of today's margarine is made entirely from vegetable oils, processed to give them desirable spreading and cooking properties. A culture of skim milk used in manufacturing is largely responsible for the appetizing flavor. Fortified with a minimum of 15,000 units of vitamin A per pound, margarine has the same energy value as butter, is nutritionally comparable, and is uniform in food value throughout the year (butter varies according to season). Many brands are also fortified with vitamin D.

New types of margarine are specifically processed to retain the original properties of the basic oils; some require frozen storage, but most, only refrigeration. Also, unsalted margarines are now available. Nationally known, quality brands are excellent and economical for table use and cooking use. Buy margarine only from a store that keeps it refrigerated. Store, covered, in the refrigerator.

Lard: Its quick-blending properties make lard excellent for pastry. It is also used in sautéing, frying, bread making, etc. The majority of brands contain small amounts of antioxidants to improve the keeping properties of pure pork fat. Such brands do not require refrigeration. Refrigerate, covered, any lard whose label does not indicate the presence of an antioxidant.

SILVERWARE |

Eating utensils such as forks, knives, and spoons are called *flatware*; silver serving dishes, platters, vases, and candlesticks are *hollowware*. A variety of flatware, as illustrated, embellishes the formal dining table, but a basic starting set may consist of the following:

12 dinner knives	12 luncheon forks
12 dinner forks	12 coffee spoons
12 salad forks	3 tablespoons
24 teaspoons	1 gravy ladle
12 butter spreaders	1 cold meat fork
12 dessert spoons	1 sugar tongs

This will serve a party of twelve, since many items may be used for more than one purpose. Salad forks, for example, double as fish forks; luncheon forks, as dessert forks; dessert spoons, as soup spoons; teaspoons, for anything served in a small dish. See illustration, next page.

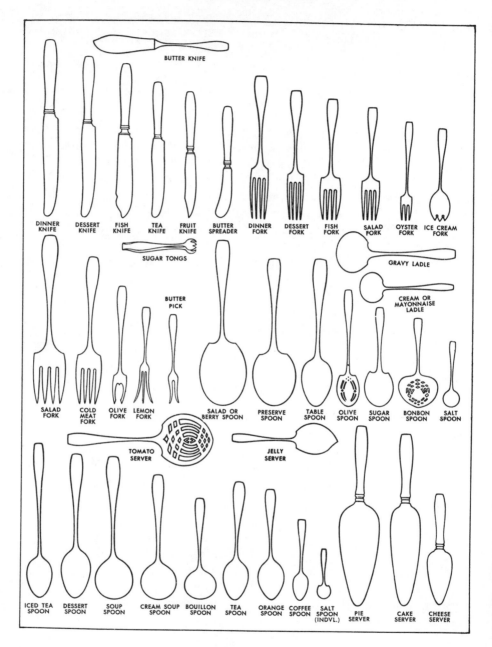

BUTTER KNIFE

DINNER KNIFE · DESSERT KNIFE · FISH KNIFE · TEA KNIFE · FRUIT KNIFE · BUTTER SPREADER · DINNER FORK · DESSERT FORK · FISH FORK · SALAD FORK · OYSTER FORK · ICE CREAM FORK

SUGAR TONGS

GRAVY LADLE

BUTTER PICK

CREAM OR MAYONNAISE LADLE

SALAD FORK · COLD MEAT FORK · OLIVE FORK · LEMON FORK · SALAD OR BERRY SPOON · PRESERVE SPOON · TABLE SPOON · OLIVE SPOON · SUGAR SPOON · BONBON SPOON · SALT SPOON

TOMATO SERVER

JELLY SERVER

ICED TEA SPOON · DESSERT SPOON · SOUP SPOON · CREAM SOUP SPOON · BOUILLON SPOON · TEA SPOON · ORANGE SPOON · COFFEE SPOON · SALT SPOON (INDVL.) · PIE SERVER · CAKE SERVER · CHEESE SERVER

Sterling silver in the United States of America consists of a single solid metal containing 92½ per cent silver alloyed with copper for strength and hardness. It is always marked "sterling" by the manufacturer. Grades and prices are determined by weight, pattern, and details of workmanship. Although expensive, fine sterling will last for generations.

Silver plate designates a base metal covered with at least two ounces of silver per gross of teaspoons; but higher grades may have two to four times as much silver plating. The grade also depends upon the base metal used, the uniformity of electroplating, and reinforcement at points of wear such as the back of spoons and forks. Since these qualities are invisible, a reputable manufacturer is the best guarantee of satisfaction. Unlabeled "flash" silver plate is never a bargain, but good silver plate will give long service with proper care.

Sheffield plate is an antique (19th century) process of electroplating copper with sheet silver.

Stainless steel flatware, like sterling, is of solid metal, not coated or plated, but made of an iron-chromium alloy that resists discoloration. Quality ranges from inexpensive "kitchen only" utensils to costly pieces of beautiful design. Stainless flatware will not tarnish or oxidize, needs no polishing, wears well, and is easily cleaned although not 100 per cent stainproof. A highly buffed finish for stain and scratch resistance, and good weight to resist bending or distortion are among the marks of quality.

Patterns of sterling silver (and of good quality silverplate or stainless) usually remain in stock for many years, allowing you to accumulate a set a few pieces at a time. During January and February of each year, many large manufacturers of sterling take orders for older, discontinued patterns. If enough orders are received, the pieces will be made up for delivery the following autumn.

Monogramming beautiful silverware makes it a personalized, treasured family possession. Either simple block initials or an elaborate script harmonizing with the silver's pattern may be used. To illustrate combinations of maiden or married name initials that are considered correct, let's assume that Miss A.B.C. has married Mr. Z.

One initial: either C or Z.

Two initials: either A C or C Z.

Three initials: either ABC or ACZ.

SINKS AND COUNTERS |

SINKS

Porcelain-enamel sinks may be of steel or cast iron. Iron is the sturdier of the two. The porcelain, whether white or a color, should be high-gloss, heatproof, acid-, stain-, and scratch-resistant, easy to keep clean. A sharp blow can cause porcelain to chip, and there's no really satisfactory way to repair the damage. Also, if the sink isn't properly cared for, the glaze can wear down, losing its gloss and getting gradually harder to clean and likelier to stain and discolor.

A new porcelain sink needs only sudsy cleaning, now and then with some baking soda; a little later on, a bleach-containing cleanser to whiten and to remove pot marks and stains. Use cleanser lightly; strenuous scouring isn't good for the glaze, or even necessary.

Stainless steel sinks. Tops in quality is nickel stainless steel (type 302, preferably #18 gauge). It's corrosion- and stain-resistant; won't chip or wear off, discolor or rust. There is no color choice, but finishes vary from high polish to satin luster and the neutral tone blends with any color.

Use leaves stainless steel with some scratches, but these soon blend together. Water spots—just marks, not stains—wipe away with a dry towel. Care for stainless steel with a sudsy sponge to remove grease and grime, plus an occasional rub with a sink cleanser. (Cleanser helps to blend scratches and produce a smooth luster.) To make the surface gleam, merely rinse well and wipe dry.

COUNTER TOPS

Next to the sink, new counter tops can give your kitchen a different personality as well as a different look. Consider these points for counter-top materials:

Laminated plastic. Most popular of the counter tops, laminated plastic (hard melamine) is one of the most durable. It resists most household chemicals and foods, temperatures up to boiling, moisture, and grease. But knife cuts may scratch it and hard blows may chip edges. A sudsy wash is the best regular care. Use a cream wax or silicone polish for a shine.

Backed vinyl. This is the same material as vinyl floor covering, but in a thinner gauge. It is quieter and not as shiny as melamine, and is almost as durable. But it may blister from hot pans, scar from cuts, and be stained by some foods. It requires the same care as melamine, but household cleanser may be used to remove surface stains.

Vinyl film. Similar to self-adhesive shelf lining, vinyl film is a satisfactory and inexpensive temporary counter-top material. Because it comes with or without adhesive and can be applied over any old, smooth surface, it is a favorite with do-it-yourselfers. Being plastic, it has good resistance and cleaning qualities, but is so thin that a knife may cut through it. Colors tend to fade after about a year.

Linoleum. This material is not frequently used today as a counter covering. Although linoleum resists stains and liquids almost as well as do plastic materials, it tends to warp and buckle from moisture. If water seeps under it, rot may start. A sudsy washing keeps it clean and a once-a-month waxing protects it.

Ceramic tile. This has traditionally been one of the most expensive counter-top materials. With the advent of new and faster installation methods, the price has dropped—although it is still expensive. New types of mortar resist decay and discoloration from grease, soaps, and cleansers. Tiles themselves last indefinitely, withstanding moisture, acids, heat, oil, and abrasion. But tile is noisy and can be hard on dishes. Washing with suds or household cleanser and water keeps tile clean.

Stainless steel. Most costly of the counter-top materials, it is also the most durable. Stainless steel is unaffected by heat, cold, acids, sharp edges, or almost any hard wear. Finger marks and water left to dry, though, will show, so towel-drying after washing is necessary. For a shine, polish stainless steel with a household cleanser or metal polish and buff off scratches with fine stainless-steel wool.

Wood. Set into counter work area, seasoned hardwoods make useful chopping blocks. Wood, of course, will stain and mar easily, but an occasional bleaching followed by a thin coat of mineral oil will restore a clean appearance. After washing, rinse wood well and dry immediately.

SNORING |

If your sleep has ever been interrupted by someone's buzzes, gurgles, whistles, snorts, or rumbles, snoring is no comic complaint. Millions of people, including men, women, and children, snore. In some cases it can be corrected. It depends on what causes the snoring.

The sound is produced by vibrations caused by the flow of air currents against the soft palate and other structures in the mouth and throat. Vibrations occur when the soft tissues are close to the throat lining. This fluttering is most likely to happen when air comes through both the nose and mouth. The membranes then can vibrate freely between twin air currents. Most responsible for adult snoring, say some doctors, is the uvula, the fleshy tip of the soft palate that hangs at the back of the throat and flutters when relaxed.

The highest percentage of cures has been in children, who usually snore because of enlarged adenoids or tonsils. The nasal pharynx (the space at the rear of the throat, behind the soft palate) is shallower in children than in adults. Enlarged adenoids can narrow this airway even more. The result is snoring. Surgery can correct this condition.

Snoring in adults may be caused by blockage in the nose or throat. A blocked nose can lead to mouth breathing, which, in turn, often leads to snoring. The nose may be blocked temporarily by any infection or allergy—a common cold, a sinus condition, or hay fever. These cause congestion and swelling in the mucous membranes. Treatment which relieves these conditions often relieves snoring. Wheezing, whistling, or snoring may also result from a deviated nasal septum, a condition in which the dividing wall of the nose is bent, twisted or deflected. Surgery may be used if the condition is serious.

The breathing passage might be partially blocked by polyps—soft, fleshy growths that hang at the back of the nose and sometimes into the upper part of the throat. This can lead to snoring, even when the mouth is closed. Again, surgery can correct this.

However, most snoring is caused by *other* factors which are much harder to eliminate. For example, jaws which do not close properly may produce mouth breathing and snoring. This condition may be corrected by orthodontia or by wearing an elastic mask around the head and jaws to keep the mouth closed. A person who has no teeth may also make a snoring sound if he sleeps without his dentures because his lips will vibrate with each breath.

Sleeping on the back may cause the tongue to drop back, partially obstructing the throat. This position also throws the soft palate backward. To stop such snoring, it may help to sleep on the side or face down.

The deep sleep that results from fatigue usually means greater relaxation and a change in muscle tone. The soft tissues in the pharynx vibrate more and the sleeper breathes more deeply. These conditions promote snoring even when the mouth is closed.

There are over three hundred antisnoring devices registered with the United States Patent Office. For example, one inventor devised a metal frame to encase the upper chest and neck, rigidly holding the wearer in a nonsnoring position. (Some doctors say you get a similar result by sleeping with a small pillow under the nape of the neck.) Chin straps have been used to keep the mouth closed. There is even a plastic strap to handcuff the snorer in a side position to the bedpost.

A simple home remedy may be as effective as any gadget. For example, one idea is to distract the listener by introducing another sound, such as a softly played radio. Nudging the snorer may also provide temporary relief by interrupting the deep breathing which causes the greatest rumbling. But make it a good-natured nudge. Much of the trouble caused by snoring is psychological: the way people react to one another's (or their own) little weaknesses. Surprisingly, it is a fact that some children find snoring a comforting sound, assuring them that father is there and all is well. It is quite possible that you snore at times, yourself, without realizing it.

And if nothing works, remember: there are always ear plugs.

SOFAS |

1. **The Lawson** sofa has a rectangular shape, and its frame is entirely covered. Usually the upholstery is divided into sections, with cushions at

the back and cushions (or occasionally one long cushion) on the seat. Cushions may be loose or permanently attached. The arms, rounded or straight, are lower than the back. The Lawson blends well with either contemporary or period furniture.

2. **The Tuxedo** sofa has arms the same height as the back; these may be straight or slightly curved. The back and seat may be divided into cushions. Because of its straight lines, the Tuxedo looks particularly good covered in stripes of any width or in geometrically patterned fabrics.

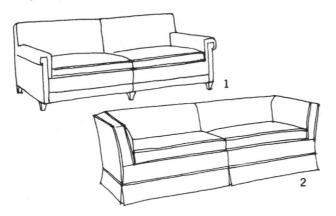

3. **The Sectional** sofa, another example of modern design, is made up of two or more sections that may be arranged to curve around or turn a corner. Like the contemporary sofa, it should be coupled with other modern pieces.

4. **The Contemporary** sofa is stripped of any excess ornamentation and may be light or bulky. Often the legs are metal; brass is popular. Textured fabrics, tweeds, and bright colors are especially effective. This style blends best with other modern pieces.

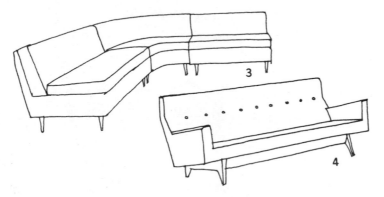

5. **The Louis XVI** sofa has an ornately carved wood frame and sturdy, tapered legs. It is usually upholstered in satin or brocade, and fits only into the most formal of rooms.

6. **The French Provincial** is a smaller, more delicate version of the Louis XVI sofa. The frame is usually fruitwood, and the design features flowing curves. The fabric is often light colored, and may be a small-scaled plaid, floral stripe, or toile. This sofa may be used with other Provincial furniture.

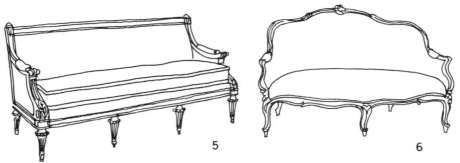

5   6

7. **The Duncan Phyfe** is an American designer's version of the Sheraton sofa, and is also carved. Legs curve outward; scroll or reed arms are typical. Fairly formal upholstery is usually used.

8. **The Victorian** sofa varies from love-seat size to a sofa large enough to seat four people. It's characterized by an oval inset in the back surrounded by carved wood. It can be used with other Victorian furniture or mixed with pieces that have a French flavor.

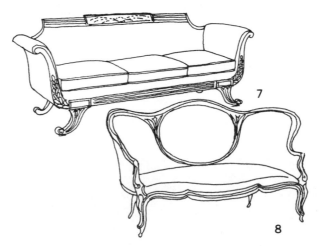

7

8

Not illustrated are two more popular styles: **The Chippendale** sofa has a curving back and arms and a wood frame (often mahogany). The legs are curved and delicately carved, and the fabric is usually damask. This sofa calls for formal surroundings. **The Sheraton** is characterized by a wood frame with bows, swags, or sheaves of wheat. Brass nailheads nearly always outline the frame. Like the Chippendale, the Sheraton sofa looks best with a background of elegance.

SOUPS | See CANNED SOUPS

SPICES | See SEASONINGS

STAIN INFORMATION | See also DRY CLEANING; LAUNDERING

Some stains, especially on badly soiled clothes or on fabrics that cannot be washed, will not respond to home treatment. They call for the technical knowledge and skill of the dry cleaner's expert "spotters." In most cases, washable fabrics can be treated successfully at home. If a dry-cleanable fabric is rough textured, not too light in color, and fairly clean over-all, stains listed on the following pages may be treated in reasonable safety. Follow these precautions:

Treat the stain promptly—before it dries, if possible.

On colored clothes, do not use any stain remover without first experimenting with a sample from the seam or other inconspicuous section.

Do not treat a stain if the result will be a clean area unsightly by contrast to the soiled remainder.

Do not tamper with light-colored fabrics, particularly in neutral or pastel tints.

Be wary of rayon or silk taffeta, moiré, shantung, and other crisp fabrics that water-spot quickly.

If in doubt, try only cool water and let the spot dry before trying a cleaning fluid. If neither is successful, do not experiment further, for the wrong treatment may set a stain. Send it to a dry cleaner.

To locate a dried stain, hold a single thickness of the fabric to the light. Or sponge the area lightly with water; the stain often will darken. Finding it now may prevent its becoming set and impossible to remove after pressing.

To prevent a ring forming, fold a clean absorbent cloth into a thick pad under the spot. Moisten another cloth sparingly with the stain remover. With grease stains, work on the wrong side of the material. With all other stains, work on the right side. Sponge from the edge of the spot toward its center. Do not let the stain remover flow; work a little of it into the cloth surrounding the stain and "feather out" the liquid to avoid a definite edge when the material dries. Pat the spot with dry cloth between applications. Move the pad under the spot from time to time as it absorbs the stain.

When a fresh stain is on an item, such as a tablecloth, that is normally laundered, the chances are good that it will "come out in the wash" if not set by hot water or the heat of an iron.

STAIN REMOVAL AGENTS |

Following is a list of the principal stain removal agents, in groups according to use. Refer to this list when looking up specific stains in the Stain Removal Dictionary (below), for guidance on the particular type of bleach, etc., employed.

ABSORBENT POWDERS

Chalk, corn meal, pepsin, talcum, cornstarch—for grease spots.

BLEACHES

Chlorine ("household") bleach, liquid or powdered—for white and color-fast cotton, linen, rayon, nylon, etc. (Do not use on resin-treated cottons, and check bleach label before using on acetates.) *Basic solution:* one table-spoon bleach to one quart water; soak fifteen minutes; rinse three times.

Oxygen ("fine fabric") bleaches, sodium perborate or hydrogen peroxide —for white wool and silk. *Basic solution:* two tablespoonfuls bleach to one gallon water; soak one-half hour or longer; rinse twice.

Oxalic acid solution—for rust stains. (Poisonous; use with care.)

Sodium thiosulfate or hyposulfite (photographer's "hypo")—for yellow-ing caused by chlorine. *Basic solution:* two tablespoonfuls per gallon of very hot water.

CLEANING FLUID OR POWDER—FOR DRY-CLEANABLE FABRICS

Caution: Use only a type that's not dangerously flammable or toxic. Because of fire hazard, do not use in a washer or put fluid-cleaned clothes in a dryer. Because of toxic fumes, do not use carbon tetrachloride.

SOLVENTS

Turpentine—for paint stains.

Denatured alcohol—mix with two parts water when using on acetate rayon or colored materials.

Acetone or amyl acetate—for fingernail polish and airplane glue stains.

Spray dry cleaner—for dissolving grease.

Soap or detergents—for water-soluble stains.

STAIN REMOVAL DICTIONARY | See also STAIN REMOVAL AGENTS

STAINS ON FABRICS

Airplane glue. *Washable fabrics (except acetate rayon).* Sponge the spot with acetone. Give it a chance to dissolve the glue, then wash in warm suds, and rinse. *Caution:* Never use acetone until you have tested it on a piece cut from a hidden section of the garment. Airplane glue on acetate rayon may dissolve the fabric. If fabric has not been affected, sponge with amyl acetate. Then wash in warm suds and rinse.

Dry-cleanable fabrics. Same as above, but do not wash.

Alcoholic beverages and soft drinks. *Washable fabrics (white).* Soak fresh stains in cool water; then wash in warm suds, and rinse. For old stains that have turned brown, use an appropriate bleach.

Washable fabrics (colored). Soak fresh stains in cool water, then wash in warm suds, and rinse. If the stain remains, make a solution of two tablespoonfuls hydrogen peroxide to each gallon of water. Test the solution. Soak one-half hour or longer, if necessary. Rinse twice.

Dry-cleanable fabrics. Sponge with cool water. Sometimes alcoholic beverages cause the dye to bleed and form a dye ring, which is very difficult to remove.

Black marks on dish towels. Black streaks from cooking utensils, particularly aluminum and cast iron, require hard rubbing with liquid laundry detergent directly on the stain. Remove as much as you can this way before the towels are washed and bleached.

Blood. *Washable fabrics (white).* Soak in cool water until stains turn light brown, then wash in warm suds. If the stains are old, add two tablespoonfuls household ammonia to each gallon of soapy water, and soak fifteen minutes. Then wash in warm suds with bleach, and rinse.

Washable fabrics (colored). As above; however, if household ammonia is used, test the solution first.

Dry-cleanable fabrics. Sponge with cool water.

Butter. *Washable fabrics.* If not removed in ordinary washing; treat like grease and oil (below).

Dry-cleanable fabrics. Use cleaning fluid or powder.

Candle wax. *Washable fabrics (white).* With a dull blade, scrape off wax; then sponge with cleaning fluid or let soak in fluid. If wax color remains, use household bleach for cotton, linen, and rayon. For white silk and wool, use one cupful of denatured alcohol and two cupfuls of water. Soak fifteen minutes. Wash in warm suds, and rinse three times.

Washable fabrics (colored). Treat like white silk and wool, above, but test alcohol solution.

For particulars on using stain removal agents, see page 326

Dry-cleanable fabrics. Treat like colored washable fabrics, except do not soak; sponge with alcohol.

Candy (except chocolate). *Washable fabrics.* Most candy stains come out in ordinary washing.

Dry-cleanable fabrics. Sponge with warm water.

Carbon paper. *Washable fabrics.* Sponge with cleaning fluid. Wash in warm suds, and rinse.

Dry-cleanable fabrics. Try sponging with cleaning fluid or use cleaning powder. If this does not work, send to a dry cleaner.

Catsup and tomato sauce. *Washable fabrics.* Soak stains in cool water; then wash in warm suds, and rinse. If stains remain, use an appropriate bleach.

Dry-cleanable fabrics. Sponge with cool water.

Chewing gum. *Washable fabrics.* Soak in cleaning fluid until gum loosens and can be scraped off. Wash in warm suds, and rinse.

Dry-cleanable fabrics. Sponge with cleaning fluid.

Chocolate and cocoa. *Washable fabrics (white).* Sometimes difficult to remove. If candy caused the spot, scrape off with a dull blade. Wash in warm suds, and rinse.

Stains from chocolate syrup or sauce, and from cocoa, should be sponged with cleaning fluid or soaked in the fluid before washing with an appropriate bleach.

Washable fabrics (colored). For chocolate-candy stains, treat like white washable fabrics. Sponge stains from chocolate syrup or cocoa with cleaning fluid. If stains remain, make a solution of one teaspoonful of sodium perborate and one pint of hydrogen peroxide. Test the solution, then sponge. Wash in warm suds, and rinse.

Dry-cleanable fabrics. Sponge with cool water. Let dry; then sponge with cleaning fluid, or use cleaning powder.

Cod-liver oil. Spots are colorless when fresh and not likely to be noticed at the time they should be removed. Examine children's clothes carefully after cod-liver oil has been given, and treat immediately.

Washable fabrics (white). Soak stains in cleaning fluid, and rub them between the fingers. Then wash in hot suds, and rinse. If stains are old or have turned light brown from ironing, use an appropriate bleach.

Washable fabrics (colored). Soak in cleaning fluid. Then wash in warm suds, and rinse. If stains remain, make a solution of two tablespoonfuls of hydrogen peroxide to each gallon of water. Test the solution. Then soak stains one-half hour or longer, if necessary. Rinse twice.

Dry-cleanable fabrics. Sponge with cleaning fluid.

Coffee and tea. *Washable fabrics (white).* Soak fresh stains in cool water. Then wash in warm suds, and rinse. If heavy cream was used in the bev-

For particulars on using stain removal agents, see page 326

erage, sponge with cleaning fluid, or let soak in fluid before soaking in cool water. If stains remain, use an appropriate bleach.

Washable fabrics (colored). Treat like white silk and wool, but test the bleach solution.

Dry-cleanable fabrics. First sponge with cool water. Let dry; then sponge with cleaning fluid, or use cleaning powder. When cream and sugar have been used, old or ironed-in stains may remain. These are impossible, even for a dry cleaner, to remove.

Curry. *Washable fabrics.* Work warm glycerin into stains. Flush out with water. Add a few drops of household ammonia. Flush out with water. If stain remains, add a few drops of 3 per cent hydrogen peroxide. Flush out with water.

Dry-cleanable fabrics. Curry rarely can be removed by home method. Consult a dry cleaner.

Dye and running colors. *Washable fabrics (white).* It is not always possible to remove a dye completely. Special color removers can be used on any washable fabric if directions on the package are followed. They are not successful on all types of dye; however, they are inexpensive and worth a try.

Washable fabrics (colored). The only way to remove streaks of dye is to remove all the color with a color remover. Then redye the garment.

Dry-cleanable fabrics. Dye stains cannot be removed by home methods. Consult a reliable dry cleaner.

Egg. *Washable fabrics.* Scrape off with a dull knife, then sponge with cold water. (Do *not* use hot water; it sets the egg.) If stain remains, sprinkle with pepsin powder and work it in with hands. Let stand one-half hour; rinse thoroughly.

Dry-cleanable fabrics. Sponge with cold water; dry; and sponge with cleaning fluid.

Fruit and berry stains. *Washable fabrics.* See alcohol and soft-drink stains. Fresh peaches, blackberries and blueberries may need a second treatment.

Dry-cleanable fabrics. First sponge with cool water. Immediately work liquid laundry detergent into stain. Let stand several hours. Then test a drop or two of white vinegar on a hidden section of the garment. If no color change occurs, apply a few drops of vinegar to stain and let it remain a minute or two. Sponge with cool water.

Glue (not airplane). *Washable fabrics.* Soak glue in warm suds until dissolved. Then wash in warm suds, and rinse.

Dry-cleanable fabrics. Sponge with warm water.

Grass. *Washable fabrics (white).* Wash stains in hot suds, rubbing well. Rinse. If stains remain, use appropriate bleach, or a special color remover.

For particulars on using stain removal agents, see page 326

Washable fabrics (colored). Wash stains in warm suds, rubbing well. If stains remain, make a solution of one teaspoonful of sodium perborate to one pint of hydrogen peroxide. Test the solution. Then soak stain one-half hour or longer; rinse twice. For very stubborn stains, sprinkle with sodium perborate while material is damp. Let stand one-half hour. Rinse twice.

Dry-cleanable fabrics. Sponge with cleaning fluid, or use cleaning powder. Make a solution of one cupful of denatured alcohol and two cupfuls of water. Test the solution. Sponge stains with solution. Sponge with cool water.

Gravy. *Washable fabrics.* Sponge with cleaning fluid, or let soak in fluid. If stains remain, wash in warm suds, and rinse.

Dry-cleanable fabrics. Sponge with cool water. Let dry. Then sponge with cleaning fluid, or use cleaning powder.

Grease and oil. *Washable fabrics (white).* For white washable cotton, linen, and rayon, soak in hot suds. Then rinse. ("Hot" means far hotter than the hands can stand. If washing does not take out stains, these fabrics can be boiled.) If stains are old, before washing, sponge with cleaning fluid, or let soak about ten minutes in fluid. Then wash in hot suds, and rinse.

For white silk and wool, sponge with cleaning fluid, or let soak in fluid, then wash in warm suds. Rinse. Do not boil silk or wool.

Washable fabrics (colored). Sponge with cleaning fluid, or let soak in fluid. Then wash in warm suds, and rinse. Do not use hot suds; do not boil.

Dry-cleanable fabrics. Sponge with cleaning fluid, or use cleaning powder.

Note: Stains are rarely seen until they have been ironed; they are then more difficult to remove. All table coverings should be inspected carefully before they are washed, so stains can be treated before laundering.

Ice cream. Ice cream is a combination of foods, so several treatments frequently are required.

Washable fabrics (white). Vanilla ice cream: Soak in cool water, wash in warm suds, and rinse.

Fruit ice cream: Soak fresh stains in cool water; wash in warm suds, and rinse. If stains remain, use appropriate bleach.

Chocolate ice cream: Before washing, sponge with cleaning fluid, or soak in fluid. Then wash in warm suds, and rinse. If stains remain, use appropriate bleach.

Washable fabrics (colored). Treat vanilla ice cream stains as described for white washable fabrics; treat fruit ice cream stains as for washable white silk and wool, but test the bleach solution. Treat chocolate ice cream stains as described for washable white silk and wool, but test bleach.

Dry-cleanable fabrics. Sponge with cool water. Let dry. Then sponge with cleaning fluid, or use cleaning powder.

For particulars on using stain removal agents, see page 326

Ink. Inks differ in composition; sometimes it is necessary to try several methods of stain removal. So-called washable inks usually are removed if washed either before or just after the ink has dried. India or drawing ink, typewriter-ribbon, mimeograph, and other inks in the "permanent" class rarely can be removed by home methods. However, promptness helps, and the following methods should at least lighten the stain on dark-colored articles. If light colors do not respond, take to a reliable dry cleaner.

Note: The old-time theory that milk removes ink stains is not only false but harmful. Milk adds a protein stain, which makes removal of the original ink spot all the more difficult.

Washable fabrics (white). Rinse freely in cool water. Then wash in hot suds to which a few drops of household ammonia have been added, and rinse. If stains remain, soak in hot suds for twenty minutes. Rinse. If stains persist, use appropriate bleach for white cotton, linen, and rayon. For white silk and wool, use oxalic acid. (Ask druggist for a 5-per cent solution. Oxalic acid is poisonous. Handle carefully.) Soak stains in solution for fifteen minutes. Rinse three times. To last rinse, add a few drops of household ammonia.

Washable fabrics (colored). Rinse freely in cool water. Then wash in warm suds to which a few drops of household ammonia have been added. Rinse. If stains remain, bleach as recommended for white silk and wool, above.

Dry-cleanable fabrics. Sponge with cool water. If stains remain, make a solution of one cupful of denatured alcohol and two cupfuls of water. Test, then sponge with solution. Sponge with cool water.

Ball-point ink stains. To remove this type of "dry" ink, place an absorbent cloth pad beneath the stain, lightly moisten stain with denatured alcohol, and blot immediately with a second cloth. Repeat several times. Then wash washable fabrics; sponge dry-cleanable fabrics with warm suds followed by clear water. On colored fabrics, test alcohol first for effect on color.

Lemon or orange juice. *Washable fabrics (white).* Fresh stains usually are removed in washing. If stains are old or have turned brown from ironing, use appropriate bleach.

Washable fabrics (colored). Wash in warm suds. If lemon juice has changed the fabric's color, rinse freely in cool water. Then hold stained fabric over fumes from a bottle of household ammonia. Have white vinegar ready to sponge on quickly if the color changes too much. Rinse.

Dry-cleanable fabrics. Sponge with cool water. If lemon juice has changed the fabric's color, use ammonia fumes and white vinegar, as above. Sponge with cool water.

Lipstick. *Washable fabrics.* The newer "long-lasting" lipstick products cannot be removed in normal washing. Soak in a full-strength general-purpose liquid cleaner, rubbing gently. Or soak in cleaning fluid; then wash.

For particulars on using stain removal agents, see page 326

Dry-cleanable fabrics. Sponge with cleaning fluid, or use cleaning powder.

Liquid makeup. *Washable fabrics (white).* Brush out as much of the powder as possible. Then, before washing, sponge with cleaning fluid, or soak in fluid. Wash in warm suds, and rinse. If stains remain, use appropriate bleach.

Washable fabrics (colored). Treat like washable white silk and wool, but test bleach solution.

Dry-cleanable fabrics. Brush out powder; then sponge with cleaning fluid, or use cleaning powder.

Mascara. *Washable fabrics.* Waterproof mascara cannot be removed in regular washing. A gentle rubbing of the stains with full-strength general-purpose liquid cleaner is the best method. Rinse completely.

Dry-cleanable fabrics. Sponge with cleaning fluid, or use cleaning powder. Then make a solution of one cupful of denatured alcohol and two cupfuls of water. Test, sponge with solution, then with cool water.

Meat juice. *Washable fabrics.* Sponge with cool water. Let dry. Then sponge with cleaning fluid. Wash in warm suds, and rinse.

Dry-cleanable fabrics. Sponge with cool water. Let dry. Then sponge with cleaning fluid, or use cleaning powder.

REMEDIES FOR MEDICINE STAINS

Medicines. Dry-cleanable fabrics, particularly if stained with dark medicines like argyrol or silver nitrate, should be sent to a dry cleaner. Medicines with a sugar-syrup base frequently can be removed by washing in warm suds. A thick, gummy medicine sometimes responds to this treatment:

Washable fabrics. Soften stain by rubbing with Vaseline. Let stand fifteen minutes; then soak in cleaning fluid. Wash in warm suds, and rinse.

Dry-cleanable fabrics. With a dull blade, scrape off as much of the medicine as possible. Sponge with cleaning fluid. Repeat several times.

Following are remedies for identifiable medicine stains:

Argyrol. *Washable fabrics (white).* Soak in cool water; then wash in warm suds. Rinse. If stains remain, use appropriate bleach for white cotton, linen, and rayon. If this fails, sprinkle on powdered pepsin while stains are damp. Work it well into the cloth. Let stand one-half hour or longer. Rinse. Put a few drops of tincture of iodine on stains. Let stand ten or fifteen minutes. Then soak or sponge with a solution made with a few crystals of sodium thiosulfate (photographer's "hypo") dissolved in one-half cup water. Rinse twice.

For white silk and wool, use two tablespoonfuls of hydrogen peroxide to each gallon of water, and soak one-half hour or longer, if necessary. Rinse twice.

For particulars on using stain removal agents, see page 326

Washable fabrics (colored). Treat like washable white silk and wool, but test bleach. If stains are not removed, treat like white cotton, above.

Cough medicine. *Washable fabrics.* Wash in warm suds. If stains remain, try the treatment suggested for removing silver nitrate.

Dry-cleanable fabrics. Sponge with cool water. If stains remain, send to a dry cleaner.

Iodine. *Washable fabrics (white).* Soak fresh iodine stains in cool water, then wash in warm suds, and rinse. If stains are old, use one cupful of household ammonia and two cupfuls of water; soak fifteen minutes. Wash in warm suds, and rinse twice.

Washable fabrics (colored). Treat like white washable fabrics. However, if ammonia is used, test the solution. Then soak 15 minutes, wash in warm suds, and rinse. (If ammonia has changed a fabric's color, it sometimes can be restored by immediate application of white vinegar.)

Dry-cleanable fabrics. Make a solution of a few crystals of sodium thiosulfate and one-half cupful of water. Test the solution. Sponge with solution, then with cool water.

Mercurochrome. *Washable fabrics (white).* Very difficult to remove unless treated before stains have dried. Rinse out in cool water. Mix one cupful of denatured alcohol and two cupfuls of water, and sponge or soak stains in solution. Wash in warm suds, and rinse. Follow with appropriate bleach.

Washable fabrics (colored). Treat as above but first test the solution. Then sponge or soak stains in solution. Wash in warm suds, and rinse with water to which a few drops of household ammonia have been added. If stains remain, use hydrogen peroxide bleach solution. Then soak in white vinegar for fifteen minutes, or until stains disappear.

Dry-cleanable fabrics. Test alcohol solution, then sponge stains with solution. Follow by sponging with cool water to which a few drops of household ammonia have been added. If stains remain, sponge with white vinegar, then with cool water.

Paregoric. *Washable fabrics.* Make a solution of one cupful of denatured alcohol and two cupfuls of water. Test for a colored garment. Then sponge or soak stain with solution, and wash in warm suds. Rinse.

Dry-cleanable fabrics. Treat like washable fabrics, but sponge with cool water instead of washing.

Silver nitrate. *Washable fabrics.* Sponge with cool water to get rid of as much stain as possible. Then wash in warm suds. If stains remain, make a solution of one part tincture of iodine to three parts of water. Test for a colored garment. Then sponge with solution. If stains remain, dissolve a few crystals of sodium thiosulfate in one-half cupful of water, and sponge. If stains are not removed, repeat applications of iodine and sodium-thiosulfate solutions. Finally, wash in warm suds.

Dry-cleanable fabrics. Stains rarely can be removed satisfactorily.

For particulars on using stain removal agents, see page 326

OTHER STAINS ON FABRICS, CONTINUED

Mildew. Mildew is a mold growth, which attacks the fibers of fabric and weakens them. It is impossible to remove unless stains are discovered before they have stood too long. (See article on MILDEW.)

Washable fabrics (white). Wash in warm suds. Then rinse. If stains remain, use appropriate bleach.

Washable fabrics (colored). Treat like washable white silk and wool, but test bleach before you use it.

Dry-cleanable fabrics. Stains are likely to be found only in very hot, humid climates. Take stained garment to a dry cleaner.

Milk and cream. *Washable fabrics.* If grease spots remain after normal washing, soak in cleaning fluid. Wash in warm suds, and rinse.

Dry-cleanable fabrics. Use cleaning fluid or powder.

Mud. *Washable fabrics.* Let mud dry. Then brush off. Wash in warm suds, and rinse.

Dry-cleanable fabrics. Sponge with cool water. If greaselike stains remain, sponge with cleaning fluid or use cleaning powder.

Mustard. *Washable fabrics (white).* Work glycerin into stains. Then wash in warm suds. Rinse. If stains remain, use appropriate bleach.

Washable fabrics (colored). Treat like washable white silk and wool, but test bleach before you use it.

Dry-cleanable fabrics. Make a solution of one cupful of denatured alcohol and two cupfuls of water. Sponge stains with solution. Sponge with cool water.

Nail polish. Follow directions for removing airplane glue.

Paint and varnish. Sometimes hardened paint is impossible to remove. Oil-base paints and varnish are more difficult than quick-drying oil-emulsion paints.

Washable fabrics. With a dull blade, scrape off as much paint or varnish as possible. Rub Vaseline into stain to soften it. Then soak in turpentine (U.S.P. quality) until stain has softened. Rub occasionally. Then wash in warm suds. Rinse.

Dry-cleanable fabrics. Sponge with U.S.P. quality turpentine. If stains remain, take garment to a dry cleaner.

Finger paints. *Washable fabrics.* Soak in cold water, then wash in warm suds. Rub lightly if paints have dried. Rinse.

Dry-cleanable fabrics: Place absorbent towel under stain, and sponge lightly with damp cloth on right side of fabric. If paint has dried, soften with cleaning fluid, then sponge with water.

Pencil (indelible). *Washable fabrics.* Sponge with cleaning fluid, or soak in fluid. Then wash in warm suds using stiff-bristled brush if stain is stub-

For particulars on using stain removal agents, see page 326

born. Bleaching is usually of no value. Do not use water first, as this spreads dye.

Dry-cleanable fabrics. See treatment suggested for candle wax. If stains remain, send to a dry cleaner.

Pencil (lead). *Washable fabrics.* If marks don't come out in wash, rub suds into them, and wash in warm suds again. Rinse.

Dry-cleanable fabrics. Mix one cupful of denatured alcohol and two cupfuls of water. Test, then sponge stains with solution. Sponge with cool water.

Perfume. Follow directions for removing alcoholic beverages and soft drinks.

Perspiration. *Washable fabrics (white).* Work full-strength liquid laundry detergent into stains; follow by washing in warm suds and bleaching.

When the garment has picked up a fugitive dye from a suit or coat lining, follow the treatment given for dyes and running colors.

Washable fabrics (colored). Perspiration frequently changes a fabric's color. Sometimes the color can be restored by holding the stain over the fumes of a bottle of household ammonia or by sponging it with white vinegar. (Sometimes both are needed.) Then wash in warm suds, and rinse. If stain remains, make a solution of two tablespoonfuls of hydrogen peroxide to each gallon of water. Test, then soak the stain one-half hour or longer, if necessary. Rinse twice.

To get rid of perspiration odor that washing in warm suds has failed to remove, soak in a solution made with three tablespoonfuls of salt to each quart of warm water, one hour or longer.

Dry-cleanable fabrics. A perspiration-stained garment should be sent to a dry cleaner. When it has an under-arm odor that dry cleaning has failed to remove, try washing underarm sections with warm suds. Gather a section in your left hand, and tuck the rest of the garment under your arm. If a suit jacket is lined, loosen lining so jacket can be treated separately. Work soiled section in suds until it is thoroughly clean. Squeeze, and rinse. Then pat as dry as possible with bath towel. Straighten garment, and place it on a hanger to dry. Then press, or send to dry cleaner if necessary.

Plastic starch. The new "permanent" starches last through many washings. If you should overstarch with one of these, soak the item, if it is colorfast, in rubbing alcohol until slipperiness disappears. Then wash in the regular manner.

Rubber cement. *Washable fabrics.* Apply Vaseline to stain to loosen it. Let stand fifteen minutes. Then sponge or soak in cleaning fluid. Wash in warm suds; rinse.

Dry-cleanable fabrics. As above, but do not wash.

Rust. *Washable fabrics.* Wash in warm suds. Rinse. If stains remain, use

For particulars on using stain removal agents, see page 326

oxalic acid. (Ask druggist for a 5 per cent solution. Oxalic acid is poisonous. Handle it carefully.) Soak fifteen minutes. Rinse three times. To the final rinse, add a few drops of household ammonia.

Dry-cleanable fabrics. Rust stains cannot be removed by home methods. Consult a reliable dry cleaner.

Salad dressings. *Washable fabrics.* Stains usually are removed in washing. If grease stains remain, soak in cleaning fluid. Wash in warm suds, and rinse.

Dry-cleanable fabrics. Sponge with cool water. Let dry. Then either sponge with cleaning fluid, or use cleaning powder.

Scorch. Heavy scorch means the fibers of the fabric have been injured and the scorch cannot be taken out. Slight scorch on cotton, linen, and rayon frequently can be removed; but silk and wool seldom can be restored.

Washable fabrics (white). Wash in warm suds. Rinse. If stains remain, use appropriate bleach.

Washable fabrics (colored). Wash in warm suds. Rinse. If stains remain, make a solution of two tablespoonfuls of hydrogen peroxide to each gallon of water. Test solution. Soak stains one-half hour or longer, if necessary. Rinse twice.

Dry-cleanable fabrics. Send to dry cleaner.

Shoe polish. *Washable fabrics (white).* Stains from paste shoe polish and white shoe dressing usually can be removed by washing in warm suds. If grease stains remain (as from a paste polish), soak in cleaning fluid; wash again in warm suds, and rinse.

Treat stains from colored liquid shoe dressing like stains from paste shoe polish. To get rid of dye stains, use appropriate bleach.

Liquid shoe dressings do not always respond to treatment, and brown shades for leather and suede are less likely to come out than black.

Washable fabrics (colored). Wash stains from paste and liquid shoe polish in warm suds, and rinse. If grease stains remain, soak in cleaning fluid. If dye stains remain, make a solution of two tablespoonfuls of hydrogen peroxide to each gallon of water. Test solution. Soak stains in the solution one-half hour or longer. Rinse twice.

Dry-cleanable fabrics. To remove liquid or paste shoe polish, sponge with cool water. Let dry. If grease stains remain, sponge with cleaning fluid, or use cleaning powder. Dye stains cannot be removed by home methods.

Tar. *Washable fabrics.* Soften stain by rubbing with Vaseline. Let stand fifteen minutes; then soak in cleaning fluid. Wash in warm suds, and rinse.

Dry-cleanable fabrics. With a dull blade, scrape off as much tar as possible. Sponge with cleaning fluid. Repeat several times, if necessary.

Urine. White washable fabrics present little problem, because fresh stains can be washed out readily. Urine may change the color of colored fabrics. This treatment should improve the appearance:

For particulars on using stain removal agents, see page 326

Washable fabrics. Make a solution of two tablespoonfuls of household ammonia to one cupful of water, and soak stains in solution. If this does not restore color, sponge with white vinegar. Wash in warm suds. Rinse. If stains remain, the dye probably has been destroyed.

Dry-cleanable fabrics. Send to a dry cleaner.

Vaseline. *Washable fabrics.* Sponge with cleaning fluid, or let soak in fluid. Wash in warm suds, and rinse.

Dry-cleanable fabrics. Use cleaning fluid or powder.

STAINS ON BATHTUBS AND BASINS

Rust stains on sinks and plumbing porcelain often are troublesome. There is a special cleanser for this purpose. Sprinkle cleanser on a damp cloth; rub discolored surface until stains are removed. Rinse, and wipe dry. The same cleanser removes rust from bathroom and kitchen plumbing fixtures and other corroded metals. Treatment has to be repeated periodically, because some of the original finish is usually gone.

STAINS ON FLOORS

Grease on cement floors. Make a strong solution of trisodium phosphate (sold in paint stores) and water. With a stiff brush, scour stains. Rinse well. If stains remain, sprinkle on some trisodium phosphate, moisten with water; let stand for several hours; then remove. Rinse.

Ink and other stains on marble floors. Marble never should be treated with acids or strong solutions, because they remove the polish. For ink stains, use a household bleach. Saturate a thick pad with undiluted bleach, and leave it on the stain for several hours. Most other stains can be corrected by using a paste of household cleanser mixed with hot water. Apply a thick coating, and let it remain several days. Then lift off. Special cleansers and stain removers for marble can be purchased in hardware stores.

STAINS ON MATTRESSES

Blood. Mix cornstarch into a paste with cold water. Apply thickly to stain, and brush away when dry. Repeat until stain disappears.

Perspiration. Sponge very lightly with warm water, to which a few drops of vinegar have been added. Then sprinkle powdered pepsin over stain, and work well into ticking. Let stand several hours, keeping pepsin slightly moist. Let dry; then brush off powder.

Medicine. For color stains, sponge with a solution of one cupful of denatured alcohol and two cupfuls of water. Sponge with warm water. Let dry. For greasy stains, sprinkle on cleaning powder, let stand until it absorbs grease; then brush off.

For particulars on using stain removal agents, see page 326

Urine. Sponge very lightly with warm salt water made with one-half cupful of salt and one quart of water.

STAINS ON RUGS AND CARPETS

Animal stains. Sponge out immediately with cool water. Repeat sponging rather than saturate cloth, for rug must not be made too wet. Then with medicine dropper, apply solution of one tablespoonful white vinegar to one cup of warm water. Allow to remain fifteen minutes; then sponge with suds made with one teaspoonful detergent to one quart warm water; rinse with damp cloth.

Beverages. Sponge with lukewarm water; repeat several times. Then sponge with suds made as above. Rinse by rubbing with a cloth wrung out of clear water.

Candy or sugar. Scrape off with dull knife or spatula. Sponge with lukewarm water, working from edges toward center of stain. Then sponge with suds made as above.

Chewing gum. Soften around edges with cleaning fluid, or cover gum with rug-cleaning powder. Wait several minutes; then lift up gum with dull edge of knife.

Food. Scrape off any sticky deposits with dull knife, then remove water-soluble substances first by sponging with lukewarm water. If grease stains remain, sponge with cleaning fluid or use cleaning powder.

Furniture or shoe polish. Difficult to remove, but first sponge with detergent solution as above. After the area dries, sponge with dry-cleaning fluid.

Mud. Allow to dry completely; then eliminate with vacuum cleaner. If stain remains, suspect some other ingredient such as road oil (see GREASE AND OIL below).

Paint, varnish, and shellac. For paint and varnish, apply turpentine with eye dropper and sponge from outer edge toward center. Then sponge in same manner with cleaning fluid. For shellac, use denatured alcohol in place of turpentine. If stains remain, professional cleaning is required.

Grease and oil. For road oil and axle grease, scrape off as much as possible with a dull blade. Then sponge with cleaning fluid. Or apply cleaning powder; let stand to absorb the grease; then brush out. Also see FOOD, above.

Ink. Only washable-ink stains can be treated with any success; permanent inks rarely respond. First, with a blotter take up as much ink as possible. Then sponge with clear water. Be sure to sponge toward center, to avoid spreading ink.

Nail polish. With eye dropper, apply amyl acetate (from drugstore) directly on stain. Wait a few minutes; sponge with clean cloth, working from outer edge toward center. *Caution:* Stains of this kind and attempts

For particulars on using stain removal agents, see page 326

to remove them may damage rugs made of synthetic fibers (acetate fiber particularly). If in doubt, professional cleaning is safest.

Rust. Requires professional cleaning.

STAINS ON UPHOLSTERY

Upholstery is difficult to treat for stains, because it isn't possible to put an absorbent pad under the material. Also, the stain remover may affect the color. Before attempting to remove any stain, test the remover on an inconspicuous section of the upholstery. Then treat as for rugs and carpets.

STAINS ON WALLPAPER

Grease. Mild grease stains can be removed by fuller's earth or a rug-cleaning powder moistened with dry-cleaning fluid. Spread paste on spotted surface; let it remain until dry. Then remove with soft, clean cloth. Repeat if necessary. Sometimes a ring is visible after powder has been removed. If so, apply a mixture of powder and water. Let dry, and wipe off. Also effective is a grease-dissolving spray cleaner used according to manufacturer's directions.

Food stains. Brush off any clinging food, and if the wallpaper is washable, sponge with cloth wrung out of warm suds. If grease stains remain, apply treatment suggested above.

STAINS ON WALLS AND WOODWORK

Grease on painted surfaces. Use general-purpose liquid cleaner in a solution of one-quarter cup per gallon of hot water for washable paint.

Crayon marks. Follow treatment suggested for removal of grease from painted surfaces. If marks are still visible, sponge with cleaning fluid. If a ring remains, apply a mixture of fuller's earth and water. Let dry, and brush or wipe off.

Lipstick. Follow treatment suggested for removal of grease from painted surfaces.

For particulars on using stain removal agents, see page 326

STATIONERY |

Writing paper, whether for yourself or for a gift, can be of many grades. Some similar grades are difficult to tell apart. Since personal stationery usually is purchased in relatively small quantities, most people can afford to splurge a little for the sake of high quality and the good impression it makes. These points can help you to select a quality paper.

Rag-content paper makes the best stationery. It should have at least 25 per cent rag fiber to qualify (ordinary papers are made from wood pulp).

Paper made from 100 per cent rag fiber is the finest you can buy. Though more expensive, it does not become brittle or yellow.

A watermark is another sign of quality. If you hold a single sheet up to a light, you will see the watermark—the manufacturer's name or trademark design.

Texture can also be checked by holding paper up to a light. Any pattern or mottling should be fairly even. Obvious spots or defects indicate poor quality.

Finishes and patterns—such as vellum, plaid, kid, suede, or linen—do not determine the quality or appropriateness of the paper. Your selection of a finish or pattern depends entirely on personal preference. If you are not sure about a gift recipient's taste, buy a more conservative style. Be particularly cautious about color. Although pastel writing paper is now considered in good taste, select white, ivory, or a subdued shade of pale blue or gray when uncertain.

Handwriting size is another factor to consider in selecting writing paper. Each style of note or letter paper comes in different sizes. A person with very fine handwriting would probably want a smaller sheet, while bold writing is best accommodated on a larger scale.

One word of warning: Order paper early if it is to be printed or engraved for a gift needed by a certain date. It may take several weeks to fill the order.

STEAKS | See also MEAT

When it's called a Delmonico or a shell steak, you may have trouble identifying the exact cut. Below is a list of common steaks, giving first the name used by the United States Department of Agriculture and the National Live Stock and Meat Board, then other names by which the cut is known in various sections of the country. To make sure of getting the cut you want, check the sketches under MEAT.

1. **Club steak.** Delmonico steak, T-bone steak, porterhouse steak, sirloin strip steak.

2. **Top loin steak.** New York cut, Kansas City steak, boneless hip steak, shell steak, boneless hotel steak, minute sirloin steak, loin strip steak, Delmonico steak, club steak, boneless sirloin steak.

3. **Porterhouse and T-bone steaks.** Tenderloin steak, club steak.

4. **Tenderloin.** Filet mignon, Chateaubriand, filet.

5. **Sirloin steak.** Hip steak, short hip steak, sirloin butt steak, rump steak.

6. **Flank steak.** London broil, cube steak, chicken steak, minute steak.

7. **Rib eye steak.** Market steak, Spencer steak, beauty steak, center cut steak, boneless rib steak, country club steak, regular roll steak, New York club steak, Delmonico steak, club steak, boneless club steak.

	TENDER			LESS TENDER	
BEEF					
VEAL PORK LAMB					
	T-bone	Rib bone	Wedge bone	Round bone	Blade bone

Tender meat cuts. Regardless of the name given to a steak (or any other cut of meat), there's an easy way to tell the tender cuts—by the shape of the bone. Study the chart, or take it along with you the next time you go shopping. (Remember, though, that there can be a big difference in tenderness of the same cut of meat, depending on the brand or grade.)

STOVES | See KITCHEN RANGES

STORMS AND DISASTERS |

In most civilized areas of the world, the violence of nature has been so tamed that people largely ignore it. Hence when disaster strikes, it catches victims unprepared. Consider, though, that earthquakes, floods, high winds, severe lightning storms, and the like occur *somewhere* almost daily, making newspaper headlines; and that they tend to hit places that have been hit before. In any area that has a history of such a disaster, even a long time ago, a few simple precautions kept in reserve can help to minimize possible injuries and property losses should nature strike again with unexpected force.

In areas which periodically are threatened by hurricanes, tornadoes, or floods, authorities such as the American Red Cross, the Office of Civil Defense, and the United States Public Health Service advise that you keep a number of items immediately available in case you must quickly evacuate your home. Among them are a first-aid kit, flashlight with fresh batteries and bulbs, portable radio with fresh batteries, portable stove, a strong rope, food that does not require refrigeration and can be eaten cold, a change of clothing for every family member, eyeglasses and currently used prescription medicines.

Know in advance various evacuation routes from your community. Most important, follow directions of the local disaster control group. Keep these points in mind:

HURRICANES

The most severe hurricanes occur in late summer and early fall, usually along the Gulf of Mexico and Atlantic coastlines. These storms and the tide and flood conditions they produce can cause heavy property losses and deaths. Follow radio and television forecasts by the United States Weather Bureau and be prepared to head for shelters set up under the Hurricane Watch of the American Red Cross. Move quickly if told to evacuate.

Even without any evacuation order, bring garden furniture, tools, awnings, and other loose or easily detached articles indoors. Board up windows or close storm shutters. Fill the bathtub, washbasins, and other vessels with water to assure a temporary supply should water be cut off or contaminated by the storm. Open windows several inches on the side away from the wind. This allows interior air pressure to match the dropping air pressure outside. Extreme differences can wreck the house.

Remain indoors, preferably in a brick or concrete house and away from windows. Every hurricane has a center or eye which brings a deceptive lull, occasionally for as long as thirty minutes. Stay where you are during this calm period. The wind will return from the opposite direction, perhaps with greater force. Do not touch fallen wires. Report them to police or power companies.

TORNADOES

These extreme wind storms are most common in April, May, and June in the south and south-central area ranging from Texas into Nebraska and Iowa. But they have struck during every month and in every state. They occur most frequently from 3 P.M. to 7 P.M.

Tornadoes may strike with little warning. However, if you are alerted, turn off electric and fuel lines. Open windows several inches on the north and east. As with a hurricane, this allows interior air pressure to drop as pressure outside decreases. Fill receptacles with water. Bring inside items that may be blown away or torn loose. Turn refrigerator and freezer controls to the coldest settings to maintain food as long as possible should power be cut off.

The safest place is a storm cellar or the southwest corner of a basement. Get under a piece of heavy furniture against an inside wall if there is no storm shelter or basement. Stay away from windows. In a school or other large building, go to the basement or stand against an inside wall on the lowest floor. Stay out of gymnasiums, auditoriums, or other large rooms with unsupported roofs. If away from a building, lie flat in a ditch or other ground depression.

In an automobile, the Red Cross advises that you may be able to outrun a tornado by moving at right angles to its path. Its direction is toward you if the funnel-shaped cloud appears to grow rapidly larger. If in doubt, stop the car and lie in a roadside ditch.

FLOODS

Flooding is the nation's most common disaster. If the flood is the flash (suddenly appearing) type, you can do little except try to get out of its path.

You can prepare, however, if you are warned of slowly rising water. Keep your radio or television set on for late reports. Move household goods to high ground or the highest floor. Food or other items from the refrigerator and kitchen cabinets should be put in baskets. Place rubber bands around cans so labels will not wash off. If dishes, bedding, and furniture are to be moved, pack them well. Write your name and address on the carton or back of each piece of furniture with crayon.

If possible, remove oil and gas burners from stoves, furnaces, and stokers, and electric motors from appliances too large to be moved. Store these parts out of the water's path. Plug electrical outlets to keep out silt. Turn off the burner under the water heater. Board up windows. Bring outdoor items inside.

Eat before you leave your home. When you leave, take along prescription drugs that are needed regularly, infant formula and special diet requirements for other family members, blankets and pillows, eyeglasses and false teeth. Then turn off the main electrical switch. Be sure your car's gas tank is filled.

EARTHQUAKES

Because an earthquake is unpredictable, little advance planning can be done by an individual. If you are indoors when an earthquake occurs, get under a piece of heavy furniture or a bed, or crouch in a doorway between rooms. Persons outdoors should get as far as possible from buildings to avoid falling debris. Those unable to get out of a built-up area should stand under the frame of the nearest doorway. Stay away from masonry walls, chimneys, power and telephone poles. After an earthquake, stay out of buildings until advised to return by authorities.

THUNDERSTORMS

Knowing how to act in a lightning storm can be important. Lightning causes more deaths each year in the United States—an average of 230—

than tornadoes or hurricanes. Most of these deaths occur outdoors. Many victims are hit while standing under trees. In addition, almost 1,000 persons are injured each year and annual property damage is more than $100 million.

Thunderstorms—which involve lightning—are most frequent during July and August in almost all sections of the country. (The Pacific Coast is an exception. Thunderstorms there usually are in the winter.) They are most likely in late afternoon or evening. If caught in an approaching storm, you should take quick and proper action.

When you are outdoors. Seek shelter in a building, preferably a metal frame one, or one with lightning rods. If neither of these is nearby, pick the largest structure you can find.

Stay away from isolated trees. It is better to lie in a ditch or to crouch in a hollow in the open than to stand under a tall tree. A cave or base of a cliff also offers some protection.

Stay away from wire fences, overhead telephone and electrical wires, isolated sheds, and hilltops.

Stay out of the water and small boats. Do not ride a bicycle, a horse, or drive a plow or tractor.

Stay in your automobile if you are driving (a car's tires insulate it). Do not stop under a tree or on the top of a hill.

Do not use metal items, such as golf clubs, fishing rods, or garden tools.

When you are indoors. Stay away from open doors and windows, fireplaces, radio and television sets, lamps and other electrical equipment, telephone, radiators, water pipes, and stoves.

Do not take showers or baths. Do not wash dishes.

Stay in the basement or lowest floor of your house.

BLIZZARDS

People in northern regions expect and prepare for severe winters, but a heavy snowfall or ice storm can wreak havoc where *not* expected. This has happened to New York in the famous blizzards of '88 and '47; to Washington, D.C.; and to many southern areas in freakish years. At times a prolonged or repeated storm may even cripple such snow-hardy states as Minnesota and the Dakotas. Today, the principal hazard is an abrupt cut-off of transportation and communication. Your home may become temporarily isolated by snow, forcing you to fend for yourself without normal services.

Automobiles bog down first, then trucks, air lines, and sometimes even a railroad. Heavy coatings of ice and toppled trees may cut overhead power and telephone lines. Without power everything stops: not only your refrigerator, freezer, electric range or heater, but oil and gas furnaces, water pumps, radio, lights. Deliveries of fuel oil and other essential supplies may be halted for days. Protect your home with these advance steps:

Provide an alternate source of heat, such as a kerosene stove, a camp stove using butane gas, or a supply of "canned heat" (a paste of alcohol in cans). The latter may be used on many kitchen ranges in place of the normal burner. Some homeowners, wary of winter storms, have built-in protection by using bottled gas for at least one appliance, such as a range or water heater. Others keep a gasoline generator to produce emergency current. If you have a fireplace, stock up on wood (or coal) around Hallowe'en time, and acquire a few utensils for fireplace cookery or water heating.

Keep the pantry full, stocking a week's supply of canned, dried, or preserved (not frozen) foods, and staples such as cereals and macaroni. If water supply comes from an electric pump, fill bathtubs and jugs with water when the storm starts. Stock candles or kerosene lamps and extra flashlight batteries. Be sure you own some warm, sturdy outdoor clothes.

Familiarize yourself in advance with ground-to-air signals, so that if you are cut off by the snow and need help you can signal to the helicopters or small planes sent out on Red Cross and Civil Defense relief operations.

Finally, winterize your car thoroughly with snow tires, skid chains, a good battery, antifreeze, and a constantly full tank of gasoline, so as to re-establish communication as soon after the storm as possible.

SUGAR |

Brown sugar, which comes in one-pound and three-pound packages, gets its color from its molasses content. There are two kinds, each with its own uses. Do not interchange in recipes. *Light-brown sugar* has a delicate molasses flavor, desirable for general cookery. *Dark-brown sugar* contains more molasses and is excellent for baked beans, baked hams, and other cookery.

An airtight container is needed to keep brown sugar soft. So transfer it from the package to a glass jar having a large opening and a lid with a rubber edging. In this way, it may be kept soft whether on the pantry shelf or in the refrigerator. A less satisfactory, but somewhat effective, method is to store the box of sugar directly in the vegetable compartment of your refrigerator, where the normal moisture content of the air will keep the sugar soft for some time.

In an emergency, you can place hardened brown sugar in a shallow pan in the oven at low temperature and heat until pliable—then use at once. On cooling, sugar becomes harder than before.

Granulated sugar. There are two kinds: common granulated and super-fine (or very fine) sugar. Superfine has tiny crystals which, because they're smaller, make it especially suitable for filling sugar bowls; easier creaming with shortening in cookies and cakes; combining with the eggs in angel and spongecake and meringues; combining with eggs and whipped cream in Bavarian cream and chiffon pies; caramelizing to use in brittles or as flavoring.

Cube and tablet sugar basically are granulated sugar pressed into a convenient dainty form for dissolving in hot drinks. They avoid the mistake of damp spoons in the sugarbowl!

Confectioners' sugar, also called "powdered," is very finely pulverized sugar with a soft, perfectly smooth, fluffy texture. It is used in cake icing, etc., for its texture and concentration of sweetening in a small area.

SWIMMING POOLS |

Constant attention to safety is necessary when you have a pool. (A 15-by-30-foot pool can be built for about $2,500.) Most families do not have pools, but millions of people will be summer guests at neighbors' pools. Unlike public swimming areas, private pools do not have constant supervision by trained lifeguards. And lack of supervision, says a Red Cross water-safety authority, is the biggest single cause of accidents. These safety practices should be observed:

No one should be in the pool alone. Use a "Buddy system"; one swimmer watches the other.

Watch the water at all times when someone is in the pool. Do not depend on your hearing, even if you are sitting by the pool. Swimmers in trouble do not always shout or make noise.

The best way to help a swimmer in distress is to use the long pole that should be by the pool as a safety aid. It can be either a bamboo pole or the pole that comes with the pool's vacuum cleaner.

Inflated mattresses, inner tubes, and floating toys are often used in swimming pools. They can give a false sense of security and are particularly dangerous to children and nonswimmers. Use them only under careful supervision.

Learn how to swim well. Encourage children to practice basic swimming skills and to learn new ones. Learn basic lifesaving techniques, including manual and mouth-to-mouth methods of artificial respiration. Training courses are available in many communities. In addition, know first aid for nondrowning emergencies, such as cuts and bruises, sprains and fractures. A first-aid kit should be kept handy.

Don't swim yourself or allow children to swim when tired, cold, or overheated. Wait at least an hour after eating a full meal (see below).

Do not allow running, pushing, or ducking in or near the pool. Keep glasses and bottles away from the pool.

To guide homeowners and swimming-pool contractors, the National Swimming Pool Institute (NSPI) has established minimum standards for residential pools. The standards include these safety recommendations:

The pool should be enclosed by a fence at least four feet high, with self-latching gates. A natural-barrier hedge, pool cover, or other device that meets local laws may be used if it gives as much protection as a fence.

A lifeline, or safety rope, should be stretched across the pool to separate the deep from the shallow end. The rope should be at the five-foot depth or shallower for small children.

In a permanent pool, the filtering system and chemicals should keep the water clear enough so that the bottom is always visible. Rescues can be made quickly in a clear pool. (This requires maintenance of the filter and use of water-treatment chemicals.)

Underwater and poolside lights, and any electrical devices used in connection with the pool, should carry an Underwriters' Laboratories (UL) label. No wires should cross over the pool.

In general, it is a good idea to insist on a provision in any contract you sign that the pool will meet all NSPI requirements or the requirements of local laws, whichever are stricter.

WHY NOT SWIM AFTER EATING?

For years, water safety experts have advised swimmers to wait at least an hour after eating. Most people assume the reason for this traditional advice is to avoid "stomach cramps" that may disable a swimmer and cause drowning. Actually, the American Red Cross says, "No one knows exactly what happens in cases of stomach cramp and plenty of doubt still exists concerning its causes." Authorities agree, though, that emotional stress may well interfere with digestion.

Most people are not good swimmers. They do not breathe properly and may swallow water. If they swim soon after eating, this can lead to nausea and panic. And, although it has no definite proof, the Red Cross strongly suspects that many drownings attributed to "stomach cramps" have actually been cases of heart failure caused by a combination of overexertion and distress from abdominal distention. Swimming is strenuous exercise for most people.

The Red Cross advises swimmers: "Do not swim or water-ski after eating a hearty meal until the process of digestion is well under way." This means wait at least an hour after a full meal (not just a snack).

SYRUPS | See also HONEY

Simple syrup, used for sweetening iced or alcoholic drinks, is made by combining equal parts of granulated sugar and cold water (e.g., put one cup of sugar in a saucepan with one cup of water). Heat to just short of boiling, until all sugar is dissolved. Cool; store in covered jar. In sweetening drinks, use equal parts of syrup and lime juice; or two parts of syrup to three parts of lemon juice.

Corn syrup, used widely in cooking and as a table syrup, comes in three styles: Dark, deep-amber in color; white or light, colorless; and maple-flavored, golden.

Maple syrup is the pure boiled-down sap from the sugar maple tree. A favorite on pancakes, waffles, French toast, in candies, on ice cream, etc. Grades are determined by delicacy of flavor and weight. Maple-blended syrup also contains cane sugar syrup. Buttered syrup is top-quality maple-blended syrup with butter added to it.

Flavored syrups that have been local favorites for years, such as blueberry, apple, coconut, etc., are spreading to the national market. *Maple-honey,* a smooth blend of honey and maple-flavor syrup, offers a unique new taste to the breakfast pancakes, or in fruit puddings, cakes, ice cream, etc.

Molasses is the thick cane syrup which drains from sugar in the process of refining, and is an important food source of iron. Dark molasses has a full, tangy flavor and deep color, excellent for all cooking in which many spices are present—gingerbread, Indian pudding, etc. Light molasses has a more delicate flavor, a lower iron content, and a golden color, is excellent for general cooking purposes or as a table syrup.

TABLE SETTINGS |

The diagrams illustrate generally accepted ways of setting a table. The rules are not rigid; many variations are possible in the contemporary mode of party giving. Basically, a table setting should make a neat, pretty appearance, and serve the convenience of guests. Silverware is placed in the order of use, from the outside in, and dinnerware is so placed as to be within easy reach of the diner's hand. These pointers will also be helpful:

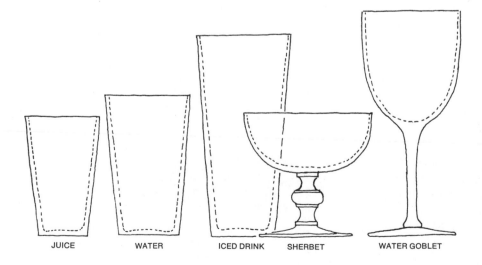

JUICE WATER ICED DRINK SHERBET WATER GOBLET

Fill water glasses about three-quarters full just before serving the meal, and place glasses for wine or juice to the right of the water glass. See illustration for types of glasses.

Place ashtrays either above the service plate or to the right. Put salt and pepper at each end of the table, or individual sets between each two places. A centerpiece for a sit-down meal should be low enough for guests to see one another across it. But candles should be above eye level, two to two and a half feet high at the flame, including holder. Use only white or cream-colored candles at a formal dinner, and only when you intend to light them.

Place mats should be one inch from the edge of the table, unless they are designed to hang over the edge. Set chairs so that the tablecloth just covers the front edge of the seat.

The tablecloth should hang fifteen to eighteen inches over the table's edges. Fold it from selvage to selvage right side out, so as to have only a single crease lengthwise down the center when it is placed on the table. With solid cloths, a table pad underneath will preserve the finish of the table (but it must be invisible; don't use a pad under lace cloths or place mats). Pads may be made to order to fit, or purchased at the same time as the table.

Linen tablecloths, whether plain weave or damask, generally give the best service, but cotton or cotton-and-rayon damasks are also durable and less expensive. All-cotton damask should have a specially treated finish to keep the surface smooth (check the label). Double damask has twice as many crosswise threads as single damask, giving it a more distinct pattern, but quality is determined by thread count and thread quality rather than by the weave. When buying any tablecloth, be sure of sturdy fabric and color-fastness able to withstand repeated laundering.

Dinner napkins are eighteen inches square or twenty-two inches square; informal napkins may be any size. Fold a dinner napkin in thirds, hems inside the fold, then in thirds again. Place it on the table with the open edge to the right. Napkins may be any color or pattern that suits your table-setting scheme.

1   2

1. **Breakfast.** Luncheon plate with cereal bowl, bread-and-butter plate, water glass and small juice glass, coffee cup and saucer, with appropriate silver in place. Cereal bowl and dessert spoon are removed before serving main course on the luncheon plate. *(Illustration on preceding page)*

2. **Luncheon.** Fruitcup (on the luncheon plate) and spoon are removed before serving main course on the plate. A dessert fork or spoon is brought in with the dessert, and a teaspoon with the coffee or tea.

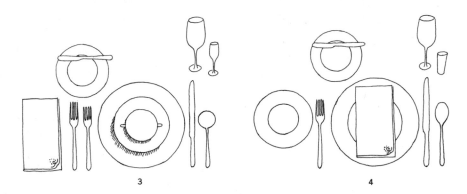

3. **Dinner.** For three courses, with soup cup and plate on the dinner plate, and wine glass to right of water glass. Main course is served on the dinner plate, with salad on a separate plate brought in at the same time.

4. **Family dinner.** Here the salad plate is already in place, as is a dessert spoon. Small glass is for juice.

5. **Formal dinner.** Note oyster fork for a seafood cocktail, next to soup spoon for the second course, and glasses for two wines. The service plate is removed before the main course is served. Bread-and-butter plates are omitted, and salad plates brought in with the main course. *Dessert service* (6) may include a finger bowl as at left, which the guest removes to the position shown by dotted circle. At right, a dessert service without finger

bowl. In either case, the guest places his fork and spoon to right and left of the plate before being served.

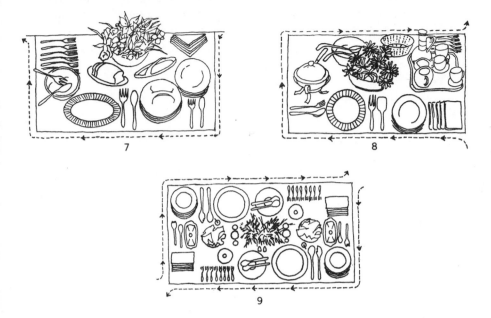

Buffet tables in three arrangements: (7) with table against a wall, (8) with table in center of the room, and (9) with duplicate servings for a large party. Guests circulate as shown by the arrows. Knives and forks are placed at the end of the line, spoons on the saucer of each coffee service. Rolls are served already buttered, while a water pitcher and glasses are provided on a side table. Decorations need not be centered as shown, but may be placed at either end of a large table. Round or oval tables are set the same way.

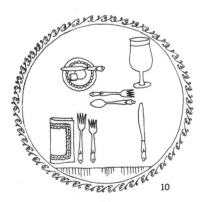

A setting for the sit-down buffet is shown on a round table (10). Guests serve themselves at the buffet and bring their food to the table. Dessert silver is ready above the space for the dinner plate. Place salad plates on the buffet table beside the salad bowl to hold both greens and bread.

The last table picture (11) shows the buffet reset with dessert and dessert plates, silver, and a coffee service, after the main course service has been removed.

Folding napkins. Some interesting, informal ways to fold a napkin are illustrated, as a way to add an imaginative touch to the buffet table.

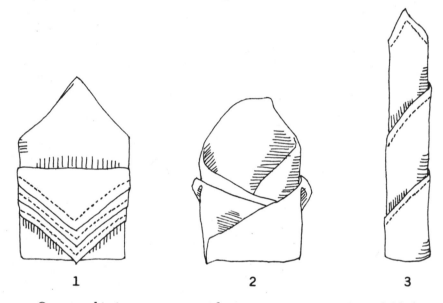

1. Open napkin into a square, with open corners at top. Now fold three of these corners down to bottom corner, so their points are one-half inch apart. Fold both sides under. Then fold back each of the three corners, making a pocket. Tuck bottom end under.

2. Fold each corner of open napkin to center, then fold each point to center. Fold in half toward you, making a triangle. Fold top corners toward center; tuck ends into each other. Turn napkin over; fold top half down.

3. Open a crisp napkin. Fold bottom left corner almost to top right corner in triangle. Fold right corner almost over to center. Turn up entire bottom about one inch. Going from right to left, tightly roll up napkin, keeping bottom even. Tuck end in last fold. It will stand up or lie in place as preferred.

TABLES |

The simplest means of recognizing tables is by their construction. The names for the various kinds depend not only on construction but also on the purpose for which they were originally designed. Since ways of life have changed, these uses, in some cases, have become outmoded. Today the specific use of a table is largely a matter of choice, convenience, and appearance.

1. **Butterfly.** English style of Tudor-Gothic era, popular in Colonial America. Usually of maple; used as cocktail or lamp table. Named for wing-shaped supports that swing out to hold leaves.

2. **Refectory.** Overhanging top, plain H stretcher at base, turned legs typify early American craftmanship. Most often used as a dining table.

1   2

3. **Drop leaf.** Sides may be raised and supported by pivoting wedges or pull-out slides. Popular dining table where space is limited.

4. **Gate-leg.** Turned gatelike legs swing out to support leaves. Style is English circa 1670. Various sizes, including dining.

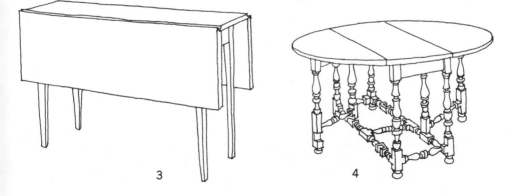

3   4

5. **Extension.** Introduced about 1750, style shown is Duncan Phyfe. It's of dining height and pulls apart at center to allow insertion of leaves.

6. **Console.** Usually attached to wall for support, but in many modern versions, back legs are used. The style shown here is Louis XV.

7. **Side table.** Designed to be placed against a wall, this style was introduced during the seventeenth century. Sometimes in pairs, to be placed together for dining. Example is Hepplewhite.

8. **Tilt top.** When table is not in use, top can be tilted upward, parallel to base. Eighteenth-century style made in wide range of sizes.

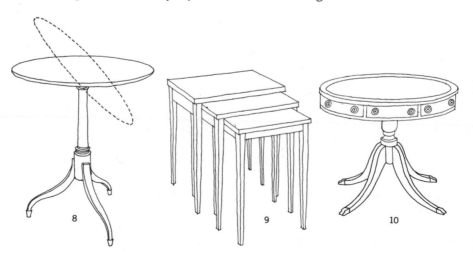

9. **Nest of tables.** Multiple units can be stacked within each other when not in use as individual serving tables. Style shown is Hepplewhite.

10. **Drum.** Features are round .top, often covered with tooled leather; a pedestal base; and real or sham drawers. Sheraton style is shown.

Cocktail (not illustrated). Available in an endless variety of periods, styles, and sizes.

SOME BASIC TABLE PARTS

Piecrust. Molding used around table top or tray; dished effect simulates pie-crust shape. Introduced during Georgian period.

Bracket. Strengthening support, usually triangular and decorative if visibly incorporated in design. Example is Chippendale.

Apron. Valance effect originally used to screen structural elements. Style shown is Queen Anne.

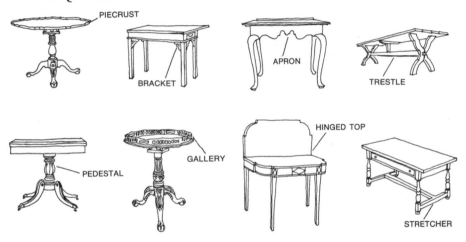

Trestle. X-shaped supports used in pairs or series of three or more. The earliest dining tables were made in this manner.

Pedestal. Single-column supporting member is called pedestal. Made in variety of sizes and styles.

Gallery. Low decorative railing around table top. May be made of metal or wood. Example shown is an English sewing table.

Hinged top. Example shown is Hepplewhite card table; with turn-about top. Usually placed against wall when not in active use.

Stretcher. Early method of providing sturdy support for four-legged table. Stretchers usually placed very close to floor.

TAXES FOR HOUSEHOLD HELP |

You do not usually think of yourself as an employer with some of the same responsibilities as a big corporation. However, in certain circumstances you are legally required to pay Social Security taxes for part- or full-time household help, just as your husband's boss may withhold and pay these taxes for him.

If you hire a maid, cleaning woman, gardener, baby sitter, etc., regularly enough to pay any one of them $50 or more during a calendar quarter, you are an "employer" under tax laws. A calendar quarter is the three-month period ending March 31, June 30, September 30, or December 31 of each year. Payment is due by the end of the month following each of these dates.

The Social Security (technically Old Age & Survivors Insurance, or OASI) tax is divided equally between you and your employee. At the 1966 rate of 8.4 per cent—subject to change by act of Congress—you would deduct 4.2 per cent (0.042) from your employee's wages, keeping it until the end of the quarter. At that time you would pay approximately twice this amount as the total tax, adjusting for the odd pennies.

For example, if your cleaning woman receives $8 a week, you would deduct 0.042 $\times$ $8, which is 34 cents to the nearest penny, and give her "take-home" pay of $7.66. At the end of the 13-week quarter, you have paid her $104 in taxable wages and have deducted $4.42. You now add the employer's contribution and pay the Government 8.4 per cent of $104, or $8.74. To equalize the contributions, add a nickel to the woman's next pay.

Note that you are not *obliged* to deduct the tax from wages. You could give the cleaning woman her entire $8 each week if you chose. But at the end of the quarter you would still owe the full 8.4 per cent tax on her wages, thus paying the employee's share as well as your own.

For information, request Circular H from the District Director of Internal Revenue (the same office that collects federal income taxes).

IRS simplifies bookkeeping by assigning an "employer number" to you and sending you a form every three months. It is easy to fill out, using a tax table for quick figuring, and can be folded to enclose your payment for mailing. The form arrives automatically until you advise IRS that you no longer have any taxable employees (that is, none receiving at least $50 per quarter).

You will need each employee's Social Security number, and also should keep a record of wages paid. Each year you must give the employee a statement of deductions, on a simple form provided in Circular H.

Sometimes a household worker will try to persuade employers to ignore this tax. Don't do it. At some future time, perhaps after the person has left your employ, the IRS could assess you for all unpaid back taxes plus fairly stiff penalties and interest. Try to convince employees that Social Security is for their own benefit, and that in any case you cannot neglect your tax responsibility.

TEA |

Black, green, and oolong teas are sold loose, in packages, or in tea bags.

Black tea owes its full flavor to the fermenting process the leaves go through before they are heated and dried. Grown principally in India, Ceylon, and Indonesia, it is by far the most popular tea in this country. Some varieties have a smoky flavor.

Green tea comes from Formosa and Japan. The leaves are not fermented, and the brew is light in color.

Oolong (Chinese) tea, from Formosa, is fermented only a short time. Color of the brew is lighter than with black tea.

Orange Pekoe indicates a particular size and type of leaf, not a kind or quality of tea. Flavored and spiced teas are blended with mint, jasmine, etc.—are delightfully refreshing, too.

Instant tea. Some instant teas are just the dried extract of freshly brewed tea; some are composed of equal parts of the dried extract and carbohydrates added to protect the flavor. Use for hot or iced tea as the label directs. Always store your teas, tightly sealed, away from cooking odors and spices. After six months they tend to lose flavor.

Ready-to-serve iced tea comes already mixed with lemon and sugar. Just add water and ice cubes.

TELEGRAMS | See also TELEPHONING

On many occasions a telegram offers the best method of fast communication. It is first of all a *written* message, more permanent than a telephone call and more impressive than a letter. Telegrams are traditional for family messages of both congratulation and condolence, and practical for other everyday purposes. It is helpful to know when and how to use the services of Western Union.

In speed, telegrams travel faster than the fastest mail, while not as fast as an instantaneous two-way telephone conversation. Sometimes, however, a one-way communication is more desirable. A telegram will reach a party who may not be accessible by phone, and it provides a legal record that the message was sent and delivered. All messages, incidentally, are private. Western Union employees are forbidden to divulge their contents.

Four principal types are used by individuals: straight or **full-rate telegrams; day letters; night letters;** and telegraphic **money orders.** In most places you may dictate a telegram over the phone by calling Western Union, charging the cost to your phone bill. Coin telephones may also be used. Or you may go to a telegraph office in person to write out the message on one of the blanks provided and pay for it there. Offices or message-taking desks are found in or near hotels, railroad and bus stations, airports, and in business districts.

Western Union transmits your message by teletype printer and in some remote areas by Morse code over a wire. At the receiving end, the telegram may be delivered, sealed in an envelope, by messenger; or the message may be telephoned and then duplicated in written form by mail. You may specify how you want it delivered.

Rates depend on the class (speed) of service desired, the distance measured in zones, and the length of the message. The address, punctuation, and signature do not count as words in domestic telegrams. Overseas messages (**cablegrams** or **radiograms**), though, count *every* word. For this reason, business firms have a one-word cable address. They use a language of "cablese" that omits implied words such as "the," and abbreviate technical data into a single code word.

The rates given below are as of 1966, for continental United States only (not including Alaska and Hawaii). Add local sales tax, if any. For telegrams to all other places, consult the telegraph company. Also note that rates are subject to change.

Straight or **full-rate telegrams** cost the most but get fastest, priority handling. They are transmitted ahead of all other messages on file at the telegraph office, in order of receipt. The minimum rate allows up to 15 words. Minimum rates within the continental United States range from $1.20 to $2.10, depending upon zone, plus a charge of 6½ to 11 cents for each additional word above 15. (For example, a straight telegram from New York to San Francisco would cost $2.10 for 15 words, plus 11 cents each additional word.) The message typically is delivered within an hour.

Day letters save tolls when your message is longer and less urgent. The minimum rate allows up to 50 words, and extra words cost less, too. A day letter is deferred until all full-rate telegrams on file are transmitted; but if the wires are not too busy, it may travel almost as fast. Rate for 50 words or less, $1.75 to $3.00, plus 14 to 23½ cents for each *five* additional words or less. It is usually delivered within two hours.

Night letters provide an inexpensive overnight service; they will be delivered the following morning if filed as late as 2 A.M. Rate for 50 words or less, $1.05 to $1.80, plus 8½ to 14 cents for each *five* additional words or less.

Messages of congratulation, condolence, etc., are sent at the same rates as above. Western Union offices provide a collection of suggested wordings as a help in composing them, but the rate is the same whether you use their words or your own. You may also "wire" gifts of flowers, candy, etc. And you may send a 15-word **personal opinion message** to congressmen or government officials in Washington, D.C., for only 85 cents.

For comparison, here are costs for a 60-word message within your local zone, showing the substantial savings possible by choosing the most appropriate service:

	BASE RATE	ADD'L. WORDS	TOTAL
Telegram	$1.20	$2.93	$4.13
Day letter (DL)	1.75	0.28	2.03
Night letter (NL)	1.05	0.17	1.22

Money orders provide a way of "wiring money" swiftly to a distant person. You deposit the cash at a Western Union office and pay the minimum message rate for the distance zone, plus a fee depending upon the amount of money. The order may be sent either as a straight telegram or a night letter. With an overnight order, you may include a 10-word personal message at no extra charge. Fees begin at 55 cents for amounts up to $20; increase on a sliding scale to $12.85 for $2,000; plus 70 cents per $200 additional.

The recipient is notified by Western Union to call at their office to identify himself and collect his money. Note that there is relatively little saving in the deferred, overnight service unless you wish to send a long personal message at the same time. A $45 money order in your local zone would cost $2.00 as a straight telegram or $1.85 as a night letter.

Collect telegrams of all classes may be sent at the recipient's expense, under certain restrictions. One is that Western Union will not accept a collect telegram asking for money.

TELEPHONING | See also TELEGRAMS

In using the telephone every day, you might call your husband at his office, find that he's out, and leave a message to call you back. He returns the call when you're out, leaving a message with Junior. You call him, miss him again—this could keep up all day. Since in many places your monthly charge covers an unlimited number of local calls, all the extra telephoning costs nothing except wasted time. But if you should follow the same blithe practice with long-distance calls, the costs in cash could be astronomical.

Properly managed, phoning long distance when necessary or convenient need not be unduly expensive. It is important, however, to understand the rate system and how to keep the charges under control. Beyond the range of your local telephone company, such calls are handled on the "long lines" of the American Telephone and Telegraph Company (Bell System). Before picking up the phone, have these points in mind:

Time of day. Bell System calls cost the most during weekday business hours, defined as from 4:30 A.M. to 6 P.M. every day except Saturdays,

Sundays, and three annual holidays (Thanksgiving, Christmas, and New Year's Day). After 6 P.M. on weekdays, and all day Saturday, rates for regular calls (see below) drop by about one-fourth. After 8 P.M. every night in the week, and all day Sunday or on the three holidays, they are cut in half. On a two-dollar call, that is, you can save one dollar simply by waiting till late evening.

Kind of call. The foregoing applies to regular *station-to-station* calls, which are the kind you would make by direct-distance dialing, or by telling the operator you will talk to anyone who answers the number called. A *person-to-person* call, specifying a particular individual only, costs up to 75 per cent more at weekday rates, and doesn't come down as much after 6 P.M. or Saturdays. (There is no further reduction after 8 P.M. or Sundays.) Which service to choose depends on the circumstances you expect to find at the other end of the line.

If you are calling a married couple at their home, one or the other will answer unless they're out, so you might as well use the less costly station-to-station service. But if you are calling your traveling husband at his hotel, a student at a university, a patient at a hospital, or an employee at his place of business, the telephone will surely be answered by someone. This automatically completes a station-to-station call even if you fail to reach your party. If he must call you back, that will constitute a second call. If you must call him at another number, that too is a second call.

If you place a call person-to-person, the call is *not* completed until you actually talk to your party. If the phone is answered but your person is not available, the telephone company operator leaves *her* number (with yours) for him to call back. When he does, only the original call is completed and charged (one call, not two). The operator also will try the number again from time to time if you so request.

If your party is reported to be available at another number, the operator will call that number at no extra charge—in fact, she will chase him all over the United States, if necessary, in order to complete your single call at the appropriate rate for the place finally reached. This extra service is the reason for the considerably higher cost.

Incidentally, while holding the phone during placement of a person-to-person call, let the operator do the talking. If you start chatting with the voice at the other end, even to leave a brief message, the operator has the right to charge you for a completed call. She may ask if you wish to talk to anyone other than your party at the answered phone. If you agree, the call will be charged as completed at person-to-person rates.

Consult the rate schedule in your phone book when deciding which kind of call to place. The following typical rates show that sometimes *two or three* station-to-station calls cost less than *one* person-to-person call. Add the local sales tax, if any. Rates are as of 1966.

	WEEKDAYS TO 6 PM	AFTER 6 PM & ALL DAY SATURDAY	SAVING	AFTER 8 PM & ALL DAY SUNDAY	SAVING
THREE-MINUTE STATION-TO-STATION RATES					
New York to Los Angeles	$2.00	$1.50	25%	$1.00	50%
Each add. minute	0.50	0.40	20%	0.25	50%
New York to Chicago	1.40	1.00	28%	0.70	50%
Each add. minute	0.35	0.25	28%	0.20	43%
THREE-MINUTE PERSON-TO-PERSON RATES					
New York to Los Angeles	$3.50	$3.00	14%	$3.00	14%
Each add. minute	0.50	0.40	20%	0.40	20%
New York to Chicago	2.20	1.90	14%	1.90	14%
Each add. minute	0.35	0.25	28%	0.25	28%

Length of call. The basic charge pays for three minutes' conversation—which is longer than you might think but not as long as a typical, chatty local call. After three minutes the charges keep piling up in one-minute units. It's not at all difficult to talk away a ten-dollar bill.

Before placing any long-distance call, it's a good idea to think through what you want to say. Jot down a few notes to keep in front of you, to avoid being diverted by small talk. Some people use an hourglass-type egg timer or kitchen minute-minder to let them know when the three minutes are reaching an end.

THREAD |

Even if you've been sewing for a number of years, you may sometimes be confused about just which type of thread to use—particularly if the fabric is a blend of several different fibers.

Mercerized cotton thread (it has a silky finish) can be used on any type of fabric, including blends. It comes in two sizes. Size 40 (heavy duty), available in a number of colors as well as black and white, is meant for heavy fabrics, such as denim, sailcloth, ticking, heavy wool coatings, etc. Size 50, in a still wider color range, is for all other fabrics. For some fabrics, however, unmercerized cotton, silk, or nylon thread is preferred.

Unmercerized cotton thread is available in black and white only. Though it comes in a wide range of sizes, it is generally used in home sewing only for very heavy fabrics or for fine handwork on dimity, voile, batiste, organdy, net, etc.

Nylon thread comes in many colors, one size. It is preferred for use on treated cottons, synthetics, and blends in which 50 per cent or more of the fabric is a synthetic, since, when the garment is laundered, the thread will dry as quickly as the fabric. (For other blends you may use cotton or silk.) Nylon may also be used on wools, silks, and rayon—but not on untreated cottons and linens. These require high ironing temperatures, which would melt the nylon thread. By virtue of its elasticity, nylon thread is especially suitable for sewing stretchable fabrics (whatever their fiber content), such as jersey.

Silk thread also comes in a wide range of colors. One size (size A) is used for all types of silk fabrics, from lightweight chiffon to heavy silk suiting. Though silk thread may also be used on wool, its luster is noticeable; many needleworkers prefer mercerized cotton thread for use on wool.

Other threads available are **buttonhole twist** (silk size D) for making buttonholes on heavy fabrics, especially wool suitings; **button and carpet** (heavy cotton with a special stiff finish); **quilting; machine embroidery; hand embroidery; basting;** and **darning.**

When buying thread, take along a piece of the fabric you intend to use it on and choose thread one shade darker. (Thread appears lighter in use.)

TIME DIFFERENCES |

For international convenience in reckoning time by the clock, the world's 360 degrees of longitude are divided into 24 Standard Time zones of 15 degrees of longitude and one hour each. **Standard Time** becomes one hour earlier for each zone traveling west; and one hour later for each zone traveling east. In general, Standard Time corresponds to local "sun time" at the central meridian of each zone.

Washington, D.C., and other Atlantic coast cities have **Eastern Standard Time.** Chicago, St. Louis, and other Midwestern or Midsouthern cities have **Central Standard Time** (deduct one hour). Denver and the Rocky Mountain states use **Mountain Time** (deduct two hours). San Francisco, Seattle, Los Angeles on the Pacific coast have **Pacific Standard Time** (deduct three hours).

In the opposite direction, toward Europe, each zone adds one hour to clock time. **Greenwich Meridian Time** (GMT), used by the world's navies and aviation, is also London time, five hours later than New York's.

Traveling completely around the world, one "gains" or "loses" 24 hours. This is adjusted at the **International Date Line,** longitude 180° in the Pacific Ocean. Flying or sailing west across the line, the calendar date changes to the next day. Traveling east, the date changes to the previous day.

Daylight Saving Time prolongs the hours of sunshine by advancing clocks one hour during summer months; i.e., by making everyone get up, go to work, have lunch, etc., one hour earlier. The idea dates back to Benjamin Franklin who, while an envoy in Paris, observed that broad daylight came at 6 A.M. He calculated that by moving clocks ahead to take advantage of this, millions could be saved in reduced use of candles at the end of the day.

The United States adopted Daylight Saving Time during World War I to promote war gardens, and in World War II to conserve electric power. Usually it begins at 2 A.M. of the last Sunday in April: before retiring on Saturday night, move clocks *ahead* one hour. It usually ends at 2 A.M. of the last Sunday in October: move clocks *back* one hour (or stop the clock and restart it an hour later). Check local times when traveling or telephoning.

TOYS |

What are the best toys to buy for children? According to authorities, primary consideration should be given to a child's age and to toys which are not dangerous for him to handle. Experts suggest these general rules for different age groups:

Infants. Babies under one year like things with bright colors, shapes they can explore, and textures they can feel. Such toys include stuffed animals and dolls, squeak toys, sturdy rattles, balls, and even nonbreakable cups or other smooth objects. Infants chew, drop, and bang these toys. Therefore, they should be washable, nonbreakable, and have no sharp edges. There should be no small detachable parts which can be put into the eye, ear, or nose. Avoid toys which are too heavy for an infant to handle.

One to two. A child now investigates things around him. Like infants, toddlers put almost everything into their mouths. Playthings that can be taken apart and put together easily (such as nests of blocks or boxes), pegboards, and push-pull toys are suitable. Stuffed animals and dolls, bath toys, blocks with round corners, a sandbox with digging toys, small chairs and table, and small wheel toys are also fine. Be wary of small toys that can be swallowed, flammable toys, or those with sharp edges.

Two to three. These children are more experimental. Things with which to build and toys that can be shared are desirable. These include building blocks, wooden animals, kiddie cars or tricycles, finger paints made from fruit or vegetable coloring, modeling clay, cars and wagons, wheelbarrows, rocking horses, picture books and crayons. Riding toys should be low and tipproof. Be sure toys are not sharp or pointed.

Three to four. This is an imitative age. Toys which encourage make-believe aid in learning. Toys should be sturdy. In this group are small brooms, carpet sweepers, garden tools, doctor's or nurse's kits, toy dishes, painting sets, and construction toys. For general fun, a wading pool may be useful in warm weather, but the water should be shallow and play supervised at all times. Costumes, which should be nonflammable, are popular at this age. Wooden trains are suggested. Electrical toys, though, are not recommended.

Four to six. Children begin to read; play becomes more complex. Dolls and dollhouses, games, craft and construction sets, blackboards, paints, blocks, hand puppets, and mechanical action toys—dump trucks, etc.— please this group. Play equipment such as jump ropes, rubber balls, scooters, slides, and swings serve increasing skills. Shooting toys and tricycles or wagons that can tip over easily should be avoided.

Six to eight. Skills are developing. Sewing materials, carpenter tools, or science toys are popular. Sleds, skates, playground equipment, kites, and more complex construction sets can be used. Kits for playing store and simple electrical toys are also suggested. Electrical toys should have the Underwriters' Laboratories (UL) seal and kites should have nonconductible lines. Use of sharp tools in carpenter sets should be supervised by an adult. Skates should have soft ankle pads and be sturdy.

Eight to ten. Hobbies develop. Model building sets and more complicated tools can be used. The National Safety Council recommends that a bicycle or an electric train should not be given before a child is eight. Craft and simple camera equipment, coin and stamp collection material can be given. Children now become keenly interested in sports equipment— gloves, balls, bats, fishing rods, rackets, etc. Musical instruments, books on history and biography, games of skill, gym apparatus, puzzles, and small phonographs are good for this age. Safe habits should be taught and encouraged as play becomes organized into games which develop speed and accuracy. The most important consideration in buying a bicycle is that it be the right size for the child and not one "to grow into."

Over ten. There is a growing interest in competition and skill perfection (e.g., archery sets, target shooting, and dart games). Toys powered with fuels and chemicals, such as rockets, should be supervised in their use. Use of chemistry sets should also be supervised; do not permit the use of chemicals not in the set.

General. Authorities divide play into four different types, and recommend that a child of any age be given a variety of toys to enjoy the whole range of experience. Never burden a child with too many toys which require adult supervision. Most playthings should be of a kind he can safely play with by himself or with other children.

The active, physical plaything includes any from a ball to a bicycle that requires physical exertion and thus aids muscular development. *Creative, constructive, manipulative, or scientific* toys encourage a child to develop his own ideas, initiative, and observation; they range from an infant's blocks through coloring books to microscopes.

Imitative, imaginative, and dramatic play is fun and instructive, too, for this is what children do with toy animals, costume dolls, toy soldiers, or miniature trucks and tools. Finally, *shared or social* play helps children learn to get along with each other, learn fair play and the challenge of competition. Its tools are any game or sports equipment ranging from checkers and baseball to word games and those that imitate travel, trading, or other phases of modern life.

UPHOLSTERY CARE | See also LEATHER CARE; STAIN REMOVAL AGENTS; STAIN REMOVAL DICTIONARY

Modern cleaning compounds and fabrics make it possible to clean most upholstered furniture at home, postponing the cost of a professional cleaning. But before trying any of the methods given below, pretest an inconspicuous area of the fabric with the cleaning product. Proceed only if you're satisfied with its appearance when thoroughly dry. Be sure to follow directions on the product's label. Then thoroughly vacuum the furniture with both the upholstery tool and the crevice tool to reach into corners.

Cleaning powder, the same as used on rugs, is best suited to upholstery that is only slightly soiled. Check the label first to see if the product may be safely used on upholstery. Spread newspapers under the furniture to protect the floor. Sprinkle powder on the fabric, brush in well with a soft brush, and leave it for at least an hour to dry and absorb soil. Then remove it with the vacuum cleaner.

Dry cleaning keeps light-colored fabric fresh if repeated often, say once a month, or before upholstery gets really dirty. Open windows wide for ventilation and wear gloves. Pour a little cleaning fluid (well chosen for safety) on an old bath towel and work it in until the towel feels just barely damp. Rub the towel over a small area in straight, even strokes, following the direction of the weave. With a second towel, also dampened with cleaning fluid, go over the same area again. Continue this process, overlapping the cleaned areas, until all the upholstery is covered. *Caution:* Foam cushions of polyurethane are not harmed by cleaning fluid, but foam rubber may soften and become sticky. Don't let the fluid penetrate through the fabric to the rubber underneath.

Shampooing is the most thorough cleaning method, but may not be used on smooth rayons, velvet, silk, or any other fabrics normally damaged by water. A prepared upholstery shampoo now comes in aerosol containers with sponge or brush attached; merely spray it on and spread as the label directs. (You may also mix a shampoo yourself from commercially packaged ingredients, which is more economical. Dip a medium-soft brush or sponge into the solution, and rub into the fabric with a circular motion.)

Stain-resistant fabrics have a protective finish added at the mill or by the store and bear the trademark of the finish used. Dust, dirt, and most watery or oily liquids stay on the surface where they may be vacuumed or wiped off easily. Spilled coffee, tea, milk, salad dressings, etc., can be blotted up with a paper towel, then sponged off with water, or if it's a greasy stain, with a dry-cleaning spot remover. Some of these finishes are available for home application in aerosol containers.

However, treated fabrics will not repel lipstick, ball-point pen ink, nail polish, shoe coloring, and certain medicines. Furniture salesmen are sometimes inclined to oversell the benefits of treated upholstery fabrics, no doubt because of the extra cost compared to the same fabric untreated. Always blot and sponge any spot while it is still fresh.

Vinyl plastic upholstery, which sometimes looks like leather, resists most stains and ordinary dirt, and may be wiped off with sudsy water. When it becomes gray looking from ground-in dirt, use a heavy concentration (very sudsy) of laundry detergent and scrub with a medium-bristled kitchen brush. There is also an aerosol foam-type cleaner made especially for vinyls. Wipe up the soil and suds with a clean bath towel; polish dry with another towel. Treat stains as you would stain-resistant fabrics. Vinyl upholstery is often used in automobiles.

Leather upholstery, now usually made of smooth leathers with a durable finish, should be dusted and occasionally washed. Perspiration areas may be wiped with a mixture of one teaspoonful of baking soda to a glass of water, then washed. Old, weathered leather must be scrubbed with saddle soap, followed by one of the special leather-softening products to bring out the luster and color. Do not wash leather-top tables or leather-trimmed lamps.

VACATIONING SAFEGUARDS |

If you leave your home unoccupied while on vacation, minimize the threat of burglary and other problems by following these rules:

Lock all doors and windows securely. Double-cylinder locks (those operated with a key outside and inside) on doors give excellent protection. Key-operated window locks—if your local fire laws permit them—are also a good safeguard. Never leave house keys outside—under a mat, over a door, etc. Shades or Venetian blinds on windows should not be left completely drawn or closed.

Police authorities recommend using an automatic timing device (one that resets itself), connected to lights in one or two rooms, to turn lights on and off at night. Cost of these units starts at about ten dollars.

Suspend routine deliveries and pickups by telephone or letter, not by a note left outside your house. If requested, the post office will hold or forward your mail. Ask a neighbor to remove circulars or notes that may be dropped on your doorstep.

Notify local police of your planned absence. In some communities, they make a special check of houses which they know are unoccupied. Inform a neighbor of your itinerary, where you can be reached, and leave your auto license number, too. It is also a good idea to leave your household keys with a neighbor or friend so that, if necessary, your house can be entered without having to break a window or lock. If you want mention of your vacation to appear in a community newspaper, arrange that it be after—not before—your holiday.

Turn off heat in summer and disconnect electrical appliances (refrigerator should be empty). Lock up outdoor tools, appliances, furniture, and ladders. An unmowed lawn may indicate to thieves that a house is vacant, so have lawns cut regularly if you will be gone long.

Finally, place valuables and important papers in safekeeping.

LUGGAGE LOSS

Most travelers by plane, train, bus, or boat arrive at their destinations with their luggage intact. Inevitably, though, some luggage is lost or misplaced. In many cases, passengers themselves are at fault because they do not mark luggage properly, or fail to check carefully when they claim luggage at the destination point.

Most lost luggage is eventually recovered, but a temporary loss may be a great inconvenience. Here are ways you can help to keep track of luggage and to insure its quick return in case of loss and recovery:

Distinguish your luggage from that of others by marking it distinctly with bright-colored plastic tape. For example, a red circle, yellow star, or white stripe will help you to identify it quickly. Mark luggage on both sides, top and ends.

Put an identification card inside your luggage as well as a tag on the outside. Include your name, complete address, and telephone number.

Use sturdy leather tags on the outside of luggage. Do not use labels on grainy luggage. They may stick temporarily, then fall off.

Tape an itinerary card inside your luggage—that is, a list of the cities you plan to visit, the dates you will be in each city, and where you will stay. If lost luggage is recovered, it can be forwarded quickly to the right place.

Remove old shipping tags from luggage, particularly stubs that list previous destinations.

VACUUM CLEANERS |

A vacuum cleaner consists essentially of a motor-driven fan which creates a suction at the point of cleaning and draws loose dirt into a closed bag for later disposal. You can spend anywhere from forty to two hundred dollars for a good cleaner. The price depends upon size and power as well as on features and attachments; choose according to the size of your storage space and the features you feel you need.

Upright cleaners place emphasis upon rug and carpet cleaning. They have built-in agitation by a revolving brush, which will deep-clean thick rugs with little effort on your part. While attachments for above-the-floor cleaning are available, attaching them is more involved than with a tank-type cleaner, and suction is generally less.

Tank or canister cleaners generally cost less than uprights, including the attachments. They are versatile; you can clean floors, walls, upholstery, blinds, baseboards, tabletops, even ashtrays. A tank cleaner will remove surface dust and dirt from rugs and carpets, and deeper dirt if you take the time to vacuum slowly in a systematic pattern.

Many women like to have both types. Some designs aim at two-in-one utility. For example, most uprights increase suction when the hose, wands, and nozzle for above-the-floor cleaning are attached. A few canister and tank cleaners provide a special power tool which plugs directly into the motor to give the same action on rugs as an upright. Of course these extras are reflected in the price. Here are features to look for in either type of cleaner:

Suction can be tested only by trying it on a dirty rug—not just by spilling a little powder and picking it up. The suction depends not only on the power of the motor, but upon design of the nozzle. Also, it declines as the bag fills with dirt; a good cleaner will maintain efficiency at least until the bag is half full.

Disposable bags. Most cleaners have them now, eliminating the messy problem of emptying a cloth bag. However, disposable bags should be changed when from one-half to two-thirds full, or every two to four weeks in the average household.

Ease of storage. It's best to keep a cleaner assembled and ready for use (one advantage of upright cleaners). Slim tank and low canister cleaners permit compact storage in small quarters, some with the basic attachments in place. Others have self-storage for tools within the cleaner; still others, a tool holder to be hung on a closet door.

Noise and weight. The former is particularly important in apartments. Light weight is a factor if you must lift the machine, but take into account whether it moves easily from room to room.

Wands, hoses, and nozzles must be easy to assemble and disassemble, but must *not* come apart by themselves in the midst of cleaning. This should be checked with particular care in second-hand cleaners.

Suction regulator permits reducing suction when cleaning lightweight fabrics, such as a hooked rug. This and the on-off *switch* should be easy to use.

Cord winding by spring action keeps the cord out of your way when cleaning and is much easier for cord storage.

Brush control on rug cleaners permits adjusting for high and low pile rugs; sometimes automatic, sometimes handled with a lever. Be sure it is easy to use.

Combination tools. If you have an area of bare floor around rugs, a single tool that cleans both in one operation is convenient.

Convenience may be checked by running the cleaner under low furniture, close to baseboards, into corners, etc.

Small hand vacuum cleaners work well within limitations; some women who own an upright prefer a hand cleaner to the upright's above-the-floor attachments. Consider one also for trailer homes, small summer homes, or for car cleaning. A lightweight electric vacuum cleaner or a carpet sweeper is handy for removing surface litter between vacuumings.

HOW TO USE THE DUSTING TOOLS

When using the **dusting brush** (1) don't stop with the furniture. Go right on to books, shelves, lamps, pictures, lighting fixtures, window screens, window shades, Venetian blinds, piano keys, records, radio, and TV sets.

The **floor-and-wall brush** (2) picks up dirt on any kind of floor, from wood to bare concrete. It takes up lint and fluff that collects in closets, and is convenient for stair treads and risers, around the fireplace, over doors and windows, for moldings and walls. For wall dusting, be sure the brush is clean. Run the end of the vacuum cleaner hose over the brush to remove dust and lint, then wash in lukewarm suds and dry thoroughly. Or buy a second brush especially for painted and papered walls.

Use the **upholstery tool** (3) in back-and-forth strokes to remove dust, lint, and animal hairs from upholstered furniture, slipcovers, sofa cushions, bed mattresses, and car interiors. For draperies, use your free hand to spread the folds of the fabric, and starting at the top, stroke downward with the tool.

The **crevice tool** (4), long and slender, is for hard-to-get-at places—cushion crevices of upholstered furniture, between the coils of radiators, along the edges of wall-to-wall carpeting, inside a piano—and inside the drawers of kitchen cabinets, dining-room or bedroom chests.

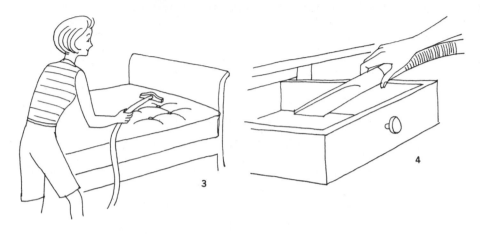

VARIETY MEATS | See also MEAT; SAUSAGES

Most meat cuts for roasts, steaks, stews, etc., are from the muscle tissues of the animal. Other edible parts are classified as variety meats. They include liver, kidney, tripe, heart, brains, sweetbreads, and tongue (and less commonly, lung and certain other organs). They are important to nutrition because vitamins and minerals are concentrated in them to a greater degree than in "red" meat. A few are classed as great delicacies; but most are considerably less expensive per meal than standard meats.

Variety meats may be bought fresh, cured or pickled, or frozen. If possible, the fresh varieties should generally be used as soon as purchased. Fresh liver, hearts, tongue, kidney, and tripe may be stored, loosely wrapped, in the coldest part of the refrigerator for twenty-four hours. Sweetbreads and brains may be precooked, then refrigerated and used within twenty-four hours. Frozen variety meats should be kept frozen until time to use; cook as the label directs in each case.

Liver, our richest food source of iron, so necessary to prevent nutritional anemia, also provides vitamin A, copper, iron, B vitamins. Veal, calf, lamb, beef, and pork liver are often sold sliced and labeled; all have about the same nutritional value. Veal, calf, lamb, and *young* beef liver may be broiled or pan-fried; pork and most beef liver are best when braised. Allow about one pound of liver for four servings.

Beef liver is tender to less tender, pronounced in flavor. Veal liver, often called calves' liver, the most popular and highest-priced, comes from milk-fed animals. It is mild in flavor and light in color. True calf liver comes from animals fed on milk and grass. It resembles veal liver in taste, but is not quite so tender or light in color. Pork liver is less tender, pronounced in flavor, and usually lowest priced. Lamb liver is mild flavored and tender.

Heart is a good buy as it has very little waste. Veal heart is the most delicate in flavor, and the most tender. In buying hearts, estimate amounts by weight as follows: lamb hearts, one-quarter pound each, one serving; pork, one-half pound, two servings; veal, three-quarters pound, two or three servings; beef, three to three and one-half pounds, eight to ten servings.

Sweetbreads are a delicate, tender meat from the thymus gland of a calf, young beef, or lamb. Each animal has two kinds: heart sweetbreads, which are rounded, and throat or neck sweetbreads, which are elongated. Veal sweetbreads are the most popular and highest priced; like lamb sweetbreads, they are white and tender. Beef sweetbreads, usually only of the neck variety, are reddish in color and inclined to be tough when pressed with fingers. Buy one pound for about four servings. Do not store fresh sweetbreads; precook, then refrigerate.

Brains are a very delicate, tender meat, the basis of many fine dishes. Allow about one pound for four servings. Veal brains, the most popular and highest priced, weigh one-half pound each; beef, about three-quarters pound each; lamb and pork brains about one-quarter pound each. Do not store fresh brains; precook, then refrigerate.

Kidneys are highly prized by epicures for delicacy and flavor. Beef kidneys weigh about one and a quarter pounds each and need thorough braising or simmering. Lamb kidneys weigh two ounces each, are very tender, and delightful broiled or sautéed. Veal kidneys weigh eight to twelve ounces each, are so tender they need very little cooking; are usually broiled or sautéed. One veal or two lamb kidneys make one serving; one beef kidney makes four servings.

Tripe is the inner lining of the stomach of beef, in three kinds: honeycomb, pocket, and plain (or smooth). Honeycomb is considered the greatest delicacy. All come fresh, pickled, or canned. Allow about one pound for four or five servings. "Fresh" tripe is cooked before you buy it, but needs more cooking. Pickled tripe is usually thoroughly cooked, but should be soaked before using. Canned tripe is ready to heat and serve.

Tongue may be bought fresh, smoked, corned, or pickled, all requiring cooking. There are also ready-to-eat whole tongues, and canned tongues whole or sliced. Tongue provides a variety of tasty main dishes as well as a popular sandwich or cold cut. Uncooked beef tongues weigh two to five pounds and come fresh, smoked, or cured. Smoked beef tongue often comes in a transparent wrapping with a packer's brand name. Veal tongue weighs one-half to two pounds and comes fresh. Lamb tongues, weighing only three to four ounces, come fresh or pickled, often in jars.

Ready-to-eat smoked beef tongue in a vacuum package, can, or jar has been completely cooked, skinned, and boned, ready to slice and serve cold, or to heat as label directs. Sizes range from one and a half to two and a half pounds. Pork tongues weigh one-half to one and one-quarter pounds and usually come in cans or jars as "lunch tongue." Lamb tongues come in jars as small tidbits.

VEGETABLE BUYING GUIDE | See also CANS AND CAN SIZES; VEGETABLE DICTIONARY

FRESH

Fresh vegetables are available all year long, but are the best buy when in their growing season in your locality. Keep these points in mind when buying:

Check on vegetable supplies in local markets through newspaper and radio reports.

Buy from a dealer who has a quick turnover and who keeps fresh vegetables under refrigeration or on crushed ice. They come to market at their peak of flavor and freshness, thanks to modern hydro-cooling at the farm (getting them cool through and through) and well-iced shipping conditions.

Go to market yourself whenever you can. In today's markets, you can quickly see daily specials, and be reminded of vegetables that seldom appear on your menus.

More and more vegetables are coming to market washed and packaged. This means they are not picked over by other shoppers.

Buy only enough vegetables for one or two days' supply whenever possible; use promptly.

To cut vitamin losses, refrigerate *at once* in food bags or your vegetable crisper. If washing seems necessary, hold heads of lettuce and salad greens, stem end up, under faucet; rinse outer leaves briefly. Shake to remove excess water before storing.

If buying potatoes, onions, or yellow turnips, store them where cool air can circulate around them. Do not clean until ready to use. (Most potatoes are prewashed.) Keep cool and dry.

FROZEN

Frozen vegetables are always in season, so you always have a wide variety to choose from, including the newer ones packed in seasoned combinations in butter sauce, cream sauce, cheese sauce, etc. The best of the crop is harvested at the peak of quality and frozen within a few hours; thus, nutritional losses are negligible.

Buy frozen vegetables from a grocer who keeps them in a freezer cabinet that maintains near 0° F. temperature. They should be frozen solid, not beginning to soften.

Watch for specials of the week—they'll be especially advantageous if you have freezer space available.

Don't waste time—once you select them. Take along an insulated bag in which to hurry them home, and store in your freezer at once.

CANNED

Canned vegetables offer a wonderful variety, too, such as green peas, green limas, green beans (Blue Lake, etc.), whole-kernel corn, asparagus, vegetable combinations, etc., and they are usually fine in flavor. Store canned vegetables in a cool dry place. If for salads, refrigerate, then use.

Never rinse canned vegetables under cold water; you lose food value and flavor. Don't turn them out of the can to be aerated before using, either; that simply adds work and does not improve their flavor.

Canned foods may be safely left in the opened can, if they're covered and kept in the refrigerator. Of course, any leftover cooked food, stored in any type of container, should be refrigerated.

Canned tomatoes. Almost until the present century, tomatoes were known as "love apples" in parts of this country, and considered unfit to eat. Today, thanks to advances in cookery, food growing, and processing, tomatoes rank as a food staple, highly prized for both flavor and nutritive value. Along with citrus fruits (a tomato actually is a berrylike fruit rather than a vegetable), they are a principal source of vitamin C in the American diet. In the fall or winter months when fresh tomatoes are more expensive and less tasty than in summer, canned tomato products become the cook's stand-by for scores of uses. This guide can help you pick the right one for a particular need.

Canned tomatoes come peeled and cored. They may be whole or in pieces. Salt, calcium salts, or tomato juice may be added. Some tomatoes are canned with a vegetable such as corn, okra, or succotash. Italian-style tomatoes are meatier and blander than usual ones.

Tomato juice is unconcentrated and strained. Salt may be added. Tomato-juice cocktail has added seasonings and may be concentrated slightly.

Tomato purée or pulp is made from crushed and strained tomatoes. Two or three times as concentrated as canned tomatoes, it has a saucelike consistency.

Tomato sauce is much like purée but contains seasonings such as pepper, sugar, onions, spices, and vinegar.

Tomato paste is the most concentrated, having four to six times the solid content of canned tomatoes. It may contain salt, spices, flavorings, and baking soda.

Tomato catsup (ketchup or catchup) is made from concentrated tomato pulp with such added ingredients as vinegar, salt, Worcestershire sauce, peppers, sugar, onions, garlic, and cinnamon. These are blended and strained to make a smooth, thick sauce.

Chili sauce is similar to catsup but contains chili peppers and has a coarser consistency. It may or may not be more spicy, depending on the brand.

VEGETABLE DICTIONARY | See also FRESH FRUITS AND VEGETABLES; VEGETABLE BUYING GUIDE

Artichokes, Italian or French (October through January). Buy compact, tightly closed heads. Cut one inch off top, cutting straight across with sharp knife. Cut off stem about one inch from base, leaving stub. Pull off outside bottom leaves. With scissors, clip off any thorny tips on leaves. Wash.

Artichokes, Jerusalem (November through January). Buy only those that are free of blemishes. Scrub well. Pare thinly. Leave whole, dice or slice.

Asparagus (March through June). Buy straight, green, brittle stalks with close, compact tips. Break off each stalk as far down as it snaps easily. Remove scales with knife. Scrub with soft brush to remove sand. (Or scrub; then thinly pare length of stalk with vegetable parer.) Leave stalks whole, or cut in long, thin, slanting, crosswise slices.

Beets (all year). Buy smooth, small or medium beets; wash them. Leave whole; cut off tops, leaving one inch of stem and root end. Or for quick cooking, pare; then slice, dice, or sliver.

Broccoli (all year). Buy with tender, firm stalks and tightly closed green flowerets, with no yellow color evident. Cut off large leaves and a bit of lower stalk. Wash well. If stalks are more than one-half inch in diameter, make lengthwise slits (about four or six) almost to flowerets.

Brussels sprouts (September through February). Buy green, fresh-looking sprouts. Avoid yellow spots or worm holes. Remove imperfect leaves; cut off a bit of stem end; then wash.

Cabbage (all year) includes green, Savoy, and Chinese varieties. Buy heads with fresh, crisp-looking leaves. Remove any wilted leaves; wash.

Carrots (all year). Buy bright, crisp carrots. Remove tops at once. (Often they come topped, washed, in one-pound film bags.) Scrub. Scrape or pare thinly. Then leave whole. Or cut into halves or quarters. Or sliver, slice, or dice.

Cauliflower (all year, peak season in fall). Buy compact, crisp white heads, as free from blemishes as possible, with fresh, green outer stalks. Remove outer leaves and stalks; cut off any blemishes on flowerets. Wash well. Leave whole, removing as much of core as possible without altering shape. Or break into flowerets. Or thinly slice each floweret.

Celeriac (September through May). Buy firm, crisp roots. Cut away leaves and root fibres. Scrub well. Pare; then slice or dice.

Celery (all year). Buy crisp stalks with fresh, green leaves. Pascal celery, with its green stalks, is especially tasty. Remove leaves; trim roots. Using soft brush, wash well. With knife, scrape off any discoloration. Dice or sliver outer stalks.

Corn on the cob (all year, peak May through September). Buy young corn that spurts milk when kernels are pressed. Refrigerate until ready to cook. Just before cooking, remove husks, all silk, and any blemishes or discoloration.

Cucumbers (all year). Buy firm cucumbers—not too plump or seedy. Cut off and discard ends down to where seeds begin. Pare. Then cut into thick slices, or dice.

Eggplant (all year). Buy well-shaped, purple, firm, shiny eggplant with no rust spots. Use soon after buying. Wash. Pare if necessary when ready to use. Eggplant discolors upon standing. Do not soak in salted water.

Endive, Belgian (September to May). Buy fresh-looking, well-bleached heads four to six inches long. Keep wrapped, to prevent light from turning endive green. Wash heads quickly in water; wipe dry with paper towel. Remove any bruised outer leaves. Cut off a small slice from the base of each stalk. Cut in half lengthwise.

Green beans (all year). Buy crisp, slender green pods that snap when broken. Wash. Remove ends and strings, if any. Then fix in one of these ways: Snapped; snap or cut into one- or two-inch pieces. Crosscut; cut crosswise into thin slanted slices. French cut; cut lengthwise into thin strips.

Green limas (all year, peak July through October). Buy crisp, full pods; snap open pods; remove beans. If necessary, with knife, cut off thin strip from inner edge of pod; push out beans.

Green peppers (all year). Buy peppers that are thick fleshed, crisp, and bright green. Buy wide, chunky ones for stuffing. Use hot and green peppers in relishes. Cut thin slices from stem end. Remove seeds and fibrous portion. Wash inside; then cut as recipe directs.

Greens (except spinach) (all year). Buy greens that have crisp, clean leaves with good color. Avoid seedy or woody stems. Discard ends, tough stems, and yellowed leaves. Wash three times in warm water, lifting greens out of water each time and shaking well so sand sinks to bottom.

Kohlrabi (all year, peak June and July). Buy small or medium kohlrabi with fresh tops and rind that can be easily pierced with fingernail. Discard stems and leaves; wash. Pare thinly; then cut into slices, slivers, or quarters.

Mushrooms (all year). Buy firm, plump, cream-colored mushrooms with short stems. For safety's sake, buy only cultivated ones. Wash well, scrubbing if necessary with soft brush. Do not peel if fresh and tender. Cut thin slice off stem end; use rest. To slice whole, slice parallel to stem.

Okra (all year, peak June through October). Buy young, tender, crisp pods. Wash. Leave whole (do not cut off stems or tips). Or cut into half-inch pieces.   [Continued on page 378]

VITAMINS AND MINERALS

Why we need them	Their richest natural sources
VITAMIN A Helps resist nose and throat infections (colds). Helps prevent night blindness and other eye diseases. Promotes children's growth.	Liver Fish-liver oils Yellow vegetables (carrots, sweet potatoes) Butter or margarine	Cream Milk (whole, evaporated) Whole-milk cheese Egg yolk Dried apricots
VITAMIN B₁ (Thiamine) Necessary for functioning of nerve tissues. Affects body's utilization of carbohydrates, fats. Promotes children's growth. Stimulates appetite and good muscle tone.	Lean pork Whole-grain or enriched breads, cereals, and flours Peanuts Dried peas Dried beans Lentils Variety meats (liver, kidneys, sweetbreads)	Lean meats Fish Chicken Milk (whole, skim, evaporated, nonfat dry) Brewer's yeast Wheat germ
VITAMIN B₂ (Riboflavin) Necessary for healthy skin and hair, good digestion, sound nerves. Increases resistance to infection, general weakness, and poor eye conditions.	Liver Kidney Lean meats Fish Chicken Eggs Milk (whole, skim, evaporated, nonfat dry)	Green and leafy vegetables (turnip greens, beet greens, kale, green limas, collards, mustard greens, etc.) Dried peas Brewer's yeast Wheat germ
VITAMIN C (Ascorbic Acid) Prevents and cures scurvy. Increases strength of capillary walls, lessening the possibility of hemorrhages. Increases resistance to infection. Necessary for sound teeth and gums.	Citrus fruits (oranges, grapefruit, lemons, tangerines) Cantaloupe Pineapple	Tomatoes Raw cabbage Potatoes Green and leafy vegetables (green peppers, mustard greens, Brussels sprouts, kale, parsley, etc.)

*VITAMIN D Aids in utilizing calcium and phosphorus in building bones, teeth. Prevents rickets in children.	Sunshine Fish-liver oils Liver Vitamin-D enriched milk and evaporated milk	Vitamin-D enriched cereals Fresh and canned oily fish Egg yolk
NIACIN Is chief factor in cure and prevention of pellagra. Helps maintain a healthy skin condition.	Liver Kidney Heart Lean meat Fish Green and leafy vegetables (green beans, broccoli, kale, cabbage, etc.)	Brewer's yeast Wheat germ Green peas Milk (whole, skim, evaporated, nonfat dry) Whole-grain or enriched breads
*CALCIUM Builds strong bones and teeth. Necessary for lactation; coagulation of blood; heart, nerve, and muscle functions. Helps maintain alkalinity of the blood.	Milk (whole, skim, evaporated, nonfat dry) Cream Cheese	Sardines Green and leafy vegetables (green beans, broccoli, kale, cabbage, etc.)
*PHOSPHORUS Builds bones and teeth. Necessary for utilization of fats and carbohydrates by the body.	Green and leafy vegetables (green beans, broccoli, kale, cabbage, etc.) Milk (whole, skim, evaporated, nonfat dry) Cereals	Wheat germ Eggs Fish Shellfish Liver Meats Brewer's yeast
IRON Helps form red blood corpuscles. Helps carry oxygen in blood. Aids in tissue respiration. Prevents nutritional anemia.	Liver Oysters Molasses Dried apricots Green and leafy vegetables (green beans, broccoli, kale, cabbage, etc.)	Egg yolk Potatoes Whole-grain or enriched breads, cereals, and flours

* The correct functioning of both calcium and phosphorus depends on sufficient amounts of both, as well as of vitamin D.

Onions (all year, depending on variety). Buy clean, hard, well-shaped onions with brittle skins. Avoid any with developed stems. In using, cut slice from stem and root ends. Peel thinly, slipping off only first and second layers (do this under cold running water to prevent tears). Or slice onion; then pull off skin.

Parsnips (all year, peak fall and winter). Buy smooth, firm, well-shaped small to medium parsnips. Soft or shriveled ones are apt to be pithy. Wash. Cut thin slice off top and bottom. Pare; halve; cut out center core. Cut into quarters or slices.

Peas (all year). Buy well-filled fresh, green pods. Just before cooking, shell by pressing pods between thumbs to open; then remove peas, discarding any with shoots.

Potatoes, sweet (all year). Sweet potatoes have yellowish, fawn-colored skins and are mealy when cooked. Yams have white to reddish skins, are moist when cooked, and have meat which is more orange in color. Buy smooth-skinned potatoes with bright appearance. Buy in small quantities; they're perishable. Scrub well.

Potatoes, white (all year, depending on variety). Buy uniform, well-shaped potatoes; scrub with brush; remove blemishes and eyes. To save food value, cook in jackets or skins. Scrape or pare thinly if necessary.

Pumpkin (October; a few in September and November). Buy bright-colored, unblemished, firm pumpkins. Halve; remove seeds and stringy portion. Cut into small pieces; then pare.

Salsify (October and November). Buy firm, well-shaped medium roots. Scrub; then scrape or pare. Slice or sliver. Plunge into cold water containing a little vinegar to prevent discoloration.

Spinach (all year). Comes washed, topped, sometimes in film bags.

Squash, acorn (all year). Buy ridged, acorn-shaped squash that are firm, green, and oval or round. Scrub well. Cut in half lengthwise; remove seeds and stringy portion.

Squash, butternut (all year). Scrub well. Cut into serving pieces; remove seeds and stringy portion.

Squash, Hubbard (September through February). Buy with hard, warted rind. Scrub well. Cut into serving pieces; remove seeds and stringy portion.

Squash, summer crookneck or yellow (all year). Buy squash with curved neck, deep-yellow color, and tender warted rind. Rind becomes rough and less tender as it matures. Scrub well. Cut slice from stem and blossom ends. (Do not pare or remove seeds if squash is young and tender.) Cut up.

Squash, Cymling or Pattypan (all year). This type is flat, scalloped, and disk-shaped. Prepare as with summer squash.

Tomatoes (all year, depending on variety). Buy large or small oval red or yellow tomatoes. Sometimes they are purchased green. Regardless of type, look for firm, plump, smooth fruit with good color and no blemishes.

"Native" tomatoes featured during your local growing season may be an especially good buy both in price and flavor.

Turnips, white (all year, peak in fall). Be sure they have fresh green tops, and are firm and heavy. Avoid those that are lightweight for size as they may be woody, pithy, strong in flavor. Scrub; pare thinly; then cut into quarter-inch slices, or into strips or half-inch cubes.

Turnips, yellow, or rutabagas (all year, peak in fall). Buy heavy, firm yellow ones. Avoid lightweight ones; they may be woody, pithy, strong in flavor. Scrub well; pare thinly; then cut into strips or cubes.

Zucchini, or Italian squash (all year). Buy small and medium ones. They look like a cucumber, but are striped and likely to be longer and more irregular. Scrub well. Cut off dark spots and stem end, but do not pare. Cut into quarter-inch or half-inch slices.

VITAMINS AND MINERALS | See page 376

WALL DECORATION | See also PICTURES AND SCULPTURES

A good way to give a room a fresh, new look without replacing or rearranging furniture is by hanging something besides pictures on a wall. Many distinctive, colorful items can be used.

Wall hangings. Almost any fabric—even a beach towel—with a striking pattern or colorful design can be used. Japanese scrolls, usually made of a parchmentlike paper, have delicate Oriental brush-stroke designs. Bright colors and bold patterns, painted or silk-screened on fabric, characterize Mexican scrolls. Serapes, actually used as blankets and ponchos, are often gaily colored and make distinctive wall decorations. American-made wall hangings are also available with screen-printed pictures of such things as sailing flags, stallions, city scenes, maps of the world and of ancient Europe. Some scrolls, with gay circus-animal designs and Winnie-the-Pooh figures, are made especially for children's rooms and nurseries. Pennants and posters are also available.

Plaques. Carved wood plaques with inlaid ceramic or mosaic designs are sold in many shops. Wall plaques from the Far East have solid brass Japanese word-symbols mounted on mahogany or ebony wood. Mexican plaques are pottery plates with Mexican designs, such as an Aztec calendar.

Handicrafts from other countries often make interesting wall decorations. From Mexico come masks of tin, brass-and-copper, and tin-and-brass. Some masks have glass eyes; some are of wood or papier-mâché. Tin figures for walls include horses, starfish, and seahorses. A Chinese abacus (counting device) with sliding beads gives an Oriental touch.

Hobby collections. Look in your attic, closets, and cubbyholes for such things as old-fashioned keys, coins, stamps, plates, butterflies, pressed flowers and leaves. A collection of seashells, mounted in a frame or on a piece of plywood covered with colored burlap, can make an attractive wall display. One collector of seashells cut quarter-inch wire mesh into free-form shapes, coated the wire by dipping it into plaster of Paris, and pressed shells onto the plaster before it dried.

Other accessories for decorating a wall include wall sconces, which are decorative bracket fixtures that hold one or several candles; trivets; copper molds and kettles; cookie molds; handmade mosaic pictures; and early American cross-stitch samplers.

WASH AND WEAR | See also LAUNDERING

The term "wash and wear" refers to a garment or other household fabric (wash and use) that may be washed, dried, and used again with little or no ironing. A more recent development is known as "durable press." The wrinkle-resistant element consists of a high percentage of modern synthetic fibers, polyester or acrylic, in the fabric; or it may be a special finish applied to cottons, rayons, or blended fibers. Their characteristics vary, and it is most important to read the labels for laundering instructions.

A durable press garment may be machine-washed and machine-dried and will need no ironing. This is not entirely true of all wash and wear. To escape ironing and hand laundering, a woman must have an automatic washer with at least a short "fine-fabric" cycle—or stand by the controls through the whole washing process. She must have a dryer, or resort to drip-drying for many wash and wear garments.

Most durable press garments, especially the heavier-weight fabrics such as poplin or gabardine, will look as good through the full cycle of the washer and with air- or line-drying as they will look if drip-dried. The automatic dryer, however, is best. If using an old dryer with no temperature selection, check frequently to be certain that garments do not over-dry.

LAUNDERING WASH AND WEAR

The most critical factor in laundering wash and wear is temperature: moderate heat of wash water, the dryer, and the iron. The following rules help to handle all types of these convenient fabrics, with any equipment.

Wash frequently. Even if a wash-and-wear garment stays fresh looking during wear, don't postpone laundering. Once heavily soiled, these fibers and finishes won't come clean easily. Pretreat stains, collar, and cuff lines with soap or detergent. Sponge grease stains with dry-cleaning fluid. (Garments may be dry cleaned if you prefer, without loss of wash-and-wear properties.)

Wash *like* fabrics together. Some fabrics tend to pick up color and lint from other types. Wash whites in a separate load.

Do small loads. Crowding the washer causes wrinkling. In hand-washing, do one item at a time, and change water frequently.

Choose correct water temperature. Cold water (below 75° F.) is surprisingly effective in removing moderate soil, using a cold-water detergent. Pretreat areas having oily soil. Cold water produces the least wrinkling, and the fabric can go through a final, short spin or squeeze to remove excess water before drying.

Warm water (90° to 110° F.) is recommended for removing light, greasy soil. It will remove wear wrinkles better than cold water; any washing wrinkles can be avoided by a cold rinse before the spin. Use any laundry soap or detergent.

Hot water (140° to 160° F.) is necessary for removing heavy soil and grease. To reduce wrinkling, cut down on the wringing or spinning as much as possible. Washers with wash-and-wear cycles do this for you automatically.

Shorten machine agitation; it shouldn't be necessary to wash more than five minutes. Use washer's slower agitation speed if provided.

Rinse in lukewarm or cold water. A fabric softener in the last rinse prevents clinging of synthetics and harshness. Don't use chlorine bleach on wash-and-wear cottons if label warns against it.

Drip dry carefully. If dryer is not available, remove garment from final rinse (without spinning unless washed in cold water, as above). Hang on a nonrusting hanger, and shape by smoothing seams, collar, cuffs, button bands, etc. Hang trousers by cuffs on spring-clip hanger.

Don't overdry. Spin or squeeze out excess water before drying by machine. Use the medium dryer setting if available; otherwise remove garments from dryer while slightly damp. With small loads, add a few clean towels to help tumbling action. Place garments on hangers immediately, or they'll rewrinkle.

Touch-up when necessary. Use a steam iron, or a regular dry iron on "low" for synthetics and blends, "medium" for cottons. Test on an inconspicuous part of garment; use a press cloth if needed to prevent shine.

Change washing methods as necessary. If wash-and-wear shirts begin to look a little gray, wrinkled, or stained, it's time for a thorough hot-water washing and complete ironing. After that, return to a gentler method as above.

LAUNDERING DURABLE PRESS

Cold water washing will produce the fewest wrinkles, but it has little effect in removing the wear wrinkles from durable press garments. Use a cold water detergent to remove light to moderate soil. Hot water is still needed for heavily soiled clothes, but it is advisable to cool them before spinning and to rinse in cold water. The spin should be slow, gentle, or short.

Dry these garments, if possible, in a dryer; the heat removes the wash wrinkles. A special wash-and-wear or durable-press setting, if provided, automatically controls both the temperature and the drying rate. At the proper time the air cools, giving fabrics time to "firm up" so that they won't re-wrinkle when the dryer stops.

Remove fabrics promptly from the dryer when they are dry and place on hangers. If the dryer has only one temperature (hot), the garments should be taken out while slightly damp and placed on hangers to complete their drying.

WASHERS AND DRYERS | See also APPLIANCE TROUBLE SHOOTING; ELECTRIC APPLIANCES; LAUNDERING

AUTOMATIC WASHERS

The price of a washing machine may vary between $200 and $400, depending mostly upon the number of automatic features. The basic construction remains about the same in all models offered by a given manufacturer. Before shopping you must find answers to these basic questions:

Where will the washer be installed? Machines range in width from twenty-four to twenty-nine inches, and you may want additional space for a companion dryer. Water supply, drainage lines, and electrical outlets are required. In some locations the weight and vibration of the machine could be a problem. For advice on these matters, consult a building contractor or inspector.

Is there enough water? Some machines can use as much as sixty gallons for the "regular" cycle of washing and rinses; minimum is twenty-eight to thirty gallons each time you wash eight or nine pounds of clothes. About half of this will be hot water. To save water, some machines may be set to use a smaller amount for less than a full load. Others permit reuse of the wash water for a second load—not the best way to get the cleanest clothes, but a good compromise where water is in short supply.

Is repair service available? Washers work hard, are complicated internally, and will need occasional servicing. Select a local dealer with a good reputation (since you must depend on him, not the manufacturer, for service) and ask for details. Normally, replacement parts and labor are free during the first year. Proper installation is important; the machine must be electrically grounded to prevent shock, and carefully leveled to prevent "walking" or jumping when in use.

A washer is one of two types: either with an agitator in the center of the tub, opening from the top; or a tumbler with a revolving cylinder, opening from the front. Both types wash clothes clean without concern about wear or damage to fabrics. The tumbler uses less water, but requires a controlled suds detergent for best results. The agitator type allows more leeway in choice of soap or detergent.

Some washers can handle two to sixteen pounds dry weight of clothes. To evaluate the difference, consider that one sheet weighs about two pounds. In deciding which machine to buy, the principal question is how automatic you want it to be. Some homemakers use a washer only for towels, shorts, pajamas, etc., sending out the larger pieces to commercial laundries and hand-washing any special items. Others want the machine to wash everything with minimum attention from them. The more features, the higher the price.

The following chart will help you decide whether you need the deluxe features or can handle your laundering adequately with a simpler machine at a lower price. It covers both washers and automatic dryers.

ECONOMY MODELS	MIDDLE OF THE LINE	DELUXE, TOP OF THE LINE
For women whose laundry consists mostly of cottons and linens, play and work clothes, with few special problems.	Models designed for the woman with a varied family wardrobe, who wants to eliminate as much hand laundering and ironing as possible.	For a woman who washes an unlimited variety of fabrics, wants complete flexibility, and the convenience of regular as well as special cycles.
Washers have a choice of hot or warm wash, one wash-and-spin speed, selection of wash time. Water levels may be adjusted while water is flowing into machine. Some are "one hose" models, which means that you adjust water temperature at the tap, then adjust it again for rinsing.	Washers offer a choice of three wash and two rinse temperatures, selection of wash time, gentle cycles for filmy, delicate or wrinkle-resistant fabrics. Some have detergent and fabric-softener dispensers, agitated presoak for extra-dirty items, choice of water levels for partial loads—all automatic.	Washers are fully automatic—instead of having to select time, action, temperatures, etc. one setting takes care of everything. Special preset cycles for wash-and-wear and washable woolens give them the best possible conditions. Dispensers for detergent, bleach, fabric softener.
Dryers have a simple minute timer which you must learn to set from experience; shut off automatically at end of drying time. One thermostatically controlled heat setting for all fabrics.	Dryers have "automatic dry" controls, sometimes also an optional timer and shut-off signal; choice of heat (or heats) no-heat or "fluff." Nonvent models are available.	Dryers also have preset cycles for various fabrics; precision controls to measure dryness. Sprinkle feature on some, damp-dry setting on most, for immediate ironing.

The special cycle for wash and wear and durable press is of particular meaning in an age of man-made "miracle" fabrics. It includes a warm or cool wash, cool rinse, and gentle washing action, and eliminates messy drip drying. Clothes come out ready to dry, requiring only touch-up ironing, if any.

Lint filters are helpful, but don't expect to wash items such as flannel, chenille, or terry cloth in the same load with dark pieces without getting some lint. Any washer should be thoroughly flushed after washing very linty loads.

A small inner wash basket in some machines permits doing basin loads such as lingerie, gloves, and men's socks as gently as hand-washing.

Don't expect miracles from any washer. Good hot water (140° to 160° F.), a good soap or detergent in proper quantity, and willingness to follow the manufacturer's instructions are the secrets of good laundry. Sort clothes properly; shake off excess dirt, and empty pockets. Some stains must be pretreated; others cannot be removed entirely but will fade with repeated washing.

AUTOMATIC DRYERS

Time studies show that a clothes dryer saves as much as three hours a week over line drying, and eliminates most of the labor at a cost of a few cents a load. Its speed and convenience also permit faster turnover; you can get along with fewer linens, play clothes, etc. Machine-dried clothes keep their shape better and need less ironing.

Dryers may be either gas or electric; find out which source of power is cheaper where you live. Also check installation costs. Either type usually requires a vent through the wall or window to carry off heat and moisture. Gas dryers must be tied into the gas line, and also need a 110-volt electric outlet. Electric ones need a 230-volt circuit for best results. Some operate on normal 110-volt house current, but drying takes from half again as long to three times as long.

Adequate venting to the outside is important—because a dryer exhausts warm, moist air which may condense on walls and windows, and because of lint. Both should be carried out of doors for your comfort, to protect furnishings, and to prevent fine particles of lint collecting on walls, floors, etc. Even a good lint trap, emptied after each day's drying, can't catch all the finer dust in the circulated air. The only exception is special non-vent dryers (see below). Some of these require additional plumbing.

Locate the dryer so as to keep the venting ductwork as simple and direct as possible. A good rule to follow is to run the duct no farther than thirty feet from the dryer to the outside, subtracting four feet for each elbow, or ninety-degree turn, in the system.

As with washers, next consider how automatic you want the machine to be. Here are some of the features to look for:

Adjustable temperature controls. Formerly, many dryers operated only above (or below) the range—135° to 170° F.—needed for wrinkle-free drying of man-made fabrics such as nylon, Orlon, or Dacron. Current models have a special setting, sometimes labeled "Wash and Wear," for these fabrics. (Or in models with only one setting, all fabrics are dried in the 135° to 170° F. range.) Some dryers also have settings for such special loads as plastics (low or no heat) and wool blankets (high heat).

Automatic timing. The trick in preventing shrinkage and wrinkling of clothes is to avoid overdrying. An "automatic dry" setting prevents this by means of a thermostat. As moisture evaporates from the clothes, the temperature in the dryer increases until it reaches a point at which the thermostat turns the dryer off. Even with this control, however, mixed loads of quick- and slow-drying items need to be watched to avoid overdrying the lighter pieces. Refinements in the self-timing feature permit automatic, uniform drying of mixed loads, by means of one or more special thermostats, or an electronic device that "feels" how wet or dry the clothes are.

Damp-dry control. With this, the dryer can be set to turn itself off when the clothes are still moist, ready to be ironed. The moisture is more evenly distributed through clothes than it would be if they had been line-dried; consequently, sprinkling is not necessary.

Automatic sprinkling provides for sprinkling of clothes that have been previously dried. You return them to the dryer, fill a reservoir with water, and set the "Sprinkle" control. The clothes are then tumbled and evenly dampened with a fine spray in about twenty minutes—instead of the two hours it usually takes for clothes sprinkled by hand to be ready for ironing.

Finish signal. Buzzers or bells signal the end of the drying cycle. These remind you to remove the clothes before wrinkles become set—as they will if clothes are left in the still-warm dryer.

Moisture-free venting. Conventional dryers give off a large volume of warm, damp air that must be vented to the outside. For homes where such venting is difficult or impossible, a condenser dryer handles the problem internally. Moisture (and lint) are collected in a chamber, which must be emptied periodically, or are washed away by a stream of cold water. The latter requires a water supply and drain for the dryer.

WASHER-DRYER COMBINATIONS

If you need both a washer and a dryer at the same time, you might consider the two-in-one, space-saving appliance. Once you have loaded this machine, clothes will wash and dry completely (or damp dry) with no further attention. Total wash-dry time may run fifteen to thirty minutes longer than in separate machines, but saved is the clock-watching and time otherwise needed for transferring the load.

Clothes come out clean, but it is necessary to keep loads small to prevent wrinkling in the dryer. Families using a combination make a habit of laundering frequently, even twice a day, to avoid a pile-up. Either the washer or the dryer operation may be used without the other. However, choice of cycles is more limited than in deluxe model separate machines.

COIN-OPERATED WASHERS AND DRYERS

The appliances in a self-service laundry have limited controls. In washers you usually have a choice of hot or warm water, and nothing else; and in dryers, a time selector, but no heat control. This means you get the best conditions only for the standard family wash—such sturdy items as white or colorfast shirts, underwear and comparable clothing, sheets, pillowcases, towels. Such machines will not do justice to wool blankets, sweaters, nylon items, or even to wash and wear if it is to keep its nonwrinkle characteristics.

White and colorfast pieces should be washed in different loads. Use the "hot" setting and full cycle for whites, *after* pretreating soiled collars and cuffs with undiluted liquid detergent. Select the "warm" setting for colors. Be sure to add enough detergent, or use premeasured tablets or packets.

In untended apartment house laundries, one of the chief problems is abuse of the machines and negligence in timing. It is inconsiderate to overload a washer to the point of breakdown in order to save a quarter; to wash rugs, blankets, etc., in machines not designed for them; or to fail to be present when the machine stops, in order to remove clothes from it promptly for the next user.

WEATHER | See also STORMS AND DISASTERS

A home barometer on a wall or desk lends a handsome decorative effect to a room—but you may overlook that the barometer is also a useful instrument in forecasting weather. It measures atmospheric pressure, or weight of the air, which is one important factor in weather changes.

A home (aneroid or "dry") barometer has a clocklike face with five or six numbers, ranging from 26 or 27 to 31. These numbers represent the equivalent inches of mercury rise in an older type of barometer which actually utilized a glass tube immersed in mercury, or quicksilver. Despite any other markings, such as "rain," "changing," and "fair," the barometer cannot, by itself, forecast the weather. *Changes* in reading are more important than any absolute number on the dial.

By reading it several times a day, you can determine whether the barometer is rising (needle moving clockwise), falling (counterclockwise), or remaining steady. Tap it lightly at each reading to detect any movement. Usually it has a second, movable needle which you can set at the current reading (so as to reveal, later, whether the reading has changed and how much).

To predict weather more accurately, you need a wind-barometer table. Some barometer manufacturers provide this, calling it a "weather chart." The table lists weather forecasts that correspond to various wind directions, barometric readings, and changes.

In general, winds from the northeast through southeast and a falling barometer indicate bad weather. Winds shifting to the west or northwest and a rising barometer usually signal the approach of fair weather. These are very general indications. They do not tell you whether it will rain today or tomorrow, or whether the rain will clear up in a few hours or a few days.

Furthermore, your particular location can influence weather—for example, in mountainous country. A good way to become expert is to compare your own barometric and wind readings with the "weather man's" radio bulletins. You will soon learn by experience what indications of local weather to look for.

A very sharp, sudden drop in barometric reading usually signals the oncoming of a severe storm. For protective measures in a hurricane, tornado, etc., see STORMS AND DISASTERS.

Simple barometers can be bought for six to ten dollars, although elaborate ones range up to one hundred dollars or more. It is not necessary to mount a barometer outdoors. Air pressure is the same inside the house.

FOLKLORE

Many people rely on various signs in nature to predict weather. Widespread publicity is given to what the ground hog sees or doesn't see in early February. How reliable are these folk weather predictions? The United States Weather Bureau says:

Lore: If the ground hog sees his shadow on February 2nd, another six weeks of cold weather will follow. If he does not see his shadow, the weather will begin to get warmer. *Fact:* Neither the ground hog nor any other animal can predict the weather. The degree to which it is cloudy or sunny on February 2nd has no effect on the next six weeks' weather.

Lore: "Red sky at night, sailor's delight; red sky at dawning, sailors take warning." *Fact:* Yes, this has some validity. A red sunset denotes clear, fair weather in the west and an absence of moisture. Inasmuch as United States weather systems generally move from west to east, this is usually a favorable sign. A red sunrise often indicates the presence of moisture and dust in the atmosphere, both rain elements.

Lore: Mackerel skies (skies covered with a thin layer of rippled clouds resembling the scales of a fish in pattern) and mares' tails (tailing wisps of clouds) foretell rain. *Fact:* This is often an accurate prediction because these cloud formations are related to a storm system. They generally precede a warm front with winds shifting and rainfall later.

Lore: A ring around the moon means bad weather is coming. *Fact:* A scientific basis exists for this belief. The appearance of a ring or halo around the moon is caused by the presence of high, ice crystal clouds which indicate an approaching warm front and low pressure area. Rain or snow very often will follow. This also applies if circles are seen around the sun.

Lore: A rainbow in the morning means rain to follow. *Fact:* This can be true. A person sees a rainbow when his back is to the sun as he looks at a rain shower. Because the sun is in the east in the morning, the rainbow and rain are in the west. Weather generally travels from west to east. Hence, the rain might move toward the viewer.

Lore: No dew in the morning foretells rain by evening. *Fact:* Dew is formed when moisture in the air near the earth's surface condenses. No dew means that the air is relatively dry, but this is no indication that it will become wet and rain later in the day.

Lore: Heavy evening dew indicates a fine day will follow. *Fact:* Generally, this is true. Early evening dew indicates clear skies and rapid nighttime cooling —a good sign that no storm or bad weather is nearby.

Lore: When the woolly bear caterpillar grows a heavy coat it means the winter to follow will be a hard one. The width of his stripe indicates to what extent this will be so (the wider the band, the harsher the winter). *Fact:* There is no scientific proof that the coat of any insect (or animal) in any way indicates future weather conditions.

WILLS | See ESTATE PLANNING

WINDOW WASHING |

The first "must" in washing windows is safety: a sturdy stepladder and willingness to leave the *outside* cleaning to professionals or to men of the family who may be accustomed to tall ladders. Never sit on a window sill to reach the outside glass. If yours is a low ranch-style home, with windows easily reached with a short ladder from the ground, place planks under the feet of the ladder to prevent toppling.

Have plenty of clean, soft, lintless cloths handy, a chamois, a sponge, or one of the nonwoven fabrics specially made for lint-free cleaning. Any of the following methods may be used:

In a pail, mix a little household detergent in warm water—very sparingly, so as not to make actual suds. Or use household ammonia, one tablespoon to each quart of warm water. Wring out a cloth or sponge in this solution, wipe the entire panel, then immediately wipe dry with another cloth. Be sure to reach into the corners and to replace cloths before they become too dirty.

Use a spray-on cleaner. Merely spray the glass evenly with one hand, immediately wipe off with a cloth in the other hand. Then polish with a *second* cloth.

Using a rub-on cleaner, shake well and pour a little of the creamy liquid on a moistened sponge. Spread a thin film over the glass, let dry to a white powder, then wipe off with a dry cloth.

Professional window cleaners make the job look easy with a rubber-bladed tool that resembles the windshield wiper of a car. Inexpensive home-size versions are sold in hardware stores. It takes skill, however, to avoid leaving streaks. You may want to remove heavy grime from a large window with a blade. Wipe the window with a fairly wet sponge, then use the blade in a back and forth motion across the glass, and from top to bottom. Angle the blade slightly as you go (let the lower end trail the upper end). Wipe off blade with a cloth as you work, and blot up excess water in corners.

WINDOWS |

Windows affect the appearance of both the inside and the outside of your house. Here are the dozen sizes and shapes you can choose from:

1. **Double-hung** window has two sashes (movable sections), both of which slide up and down in grooves in the window frame. It is the most common type of window and is easy to curtain and screen. New types of double-hung windows have a maintenance-free device that replaces weights and sash cords.

2. **Casement** window has a sash or sashes that swing outward. Sometimes there is a lower horizontal section, hinged at the bottom, that opens inward like the top of a hamper. Some casement windows also have muntins or mullions—strips of wood or metal between the sections of glass.

1   2

3. **Dormer** window is one that projects outward from a pitched roof in order to bring light into an upper story. It is covered by a little pitched roof of its own, which may contain one or more windows.

4. **Awning** window is made up of three or more horizontal sashes, each one hinged at the top to open outward. Because the sashes act as a kind of awning, such windows can often be left open when it's raining.

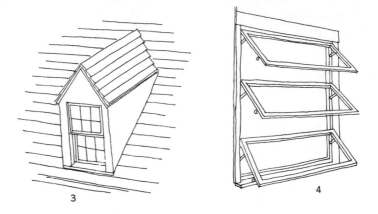

3   4

5. **Bay** window is composed of a group of units, which may be double-hung, casement, or fixed windows. The bay projects from the house and has angled sides. Bay windows are appropriate to traditional houses but usually are not compatible with modern architecture.

6. **Bow** window is similar to a bay window but instead of being angled, it is curved. Usually the window is fixed and has many muntins. Like the bay, the bow window usually is suitable only to traditional architecture.

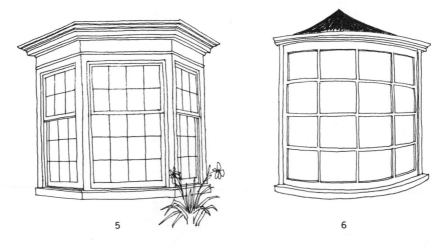

5   6

7. **French** window is often called a French door. Pairs of these windows begin at the floor and are high enough to walk through. They open inward and are sometimes flanked by fixed sections of glass.

8. **Fixed** window is a window that does not open. It is used to provide light and a view in a room where ventilation is otherwise provided. Panes of glass or Thermopane may be fairly large.

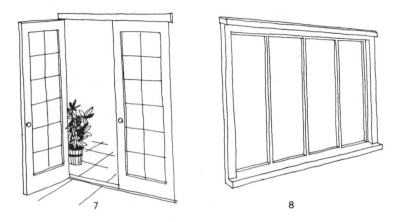

7   8

9. **Clerestory** window is installed under the roofline at the top of an interior wall. Such windows give a high horizontal line of light and may provide ventilation without sacrificing complete privacy. Some clerestory windows open like a transom; others are fixed.

10. **Louvered** window, sometimes called a jalousied window, is made up of narrow slats of glass installed horizontally. The slats are all movable, overlap when closed. This type of window makes it easy to control ventilation and is popular in warm climates.

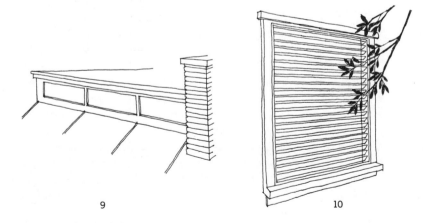

9   10

11. **Picture** window is composed of one or more units that cover a large area of wall and provide a maximum of light and view. Usually picture

windows have one large fixed pane in the center, and casement or double-hung windows at each side for ventilation.

12. **Window wall** is just what it sounds like—an entire wall of windows. Often floor-to-ceiling panels of glass open onto a terrace or patio and slide aside for indoor-outdoor conversion. However, a window wall may be composed of any one of several types of window or a combination of two or more types.

11   12

WINDOW TREATMENTS | See also CURTAINS; DRAPERIES AND DECORATIVE FABRICS

The popular picture window, sometimes a whole wall of glass, has resulted in a new window-treatment style and new furniture designs. Study the types shown in this section and adapt your ideas to any special problems offered by your windows. First, ask yourself these questions:

Are the curtains and draperies sufficiently flexible to permit control of light and air? Do they provide privacy? Do they improve the view? Will they launder or clean? Do they present a pleasing exterior aspect? Do they suit the climate? Are they appropriate to the house's scale, quality, and uses? Do they look as good at night as in the daytime?

A window is one of the chief centers of interest in any room. With proper handling, a window can accentuate the mood of a room—formal, traditional, colonial, or modern. And window treatments can help to correct architectural flaws. For example, a small window can be made to appear larger, an unattractive window can be masked, or an ordinary window can be made elegant.

The double-hung window is probably the most common type. It lends itself easily to a variety of drapery treatments.

1. **Floor-length draw draperies** extended beyond the sides of the window give a small or narrow window added width and importance. Café curtains

over the lower portion of the window afford privacy. Solid-color drapery and patterned curtains can also be used.

2. **For informal effects,** tie-back curtains edged with ruffles add a cheerful note to a room. They can also be of solid-color fabric to complement and accent a printed wall covering.

3. **Sheer floor-length draperies** coupled with a rich swag give a formal effect and add height. A length of fabric draped or pleated and hung at the top of the drapery forms the swag. It can match or contrast with the drapery fabric. Note how the first window looks wider and this one taller as a result of the way they are draped.

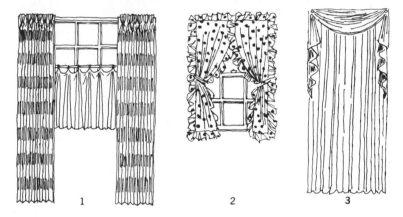

4. **A picture window** practically insures a light-filled room. Such windows often consist of a large, fixed pane of glass with two smaller side windows that can be opened.

Traverse rods enable draperies to be pulled open and closed affording a maximum view during the day and privacy at night. Sheer, sill-length draw curtains under draw drapery permit daytime privacy.

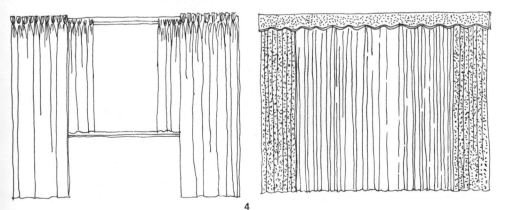

4

The combination of floor-length drapery on traverse rods and a sheer draw curtain with a cornice also complements a picture window. The cornice is made of painted or fabric-covered wood cut to the desired shape. If a sliding glass door is incorporated into the picture window, the drapery and curtains should open wide enough to clear the door area, even if this means extending them beyond the window areas.

5. **A bay window** projects out from the room and usually has windows on three sides. Any of these treatments, using a curved rod, would also suit a bow window—one that curves out.

Draw draperies and a valance frame the window area. For privacy, full floor-length curtains can be added. These draperies can be straight panels; pulled closed across the bay area, or closed along the angle of the windows. The valance is made of a strip of pleated fabric. For proper balance it should be about one-eighth the length of the draperies.

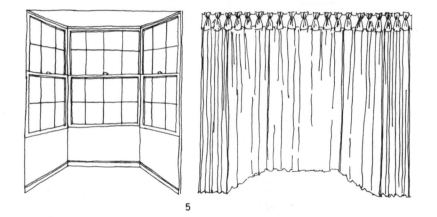

5

6. When a **seat, shelf, or radiator** fills the bay area beneath the windows, two pairs of short draperies can be used, one pair at the center, another pair divided between the two side windows. Short transparent curtains or café curtains are also good here. Floor-length drapery panels can be hung at either side of the bay area to add emphasis to the window.

7. **French doors** can often be draped to look like the windows in the same room. When this is done, the height of the drapery should be the same for doors and windows. It is sometimes necessary to use a cornice or valance to accomplish this illusion. If one is used on windows, the doors should receive the same treatment.

Shirred curtains attached to rods above and below the glass panels on the door screen out bright sunlight and afford privacy. Such curtains do not interfere with opening the door and they are often a good solution where the door is used frequently.

Traverse rods and drapery should extend far enough beyond the sides of the doors to permit easy opening. If a valance or cornice is used, it must also clear the top of the door.

The same shirred curtains can be sashed at the middle—another easy and interesting treatment for French doors. These can be of sheer fabric or of chintz, polished cotton, or other light, colorful material.

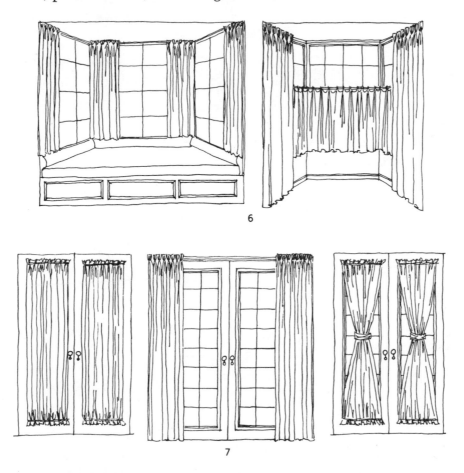

6

7

8. **Ranch windows** are usually high up in the room so that privacy is no problem.

Ruffled tie-back or Priscilla curtains add a gay touch in decorating single, small ranch windows.

Short draw draperies in a color and fabric that blend into the wall make these windows unobtrusive. Sheer draw curtains let more light into the room while masking the window. Again, if the window opens in, be sure to extend the drapery or curtains beyond the window edge.

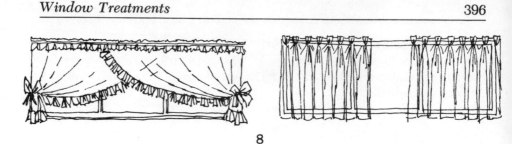

8

HOW TO MEASURE WINDOWS

Carefully measure from the top of the rod wherever it is placed, on the frame, above the frame, or on the ceiling. Windows vary slightly, particularly in old houses, so measure each one. The curtains may hang to the sill, the bottom of the apron, the floor, or in tiers (as with café curtains).

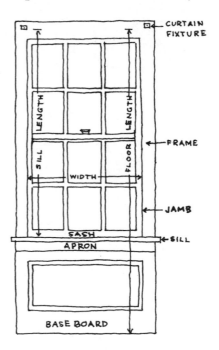

After you decide the finished length, add the depth of the bottom hem, top hem (casing wide enough to hold rod), and heading (usually a minimum of six inches). If you do not know whether or not the material has been treated to control shrinkage, allow one inch per yard and make double hems. Some materials such as fiber glass do not need a shrinkage allowance.

For the average window, two widths of thirty-six-inch-wide material, and one width of fifty-inch-wide material are sufficient; but if the window is oversized, measure the width (see above) and make the curtains and draperies two to three times as wide. The sheerer the fabric, the fuller the curtain and drapery should be. The lengths may be sewn together or hung in separate strips.

WINES AND LIQUORS |

Many people do not drink or serve alcoholic beverages, and this section implies no recommendation. In giving a party, however, a hostess who desires to serve a wine or liquor may have questions about observing the amenities. Actually, a few common-sense rules suffice for all but the connoisseur—although, of course, the proper mixing of a cocktail or the genealogy of a wine are always good makers of conversation.

TIPS ON COCKTAILS

Cocktails containing spirits such as gin, vodka, rum, whiskey, or brandy are served before dinner, never with the meal or afterward. Because of this timing, some people consider a cocktail an appetizer, but gourmets disagree. They frown on iced spirits as dulling to the taste, preferring an aperitif wine such as dry sherry or vermouth. If cocktails have been served, a hot soup is recommended as the first course of the meal to reawaken taste buds.

Look upon cocktails as a social custom intended to loosen tongues a bit and put guests at their ease. Needless to say, plying people with potent drinks before dinner can be overdone. The host is not obliged to urge "seconds" on anyone against his better judgment, and the hostess may call a halt to the cocktail hour at any time by announcing dinner.

What kind to serve is a matter of taste and of current fashion. If uncertain, avoid any elaborate, sweet, or rich concoction except, perhaps, at a party for ladies who will enjoy the extra fuss. The simpler, standard drinks of somewhat dry (not sweet) flavor, such as a martini, Manhattan, daiquiri, etc., are generally acceptable. All of these may be purchased ready-mixed, needing the addition only of ice, or sometimes of the liquor. The bottled cocktails are always uniform in flavor.

To mix a good cocktail, remember that the end result is psychological rather than gustatory: a subtle blend of flavor, aroma, temperature, color, and a gleaming glass. One common mistake is to skimp on the quality of the vermouth or other "mixings," despite their low cost compared to the cost of spirits. Actually the quality (age or purity) of the liquor itself is disguised in a cocktail. Lower priced blends of good flavor may give excellent results with good quality mixers. If you add olives, fruit, or whatever, use the best obtainable.

Another mistake is to skimp on the ice. A good cocktail should be chilled not only thoroughly but *quickly*; load the mixing glass or shaker with as much ice as it will hold. After pouring off the drink, you can preserve the remaining ice for second use by putting the shaker in the refrigerator. It's also a good idea to prechill the glasses by filling them with ice. Almost as

WINE AND LIQUOR GLASSES

PONY BRANDY BALLOON BRANDY SHERRY SPARKLING BURGUNDY HOLLOW STEM CHAMPAGNE

CLARET SAUCER CHAMPAGNE PARFAIT OR STEM WHISKEY SOUR COCKTAIL

MARTINI DELMONICO OLD FASHIONED HIGH-BALL PILSENER

effective: pour the drink twice, once to cool the glasses, then back into the shaker before again filling the glasses for serving.

In measuring, first decide how much of the basic liquor to include per drink. Check the "proof" shown on the label—normally about 86 proof, or 43 per cent alcohol. One and one-half ounces of this makes a normal portion. But if the liquor is 100 proof (50 per cent alcohol) or stronger, you can and probably should allow less. Add other ingredients in proportion according to the recipe. For example, ¾ of a measuring cup of gin or vodka topped with ¼ cup dry (French type) vermouth will make up to five so-called 3-to-1 martinis.

Cocktail recipes are variable because every brand of liquor, vermouth, etc., has a distinctive flavor, and blending them well can become quite an art. In general, when mixing all but the very sweet or fruity drinks, lean to the dry side (less vermouth, sugar, grenadine, etc.) for best results.

Cocktails should be sipped, not gulped. The longer the time taken to consume one, the gentler the effect. Serve "nibble" foods, such as nuts or canapés, to preserve guests from drinking on an empty stomach. And always have soft drinks or fruit juice available for nondrinkers.

The stemmed, inverted cone-shaped glass is correct for all cocktails other than those containing ice cubes (i.e., served "on the rocks"), which take the flat-bottomed old-fashioned glass. Clear rather than colored or decorated glass is smart. Highball glasses, the size of a juice glass, are traditional for straight liquor (or wine) mixed with soda or plain water; use tall "cooler" glasses for summer drinks such as a julep or planter's punch.

WINES

Wines require no mysterious ritual, either. Three standard glass sizes suffice for most people: the stemmed, inverted bell-shaped type, small for sherry or other aperitif wines, and six- to eight-ounce size for table wines; and a fluted glass for sparkling wines. Fill glasses no more than two-thirds, since the bouquet or aroma that fills the remaining space is part of the enjoyment of wine.

The temperature of wine is important; practically none except sparkling wines are at their best ice cold (see Wine Dictionary, below). Most red table wines are drunk at cool room temperature; rosé or white wine is served chilled. Unless you are mixing a punch or a summer "spritz" of wine and soda, never put ice into the glass. Here's a European secret, however: if you find a wine too tart for your taste, there's nothing wrong with diluting it in the glass with a little cool water.

Selection of wine depends upon the food being served, but again there are no rules so long as the combination seems pleasing to you. The traditional matings go like this: [Continued on page 405]

BRIEF U.S.A. WINE DICTIONARY

WINE	CHARACTERISTICS	WHEN TO SERVE	TEMPERATURE
Appetizer Wines			
SHERRY	Appetizer or dessert wine, with nutty, or *rancio*, flavor. Color ranges from pale to dark amber. Made dry, medium dry, and sweet. Dry sherry is the most popular appetizer wine.	*Dry sherries:* Before meal as appetizer. *Sweet sherries:* Usually served with dessert, with between-meal refreshments, or with biscuits, crackers, etc.	Chilled or at room temperature
VERMOUTH	Appetizer wine flavored with aromatic herbs. There are two kinds: *Sweet* (Italian type) is dark amber. *Dry* (French type) is pale amber.	Before meal as appetizer.	Well chilled
White·Table Wines			
CATAWBA	Made in Eastern and Midwestern states from native hybrid grapes that give it characteristic flavor and aroma. Both dry and semisweet.	Same as sauterne.	Well chilled
CHABLIS	Straw-colored wine, similar to Rhine wine but less tart than most wines in that group, and with fruit flavor and body.	With main course. Especially good with fish, shellfish, poultry, veal, lamb, etc.	Well chilled
DELAWARE	Made from Delaware grapes grown in Eastern states.	Same as Rhine wine.	Well chilled
FOLLE BLANCHE	Chablis type. Made from folle blanche grapes.	Same as chablis.	Well chilled
LIGHT MUSCAT	Dry or semisweet. Also called dry muscat. Light wine of muscat grapes with characteristic flavor and aroma.	*Dry types:* With white meat or sea food. *Semisweet types:* With or after dessert; or with between-meal refreshments.	Well chilled
PINOT BLANC	Chablis type. Made from pinot blanc grapes.	Same as chablis.	Well chilled

RHINE WINE (Hock or Moselle)	Thoroughly dry. Sometimes on acid side, with delicate pale-gold, slightly greenish color. Eastern Rhine wines are flowery, fruity.	With main course, especially white meats or sea foods.	Well chilled
RIESLING	Rhine-wine type made from Riesling grapes.	Same as Rhine wine.	Well chilled
SAUTERNE	Golden-hued wines, sometimes dry but often semisweet. *Very sweet sauternes*, also labeled haut sauterne or frequently chateau sauterne. *Eastern sauternes*, often less sweet, with characteristic aroma and grape taste.	*Dry:* With white meats and sea food. *Sweet:* With dessert, between meals, or with white meats and sea food. *Very sweet:* After dessert, often with meals.	Well chilled
SEMILLON	Sauterne-type wine made from semillon grapes. Either dry or semisweet.	Same as sauterne.	Well chilled
SYLVANER	Made from sylvaner (also called Franken Riesling) grapes. Rhine-wine type, but fruitier and more fragrant. Resembles Alsatian wine.	Same as Rhine wine.	Well chilled

Red Table Wines

BARBERA	Heavy-bodied—typical Italian. Made from, and with distinct flavor and aroma of, barbera grapes. Strong in flavor. Burgundy type.	With main course. Delicious with highly seasoned food, rice and spaghetti dishes, etc.	Room temperature or slightly chilled
BURGUNDY	Dark ruby in color, stronger in flavor, body, and bouquet than claret. (Made from a number of grape varieties.) Eastern Burgundy has characteristic "grapy" perfume and flavor of Eastern native grapes.	With main course, especially red meats, turkey, or dark-meated birds.	Room temperature or slightly chilled
CABERNET	Made from cabernet sauvignon grapes, famous Bordeaux grape of France and one of the best red-wine grapes of California. Has distinctive flavor. Stronger flavor and body than most clarets, sometimes heavier than California Burgundy. Harsh when young, very fine cabernet becomes really great with age.	Same as claret.	Room temperature or slightly chilled

BRIEF U.S.A. WINE DICTIONARY

Wine	Characteristics	When to serve	Temperature
CHIANTI	Medium-bodied, ruby-red wine, strongly flavored, dry, fruity, slightly tart.	Same as claret.	Room temperature or slightly chilled
CLARET	Medium-bodied, with tasty dryness. Often less expensive than other red wines.	With steaks, roasts, chops, spaghetti, game.	Room temperature or slightly chilled
GAMAY	Made from gamay grapes. Light in body. Often made into rosé wine.	Same as Burgundy.	*Red:* room temperature *Rosé:* chilled
PINOT NOIR	Made from famous pinot noir grapes (Burgundy type). Varies greatly with amount of this grape present (by law, at least 51 per cent). Finest are velvety to taste, beautiful red in color. Can be aged into wonderful wine in bottle.	Same as Burgundy.	Room temperature or slightly chilled
ROSE	Lightest of red table wines, being light in color, body, and alcoholic content. Dry, fruity wine.	Ideal for luncheon or picnic.	Chilled
ZINFANDEL	Claret type. Made from, and has distinct taste and aroma of, zinfandel grapes. Somewhat coarse, fruity, medium-bodied.	Same as claret.	Room temperature or slightly chilled
Dessert Wines			
ANGELICA	Sweet; straw- or amber-colored; mild and fruity in flavor; originated in California.	With or after dessert, or with between-meal refreshments.	Room temperature or chilled
MADEIRA	Deep amber. Semisweet. Resembles sherry, but is sweeter and darker. Drier than Tokay.	With or after dessert, or with little cakes as refreshments.	Room temperature

MARSALA	Deep amber. Resembles sherry but is sweeter and darker. Usually sweeter than madeira but drier than Tokay. Medium-bodied.	With or after dessert or with cheese and nuts.	Room temperature or chilled
MUSCATEL	Has distinctive flavor, aroma, and sweetness of muscat grapes from which it is made. Ranges in color from golden to amber. Medium-bodied.	With or after dessert, or with between-meal refreshments, biscuits, crackers, or cheese and nuts.	Room temperature or chilled
PORT	Rich, heavy-bodied, sweet wine, ranging from deep-red to tawny color.	With or after dessert. Especially good with cheese and nuts.	Room temperature or chilled
TOKAY	Amber-colored, sweet dessert wine. In no way resembles Hungarian Tokay in flavor. Usually made by blending angelica, port, and sherry.	With or after dessert; or with fruit cake, nuts, raisins; or as between-meal refreshment.	Room temperature or chilled
WHITE PORT	White dessert wine. Usually straw colored. Sweet, heavy-bodied.	With or after dessert, or with between-meal refreshments.	Room temperature or chilled
Sparkling Wines			
CHAMPAGNE	Made sparkling by secondary fermentation of finished wine, creating natural effervescence. Comes *dry*, usually labeled brut; or *semidry*, labeled dry; *extra-dry*, or *sec*. There are pink champagnes.	*Dry type:* As appetizer. Or with main course—especially poultry, game, sweetbreads, fish. *Sweet type:* With dessert.	Very well chilled
SPARKLING BURGUNDY	Red wine made naturally sparkling by same process as champagne. Smooth, slightly sweet, light-bodied.	With main course—especially poultry, game, sweetbreads.	Very well chilled
Flavored Wines	As sweet as dessert wines, with added natural flavors varying from orange and lemon to vanilla.	For afternoon or evening refreshments, with or without food. Useful in fruit punches, too.	Chilled or at room temperature

LIQUEURS TO SERVE WITH AFTER-DINNER COFFEE

ANISETTE
From France, Italy, etc. Colorless, mild, and sweet. Has an aniseed flavor (also an aperitif when diluted with ice and water).

APRICOT LIQUEUR
Sweetened brandy plus crushed dried apricots.

AQUAVIT
From Scandinavia, based on unsweetened neutral spirits, caraway flavored (light kümmel).

B & B
Brandy and Benedictine, already mixed.

BENEDICTINE
From Normandy, France, from secret formula. Trademark ("D.O.M.") comes from the Benedictine Monks' inscription "To God, most good, most great."

BLACKBERRY LIQUEUR
Blackberries with brandy (sweet).

BRANDY
Undisputed after-dinner drink—distillation of fermented juice of a fruit; grape, apples, etc. Famous grape brandy comes from Cognac, France; is so labeled.

CHARTREUSE
Yellow and green. (Green, stronger with a more herbal taste, is considered finer.) From secret formula of the monks living in French Alps.

CHERRY LIQUEUR
Made from bitter cherries in U.S. and abroad.

COINTREAU
A colorless liqueur with an orange flavor and brandy base made from orange blossoms or peel.

CRÊME de CACAO
Brown liqueur with chocolate flavor, made from cocoa beans. Also a white variety with same flavor.

CRÊME de MENTHE
Green or white, made from fresh mint and spirits. Very popular.

CURAÇAO
Colorless or burnt orange. Orange flavor from skins of bitter oranges, largely grown in Curaçao in West Indies.

DRAMBUIE
A popular liqueur made with Scotch whiskey base. (Honey and herbs are added.)

FIOR d'ALPE
From Italy. Distinctive blend distilled of herbs (mint, wild marjoram, and hyssop). Twig, encrusted with rock sugar crystals, in each bottle.

GRAND MARNIER
Orange-flavored liqueur based on Cognac.

KUMMEL
White, sweet, tastes of caraway seeds.

STREGA
From Italy. Sweet yellow liqueur with an orange flavor, and added herbs.

TEQUILA
From Mexico. Spirits made from maguey plant. Served with lemon wedge and salt.

TRIPLE SEC
Colorless, like Curaçao, but less sweet.

Dry fortified wine, such as sherry or vermouth: as appetizer before meal, or with hors d'oeuvres or soup.

White table wines, such as chablis, Rhine wine, dry sauterne, etc.: with seafood, chicken, veal, omelets, other light-flavored dishes.

Red table wines, such as Burgundy, chianti, etc.: with red meats, game, cheese, macaroni dishes. (*Note:* rosé wines fit into either category.)

Sweet fortified wines, such as port, muscatel, etc.: with dessert, cheese, nuts, fruit, etc. Sweet flavored wines (orange, cherry, etc.) belong here, too.

Sparkling wines: if dry, before and during the meal with any kind of food. If sweet, with dessert or between meals. In a formal dinner including a different wine for each course, dry champagne might be served with oysters or fish, sweet champagne with the dessert. The word "sec" indicates dryness.

If you are serving a single wine with dinner, bring the bottle to the proper temperature (see chart), uncork, and place it with cork loosened on a small tray on the table as the meal begins. When the main course is served, the host begins by pouring a little wine into his own glass, to make sure no bits of cork remain in the bottle. He may then fill the glass of each person in turn, ending with himself, or pass the bottle from hand to hand.

If the wine is chilled, wrap a cloth around the lower part of the bottle only, leaving the label exposed. Guests enjoy knowing what wine they are drinking, and it makes for pleasant table talk.

WOOL |

In shopping for woolen clothes there is a great variety of fabrics to choose from. This glossary explains how these fabrics differ.

Woolens are woven from yarns of comparatively short wool fibers with a low or soft twist. There is noticeable nap and individual threads are indistinct. These fabrics are warm, soft, and luxurious.

Worsteds are woven from yarns of long wool fibers with a high or hard twist. Their surface is hard, smooth, and unnapped; individual threads are quite distinct.

Serge is made from worsted yarns and has prominent diagonal lines (twill) on both sides of the fabric. Its finish is usually soft and smooth.

Sharkskin is a hard-finished worsted. Typically, it has small dots of white on a colored ground, with a white and a colored thread alternating in the length and width of the fabric.

Covert is made of tightly woven worsted yarns. It feels firm and has sharply angled twilled lines. This cloth is found in suiting and coating weights.

Homespun is usually woolen and is a plain-and-loose-weave fabric.

Tweeds are sometimes called homespun even though they have a twill construction.

Tweed varies according to the type and color of the yarn and filling threads used.

In Scotch tweed, irregular yarns and fibers of varying lengths give a rough look to the fabric—which usually has white warp (lengthwise threads) and the heather-toned or vividly colored filling threads.

White yarns in the warp direction and black or dark shades of gray, blue, and brown in the filling direction characterize Irish tweed.

The distinctive, loosely woven Cheviot tweed is woven from warp and filling yarns of the same color.

Colored nubs on the coarse yarn of Donegal tweed, a firm, hand-woven Irish fabric, dot the cloth with tufts of different colors.

Another woolen twill, Harris tweed, is made only on the Outer Hebrides Islands off Scotland and is always hand woven.

Melton cloth, a thick, heavyweight fabric, looks like felt. Usually dyed in solid dark colors, it has a short nap and a dull surface.

Crêpe may have a flat, grainy, or crinkled surface, depending upon the way the yarn is twisted. Sheer wool crêpes have different names such as crêpe de laine, wool voile.

Doeskin is a smooth, closely woven fabric that feels life soft peachskin. Its dense nap completely conceals the weave.

Flannel, a soft, lightweight fabric, has a weave only partially concealed under a slightly napped surface.

Gabardine is a worsted fabric, firmly woven, distinctly twilled, and clear faced.

Jersey fabrics are knitted on machines with fine-gauge needles. They come in a variety of weights and patterns.

Virgin wool is new wool, used for the first time in any yarn or fabric so labeled. **Reprocessed wool** has been woven, knit, or felted. Never used by consumers, it is reduced to fibers and manufactured again. These new fibers keep most of their original resiliency. **Reused wool** is reclaimed from products that have been used and then shredded into fibers which are made into yarns and cloth. The process thoroughly cleans and disinfects these fibers.

WORKING WIVES |

One of every three married women works, and that number is increasing daily. The main reason most women work, on either a part- or full-time basis, is to supplement family income. Numerous cases have been noted in government surveys, though, in which working wives, particularly mothers of young children, actually netted little money after deducting the expenses incurred by employment.

COSTS

United States Department of Agriculture surveys reveal that average work-related expenses consume one-third of the wife's earnings. When there are school-age children, these expenses average one-half of the earnings. Consequently, if you are considering going to work, know what costs are involved. Among them:

Taxes. You will have to pay federal and possibly state income taxes. Your earnings may also place total family income in a higher rate bracket. Social Security taxes will be deducted.

Occupational. These expenses differ for each job and range from dues for unions or professional organizations to costs for uniforms, job-related publications, or attendance at meetings. Don't forget to include transportation to work.

Food. Home meal expenses have been shown to rise about 10 per cent for the cost of time-saving convenience items when wives work. In addition to lunches and snacks you may purchase, lunches may have to be bought by children because you are not at home to prepare them.

Child care. Where there are children, particularly preschool or school-age youngsters, costs increase sharply. If a good day-care center is available, you can plan on spending up to $15 weekly, some authorities say. Otherwise, costs can go as high as the bill of a full-time sitter or maid. Too, realize that someone may have to do household chores for which you no longer have time.

Personal. Working wives spend more on personal grooming and twice as much, experts say, on their clothing.

BENEFITS

Keep in mind that many employers offer fringe benefits, ranging from hospitalization and major-medical insurance (sometimes for your family as well as yourself) to paid sick leave, use of company medical facilities and company store, and discount privileges if you work for a retailer.

If you work long enough to be insured, a variety of important benefits will come from Social Security. These include increased monthly retirement payments, up to a maximum of $127 at retirement in contrast to the maximum $63.50 that a nonworking wife would receive at 65 if her husband had retired.

PART-TIME JOBS

A part-time job is an appealing possibility to many women. For some, it is a way to earn money for current family needs. For others, it represents additional income for future expenses, such as a child's college education, or for items that normally would not fit into the family budget. In addition, many women are reluctant to lose previously learned and used skills. For them, part-time work can be an ideal solution. They can handle their family and household responsibilities and at the same time stay active in the business or professional world. A basic attraction of this work is that hours frequently can be arranged so that women are home when children leave for and return from school.

More than six million women now work part time in nonfarming jobs. Furthermore, government experts predict that additional millions will go to work on a part-time basis in the next ten to fifteen years. (By government definition a part-time job is for less than thirty-five hours a week on a regular basis. Temporary or seasonal employment involves jobs for thirty-five or more hours a week, but for less than a year.)

Household work, including baby-sitting, comprises one of the largest segments of the part-time job market. Other opportunities—and the salaries they pay—tend to be linked to the over-all employment situation in an area. For instance, many employers will not hire part-time workers until the available supply of full-time employees is exhausted. Nevertheless, specific openings do exist for part-time work, the greatest number in two general areas: businesses with peak customer hours (e.g., department stores, restaurants, supermarkets); and fields in which there is a shortage of qualified personnel (e.g., teaching, nursing, skilled office work).

Obviously, special skills and training can increase chances of finding employment. Typing, for example, is an advantage for job seekers in many fields. Few jobs are open to the completely inexperienced person, although some employers will train new workers. (An example is on-the-job training of sales clerks in department stores and specialty shops.) Consequently, it may well be worth the investment in time and possibly money to take adult education or other courses to acquire employable skills or to brush up former ones. Free government-sponsored training in about five hundred occupations is available to eligible trainees under the Manpower Development and Training Act and other legislation.

Public schools and some YWCA's offer courses in typing, shorthand, and operation of business machines. Home correspondence courses are also available. A few communities offer refresher courses in professional fields such as social work, nursing, and teaching. For women who want college training, some colleges have worked out plans that enable students to take courses over a period of years and they do not require the normal one-year residency on the campus for a degree.

WHERE TO LOOK

A favorite starting point is an employment office—either state or private. However, don't overlook former employers, family, and friends as good sources of information. State employment services frequently counsel and test applicants before trying to place them.

Classified newspaper advertisements are another excellent source. Some women who believe they are especially well qualified may place job-wanted ads in newspapers or on community bulletin boards. If you are interested primarily in clerical, secretarial, or sales work, first check with businesses and professional offices in your neighborhood.

An advantage of neighborhood work is that it can reduce both transportation expense and time. Keep in mind what any job will cost you—in transportation, possibly extra clothing and cleaning, lunches, etc., and income taxes.

WORKSAVERS |

A wide variety of useful materials which were unknown a generation ago have become standbys of the modern American kitchen. Among them are paper products, metal foil, plastic film, cellophane tape, freezer tape, and steel wool. It is helpful to know the special features of each, not only for kitchen use, but for other household jobs as well.

FOOD WRAPS

When storing leftovers or other perishable food, don't just grab the handiest roll of wax paper, aluminum foil, or plastic film. All are good, all protect against loss of flavor, drying out, and transfer of odors—but there are differences in cost, and for your immediate purpose, one may be a better choice than the others.

In price per square foot, heavy-gauge aluminum ("freezer") foil costs most, but is a good choice for long-time food protection in the home freezer. Regular household foil comes next in cost, and like the heavier gauge may be used in cooking as well as in the refrigerator (but not in the long-term freezer). Wax paper costs about one-fifth as much as foil, plastic film slightly more than wax paper. All are inexpensive enough for one-time, throwaway use.

Versatile **aluminum foil** is a major kitchen asset. Properly utilized, following the carton directions, it protects the oven and broiler pan from spills, eliminating strenuous cleanup (for methods, see below). In roasting a turkey, ham, or pot roast; steaming frozen vegetables and heating leftovers; baking potatoes; as a cover for casseroles and a pan liner—there are many ways foil makes cooking easier while giving tasty results. A sheet used for wrapping food in the refrigerator may often be smoothed for reuse in the oven, after which it is discarded.

Plastic films, whether heavy or light in thickness or gauge, have the distinctive feature of letting you see what's stored. Because they cling tightly, they make an excellent cover for bowls, platters, jars, and irregularly shaped items ranging from half a leftover turkey to a sprig of parsley.

Bags of plastic film are extremely handy, in small size for wrapping sandwiches or storing small items, in larger size for leftover roasts, corned beef, etc. The cold meat may be pushed out enough for slicing, then pushed back into the bag for further storage. Use a plastic bag also to store extra ice cubes for a party.

Wax paper, the old standby, is the best wrap for uncooked meats (keep the wrapping loose). It also gives good refrigerator protection of cooked meats, sandwiches, or baked goods. Don't count on it, though, to perform well in the freezer. And keep both wax paper and plastic film away from the range.

Freezer wrap, a heavy-duty paper, comes on a roll, for storing foods in freezer. Use freezer tape and label the packages.

CONTAINERS

Housewives used to save the screw-top jars that jams, pickles, etc., come in; and while they're all right for storing liquids and other foods, modern plastic refrigerator-freezer containers are better. They are regular in shape and may be stacked, saving space; and their tight-fitting covers make them ideal for any moist food. Unbreakable and lightweight, they may double for transporting picnic or station-wagon tailgate lunches.

Treated paper bags, and particularly plastic bags, simplify many messy jobs: lining the garbage pail and wastebaskets; transporting wet bathing suits or diapers; holding dampened clothes until ready to iron.

PAPER TOWELS

Besides their obvious uses to dry hands or wipe out a pan, paper towels are a worksaver for:

Wiping off meat, fish, or poultry before cooking. Skimming fat from soup or stock (simply draw towel across the surface). Handling hot foods or pot handles. Draining berries, and other things that leave stains. Draining grease from bacon, and other fried foods. Picking up spills on hot range enamel (which might be damaged by water). Applying cleansers, silver polish, etc., to save cloths.

USES OF ALUMINUM FOIL

To line a broiler pan, fit one sheet into the bottom pan, and cover the broiler rack with another. Slash the foil between rack openings to let grease drain. After broiling, and when the pan is cool, remove the foil, keeping grease intact. Soak pan and rack with hot water and detergent for easy cleaning.

Also use foil to make a reflector pan under a range burner; to line drip trays or spatter areas; to make a loose-fitting skillet cover that lets steam escape but catches spatters; as a liner for cookie sheets, casserole dishes, etc.

ZIPPERS |

Getting the best performance from a slide fastener or "zipper" involves some basic precautions:

Close the zipper before washing, dry cleaning, or ironing.

If a wringer is used, be sure the zipper is straight and folded inside the garment so that it does not touch either roller.

Paraffin, beeswax, or a commercially prepared product can be applied to the chain or teeth of a metal zipper that does not open and close smoothly.

If fabric or threads become enmeshed in the teeth of a metal zipper, work gently to avoid damaging the fabric or the zipper.

A neck-, dress-, or skirt-opening zipper is probably too short if the slider seems about to come off the chain (or track) at its bottom. Replace the zipper with a longer one.

A zipper should be replaced if a tooth is broken or bent. This can be done at home or by a tailor or seamstress. Some damaged zippers can be fixed by repair services listed in the telephone directory.

Synthetic (such as nylon or polyester) coil zippers require much the same care as metal ones. However, care must be taken when ironing that the temperature is not too high, because the fiber coils which replace metal teeth can be damaged. Set iron at a low heat setting or use steam heat. If the fabric requires a higher temperature or if the zipper must remain open while ironing, cover it with a press cloth or similar fabric covering.

An advantage of the synthetic fiber zipper is that it can be opened easily if threads or cloth catch in the coils. Simply fold the zipper lengthwise, pinch and twist on the fold, and pull the coils apart at the snag to release the cloth. The zipper can then be opened fully and rezipped.

Synthetic zippers can be dry-cleaned, machine-washed, and tumble-dried.

INDEX

413

Format by Katharine Sitterly
Set in Linotype Caledonia
Composed by The Haddon Craftsmen, Inc.
Printed by The Murray Printing Company
Bound by The Haddon Craftsmen, Inc.
HARPER & ROW, PUBLISHERS, INCORPORATED

HOW TO MEASURE

Correct measuring of ingredients is a must. All measurements are level!

Choosing Measuring Cups

For Dry Ingredients: Buy 2 1-cup measuring cups, each with the 1-cup line at the rim. Or for one of these cups, buy a nest of 4 graduated measuring cups, consisting of a ¼-cup, ⅓-cup, ½-cup, and 1-cup measure. Such a nest of cups makes accurate measuring easy.

For Liquid Ingredients: Buy a 1-cup measuring cup that has the rim *above* the 1-cup line to avoid spilling. The 2-cup and 1-quart measuring cups are also very convenient.

Choosing Measuring Spoons

Buy one or more sets, attached to a ring, containing the following spoons: ¼ teasp., ½ teasp., 1 teasp., and 1 tablesp. In a good set, 16 tablesp., or 48 teasp., should equal 1 cup.

Measuring Dry Ingredients

Use a measuring cup with the 1-cup line even with top. Or use a nest of graduated measuring cups. Use a set of measuring spoons.

Baking Powder, Salt, etc.: Dip measuring spoon of correct size into dry ingredient until full; lift out and level off with edge, not flat surface, of knife or spatula.

If it's necessary to measure half spoonfuls, first measure a level spoonful; then divide contents lengthwise with knife, and push off half.

Brown Sugar: Roll out lumps with rolling pin. Sift. Spoon into measuring cup, packing firmly enough to hold shape.

Granulated and Confectioners' Sugar: If lumpy, sift. Spoon lightly into cup, leveling off with edge, not flat of spatula or knife.

Flour: 1. Sift onto waxed paper or into bowl. Do not sift directly into measuring cup.

2. Spoon sifted flour lightly into cup until cup is full. Do not pack or shake.

3. Level off with edge, not flat surface, of spatula or knife, without packing it down.

Measuring Liquids

Milk, etc.: Set measuring cup (one with rim above 1-cup line) on level surface, keeping measuring line at eye level. Fill cup as desired.

Vanilla, etc.: Pour extract into measuring spoon. If thick, like molasses, level off with edge, not flat surface, of spatula or knife.

Measuring Shortenings

Shortening: Scoop from can or package and pack firmly into graduated measuring cup. Level off with edge, not flat surface, of knife or spatula; remove from cup.

Butter or Margarine: Measure as for shortening. If you're using a 1-lb. print of butter or margarine, each ¼-lb. stick equals ½ cup, or 8 tablesp. Half of a ¼-lb. stick equals ¼ cup, or 4 tablesp. For 2 tablesp., cut off one fourth of ¼-lb. stick.

Melted Fat: Measure before or after melting—the amount will be the same. However, it's simpler to measure it after melting.

Salad oil, often used instead of melted fat, is measured in a measuring cup or spoon.